The Non-Orthodox Jew's Guide to Orthodox Jews

Why We Do What We Do, Wear What We Wear and Think What We Think

---

David Baum

Veracity Press

Book design by:
Arbor Books, Inc.
www.arborbooks.com

Printed in the United States of America

The Non-Orthodox Jew's Guide to Orthodox Jews
David Baum

1. Title 2. Author 3. Religion

Library of Congress Control Number: 2009943625

ISBN 13: 978-0-615-34273-3

Table of Contents

PART TWO: The Jew and His Society

PART THREE: The Jews and the World

Acknowledgments

The writing of this book has been a much longer process than I could have anticipated and there are many people I would like to thank for helping me get through it.

First of all, my wife and children, for their constant encouragement and sincere excitement for this project. My children earn a special thanks for being the guardians of my secret. This book was nearly complete before anyone knew I was even writing it. Anyone, that is, except my children (some still in elementary school) who discovered almost immediately that something was up but did not utter a peep for years, not even to their closest friends!

I would like to thank my friends and colleagues, Rabbis Shimon Apisdorf, Chaim Dubin, Reuven Sarett and Eliezer Weisenfeld for reviewing earlier versions of the first few chapters and Rabbi Shmuel Kaplan, Michael Shavelson and my sister-in-law, Jodi Bloom for their pertinent observations. Later, my wife Laurie, my mother, Mrs. Gladys Baum and my son Yitzchak reviewed the entire manuscript and were instrumental in helping to clarify the text, eliminate inadvertent errors and improve the flow and feel of the book. Without their input, this book would seem amateurish.

I would also like to thank everyone at Arbor Books for their expertise and professionalism and especially my editor, Elise Vaz and my typesetter, Jessica Gorham for their patience and flexibility. And a special thanks to Jonathan Ehrman for getting the project started, Dennis Berman for helping it along and to my anonymous friend for really making it happen.

I owe a debt of gratitude to HaRav Aharon Feldman for reviewing the manuscript and offering perfect suggestions and improvements. Rabbi Feldman runs one of the largest Yeshivot in the world, the renowned Ner Israel in Baltimore, Maryland, and carries a monumental load of communal responsibilities as one of the leaders of Agudath Israel of America. Yet once he understood why I had written this book, he dedicated his time and his attention to its publication. It has been a great example to me of how to bear the weight of great responsibility with joy and selflessness.

Lastly and most consequentially, I want to acknowledge my main teacher and mentor, HaRav Noach Weinberg zt"l and his older brother who also became a teacher and mentor to me, HaRav Yaakov Weinberg zt"l.

Rav Noach was a man whose humility can only be understood by those who spent time with him. His love of G-d and the Jewish People was contagious and he dedicated his entire life to improving the spiritual lot of the Jewish people without ever considering his personal needs or honor. All he ever asked of his students was to take responsibility for the Jewish people. There is little in my life that cannot be directly attributed to him in some way.

While studying at Aish HaTorah I met Rav Yaakov, as we called him, who would visit at least once a year and give a series of lectures. When I first entered Aish in December 1981, people were still talking about Rav Yaakov's visit of the previous summer. His Torah scholarship was without peer and he conveyed the most profound ideas with simplicity, crystal clarity and the eloquence of an Oxford don. Although it has been over ten years since his passing, there is rarely a day that I don't wish I could call him to ask a question or for clarification on some matter.

Students of both Rav Noach and Rav Yaakov will recognize their words and even hear their voices in the pages of this book. This only demonstrates the Talmud's statement that the righteous, even in death, are considered to still be alive.

Introduction

I have always been pained and dismayed by the rift which exists between Orthodox and non-Orthodox Jews, two parts of one family who share the same fate and the same history.

In the forty-plus years that I have been involved in Jewish education teaching both Orthodox Jews and non-Orthodox Jews, I have found that this rift, which has led to a painful alienation within Jewry, is usually a result of a lack of awareness of the value system of Orthodox Jews, a system based on a profound intellectual tradition that stretches back over 3,300 years and represents a very real and very specific philosophy and world view.

I have always believed that if non-Orthodox Jews had an understanding of their Orthodox brethren's beliefs, there would be more harmony and peace within the Jewish family. I am happy to see that a book with that specific goal has now been published.

David Baum has written a book which should make an immense contribution toward healing this fracture within our family. It presents the beliefs and practices of Orthodox Jews in a cogent, well-researched form. It is at turns fascinating, poignant and humorous, and it broaches nearly every conceivable topic in Judaism without judgment or ill-will.

All Jews, both Orthodox and non-Orthodox, who read this book will benefit immensely from it. Orthodox Jews will come away with a refreshed perspective on the meaning of their way of life and their performance of the commandments. Non-Orthodox Jews will come away with a deeper respect for their heritage and for the observant members of their extended family. They will also discover, perhaps for the first time, the age-old definition of what it means to be a Jew.

—Rabbi Aharon Feldman
Ner Israel Rabbinical College
Baltimore, Maryland

PART ONE

The Jew and Himself

Chapter One
Why

In the spring of 1986, I was fundraising in Kansas City for Aish HaTorah, a Jerusalem-based, international outreach organization for Jews with little or no Jewish education. I had a list of names and was cold calling them to make appointments. I was in town for only a few days, so if I could not reach a prospective donor on the phone, I would stop by his office to see if I could grab a few minutes with him.

One man whose name I have forgotten was just leaving his office as I was stepping out of the elevator, and he said I could ride down with him. In the elevator, I started to explain why I had stopped by, but he cut me off rather brusquely and said, "I won't give you any money."

Surprised at his reaction, I asked why, and he answered me with a statement that I have never forgotten. His answer was, "Because I think the Orthodox are the death knell of Judaism."

At first, I thought he was kidding and I actually started to laugh, but then realized that he wasn't laughing—he was dead serious. The elevator doors opened, and he turned his back to me and walked away.

It has been many years since that incident but I have never forgotten it. It has stayed with me because his statement was so incredibly absurd and at the same time, so incredibly sad. How could he honestly believe that the Orthodox are the death knell of Judaism? The Orthodox who have, on the average, six children who all go to Jewish schools, who all have Hebrew names and who study Jewish thought and practice as the main components of their curricula. The Orthodox who have an almost nonexistent rate of intermarriage and who are so committed to Judaism and the Jewish people that today, they produce the only significant *aliyah* to Israel and make up the majority of the officer corps in the Israel Defense Force.

Does this group sound like the death knell of Judaism?

And who exactly did he think was the future of Judaism? The millions of unaffiliated Jews? Or perhaps the over sixty percent of Jews who were marrying non-Jews? An unbiased observer could easily conclude that on the contrary, the Orthodox were the future of Judaism.

This man was intelligent and very accomplished, yet his thoughts about the Jews and their future were so convoluted. One thing was abundantly clear: He was very confused. And confusion leads to frustration, which leads to anger. The result was an enormous and yet artificial divide between us and a good deal of hostility towards me. For him to think as he did meant that he had no idea what I believed in or why I believed what I did. We had almost no common ground. His response also indicated that he was unfamiliar with Jewish history or what the Jewish people have stood for or accomplished over the past three millennia.

Ever since that encounter, the idea for this book has been percolating in my mind. That this type of book is needed is an understatement. Every non-Orthodox Jew has, at one time or another in his or her life, wondered why the Orthodox are the way they are. Why do they seem so unbending to the times? Why do their lives seem so restricted and regimented? To many secular Jews, an Orthodox Jew—and especially a Hasidic Jew—is no different than the Amish except that the Amish aren't as irritating. And while many secular Jews might look upon the Orthodox through sentimental, *Fiddler on the Roof* lenses, they still have no understanding of their beliefs or motives.

And on the other end of the spectrum—how often has an Orthodox Jew wished he had a book—one book—to give to non-Orthodox Jews to reintroduce them to their own birthright and give them an idea of the beauty and wisdom of the Torah? A book that would explain so many of the seemingly incomprehensible traditions and beliefs of Judaism and somehow bridge the widening gap between the observant and the nonobservant? I had hoped that someone more qualified than I would publish this type of book, but, unfortunately, no one ever did.

The final catalyst that made me sit down and start writing was a near tragedy that hit my family a few years ago. A few of my children were playing in the basement. My infant daughter was sitting on the lap of one of her sisters, in front of a computer screen. She had picked up a small, handheld electronic game and was chewing on it. No one in the room thought anything of it because they mistakenly thought that it did not have small parts that would pose a danger to her. They did not see her bite off the small door that covered the compartment for the watch-type battery that powered the toy.

How long she had the piece in her mouth, no one is sure, but eventually, someone noticed that she was choking and gagging. As she gagged, she sucked the piece deeper into her throat until it completely blocked her airway. As her sisters ran her upstairs to my wife, the little girl was already turning blue and her eyes were rolling up into her head. Then, she stopped breathing altogether and passed out.

My oldest child, then a young man of fifteen who had learned CPR and first aid in Yeshiva, grabbed her out of my wife's trembling arms, performed the proper technique to dislodge the hard piece of plastic and revived her. We all believe that he saved her life. I was at my office and not at home when all this happened. When my son called me to come home, I could hear the police and emergency personnel in the background. I arrived to find six shaken, crying children and an hysterical wife. The only one completely unaffected by the incident was my little girl, who was thrilled by the commotion and totally enjoying herself.

The traditional Jewish reaction to escaping a catastrophe—and this is still practiced by Orthodox Jews today—is to undertake something that will benefit the community, to do something that will do well for others. Some give to charities, some start charities. Some perform acts of kindness for others, some write scholarly texts. We do these things as acts of gratitude to G-d, to show him that we acknowledge and appreciate his kindness toward us.

For reasons that are not clear to me, the thought of writing this book immediately came into my mind when my daughter's life was spared, and I committed myself to it on the spot. I hope it does some good. It is truly a heartfelt response to the irrational and depressing situation that exists today within the worldwide Jewish family. And it is my way of thanking G-d for the deliverance of my daughter, for the many undeserved kindnesses he does for me, and for the generous blessings I have received in my life.

I have approached the task of writing this book with a unique perspective. I did not grow up in an Orthodox home. I grew up in a suburban, Jewish home in Fair Lawn, New Jersey, that was typical for the 1960s and 1970s. I had a Bar Mitzvah in a conservative synagogue and even had some Jewish education afterwards (we called it "Hebrew high school") but my Jewish education was finished effectively by the time I was fifteen. I was culturally Jewish; all my close friends were Jewish and in school I hung out primarily with Jews, but by the time I was in college my connection to anything Jewish was minimal and my crowd was much more mixed. I had no connection with anything Jewish on campus.

It was not until I was twenty years old that I began to explore my roots. In the summer of 1980, after my freshman year in college, a friend called to tell me that a mutual friend from high school was in town; he would be stopping by to visit her that night, and she asked if I would like to come over as well. This mutual friend, let's call him Scott, had not gone to college after high school, as had almost every other Jewish classmate of ours. Instead he had gone to Israel and spent a year on two different *kibbutzim*, six months on each. During a visit to Jerusalem, Scott had wandered into Aish HaTorah and stayed, fascinated by the intellectually challenging environment and the open, freewheeling debates about moral issues and the meaning of life. This type of place was right up his alley—Scott had never been a mainstream type of guy.

He and his two sisters were products of a marriage between two people from two different planets. His mother had grown up in the Bronx and spent her teenage years listening to the radio, going to movies and giggling with her girlfriends; at the same time, his father, from a small *shtetl* in Poland, was surviving starvation in the Lodz Ghetto as well as heavy labor in the work camps, forced marches and several concentration camps, including Auschwitz. It would be an understatement to say that they did not relate to each other. Eventually, they divorced.

When we were teenagers, Scott always seemed to be on a different path. He was more worldly than our peers, more well-read, and he loved discussing ideas. As we grew up, he veered politically towards the radical left; I did not. In our many years of friendship we had had many knockdown, drag-out, thoroughly enjoyable battles. In our high school yearbook, his quote was, "He who walks in another's footsteps leaves no footprints." When I signed his yearbook, I wished him good luck in Israel and informed him that I was staying behind to become part of the military-industrial complex.

When I arrived at our friend's house on that summer day in 1980, Scott was sitting in the living room. I hadn't seen him for about a year. He was wearing typical teenager clothing—a T-shirt and jeans—but on his head was a straw, fedora-type hat. I made a joke about his trying to look cool and went to take it off his head. He wouldn't let me. It turned out that he was wearing the hat in lieu of a *yarmulke* (skullcap), and it had to stay on his head.

I was speechless. Scott was the absolute last person I'd expected to become religious. (I was next to last. In fact, a few months later, when I was about to leave for an extended visit to Israel, my mother asked me, "Are you planning to become religious like Scott?" I replied, "Mom, I am way too cool to become religious.")

That night, the three of us talked about many things, but mostly about what it meant to be Jewish. Scott gave me a reprint of a *Rolling Stone* article by a well-known writer about her trip to Israel to visit her brother, who was studying at Aish HaTorah. He also lent me some cassette tapes of classes, one of which, entitled "Happiness," was by Rabbi Noach Weinberg, the founder and head of Aish HaTorah. I remember thinking, *what would a rabbi know about happiness?* I had known a few in my life and they hadn't seemed particularly happy.

I never did listen to those tapes because I was too busy that summer going to the beach, to parties, to rock concerts and to other important social engagements. But my discussion with Scott that night did convince me of one thing: I wanted to go to Israel.

So, six months later, I was on an airplane. I spent six months on a *kibbutz*, working in the banana fields and learning Hebrew, and then two months traveling throughout Israel and the Sinai, which was still under Israeli control. Scott was in Jerusalem during that time, and I dropped in on him from time to time; I also sat in on classes and lectures at Aish HaTorah. The more I heard, the more I wanted to hear, and just days before I was to return to the States, I decided to change my plans. Instead of continuing my college education right away, I would take off a year or so to study my own heritage, which was turning out to be much deeper and richer than I could have imagined.

That year or so turned into six and a half years, and when I did eventually return to the States, I came with my wife, my firstborn and my rabbinical ordination.

Given my experiences in Israel, and having been a typical American teenager immersed in pop culture and exposed to the prevalent social mores of the times, I understand both sides of the Jewish divide. I understand why a non-Orthodox Jew would see an Orthodox Jew as backwards and ignorant, and I understand why the Orthodox would see the non-Orthodox as brainwashed by secular culture and living with one foot out the door. (What is not known to most non-Orthodox Jews is that Orthodox Jews view them only with great sadness, basically considering them lost to their people as more and more of them drift off and marry out. There is an almost unbelievable lack of animosity towards non-Orthodox Jews.)

While reading this book, I would like you to keep three things in mind. First, read this with an honest and open mind. Many prejudices have been artificially created and ingrained by society; if you acknowledge yours at the outset, you will gain much more from this book.

Second, acknowledge your level of knowledge of Judaism, even if it's limited or nonexistent. Think about how often a non-Jew has posed a question to you about Judaism and you had to admit that you weren't sure or didn't know. Most of us finished our Jewish educations, if we had any at all, at the age of thirteen. Not only did we hate going to Hebrew school in the first place, but we probably left with only a smattering of knowledge.

Lastly, be objective, fair and committed to the truth. We should always be fearless truth seekers and not afraid of intellectual challenges; putting our beliefs to honest scrutiny ensures that we are always doing what is right and true. In these pages, there will be no kowtowing to political correctness—that's just an intellectual shackle that prevents honest discourse, and there is no place for it in this type of book.

Many of the issues raised in these pages are super-heated, and it is inevitable that some points will cause discomfort because I have not tried to avoid ideas that might cause controversy. But neither have I written anything with malice; my only intent is to inform and educate and so my criticisms should not be taken personally. I ask you to give the ideas in this book a serious hearing. I did not dumb down any of them, because Judaism is not dumb nor are Jews. This is neither an "Idiot's Guide" nor a book for "Dummies."

I also want to emphasize that this book is not intended as an apology. I did not sugar coat anything to make it more palatable, and I did not attempt to explain away difficult issues with platitudes. Please be committed to the truth because otherwise, this book will just be another "he said/she said" waste of time.

While it is absolutely impossible to take all of Jewish thought and practice and encapsulate it into one small volume, I nevertheless tried to reach across a breadth of topics and tie them together into a coherent narrative. Many topics, such as the Shabbat and holidays or the Jewish lifecycle, were only briefly touched upon because to give them decent explanations would require separate books. I also wanted to discuss those issues that I felt would have more personal relevance to readers.

The chapters of the book are built as a progression, each building on the previous one, and they should be read in order. Each chapter assumes that you have acquired certain knowledge and a certain understanding from the previous chapters. I have chosen to refer to biblical figures by their Hebrew names, with their more commonly known English names following in parentheses. No man named Moses ever lived; his name was Moshe, and I figure that a book by a Jew for Jews and about Jews should use the Jewish names. When I use Hebrew terms to introduce concepts and practices, I also translate and explain them.

It is my fervent hope that this book will create some understanding and, hopefully, generate even a small amount of brotherhood and unity amongst the Jewish people. If that could be accomplished, it would make this effort all the more worthwhile. I also hope that a copy of this book finds its way to my friend in Kansas City.

Please fasten your seat belts; it might be a bumpy ride.

Chapter Two

What Really Happened
at Mount Sinai?

Bottom Line

This book is intended to bridge a gap and there can be no reconciliation without understanding. Therefore I must begin this book with an explanation of the basis for everything Orthodox Jews do and think.

Orthodox Jews believe that G-d gave the Torah to the Jewish people at Mount Sinai. They believe this literally happened; it's not a metaphor, nor a fairy tale. It was a real, live occurrence witnessed by the entire nation in the Hebrew year 2448, corresponding to 1312 BC.

Everything in this book begins and ends with the Torah. What the Torah is, exactly, will be discussed in chapter four, but until then, let's think of it as the Five Books of Moshe (Moses). It is the foundation of everything that Orthodox Jews believe and every act they perform.

There is absolutely no way to understand anything about Orthodox Jews unless you understand the basis for their unflinching commitment to the Torah and why, since that day over 3,300 years ago no matter what part of the world we have lived in and through the most trying of circumstances, the Jewish people—and for the last 250 years, Orthodox Jews—have maintained an ironclad belief in a G-d-given Torah.

In this chapter, I will briefly and succinctly explain the foundations for this belief. But first, let me tell you how I came to the fork in the road that took me to a place I could never have imagined.

Bananas

When I arrived in Israel in January 1981, I honestly thought I was going to a country where people were proud of being Jewish. What I quickly discovered was that whatever pride I was seeing was not in being Jewish but rather in being Israeli. In fact, most Israelis I encountered knew next to nothing about Judaism or Jewish history.

I didn't get to speak with any Israelis my age because when I arrived on the kibbutz I was nineteen, and my peers were still in the army. The girls my age were being discharged because they only serve two years but they were also never around. In fact there weren't too many young men from the kibbutz working there at all. I only learned later that most Israelis, especially those from kibbutzim, head for the airport as soon as their army service is over.

I had signed up for an "Ulpan" which was a six month work/study program. I was assigned to a Kibbutz that was located on the Mediterranean coast. The work was whatever the kibbutz needed; the study was conversational Hebrew. I was chosen to work in the banana fields because I was tall and athletic and the *bananot* was the most physically demanding job next to the fish ponds which didn't take *chutzniks* (people from abroad).

When I was given this job at the beginning of the program, I was thrilled. I thought that I'd be working alongside *sabras* my age. But there was only one, Doron, who was in his mid-twenties and had just been discharged from an extended tour in the army. He has been in the assault group that flew into Entebbe in 1976 and the forces that invaded Lebanon in 1978. He had great stories. But within a month he was off to South America and didn't return while I was there. So for six months I worked with older people and *ulpanists*.

The view of the older *kibbutzniks* with whom I spoke was that Jewish practice was a thing of the past; it was silly and outdated. The younger Israelis, to my chagrin, were primarily interested in listening to Bob Marley and moving to Los Angeles. They never tried to convince me to stay in Israel; they just wanted to hear about life in America. During this time, I read an article in the *Jerusalem Post* that reported that in polls of Israeli high school students, the overwhelming majority would choose, if it were possible, to be reborn as non-Jews.

The *kibbutz* was physically beautiful and the people friendly but it was spiritually barren. After months of living in Israel, I came to realize that most Israelis had no idea what being Jewish meant. Neither did I, but I'd thought I would gain something deeper just from being in Israel. The only thing I gained, however, was more questions. For me the godsend, literally, was the fact that my friend Scott was learning in Aish HaTorah in Jerusalem and I would visit him when I was in town. It was the only place in my eight months in Israel where I discussed real issues: Why be Jewish? Why marry Jewish? Why should there be a state of Israel? What is life about anyway? This was why I had come to Israel in the first place. Subconsciously, I had been searching for answers.

What I discovered almost immediately was that Orthodox Judaism—or

Torah Judaism as it was usually called—was significantly different from what I had always assumed it to be. I'd had the impression that Judaism did not add any enjoyment to life and, in fact, interfered with the pursuit of pleasure. I also thought that Orthodox Jews spent their time studying ancient texts that had no relevance to the modern world, that they were intolerant and judgmental and that they were locked in the past, their societies rigid and their women suppressed.

I also could not grasp why Scott—and, from what I was seeing, many other intelligent, successful, put-together young men and women—would embrace a lifestyle that on the surface seemed so old fashioned and restrictive. Why go backwards when mankind is progressing? Why would women accept being second-class citizens now that they were finally on the cusp of achieving equal rights?

But instead of finding evidence to support these negative characterizations, I found the opposite: Everyone—students, rabbis and the families with whom I spent Shabbos—were accepting and friendly. No one tried to force any beliefs down my throat or demand any type of behavior. The only thing they asked for was independent thought: How did I justify my beliefs and opinions? Why did I believe what I did? Had I put it to any scrutiny or was I following blindly?

I had never experienced such an intellectually rigorous environment even though I was a college student when I first came to Israel. In fact, I considered myself an independent thinker. But, in truth, college students are the ultimate followers. "Doing your own thing" in college is really just a way of following the crowd; it's conforming to the idea that you have to do your own thing. In college, rebellion is really just an act of obedience.

I quickly learned that independent thinking requires a person to understand three things: a) that we come with prejudices because we are products of our society, b) that we each have an intuition that checks and balances our thoughts, and c) that without using our sense of reason, our ideas can get ridiculous and even dangerous.

This is how a human being is supposed to use his or her mind. Let me explain each of these points a little bit further.

Products of Society

Every human being on this planet is a product of the society in which he or she grew up. Our beliefs, thoughts and opinions are molded from a very young age by what is happening around us and what we are taught. Without effort, we could easily coast through life on autopilot and never question what we are being taught or what we accept as the truth. That is why it is common to see millions of people believing diametrically opposed ideas—and believing them passionately.

This phenomenon leaves us with two ways to view the nature of human existence. In the first, we are products of our society, and that is the beginning and end of it. We cannot change. Right and wrong are determined by either numbers or strength, and peace and understanding amongst the nations of the world is a fleeting goal, since mankind's opinions vary so greatly and, in many cases, are in conflict.

In the second option, we start out living in a society with a fundamental set of beliefs but are able to evaluate everything we are taught in both the civic and religious spheres. With proper questioning and evaluation, we can choose the correct and moral path in life even if it defies the mores of our society or what we have been taught.

It is clear that the second option is the true one. Many people change their ideas and opinions. Human beings, when open-minded, can discard their pasts and embrace new ideas and philosophies and even a new culture or religion. However, any change requires one to challenge all assumptions, principles and doctrines, both old and new, and while some people do this naturally, others find the very idea terrifying, and so they do nothing. Unfortunately, most of humanity simply accepts what their society believes and practices because going with the flow is the easiest thing to do; even dead fish go with the flow.

But going with the flow has risks if the flow is going in the wrong direction. Under the right circumstances, seemingly normal people can turn into inhuman beasts, as was exemplified during World War Two. During the war-crimes trials that were held after the war, all the Nazis, including the ten leaders tried at Nuremberg, claimed that they had been just following orders. Most Nazis had operated in a virulently anti-Semitic environment where the demonization of Jews permeated the political system, the educational system and all modes of entertainment. The younger ones had been raised in that environment and knew nothing else; they had been intoxicated by the Hitler Youth movement and believed in the superiority of the Aryan and the need to eliminate the Jew.

So, why do we expect them to act in any way differently than they did? Why do we consider them culpable for following orders? The answer is because deep down, we believe that everybody is responsible for evaluating their own beliefs and that unless they do, they are making a proactive decision to remain brainwashed. We admire and hold in high regard those who have rejected false ideologies, such as dissidents who resist totalitarian regimes and we abhor brainwashing and expect people to be able to recognize and reject it.

What people in the West don't recognize is that we also have been programmed with certain ideas, philosophies and prejudices, and we need to dig into them to make sure that we are not blindly swallowing the party line, even if it preaches free love. It is easy to spot a herd mentality when we view footage of people marching for their fatherland whether it be Germany, the Soviet Union, Iran or North Korea. But the reality is that citizens of western democracies are just as passionate and just as "programmed" to believe certain "truths" as are the goose-stepping hordes. It's just that our style is different.

Therefore, until we examine and evaluate our beliefs, we are not really living our own lives—our ideas and opinions are being chosen for us by others. To avoid living with pre-programmed minds, we, as well as every single person on this Earth, must evaluate our beliefs and determine whether or not they are true. Every single one of us, including Orthodox Jews, must do this with every single one of our beliefs.

What it comes down to is that if G-d wanted us to be zombies, he would have created us that way. Instead, He gave each one of us a probing, delving, questioning, expansive, examining intellect. Using it is an obligation.

Intuition

But how are we to know what is true? How is a person supposed to know better than to swallow every lie that is fed to him? Why shouldn't a German teenager during World War Two have believed that killing the Jews of Poland was a great benefit to the German nation and all of mankind? How can we expect an Arab youth, raised in misery and subjected to constant hate speech, not to believe that Allah actually wants him to kill American women and children?

The reason why we expect them to reject such insanity is because we have an intuition. In traditional Jewish thought, intuition, which can be defined as an inner sense of right and wrong and an awareness of a higher truth, is a universal quality of all of mankind. It is a connection to the soul, and we all have it to one degree or another. In some people it is very strong; in others it is weaker. But we all have it. And because we know it is there, we expect people to recognize unvarnished evil when faced with it, and to see clearly a choice between what is right and what is wrong.

The Requirement of Reason

This third point was stressed repeatedly and, unbelievably, it is the basis for the Orthodox belief in a G-d given Torah. Reason! To me, religions were inherently unreasonable and that's why they resorted to violence and repression. And, although, I knew that the Jewish people had never been violent towards other peoples and had never acted against another people in an attempt to impose our religion, I still thought that a belief in Judaism necessitated a leap of faith. But there I was, being told to use my sense of reason to evaluate Judaism. In fact, in Judaism, thinking is synonymous with reasoning.

Reason is actually a type of thinking that is distinct from intelligence. It is the ability to identify and accept truth without bias. A person can be very intelligent and reasonable or very intelligent and unreasonable. And some people of limited intelligence are very reasonable while others are not. Usually most people are reasonable in most of their dealings but will become unreasonable when it comes to a cherished belief that cannot be reasonably defended. Many times such a belief is religious in nature, but this could apply to anything that a person feels strongly about such as politics or morals. We all have seen very reasonable people become very unreasonable in situations of need or when strong beliefs are challenged. The emotional need to believe, more often than not, will trump reason.

Belief that is based on an emotional need and without regard to reason is the definition of a leap of faith. And what is usually the most shocking revelation to new students of Judaism is that while it is considered axiomatic that religion is a matter of faith, this is not true of Judaism. The Torah actually considers it a transgression to live with one's mind shut off because it is through our minds that we accomplish our lives' purposes. Our minds were given to us by G-d, and they are what differentiate us from animals.

Where else in life is it required or meritorious to shut off one's mind? It is self-evident that we should not shut off our minds when it comes to choosing careers or deciding how to invest money. It is also self-evident that we should never shut off our minds when deciding to get married or when raising our children. So, why would it be a requirement for a person to shut off his mind in order to have a relationship with G-d? Certainly, religion, which defines our relationships with G-d and requires sensitivity and ethical behavior towards others, would require that our minds be engaged. In fact, the first of the Ten Commandments is "*know* there is a G-d"—not "*believe* there is a G-d." It is a required knowledge.

This foundation of Judaism is the diametric opposite of blind faith. The most fundamental requirement of any Jew is to think and to learn, and learning requires questioning. Further, there are no questions that are off limits or cause for rebuke, though this is not so for all religions and cultures. It is clear that phony religions and philosophies forbid questioning lest they be exposed for the shams they are. Christianity and Islam obviate the need to protect themselves from questions by outlawing questioning as the work of the devil. A citizen of the Soviet Union did not question how exactly the worker and the peasant were better off under Communism, for such questions would earn him a free trip to Siberia.

But Judaism wants the questions, because inquiry is the only way to learn. The Torah itself is written in a way that provokes questions, and, in fact, the entire Talmud is a series of questions and answers. Think about the Passover Seder—it is built around the Four Questions that are asked by the children. The rest of the Haggadah is the answers.

So, to understand and evaluate our original statement that Orthodox Jews believe that G-d gave the Torah to the Jewish people at Mount Sinai, we need to phrase the question with a slight difference. The proper phrasing of the question is not whether a person can believe in a G-d-given Torah but rather whether a person can believe in a G-d-given Torah *while using his reason.* In other words, can a Jew believe that G-d Himself gave the Torah to the Jewish people at Mount Sinai 3,322 years ago *while using his reason and without resorting to leaps of faith?*

On this one point, everything will hinge.

For most of our 3,322 years, all Jews believed in a G-d-given Torah. Beginning in the late 1700s, the Reform movement, for reasons to be explained later in this book, endeavored to uproot the foundation of Jewish existence—the belief in a G-d-given Torah. In this they were wildly successful. Most non-Orthodox Jews today view the idea that G-d spoke to the Jewish nation at Mount Sinai as nothing more than folklore.

But the Orthodox never budged. And that is because there is a significant body of evidence that points a person *using his reason and without resorting to leaps of faith* to reach a vastly different conclusion than the one that is commonly accepted.

Keeping this in mind we are ready to explore a world of thought that I hope you find new, exciting and inspiring.

The Four PERLs

I will acknowledge that the idea that G-d Himself wrote a "book" and gave it to His creations can sound a little odd to a modern, secular Jew. But let's put that thought to the side for now; the purpose of the Torah will be addressed in chapters two and three. For the purpose of this chapter, we need to see whether the basis for Judaism has any validity—i.e., whether the foundation of the Jewish religion is the same as the foundations of millions of other religions that have come and gone—or come and stayed—throughout history.

Are the Torah and the thousands of volumes in our unbelievably rich and prolific, 3,300-year-old literary history merely an antique collection of ancient writings, wise sayings, folklore, tales and poetic verse? Is the Torah no different than the Code of Hammurabi or the *Iliad* or the Scandinavian Eddas? Or even the New Testament or the Koran? If this turns out to be the case, then I will be the first to say, "Why bother with it all? There is no reason why the Torah should have any relevance to our modern lives except as a source of entertainment and, perhaps, inspiration."

On the other hand, if G-d truly authored the Torah, it should be self-evident to anyone reading it. In other words the Torah should contain information attesting to the fact that a human being could not have written it. Granted, this information is very hard for someone unfamiliar with the Torah to evaluate and so I have synopsized the points into what I term "the four PERLs," which is an acronym for:

> **P**rophecies that a human being could not predict.
> An **E**vent that a human being could not fabricate.
> **R**ewards that a human being could not promise.
> **L**aws that a human being could not decree.

None of this understanding is new, in fact much of it has been discussed in rabbinic writing since the Middle Ages when Jewish communities were forced by the Catholic Church into disputations to discredit Judaism and prove that Christianity was the "true religion."

An Event That a Human Being Could Not Fabricate

Let's first look at the second PERL (I am purposely leaving the first PERL for the end). In the second book of the Torah, Shmot (Exodus), our experience at Mount Sinai is clearly laid out. All Jewish people, numbering between two and three million, were camped around Mount Sinai—every man, woman and child. There was a tremendous display of thunder and lightning, and the sound of a *shofar* (ram's horn) growing louder and louder. The first two of the Ten Commandments were spoken directly to the entire nation; the last eight, at the Jews' request, were given to Moshe to transmit to the rest of the nation.

To receive the rest of the Torah on behalf of the Jewish people, who had already agreed to receive it, Moshe ascended the mountain and entered the thick cloud resting on the summit. While he was in the cloud, the entire nation heard him speak to G-d and heard G-d speak to Moshe (Exodus, chapter 19, verses 9-19).

This is what it says in the Torah. The issues that a thinking person needs to address are whether this account can be verified and/or whether Moshe could have fabricated the entire story and then convinced approximately three million people that they had experienced something that they did not. Our first instinct is to doubt that he could have pulled off such a hoax. How do you convince someone that they experienced something they do not remember? Furthermore, how do you convince an entire nation?

In the fifth book of the Torah, Dvarim (Deuteronomy), Moshe reminds the Jewish people of their experience. In an address he makes to the nation before he died (forty years after the event) he specifically exhorts them three times to remember and to teach their children that they stood at the mountain and heard G-d speak to them "out of the fire" (Deut. 4:9-12, 4:32-36 and 5:1-4). In 4:32, he asks specifically if any other nation has ever heard G-d speak to them—"*Has a people ever heard the voice of G-d speaking from the midst of the fire as you have heard and survived?*"

But for the sake of argument, let's try to re-enact such a scenario. Imagine that someone today would attempt to convince a large group that they had experienced G-d's revelation when, in fact, they hadn't. To try this experiment in a modern society, where the media records our lives, would be futile so this person's first requirement would be to find a population living somewhere in isolation, perhaps somewhere in Africa or the Pacific Islands, or maybe in Central America.

Next, to make this attempt analogous to the Torah's account, he would need a compendium containing the philosophy and laws of a new religion. To be analogous to the Torah, this book would have to be so comprehensive, containing laws of personal conduct, commerce, agriculture and justice and even laws of worshipping a god, that it would be disruptive to any potential followers. That is, they would not be able to follow its laws without suddenly and drastically changing their lives. In short, getting them to buy it would be difficult.

Essentially, there are only two ways for this person to approach such a sale. The first would be to tell the people that G-d sent him to bring them the happy tidings. The second would be to tell them that G-d had previously given the book to all of them or to their ancestors in a national event.

The first approach certainly has potential for success—just look at all that missionaries have been able to accomplish throughout history. They arrive bearing the message of G-d's love and the redemption of mankind. They speak of wonders and miracles and the rewards in the afterlife. For the average pagan, this is truly good news.

Now, let's watch our intrepid lawgiver try the second approach.

This fellow shows up one day in a village and tells the people he finds there the following: "One day, years ago, the mountain outside this village was completely engulfed in smoke. Lightning was striking the mountain from above, and deafening peels of thunder resounded throughout the heavens. All of you camped around the mountain while I ascended it to receive this set of laws. G-d himself spoke directly to your entire tribe—men, women and children—and gave you this book. And you all agreed to accept it as binding forever. Now, you must follow my teachings."

How effective do you think that approach would be? I think that the natives would split their sides laughing—and, if they were cannibals, would start building a fire on which to roast the stranger. Why is this approach such a non-starter? Because it is impossible to tell a normal person that he has experienced something that he has not. And, it's even more impossible to tell a large group of people that they have experienced something that they have not.

Okay, lets adjust the scenario slightly. This time, instead of informing the people that *they* had this awesome experience at the mountain, he will inform them that it was their ancestors who experienced it. Will this new approach really work? Let's see.

One day, he shows up in another village and tells them the following: "One day, years ago, the mountain outside this village was completely engulfed in smoke. Lightning was striking the mountain from above, and deafening peels of thunder resounded throughout the heavens. All of your ancestors—the entire nation—camped around the mountain while the leader of your tribe at that time ascended it to receive this set of laws. G-d himself spoke directly to your entire tribe—every man, woman and child—and gave your ancestors this book. And they all agreed to accept it as binding forever."

Before barbequing him, some members of the tribe might taunt him with a few obvious questions, such as: If this momentous event occurred in the history of our tribe, why is it that absolutely no one has any recollection whatsoever of ever hearing anything about it? Such an event would surely not be forgotten. Why wouldn't our ancestors have spoken about it to their children and their children's children? And why don't we have any semblance of any of these laws? No one has ever heard of any of them. And how is it that you, a stranger, wound up in possession of this book of laws?

It's apparent that it is impossible to invent a story of a national occurrence. It is impossible to approach a group and convince them that G-d had spoken to them or to their ancestors. The only way you can get people to accept a new religion (without resorting to violence) is to claim that G-d spoke to you and you are spreading His word. There is really no other way.

This is why, out of all the thousands of religions that billions of people have practiced from the dawn of time until today throughout the entire world, there is only one—**one**—that claims that G-d spoke to an entire nation: Judaism. Every single other man-made religion that claims to represent the will of G-d, including Christianity and Islam, bases itself on the vision or revelation of one man, and all of these new religions were spread using force, charismatic persuasion or a combination of both. Mohammed can emerge from a cave and claim that G-d spoke to him; Moshe cannot descend from a mountain and claim G-d spoke to everyone.

But there is a deeper point to be stressed. As I mentioned earlier, leaps of faith—i.e., turning off one's mind—is not an accepted Jewish practice and is, in fact, the opposite of what G-d wants of us. This is why He did not send Moshe to sell the Torah to the Jewish people. If Moshe had come to us and told us that G-d had sent him, we would have been left with only two choices: Reject him as a liar or turn off our minds, take a leap of faith and blindly accept what he said. G-d would have to put us in an untenable situation.

A parable will help illustrate this point. There was once a king who had two sons. The older son was not too bright and not too motivated. He enjoyed the perks of palace life but wasn't interested in the responsibilities; his idea of a full week was seven nights of parties.

The younger son was much brighter and much more motivated, and wasn't interested in wasting time. Instead, he spent his time shadowing his father and absorbing the lessons of his example.

One day, the king suddenly died, and he had not appointed an heir. The older son, naturally, felt that the throne was his by right of birth. The younger son felt that he had prepared himself for such a day and that he was eminently more qualified than his irresponsible and incapable older brother.

The people of the kingdom were split. Part of the nobility backed the older son out of respect for the tradition of primogeniture. Another part backed the younger son, feeling that the older son was a worthless drunkard and that the younger would be a far better king. Still another sizable part of the nobility could not decide. For weeks, the debate went on until civil war seemed imminent.

Suddenly, one morning, the older son made it known that he had a major announcement to make, and that he would do so at noon in the banquet hall. The palace was abuzz with rumors. What would he announce? Would he make an ultimatum? Would he throw his support behind his younger brother?

Noon came, and the son strode into the room and stepped to the front. He cleared his throat. "Ladies and gentlemen," he began. "These past few weeks have been a difficult time for all of us. It has certainly been hard for me personally, and I am sure it has been hard for my dear brother. And, I know it has been hard for each and every faithful subject of my late father and for the kingdom as a whole. What I didn't know until last night was that this most unfortunate situation has been paining my late father in the world beyond. It seems that he can no longer stand to watch his faithful subjects tear at each other over this issue. So, I am here to say that last night, our beloved king came to me in a dream.

"'My son,' he said to me, 'this fight prevents me from resting in peace. It must stop. And so I am reaching out to you from the world beyond and asking you to please put a stop to it. Please announce to the entire kingdom, and of course to your brother, that I have selected you to sit upon my throne in my stead. I know that this will come as a bitter disappointment to your brother, but only one man can rule and it is my firm belief that it should be you.'

"Ladies and gentlemen, you can imagine my shock! How painful it must have been to my father that he would have to take such extraordinary action. But, nevertheless, we must accept his will." Bowing his head, he whispered, "I stand before you humbled by his trust in me."

The room was utterly still. For what seemed an eternity, no one stirred until finally, the younger brother spoke up.

"My dear brother, I am sure that these past few weeks have been painful to our father. But I have just one question. If our father wants the fighting to stop and you to be the king, why would he come to you in a dream and tell it to you? We have no way of knowing if you are telling the truth. If he wants me to accept you as king, shouldn't he have come to me to announce it? If he wants all of us to accept you, shouldn't he have come to all of us?"

Similarly, if G-d had wanted the Jewish people to listen to and follow Moshe, the only reasonable way for Him to accomplish that would have been for Him to come to us and tell us to do so. He could not have told Moshe to convey the message because there would have been no way to confirm such a story and no way to reasonably believe him. The only reasonable way for G-d to establish Moshe as his prophet was for Him to directly inform the entire nation, which is exactly what He did.

It has been suggested that perhaps, during the time in the desert or even at a later time, some people decided to concoct the story and pass it down to their children. I think this idea ignores two truths. The first is that it is impossible for large numbers of people to lie in unanimity; stories would vary, and the conspiracy would be exposed. The second is that people do not lie to their children about real issues or important things unless they feel that by doing so they are helping them. If the parents spent an afternoon looking for a bicycle to give their child as a birthday gift, they would not truthfully tell the child where they had been so as not to ruin the surprise. But the same parents would never concoct a story about meeting Bigfoot on a camping trip and continue with the lie throughout their child's entire life. Some Holocaust survivors hid the truth about being Jewish from their children because they felt it would protect them. But even if a few sets of parents would concoct a story and lie about it to their children, is it reasonable to believe that millions would do so?

For the sake of comparison, let's look at the other two religions that claim to represent G-d's will for mankind—Christianity and Islam. Neither of them claims a national revelation; in fact their origins are quire similar. Jesus claimed that he was the son of G-d. But how can one know if he was telling the truth? Christians will point to miracles but to the Jews that is no big deal—the Old Testament is full of miracles and Moshe, Yehoshua (Joshua) and Eliyahu (Elijah) performed much more impressive ones than

Jesus is purported to have done. In fact, in Jewish philosophy, miracles hold no special place as evidence of anything except G-d's love for the Jewish people. They don't prove truth.

According to Islam, Mohammed emerged from a cave and announced that G-d had spoken to him. How can a person know if he was telling the truth? He can't. So, he has two options: Blindly accept it or reject it, which amounts to believe him and be allowed to live, or don't believe him and be killed.

Christian and Moslem adherents have no choice but to blindly accept the words of either Jesus or Mohammed. It is one man's word against another's.

Similar to Christianity and Islam is the Mormon religion, which began in the United States nearly 150 years ago. The Mormons believe that G-d sent an angel to Joseph Smith to tell him where to find the Book of Mormon and the secret tablets needed to translate it (which were conveniently lost immediately after he finished). This claim is just as unreasonable as the stories of Jesus and Mohammed, but it doesn't matter; if people have an emotional need to believe, they will find a way to do so as evidenced by the billions of people who believe in these faiths.

This means that one cannot be a Christian, Moslem or Mormon and accept the stories and doctrines of these religions in the face of the logical arguments or empirical evidence against them without making great leaps of faith. And because these religions cannot stand up to the test of reason they have raised blind faith to a doctrinal virtue—something Judaism vigorously rejects.

This account of a national revelation is the first indication that a human being did not write the Torah. In fact, of all religions, Judaism stands apart as unique: It is the only religion in the history of mankind that is based on a national event and not the words of an individual.

Laws That a Human Being Could Not Decree

If you were creating a religion, would you include laws that would seem ridiculous or be impossible to fulfill? I wouldn't. What would be gained from making irrational decrees that would seem insane or elicit laughter?

For example, would you decree that every seven years, people had to quit their jobs and not earn money for an entire year? Or that three times a year, every single citizen, even those in the armed forces, had to abandon their towns, villages and bases and assemble in one city in the center of the country? Such laws are ridiculous and irresponsible, even dangerous, and that's why you don't find anything like them in Christianity, Islam or any other religion.

But there are such laws in the Torah, in black and white, for everyone to see.

In chapter 25 of third book of the Torah, Vayikra (Leviticus), the Jewish people are commanded to let the entire Land of Israel lay fallow for an entire year every seventh year. This is not a rotating cycle where only one-seventh of the land goes unused each year, allowing for cultivation to continue uninterrupted so the people can have food. It is a commandment that stipulates that every seventh year, every square inch of the Land of Israel must remain untouched for a full calendar year. This means no farming, no harvesting, not even the clearing of weeds. In other words, this decree basically tells the Jews, "Every seven years, you and your family should starve yourselves to death."

The obvious question is, if the people don't plant, what will they eat? Not to worry, says the author of the Torah, he has anticipated the question. The Torah states: "And if you ask 'what will we eat in the seventh year being that we will not sow or harvest our crops?' I will command my blessing to you in the sixth year and the crop will suffice for the three years. You will sow in the eighth year and [continue to] eat from the old crop until the ninth year, until the arrival of its [the ninth year's] crop you will eat the old."

This commandment was given to an agrarian society; let's adapt it to the modern world. Imagine that you are commanded to quit your job at the end of every sixth year and earn no money during the seventh year. You are also told not to worry because either:

a. checks will miraculously come in the mail
b. no bills will come that year
c. everything will suddenly be very inexpensive so you will spend very little money that year
d. somehow you will be able to afford your current lifestyle without earning a penny

Or whatever. Does it really matter what any self-styled prophet would guarantee? After he tells you to quit your job, you're not going to listen anymore. Your reaction will be, "This guy is nuts. Where's the door?"

But as if this commandment weren't audacious enough, the author of the Torah threw in another: After seven cycles of seven years—that is, in year number fifty—the entire Jewish nation is to celebrate the *Yovel* or Jubilee Year and observe the same agricultural restrictions again. This means absolutely no farming of any kind in the forty-ninth year due to the first seven-year requirement, and then no farming again in the fiftieth or *Yovel* Year. (There are other aspects to the *Yovel* Year but I am only focusing on the agricultural laws for the purpose of this illustration.)

There is another seemingly irrational commandment. In Exodus 34:23, the Jewish people are commanded to join together in the celebration of the three major holidays: Pesach (Passover), Shavuot (when we received the Torah at Mount Sinai) and Succot (Feast of Tabernacles). To do so, all men, women and children are to travel to Jerusalem.

This means that that three times a year, every year, all citizens of Israel shall abandon their cities and towns, leave the entire country uninhabited and all assemble in one specific city. This includes the entire armed forces, which should abandon their bases, forts, early warning systems and outposts and also assemble in that same city. That city was later designated as Jerusalem, which happens to lie near the geographic center of the country, meaning that any would-be invader from any direction would be able to drive through much the country unopposed.

And remember, Israel is located in the Middle East, which has always been as volatile as it is today. Lying at the crossroads of Europe, Asia and Africa, it has seen more than its share of invaders and occupiers. Even way back, Israel had unfriendly neighbors; the Ammonites and Moabites to the east, the Edomites and Midianites to the south, the Canaanites and Arameans to the north and the Philistines along the coast. To the southwest lies Egypt and farther east lay Assyria, Babylon and Persia. Later in history, Greece and then Rome would threaten from the west.

To what nation in today's world would a sane person make this suggestion? Even Switzerland maintains an army. But the author of the Torah tells us not to worry. We are promised outright that no other nation or power will have any aspirations for our land, nor will anyone attack while we are in Jerusalem, celebrating the holiday (Exodus 34:24).

Had millions of Jews not experienced the national event at Mount Sinai and instead were hearing all this from a single, charismatic individual, how long would it take for someone to assassinate him in his sleep to prevent a national catastrophe?

Alternatively, once the surrounding nations caught on to this thrice-yearly cycle, how long would Israel last?

And there is another fact that makes this commandment even more incredible. Assuming the people were to accept such a decree, what would be its effect on the nation's agriculture? In the Gregorian calendar, Passover comes in either March or April, coinciding with the harvesting of the winter grain crops and the planting of the summer grains. Shavuot is in May or June, just when the summer fruits are ripening. And Succot is in September or October, when the summer grains must be reaped and the grapes harvested. Every farmer knows that any crop left in the ground, on the tree or on the vine too long becomes ruined—and yet it is precisely at these critical junctures in the agricultural cycle that the Jews are told to lay down their sickles and baskets and travel to Jerusalem. Though it defies all sense and logic, after toiling all season in their fields, they are expected to trust the author of the Torah, who promises that everything will be okay.

These two commandments also seem to indicate that a human being did not write the Torah. There are no such decrees or requirements in any other religion in the world. Again the Torah stands apart—it contains laws that no rational human being could decree.

Rewards That a Human Being Could Not Promise

If a person were to claim that G-d gave him a set of laws and wanted people to follow them, he would need to establish some type of system of reward and punishment. Without rewards, no one would follow, and without some system of punishment for transgressors, what would keep people in line? But how would a human being structure such a system? Would he have these consequences occur in this lifetime, or would he have them play out in the next life, after a follower has died? This is not just an academic question because, eventually, the leader's entire credibility will rest on it.

Think about it this way: If he would promise results in this lifetime, they'd better happen or he would quickly be exposed as a phony. Therefore, it would seem much safer to script the religion in such a way that the consequences, both good and bad, occur in the afterlife, far from the eyes of the living. This way, he could promise all types of eternal pleasures for believers and pain and suffering for the disobedient, and whether or not any of it is ever actually delivered, no one will be the wiser. Promises like these are hard to disprove since, so far, no one has ever come back. The dead are very good at keeping secrets.

The Torah is quite unique when it comes to reward and punishment: It unequivocally states that our actions and behavior will affect the blessings the Jewish people receive in this life. It specifies—*in detail*—the consequences that will occur in this life and in this world for those who obey its laws. In fact, the Torah makes no explicit mention of an afterlife. This does not mean that an eternal life is not a basic tenet of Judaism; it is, as you will see in chapter five. Rather, the Torah emphasizes this life because the purpose of our existence is to be found in the here and now, not in the next world.

In chapter eleven of Dvarim (Deuteronomy), the Jewish people are given a very clear choice. They are told, if you "love Hashem and serve Him with all your heart and all your soul, then I will provide rain for your land in its proper time, the early and the late rains, that you may gather in your grain, your wine and your oil. I will provide grass in your field for your animals and you will eat and be satisfied."

It continues: "Beware lest your heart be seduced and you turn away and serve other gods and bow to them. Then G-d will become angry with you. He will close up the heavens so there will be no rain and the ground will not yield its produce. And you will be quickly banished from the good land that Hashem has given you."

The author of the Torah promises rain for our crops, an abundance of grain, wine and oil, and plenty of grazing for our flocks. He also threatens to withhold rain, cause a famine and eventually exile the people. It seems unreasonable for a human being to make such statements and expect anyone, let alone an entire nation, to believe in and follow him. As human beings, we understand our limitations and so will our followers; we will know when a leader is making a promise—either of punishment or reward—that he could not possibly fulfill.

Not surprisingly, and again only for the sake of comparison, all of the promises of reward made by Christianity and Islam occur in the next life. Neither makes any mention of any consequences occurring in a person's lifetime. Believe and you will merit eternal paradise; don't believe and it's eternal damnation for you.

In this regard as well, the Torah stands apart as unique. Judaism is the only religion that contains promises of rewards in this lifetime which, by definition, cannot be provided by a flesh and blood person—another indication that the Torah was not authored by a human being.

Prophecies That a Human Being Could Not Predict

I saved this "PERL" for the end because it is really the most awesome of the four.

The idea that a human being can predict the future in great detail is very farfetched. How many of us would feel comfortable declaring how the world will look in 100 years? Or 1,000 years? Imagine someone standing up and making self-assured predictions about the future of the Indian tribes in the Americas or the worldwide dispersal of the Tibetan exiles in, say, 2,000 years. No one would take such a person or his assertions seriously.

And yet, this is exactly what Moshe did. In a series of public pronouncements, many taking place just days before his death, he informs the Jews of their entire future, laying out in fantastic detail a sweeping overview of what was in store. He made eight individual prophecies that are each unbelievable in their own right and when combined into a narrative, become absolutely mind boggling.

He told the Jewish People that:

- They would inevitably stray from the path of Torah (Deut. 31: 15-18, 32:15-18)
- They would be exiled from the Land of Israel (Deut. 28:63),
- They would be scattered to the far reaches of the Earth (Deut. 28:64)
- They would be few in number (Deut. 28:62)
- In exile, they would be harassed and persecuted and find no rest (Deut. 28:65-67)
- Israel would be barren and devoid of any significant human settlement during the Jews' absence (Deut. 29:21-27)
- They would eventually return to the Land of Israel, (Deut. 30:3-5)
- After their return, the land would experience a fertile rebirth (Deut. 30:5-9)

There are so many questions that jump to mind when reading this list.

First of all, what person who wanted to attract followers would make such statements? What would he gain? He could only lose credibility. Such dire warnings might, through sheer terror, keep people in line, but the risks of being exposed as a charlatan far outweigh any such gain. And why eight horrible predictions? Wouldn't one or two suffice? They are also very specific; a general "you will burn in hell" might accomplish the same thing.

Also, such threats are rarely effective. Human beings employ cognitive dissonance when faced with uncomfortable situations; people listening to such predictions would either doubt that such catastrophes would ever occur or believe that they could happen to another generation, but certainly not theirs.

A closer look at these predictions raises additional questions. Why would a human author threaten to exile an entire nation? Historically, such a thing is extremely rare. Besides those that occurred under the Assyrians and Babylonians—over 800 years after the giving of the Torah—and perhaps the exile of the Crimean Tatars to Siberia under Josef Stalin, there aren't too many examples of entire populations being relocated *en masse*. Thus, it seems strange that a human author would threaten to do so, especially when such an occurrence was unheard of at the time.

Further, why would Moshe bother threatening a worldwide dispersal of the Jewish nation? Or that the Jewish people will be few in number, will be targets of relentless and irrational violence or will find no peace in exile? These were unknown occurrences at the time of the Torah and thus held little weight. A human author could have created much more realistic and therefore scarier scenarios, like a foreign power swooping in and stealing their wives and daughters. That they would have understood. But harassment and wandering from one end of the earth to the other sounds a little over the top.

Another question is why, after prescribing what sounds like a national death sentence, would Moshe go on to say that the Jewish people would ever return to the Land of Israel? How could a people scattered to the four corners of the world, harassed, murdered and in a constant state of uncertainty be expected to survive at all?

The last two statements are, in some ways, the most unbelievable: The Jews would return to Israel and upon their return, the land, which he states will be utterly barren during the Jews absence, will once again become fertile. Why would anyone believe that such an abused and widely dispersed nation would have the ability to reclaim its long-lost homeland? A nation with military power might have a chance, but a people without any physical power living in restricted ghettoes and under discriminatory restrictions throughout world? Not very likely.

And why would anybody believe that the Land of Israel would become a wasteland? Israel lies on the southwestern tip of what is known as the "Fertile Crescent." Is it conceivable that the land would dry up and die as if someone suddenly shut off a switch? And then, when the Jews returned, turn the switch back on again? It is not believable—and yet, it is exactly what transpired. Despite present-day Arab propaganda, the fact remains that the Land of Israel was, until recently, a barren, empty wasteland.

Mark Twain in his travelogue *The Innocents Abroad*, noted that his party traveled for miles in the land without seeing a village or even a single human being. Further, the accounts of the British and French archeologists who traveled and worked throughout the land in the 1800s told the same tale of a denuded land void of inhabitants. The Jews, it seems, don't make the desert bloom only through hard work; it happens through their sheer presence.

All of these questions pale in comparison to the one gargantuan fact that is staring us in the face—every single one of these prophecies actually came true. The statements in the Torah are not vague, two-line statements, *a la* Nostradamus, that can be constantly reinterpreted to fit current events. They are very detailed predictions involving a large part of humanity, a big area of the world and an enormous span of time. For them to be fulfilled over a course of 3,000 years is statistically beyond impossible.

- Did we not veer from the proper path? (The rest of the Bible chronicles it.)
- Were we not exiled (not once but twice!)?
- Were we not scattered to the four corners of the world?
- Are we not few in number?
- Are we not harassed and persecuted? (While all other hatred is lumped together as "bigotry" or "racism," only prejudice against Jews has its own name: Anti-Semitism.)
- Have we found any repose in this exile? (Most Jewish-population centers in the world today are less than 100 years old.)
- Despite numerous attempts against us, were we ever annihilated?
- Did we not return to Israel? (In fact, Israel is the only nation in the world that governs itself in the same land, with the same religion, same language and same name, as it did 3,000 years ago.)
- Has the land not flowered?

When Jewish history is viewed through the prism of these prophecies, it becomes obvious that the entire narrative of Jewish history and survival is, in fact, supernatural because we simply never had the natural means to survive. The Chinese have lasted for thousands of years because they are settled in their land in great numbers, have a common language and culture, and have not fallen victim to intense, irrational, murderous hatred. For the same reasons, the French, the British and the Russians can trace their roots back over 1,500 years.

But the Jewish people, throughout the last 2,000 years of exile, have had none of these advantages. We've had no common land or language, no strength in arms or numbers, and no lasting peace in the lands in which we have found even temporary shelter.

Again for the sake of comparison and to show the uniqueness of the Torah, we can draw a contrast with the New Testament and the Koran to see if they share the Torah's ability to predict the future with the same sharpness of vision. But they do not; in fact they are oddly silent on the subject. It's almost as if their human authors said nothing because they had absolutely no idea what the future would hold. And how could they? Does any man? To say that they knew the future, to make wild statements that would certainly be proven untrue, would have blown their credibility.

This last PERL also indicates that the Torah is ultimately unique. It alone, among countless religious texts throughout history, has the ability to lay out in detail the course of history before it happened.

Improbable and Impossible

Each of these four PERLs is fantastic in its own right; all four together in one document is nothing short of phenomenal. I say that because if similar examples would be found scattered amongst the world's religions, the Torah would not be so different. But not one of these PERLs is found in any other religion; not one of the thousands of religions in recorded history contains even one of them, yet the Torah contains all four. They are entirely unique to the Torah.

This means that the author of the Torah is claiming to have the ability to control nature, the fate of entire nations and the future of mankind. So either the Torah was written by the one omnipotent G-d or a very ambitious but unbalanced human being whose religious experiment would very quickly crash and burn. It doesn't seem likely that Judaism, which has given the world so much enlightenment as we will see in later chapters, would be the product of craziness and even if it had been, we have seen that there would have been no way for Moshe to have foisted it upon an entire nation.

Some people have proposed that Moshe forcibly seized power and then, as a way of justifying his rule, concocted the story and forced it to be taught. But this theory is not reasonable because although we know of such cases in history, rarely do such established "facts" survive the dictator himself, let alone last thousands of years. And from the narratives in the Torah, we clearly see that Moshe was not a dictator—the people were not afraid to challenge him and there were times when he even feared for his life.

I have also heard the suggestion of mass hysteria, but, again, it is not reasonable to believe that mass hysteria could have happened to three million people with complete unanimity—and that the result of the hysteria was a detailed law book that eventually changed the morality of the world.

These last two suggestions also ignore one fact of our existence: Throughout our history, we Jews have been called almost every insult possible, but "stupid" and "simple minded" have never been among them. In fact, the Torah itself describes us as a "stiff-necked" people, meaning that we are not easily swayed. We are so renowned for our cleverness and sagacity that kings and emperors consistently turned to us to manage their kingdoms and fortunes. Today, we are still the doctors, lawyers and financial advisors of choice.

All of these points create a stark difference between Judaism and other religions: Other religions need to be proven true while the Torah needs to be proven *not* true. Much ink has been spilled by so-called "Bible critics" attempting to do just that. One of their favorite arguments centers on the exodus from Egypt, and specifically on the splitting of the Red Sea. They say it was the result of an unusually strong windstorm—some very intelligent people have written long, scholarly papers detailing how it could have happened. The irony of this argument is that the Torah itself specifically says that a strong wind blew all night and parted the waters. To claim it was purely a natural occurrence would mean that the Jewish people benefited from a remarkably fortuitous coincidence—just when they were trapped against the sea with no means of escape, a mighty windstorm suddenly blew the waters apart just long enough for them to escape before crashing down on their Egyptian pursuers. It also begs the question of why no other body of water in any time or place has ever been parted by similarly strong winds.

Still, even if the Red Sea did part by completely natural means, it only explains one small detail of the entire exodus from Egypt. Did the Jews imagine the destruction of the pursuing Egyptian army when the waters came crashing down on them? Did the Jews imagine that they crossed on dry land? Did they imagine the booty they collected on the shore and the ten plagues that ended their slavery and decimated the Egyptians? Did they also imagine the Manna that fell for forty years?

Another very compelling argument to be made for the Torah's divine origin comes to us through a strange and ironic piece of information—both Christianity and Islam officially accept the revelation at Mount Sinai as an unassailable fact. Why is that so? Why didn't the founders of these religions just claim that Judaism was nonsense and that they had the truth? Why tie the new religions to the Torah? The answer is obvious; the evidence of the giving of the Torah on Mount Sinai was so strong that they could not discredit it. Rather, in order to have any credibility at all, they had to attest to the truth of the Jewish claim. But then they employed what in sales jargon is called a "bump and roll" or a "yes, but." The Christians said, "Yes, of course G-d gave the Jews the Torah, but it was too hard to fulfill, so he sent his only son, Jesus." The Moslems said, "Yes, of course G-d gave the Jews the Torah, but it was only meant to be temporary until He sent his final prophet, Mohammed."

So remarkably, if you put a religious Jew, a religious Christian and a religious Moslem in a room, they will be in complete agreement that G-d gave the Torah to the Jewish people on Mount Sinai. (The first group in history to officially reject the revelation at Mount Sinai was the Reform movement. So ironically, if you put a religious Christian, a religious Moslem and a *secular* Jew in a room, the Christian and Moslem would both say to the Jew, "G-d gave you a Torah on Mount Sinai," but the Jew would protest and insist that G-d had not.)

And what is also very revealing is that the founders of Christianity and Islam didn't mimic the Jews and claim their own national revelations. This omission only proves the fact that such a story could not be made up. Neither Christianity nor Islam claims that G-d spoke to an entire nation or even to a large group. I think that if they could have made such a claim, they would have. But since it is impossible to do so, they simply used the legitimacy of the Torah as the basis of their new religion.

Playing the Odds

Based on the all the information I've presented in this chapter, the Jewish people have always known that we possess a G-d-given Torah. (Since the early 1800s, those who maintained the belief have been termed "Orthodox Jews"; how this came to be is fully explained in chapter eleven.) We know this as a fact because we live according to statistics—what some might call "odds" or "chances." We are always making calculations to determine what is safe or risky, or what might happen or probably won't. Driving a car can be dangerous but the odds are very favorable. Most people are not afraid to fly for the same reason—the odds are long against a crash. On the other hand if even ten percent of all flights ended in a crash no one would fly.

In the same vein, what if human authorship of the Torah were statistically impossible? What if the odds that a person or people wrote the Torah were the same as a human's chance of breathing underwater? Or teaching a dog to speak a human language? Or jumping from a plane eight miles up and landing on your feet and walking away? All of these are so statistically improbable as to be considered impossible but so is the possibility that a human being could convince millions of people that they experienced something they did not or that they should accept a law book that requires them to abstain from farming for a full year every seven years and abandon their towns, villages and borders three times a year. One does not have to be a statistician to know that it is impossible for a human being to guarantee rain and abundant crops or make eight extraordinary predictions about the course of human events, all of which would eventually ensue.

The threshold that applies to all of our lives' decisions—whether it be beyond a reasonable doubt or just a preponderance of evidence—also applies to the test of whether the 3,322-year-old Jewish understanding of the event at Mount Sinai is true and accurate.

It is not a stretch to state that it seems impossible that the Torah is the work of a human being. And I don't think it is hyperbole to state that what happened in the Sinai desert on that spring day 3,322 years ago was an unparalleled event in human history.

Which leaves us with one very fundamental question: If the Torah is truly G-d-given, what is the point of it all? Is the meaning of life to be bound by thousands of laws? Why would G-d bother with any laws at all? Why forbid certain foods, activities and hedonistic pleasures? Why not just let us enjoy ourselves?

It is certainly not reasonable to think that G-d created us just so we should be circumcised and avoid eating shellfish. There must a greater purpose to the Torah. But what is it? This question can only be answered by first answering a larger and even more fundamental question: What is the point of life itself?

Once we answer this question, we will be able to understand why G-d gave us the Torah and why is it so powerful that it has brought down empires, altered mankind's thinking and changed the course of history.

Chapter Three
Free Will
and the Meaning of Life

Who Is G-d?

Any discussion about the meaning of life must inevitably begin with a discussion about G-d because the two are inextricably linked. Unfortunately, this can be problematic for some because, let's be honest, G-d has been given a bad reputation; He's been hijacked by an assortment of lunatics, lowlifes, manipulators and thieves. Because of this, the average secular Jew finds it a little uncomfortable to have a serious conversation about Him and cringes at statements like "G-d loves you," picturing it coming from someone with a Southern drawl, tasteless clothing and a plastic smile or from some emotionally disturbed person handing out leaflets in a bus station.

To further complicate matters, the people screaming most about G-d nowadays are also slitting the throats of innocent people, blowing themselves up in crowds or foaming at the mouth in yet another Third World street demonstration. It is very hard to have a sincere conversation without seeing these images somewhere in the background. But it is imperative to understand from the outset that the Jewish concept of G-d and His relationship with us have nothing in common with these distorted philosophies, and that nothing in this book should be seen through those lenses.

So who exactly is "The G-d of Israel"? Here is the Jewish view in a nutshell: He is completely altruistic and benevolent, and He created us in order to bestow goodness and kindness upon us. He can do only good and everything He does is for the good. His love for us is beyond human understanding. He only wants to give to us and created the world only to give us pleasure. (A mean or uncaring god would not create the concepts of love or pleasure. Nor would he create a beautiful world or adorable children.)

He is infinite, without needs or limitations. And not only is He acutely aware of what is happening to every molecule in the universe, He is also continuously willing each one of them into existence. Because G-d is infinite, He is ultimately unknowable, so He describes Himself using human attributes, feelings and even physical characteristics so that we can relate to

Him. The Torah mentions "His voice" or "His outstretched arm," but those are allegorical. This idea will be developed later in this chapter and in the following chapters, and every topic discussed in this book is based on this definition.

The Big Question: Why?

Why are we here?

The Torah describes our beginning in a narrative of continuous generosity. For six days, G-d created the world for man, preparing the universe, putting everything in place and setting up a self-sustaining system called "nature" to provide beauty, sustenance and enjoyment. As His final act, the one He had been building towards, He created man and woman, and placed them in the perfect environment, one in which they would thrive: *Gan Eden* (the "Garden of Eden" in English).

What was the purpose of all of this? It certainly can't be malevolent. A parent doesn't conceive a child in order to cause it sorrow. A mother doesn't carry a child for nine months of discomfort, and give birth to it in great pain, in order to later make its life miserable. (True, there is pain and suffering in life but they play a role as we will see in chapter five). The Torah's description leaves no doubt that forethought went into creation. This means that there is a benevolent purpose to the existence of the universe. What could that purpose be?

Some people will acknowledge G-d as the creator but choose to believe that He left the world on its own after He finished creating it. However, it is fundamentally unreasonable to think that G-d would create the world with all its ingenuity and beauty—which implies a purpose—and then just abandon it. Such a belief removes any purpose from creation and is usually voiced by those who prefer to avoid discussions of morality.

It has been suggested that perhaps G-d created us for his amusement or entertainment. This idea seems a little ridiculous for two reasons: First, who in his right mind thinks he is so interesting that G-d would enjoy watching him live his life? Most of the time, our lives involve mundane, excruciatingly boring activities. And second, with all the horrible things that happen in the world, how could it be so amusing?

It has also been suggested that perhaps G-d created the universe for His benefit. But what benefit could He possibly receive? Is it logical to think that G-d could gain anything from ruling a world in which He is omnipotent? How could He benefit from something that He could create with mere thought? What could human beings provide Him that He couldn't just will into existence?

Maybe He created us in order to rule over us. Maybe he needed subjects. This idea is akin to buying an ant farm in order to rule over it, or buying a remote-controlled toy car in order to feel all powerful—except that you didn't create the ants and can't really control them, and you are only omnipotent as far as the car is concerned until its batteries run out.

Besides, there is an even deeper problem with this suggestion. If G-d really *needed* to rule over us, why would He create us with the ability to rebel against Him? No ruler wants mutiny; above all he wants obedience. And yet, we are not forced to obey G-d. He did not make us robots, slaves or puppets. We gave us ability to choose to defy Him and the ability to carry out that defiance.

So where does all of this leave us? With a big, wonderful universe that provides no benefit to its creator and faced with the fact that we can do nothing for nor provide any benefit to Him.

The Big Answer: Pleasure

Our original question is still unanswered: Why are we here?

Since this universe can provide no benefit to its creator, it only follows that it is here to provide benefit to those whom He created. And since, as we have seen, we cannot *give* anything to G-d, it is only logical that we are here to *receive*.

The narrative of creation in the Torah clearly points to this conclusion. But what is it that we are here to receive? The answer is that G-d created us to have pleasure. Yes, pleasure—when I said Judaism is fundamentally different from other "religions", I meant it. G-d, it seems, is no different than a parent in this sense: What greater desire do parents have than to see their children enjoy life? An unhappy child is a source of great pain to a parent.

But what kind of pleasure are we here to experience? The Torah describes G-d creating man and placing him into paradise, or *Gan Eden* where all of his physical needs were taken care of. So, maybe we are here to indulge in physical pleasures. Perhaps the meaning of our lives is to be plied with food and drink and good times. Maybe G-d created a beautiful world full of delicious, enticing, hedonistic pleasures so we could just dig in. Could that be the meaning of our lives?

This question can be answered from two directions. First is from the account of our creation in the Torah. G-d formed Adam's body out of the soil and then "blew" a soul into it, positing that a human being is an amalgamation of two parts—one spiritual and one physical, the soul and the body. To be called a "human being," both parts must be present; a soul without a body is not a denizen of this world and a body without a soul is a corpse. This presence of a spiritual component in our makeup indicates that physical pleasure is not the sole purpose of our existence. It definitely plays a part in our lives, since we are partly physical, but it does not define our purpose.

The second approach to the question involves looking at those people and societies that pursue physical pleasures exclusively—and seeing, quite obviously, that decadence does not provide happiness. If it did, there would be a direct correlation between wealth and happiness; the richer people would all be happier. The more homes or cars a person owned, the happier he would be. A woman's happiness would be in direct proportion to the size of her walk-in closet.

But every rational person knows that this is far from true. Clearly, wealth does not bring happiness and, in fact, very often, the lives of the "rich and famous" are really messed up and they seem pretty miserable. Focusing on physical pleasure as the meaning of life—hedonism—actually brings deep unhappiness because it leads one *away* from the true purpose of life: Spiritual pleasure.

An indication that our nature is to be pleasure seekers is the fact that we find it almost impossible to do things that we do not enjoy on some level. A person forced to live a life wherein he finds no pleasure is miserable; he feels as though he is not really living but only existing. We must find pleasure in what we do in order to feel alive. Even when we act altruistically, we still do so in a way that will give us spiritual pleasure.

What Is Spirituality?

Let's stop for a moment and define what we mean by "spirituality." The Western world has trouble with the concept of spirituality and as a result, has difficulty reconciling it with the physical aspect of life. The result tends to be a lurching from one extreme to the other.

Being a spiritual person does not require doing yoga on a mountaintop or eating organic foods. One can live a regular, everyday life and still be very spiritual. One can be an investment banker or a boom crane operator and still be a spiritual person. We all have needs and desires that have nothing to do with anything physical. We all need love, friendship, self-esteem and the respect of our peers. We all want to love, to give and to make others happy.

These are spiritual needs. They cannot be weighed, measured or counted. They are not subject to the physical laws of nature. They are infinite; they do not run out or expire. You can eat too much and sleep too much, but you cannot love too much or have too many friends. In fact, people are so in need of giving love that if it is absent from their lives, they will buy a pet and treat it like a human being, lavishing affection on it.

Our spiritual half compels us towards spiritual pleasure while our physical half drives us towards physical pleasure. This duality can be compared to a horse and a rider. The horse and the rider each have different desires and different goals. When you see someone on horseback, it looks as if the rider and horse are operating as a team, but in reality the horse couldn't care less where the rider is going or why. It only knows that it has been trained to obey the rider's directives. They are operating as a team because the rider is controlling the horse. Before it was trained, the horse was a wild beast that would take no direction at all. It took many months of breaking the horse's independent will before it became a compliant servant. Once a horse is broken in and put in the hands of an experienced and knowledgeable rider, however, it becomes almost an extension of the rider; only then do they act as one.

In this way, our bodies are the horses, our souls the riders. An undisciplined horse in the hands of an inexperienced rider will run amok and follow its own desires and instincts, dragging the rider along. It's very telling that in English, we refer to unchecked desires as "unbridled passions"—if our bodies' desires are not controlled, they will run wild and inevitably ruin us. Our souls—our spiritual sides—are supposed to be in control, leading our bodies and directing them. The horse is clearly meant to serve the rider.

This does not mean that we denigrate physical experiences; they play a major role in our lives and can be quite enjoyable. But, they only exist to support our spiritual endeavors. All physical pleasures are meant to serve a deeper spiritual purpose and without that component, they leave us feeling unsatisfied or without real happiness.

All of the physical pleasures we seek—food, careers, status, companionship, luxuries, exotic travel—are tied to an underlying need for spiritual pleasures, such as transcendence, meaning, love, esteem, friendship, the need to be good or even a longing to be in touch with G-d.

Actual physical experiences are short lived and quickly forgotten. The spiritual experiences that they are tied to are what we remember.

We see in the Torah that these two elements are not meant to be indulged equally. The laws, ethics and principles of the Torah operate under the philosophy that life is inherently a spiritual experience. The definition of a spiritual person is one who understands that the spiritual elements of life are much more important than physical needs or pleasures and *lives his or her life accordingly*.

When we identify with our souls and live accordingly, we are lifted out of our immediate and mundane existences. Identifying with our bodies and living accordingly leads to frustration, boredom and depression. Frustration, because there is no possible way for a person to fulfill all his physical desires in his lifetime; boredom, because we are never satisfied and the thrills from new experiences decrease with time and frequency; and to depression, because such an existence is degrading. A human being cannot successfully live the life of an animal.

Gan Eden, man's original and intended state, was a place where the spiritual world was more powerful than the physical world; the physical was subservient to the spiritual, playing a supporting role. Adam and Chava (Eve) had all of their physical needs provided for them. The requirement for man to eat by the "sweat of his brow" only came as a result of their having to leave the Garden.

And when a person leads a spiritually oriented life, whether or not he or she admits it or is even aware of it, he or she is someone who believes in G-d.

Why? Because these are drives that have no explanations in the physical sciences. In fact, until very recently, medical science scoffed at the idea of including a spiritual component in the science of healing, though the mountains of evidence pointing to its very real healing power has started to alter opinions. Science, the study of the physical world, can tell us how many calories we need to stay alive but cannot tell us how much love we need. If a person understands that the spiritual side of life is more important, he inherently believes in more than that for which science can account. He is acknowledging that there is more to the world than mere physical existence and, in a roundabout way, that there is a greater power.

There is one place where this truth is almost universally recognized—a funeral. A eulogy focuses on spiritual matters—what kind of person the deceased was, what kind of friend or spouse or parent, how he was loved by his neighbors and co-workers, how he was always cheerful and helpful. I have heard eulogies that instead elaborated on how the deceased loved food or sports, and they were embarrassing for everybody present. We want to be remembered for our spiritual attributes, not our physical ones, unless the physical ones contribute to the whole picture by augmenting or embellishing our spiritual virtues—for example, if a person was very physically strong yet kind and gentle, this would demonstrate humility, a wonderful character trait. (By the way, as an exercise, write your own obituary. It will help you focus on what is important to you. Then, use it as your life's game plan. You'll be surprised how spiritual your real goals are.)

This need for spiritual fulfillment also explains why so many people in modern society feel that they are not living their own lives. It is common for people to describe themselves as living on autopilot or as mere observers, watching their lives from the outside. This is because the more important components of their beings—their spiritual sides—are not engaged. They are eating, sleeping, working, even raising children, but the underlying meaning of it all is missing.

We have all heard the expression "man cannot live by bread alone," but it is misunderstood to mean that in order to have a full life, man needs physical luxuries, not just plain old necessities. The actual quote is in the Torah; it was stated by Moshe when he was recounting the previous forty years in the wilderness in a series of public orations before his death. The full quote is: "He [G-d] afflicted you and let you be hungry, then fed you with the Manna that you did not know and that your forefathers did not know, in order to make you aware that not by bread alone does man live but by the utterances of the mouth of G-d does man live" (Deut. 8:3). In short, man needs more than physical existence; he needs spirituality.

This might explain why Orthodox Jews do not seem, at first glance, to be very spiritual. Unlike the philosophies of both the West and the East, we do not separate from the physical in order to be spiritual. Rather, the Torah life is the true merger of both the physical and spiritual worlds; our spirituality is extruded through each and every physical act we do.

If you take some time to observe a Torah life, it will seem strikingly average. Those of us who live by the Torah go to work, shop in supermarkets and malls, check our stocks and investments, worry about our children, try to look good for our spouses, like a good meal and so on. But despite all these mundane activities, there is something elevated and sublime about our lives.

The Key: Free Will

So let's review for a moment. We are formed from physical matter and then imbued with souls. The Torah teaches us that these two elements have two distinct drives: The soul desires spiritual pleasure and the body desires physical pleasures. Unfortunately, the bad news for those who want easy lives is that these two drives are diametrically opposed to each other, are in constant conflict and want to lead us in opposite directions. We have all felt this within ourselves. This naturally leads to another question: Why would G-d create us with this ongoing conflict?

The answer lies in the very purpose of our existence and can be summed up in two words: Free will. Life is not designed to be easy; it's designed to make us great. G-d created us as pleasure seekers and, by definition, the greatest pleasure we can experience is to be like Him, since He is the source of all good. I think that most atheists would agree that if there were a G-d, experiencing Him would be the most awesome experience possible.

And this is what G-d did when He created us "in His image." This phrase does not mean that we resemble Him physically, since He is not a physical being. He cannot be composed of matter because He created matter; He cannot be bound by time and space because He created time and space.

"In His image" means that we are godlike in the sense that we have complete freedom of decision—we have independence. It is *the* fundamental definition of what we are. Man has the autonomy to choose the moral course of action in any given situation or circumstance. Despite how strongly any external or internal pressures are pushing or pulling in one direction, our actions and decisions are ours and ours alone. Just as G-d acts without coercion, so do we. Just as G-d is free to choose to do good, so is man. The entire rest of creation is compelled by instinct to fulfill its purpose. Man alone chooses.

A Polish farmer who found a Jew hiding in his barn during the Holocaust had complete range of choice as to what to do—kill him, turn him in or hide him and feed him. Because we understand that the choice was solely his and he had complete independence of action, we despise those who did the wrong thing and praise those did the right thing. If they didn't have freewill, their choice would be no different than a hyena chancing upon a wounded zebra. The outcome would be predetermined by instinct. But we understand that a human being is fundamentally different from a hyena.

In Jewish philosophy, free will is defined as the ability to choose between right and wrong, i.e. to listen to G-d or to defy Him. In other terms, it is the battle between listening to the body and listening to the soul. Free will is very often mistaken to mean the freedom and ability to do what ones wants—to choose what to eat for dinner, what color dress to wear or what profession to pursue. But in truth, these choices can be more accurately defined as license, which is amoral. It is just permission without a moral component. The definition of true freedom is the ability to do what the soul wants to do unbound by the passions of the body.

The Mission

We are born into this world to fulfill a specific purpose, and to do this we must use our free will. In a sense, we are born as lumps of clay with enormous potential, and through our free-will decisions we actually create ourselves. Where, when and to whom we are born makes a world of difference, but in the end it is our choices that determine what we become.

To more clearly understand our purpose in life, I'd like to use a story as an illustration. This story involves a British frigate on a mission in the South Pacific.

One morning, the captain calls his crew to attention on the deck and makes the following announcement: "Unbeknownst to you all, His Majesty has sent us on a secret mission. The beaches of the island now visible off the starboard bow are rumored to be littered with gems. It seems that the island possesses unique geological qualities. Obviously, the existence of this island must be kept an absolute secret.

"Two of you will be chosen by lots to row to the island and investigate. This ship will continue on its course and rendezvous with the landing party on our return voyage in approximately two years' time. Should the rumor about the island prove to be true, the two men selected are hereby commissioned by His Majesty to collect as many gems as is humanly possible over the course of the two years on the island. You will, of course, be richly rewarded for your efforts on behalf of the crown. Should the rumor prove to be false, then you will have experienced a long and restful holiday courtesy of His Majesty."

The lots are cast, and two sailors pick the short straws. Despite their pleas for mercy, they are lowered into the rowboat, given provisions and water for a few days and a load of burlap sacks, and wished Godspeed. Left with no choice, they row towards the island, cursing G-d, their mothers' wombs and the days they were born for their being exiled to a remote island for two long years.

Soon, they approach the island and something on the beach catches their attention. They blink in disbelief, certain that their eyes must be playing tricks on them. Can it be? Yes, it's true! As far as they can see, the beach is awash in gems, glittering like a jewel case! They hug each other in unbounded joy and, dropping to their knees, thank G-d for his kindness and bless their mothers' wombs and the days they were born for this unbelievable stroke of good fortune.

Desperately, the two sailors row with all their strength to get to shore and dive into their task. Through their minds race visions of their lives in just two short years; the servants, cooks, gardeners and drivers they will employ; palaces with grounds that stretch for miles; stables for a hundred horses. They waste no time, furiously shovel gems into their sacks. They do not stop to eat or even to drink.

Meanwhile, a band of curious onlookers forms on the beach. Half-naked natives watch with amusement as these pale-skinned strangers madly collect what are, to them, worthless rocks. The men and women point at the sailors, and the children laugh and imitate them. How mad the two are! Why would anyone want those rocks, and why are the men so impatient? Isn't tomorrow another day? The rocks will surely be there. So, what's the hurry?

Soon, the sun begins to set and the two sailors collapse into a deep sleep. They have more wealth in their sacks than they have ever laid eyes on—and it's only the first day. At the first crack of light, they jump up and once more plunge into hours of frenetic, almost maniacal collecting, lunging at anything that glitters.

Soon, however, the sun is directly overhead and oppressively hot. They're hungry, and their bodies ache. Their hands are so sore that it hurts to make a fist. Sitting down in the shade of a palm tree to take a break, they notice that they have been entertaining the locals. A group of boys approach them with some fruit, which the men gulp down.

Then, the boys motion for the two weary sailors to follow them to their village, where they are welcomed and treated with hospitality. They are given food and drink and even a hut to sleep in. The natives cannot help but be amused at how tightly the two men grip their sacks of worthless rocks; they will not let anyone near them.

For days, the men get up with the dawn and head for the beach. But as the days go by, their pace slows considerably. They sleep longer in the morning, they quit earlier and they take more breaks during the day. They also begin to learn the native tongue and before long, they are communicating with the villagers.

They also come to learn that the natives view these gems as worthless. A sack of gems can't even buy a coconut on this island. What the natives *do* value is a certain shell they call the "klume," from a type of shellfish that lives on the seabed far out to sea. It only washes up onto the shore infrequently, and these people use it as their currency.

This only seems silly and primitive to the Englishmen, and they continue their mission. After a few weeks, though, they look at each other and laugh. "Why are we killing ourselves like this? We're not going anywhere for another two years. What's the rush?" one asks the other.

The second man agrees. "It won't take more than two or three months to collect all the gems. Let's bury our sacks and finish the job in a few months. In the meantime, we have a tropical island paradise to enjoy."

So, the men decide to bury their loaded sacks and do absolutely nothing for the next few months. As they watch the natives go about their lives, they soon realize just how valuable the klume shells are to the natives; those with the most shells are given great honor and prestige. People constantly walk the beaches, looking for klumes, and every once in while someone drowns while trying to retrieve them from the seabed.

The sailors realize that they can anchor their rowboat farther out than the natives are able to swim. Using the anchor line as a guide, they can dive down deeper and stay down longer. They rig up a rudimentary breathing tube out of reeds and head out to sea, locate a spot with a concentration of klumes and get to work.

Taking turns, they weigh themselves down with rocks and descend to the bottom. Once on the seabed, they tie themselves to the anchor line and breathe through the tube. In one day, they collect more klumes than the natives could collect in a month.

The natives are astounded and after just a few more trips to sea, the two Englishmen become royalty in the village on account of their wealth. They start collecting so many shells that they have nowhere to store them, but then they remember that they came with sacks. But where did they bury them? It seems so long ago.

Retracing their steps, they find the hiding spot and quickly dig up the sacks of gems. But what should they do with the gems? They find a secluded cove on a beach and stack them up. What's the difference? Nobody will take them.

Taking the sacks, they head out to sea at dawn. They locate their original spot and get to work. Dive after dive brings new riches, and they amass a fortune never before seen on the island. When darkness falls, they reluctantly give up their prospecting—but they are by now the richest men on the island.

In no time, they use their fortune to acquire land and animals and to marry the daughters of the most important chieftains of the surrounding villages. They settle in to lives of honor and comfort.

One day, a ship appears in the lagoon flying the Union Jack. It is quite a shock at first. Has it been two years already? It doesn't seem that long. Maybe it's a different ship, they think. Maybe it's their ship but it's arrived early for some reason. They watch as a rowboat full of men is lowered from the ship and makes its way towards shore. And in it they see their captain!

They run to meet the party as it wades ashore and the captain, recognizing them, gives them a wide grin. "Good to see you again, men. I'm happy to see that you are well. So sorry that we're late, old chaps, but the French were giving us trouble again around the Solomons and it delayed us a bit. But that's all been straightened out now. I'm sure you men are eager to get back to civilization, so let's start loading up. The sooner we're finished, the sooner we sail for home."

The captain looks around himself, at the gems that still glitter in the sand. "I see that the rumors were indeed true. These beaches hold more wealth than the king himself would be able to spend. Well, let's not tarry. Show these men where you've stockpiled the fortune you've collected and we'll begin loading the ship forthwith. If there's too much for one trip, we'll send as many rowboats as needed until all the sacks have been transferred to the ship."

The men are dumbstruck. Suddenly, they clearly see that they have blown their mission. They look at each other and wonder what they have done. How could they have strayed so far? The gems, which they were supposed to have collected and would have provided them magnificent futures, still lie on the beach undisturbed. All that the men possess are bags of shells that are absolutely worthless in the place they are heading.

The men realize that they have wasted their time on the island and squandered the great opportunity they were given. How can they explain themselves to the captain? They allowed themselves to be so influenced by the society in which they were living that their ideas and their values were turned inside out. They came to view something valuable as worthless and vice versa. How could they have been so brainwashed that they looked at a gem and saw a rock, and looked at a seashell and saw treasure? How could they gone so wrong?

This story is the story of our lives. Our souls are sent to this world to accomplish great spiritual things and yet it is easy to be caught up in the craziness of society and wind up chasing the wrong goals. It is said in jest that the one who dies with the most toys wins. The Torah's view, however, is that the one who dies with most toys is the biggest loser. He has squandered his time and his potential.

The battle for sanity—keeping our eyes on the prize and not getting confused—is the true battle of life. To win this battle we first need to understand how it is possible to be led astray.

The Negative Inclination

Using our free will, each of us should be able to look with an unbiased view at this world, see the options clearly and be able to choose right from wrong. It seems pretty easy. So why are some decisions so difficult? And why do we sometimes make incorrect choices? Hmm… Should I take that purse that was left on the counter or return it to its owner? Such questions seem simple—almost too simple. If all of our moral choices were so black and white, being a good or righteous person would be no great accomplishment.

And not every free will choice is a simple yes or no dilemma. Many of them involve the paths we choose in life. For example, which is more important in life—being happy or being rich? If a person thought about it, it's obvious that being rich and unhappy is no way to live. On the other hand there are many people who are not rich yet very happy and enjoying life. I know, I know both is better but if you could only choose one, which would it be. I think any sane person would choose happiness over wealth. Yet most people spend almost no time working on happiness and a great deal of time trying to get rich. How can we be so confused?

To understand how we operate our moral machinery, we need to go back to the Garden, to where the first moral choice in human history was made.

Adam and Chava were told that they could enjoy all the trees of the Garden with one exception: They were told not to eat from the Tree of the Knowledge of Good and Evil. Through obeying this one commandment, Adam and Chava would "complete" the act of creation and permanently subjugate their physical or animal natures. In doing so, they would permanently establish their existence as spiritual. But to make the proper choice they would have to subjugate their will to G-d's, to listen to G-d instead of their own desires and impulses.

We already know the ending: They chose to eat the fruit of the Tree of the Knowledge of Good and Evil and defy the very G-d that had molded them, so to speak, with His own hands. But how in the world did they come to that point? How was it possible to defy G-d when His existence was so crystal clear to them?—He spoke directly to them! The answer to this question will explain why we do not always do the right thing, even at times when it should be crystal clear.

For a person truly to have freewill, the truth cannot be perfectly obvious; if it is, he actually loses his free will. For example, could you actually kill someone who insulted you? Or knock down an old woman and steal her pocketbook if you needed money? If everything that was wrong were so *clearly* wrong, we would be forced to act righteously in every case and would have no free will. We would no longer be able to be "godlike" but rather would resemble an animal forced to act by its instincts—albeit good instincts.

Because of this, G-d created what is called in Hebrew the *yeitzer hara,* which translates as the "negative inclination"—so named because it's advice is always bad for you. In the Torah, *yeitzer hara* is personified by the snake that convinced Chava that she had every right to eat the fruit that G-d told her not to eat. Each of us has a *yeitzer hara* that always tries to convince us that the wrong thing is the right thing. We also have a *yeitzer hatov,* or positive inclination, that amplifies the desires of the soul. This set of discordant voices, of which all human beings are aware, are often portrayed in popular culture as an angel and devil on someone's shoulders.

And this is where our freewill challenges lie. The *yeitzer hara* is the great rationalizer, the great justifier; it will always attempt to cloud your judgment. When you will be faced with a choice between going with your body or going with soul it will always interfere on the part of the body. Take, for instance, a chaise lounge in a Caribbean resort. If the body had its way, it would spend its entire existence lolling by the pool sipping a perfectly chilled margarita, stopping only to eat or take a dip in the water to cool off. It does not have any higher goals or ambitions. The *yeitzer hara* will try to convince you that this is the ultimate life and a worthy use of your time.

But the soul sees this type of life for what it is—shallow and meaningless. The soul wants to accomplish something and even while you're lounging by the pool, it is driven to understand everything on a deeper level. It wants to know the creator of the palm trees, the warm breezes, the hibiscus, the hummingbirds and the lemon and the lime. This does not mean that some time by the pool is not a wonderful thing. It can be, if it is used properly.

Each of our free will choices are uniquely our own, and the *yeitzer hara* uses different arguments depending on what each of us will hear. This is why prisons are filled with people who perpetrate acts that are inconceivable to others—because their *yeitzer hara* spoke only to their specific desires and they chose to listen to it. This also explains why talking out issues and problems with friends or family members is so helpful. Another person's *yeitzer hara* is not engaged with your problems, and therefore this other person can be objective regarding them. Another person can very often see things that your own *yeitzer hara* has clouded for you.

Each time we are faced with a moral dilemma, if we choose correctly, we become more like G-d; this is the purpose of our lives and concurrently our greatest pleasure, because our greatest pleasure come from doing good. In essence, we mold ourselves with each choice and, by the end of our lives, we have created what we are through the use of our free will.

Adam and Chava had souls that wanted to listen to G-d and make the correct moral choices, but they also had bodies that wanted to eat the forbidden fruit because it was so tempting. They had to make a choice; unfortunately, the *yeitzer hara* convinced them that their bodies were correct.

At that moment they ate the fruit, they experienced a physical pleasure that had no spiritual root; since it defied G-d's will, it could not have a deeper spiritual purpose. Thus their entire existences changed, and from that moment on, it was as if their bodies had minds of their own, pursuing their own agendas that **would not benefit the soul**. Adam and Chava had created desires within themselves to do wrong, and this meant that instead of being a purely intellectual choice, free will would now contain an emotional element.

We can see in our own lives that when the body acts on its own, it is very embarrassing to us. Body odor, bad breath and flatulence are all natural occurrences, but they also are very humiliating. The Torah states that originally, Adam and Chava were naked, and they were not embarrassed. Why should they have been? Their bodies were still only extensions of their souls. But once they ate, they felt the need to hide in the bushes until G-d made them clothes.

Similarly, children, before they reach an age of awareness, have no problem using the bathroom with the door open or spitting out food they don't like. A two-year-old who runs through the house screaming, "I'm naked, I'm naked!" is cute. But if your twelve–year-old acted that way, you'd be taking him to all kinds of specialists. At a certain age, we become aware of our body's "independence", and it embarrasses us.

This understanding of human composition is why, to an Orthodox Jew, child raising is not just a litany of do's and don'ts. Child raising is a process wherein a person is molded to be humble enough to be willing to listen to G-d's commandments. By guiding a child on the path of pleasantness and good character traits, teaching him to treat others with respect and consideration, giving him a sense of self-worth and requiring him to conduct himself with discipline and self-control, a parent trains a child to subjugate his physical passions. The parent is giving the child life itself.

Sure, G-d Knows

A standard question posed about the concept of free will is the following: If G-d can see the future and knows what we will do, how do we truly have free will and freedom of action?

This question arises because we mistakenly assume that G-d lives the same type of existence that we do but this is not the case—G-d lives in a very different reality. He is not bound by time or place; they are mere creations of His, no different from rocks or trees. We clearly do not think that G-d gets hot or cold or that He ages or tires out. G-d can see the before, during and after of any situation, but He sees them all as "is"; when you or I face a freewill decision, G-d watches us with a complete knowledge of our future just as He has a complete knowledge of our past. It all just *is* in His eyes. But His knowledge does not affect what we decide.

This is impossible for a finite human to comprehend, and it's a waste of time to try. (Similarly, people who believe in an afterlife assume that once a person leaves this world they are no longer in the realm of time and don't continue to age. We intuit that time is only present in a physical existence.)

But G-d's vantage point does not affect what our souls and bodies are grappling with in any given situation. Nothing is pre-decided. If it were, how could we ever praise or condemn a person's actions? He would just be acting out that which was already decreed. Similarly, why would we seek out medical help, prepare for a coming storm or store food for the winter? Our actions, words and even thoughts would be no different than our beating hearts and reproducing cells—natural functions over which we had no control.

Taking this idea even further, why would we even need to live out our entire lives if G-d was going to preordain our fates? He could just create us in our final destination in the afterlife and save us the bother. If we had no real freedom of thought or action, why this elaborately choreographed existence?

And even though we might have these questions in our heads, we do not believe them in our hearts. Do we really believe that the choice between being industrious or lazy makes no difference in a person's economic situation, or that the choice between being selfish or generous makes no difference to a person's marital happiness?

Of course not. We all know that our fate is in our hands. But to some, it can be a little disconcerting that G-d knows what we will decide before we do. But this is only a function of the difference between an infinite, all-knowing G-d and a finite, limited human being.

Self-Made

Another aspect of free will is the fact that we only appreciate what we earn. A person who works for his wealth gains infinitely more satisfaction from it than someone who inherits money or wins the lottery. Alternatively, things that are given to us, even if we need them, can actually cause us shame. A beggar is often too embarrassed to make eye contact; a rich kid living off his parents' money might feel embarrassed. In fact, the self-destructiveness and jadedness of wealthy youth is a result of having been given everything, which in turn destroys their self-esteem and their feelings of self-worth.

On a deeper level, a human being only appreciates the good he does if it is a choice and not coerced. Imagine standing on the beach and suddenly seeing a young man struggling to stay above the waves. Without thinking, you dive in and pull him to safety. Such a moment will stay with you for the rest of your life. Now, imagine the same scene but this time, a man with a gun runs up to you, puts it to your head and says, "That's my boy out there. Get in the water and save him or I'll kill you." You still dive in and save the kid, but which act would give you more pleasure? Obviously, the first one, because it was a freewill choice. We only appreciate what we accomplish through our freewill decisions, and the more difficult the challenge we overcome, the more satisfaction it gives us.

Choosing correctly is a challenge that requires intellectual and moral effort. And because we make such efforts and overcome challenges, we can appreciate our gains. In this way and this way alone can a person ever be referred to as a "self-made man." We make what we are in this world and we create our own eternities. We are all self-made—for better or worse.

The Existence of Evil

The flip side of our awesome freewill ability to create is our awesome free-will ability to destroy. For human beings to have true free will, there must be real consequences to our actions, and this allows for the existence of evil. The general issue of suffering will be discussed in chapter five; however, we must first acknowledge that the vast majority of suffering in this world is caused directly by man's actions. In this category, I include not only wars, political oppression, terrorism, the Holocaust and crime but also selfishness and cruelty towards others.

Because free will always requires an even playing field, our potential for evil must be equal to our potential for good. If there were no consequences to our actions, our decisions would have no meaning and life would be a mere charade. If G-d intervened every time someone chose to do something wrong or evil, we would only have the ability to choose to do the right thing. His outright intervention would reduce or even eliminate our ability to choose freely. We would be reduced to moral drones forced to choose only one way—like voters in the former Soviet Union, who were given a choice of a single candidate. That is not a "free" choice because there really is no choice.

And just as the extent to which we can choose to do good or evil on a personal level indicates our potential for greatness as individuals, so too does humanity have unlimited potential on a cosmic level to rise to unbelievable heights or be utterly debased and savage. It is all in our hands.

The Soul, False Gods and Drugs

The fundamental principle of Torah Judaism, that we are each comprised of a body and a soul, is not shared by modern society.

The modern world, which is based on the Greek school of thought, negates anything that cannot be proven in a laboratory. The Torah, on the other hand, says that it is precisely those things that cannot be scientifically proven, or that cannot be discerned by the five senses, that are the most essential and fundamental aspects of life. Spirituality, not physicality, is what life is about. In the absence of spirituality, people feel that their lives are empty. All of their physical needs can be met, yet they still might not feel fulfilled.

This is the real underlying cause of modern angst and social ills. The soul is very real, and it has drives just as our physical bodies do. The soul craves meaning the way a body craves food, and it cannot be ignored. This drive for meaning explains why human beings have a need to be good even at the expense of their physical welfare. How else can we explain the super-human sacrifices that some people make?

Every human being who has ever stepped foot on this planet wants to be good. In fact, everyone is willing to die to do the right thing. (Knowing what we are willing to die for immeasurably helps define our lives.) No one in his right mind ever chooses to do bad or be evil even if he claims that he does; such a person's definitions are just so twisted that they become inverted. An evil man will convince himself that he is doing good, and will insist more loudly and more virulently than anyone else that he *is* good. Ironically, a truly good man, when asked if he is good, will reply with something like, "I try."

The drive for meaning is really a drive to be in touch with the transcendental. All human beings need something outside of themselves to which they can dedicate and devote themselves, and if this drive is not oriented toward the true G-d and true meaning, it will aim at a substituting idea, ideal or object. This means that if a person is not in touch with G-d, he will need to create a god, a religion or a cause as a replacement.

Without transcendence, life devolves into a murderous cycle of eating in order to live in order to go to work in order to earn money in order to eat in order to live in order to go to work. When true meaning is removed from our lives, there is no purpose to any of our activities be they mundane or heroic. Even meaning derived from noble causes or professions eventually runs out; doctors who save lives or relieve suffering on a daily basis can still be unhappy people when they become detached from the higher meaning of their efforts.

Throughout much of history, false religions have been the drug of choice for those seeking meaning. In modern society, secular causes, both good and bad, have taken the place of religion, often becoming objects of devotion.

However, ideology can become idolatry when there is an irrational dedication behind it. When, for example, people are dedicated to the idea of the welfare state when all empirical evidence proves that ongoing government handouts are not beneficial to the recipients, the belief becomes a false god demanding blind obedience. Others might have similar but more modest devotions, such as their careers or their families. To others, it can be as base as a sports team or a celebrity or music group. Ironically, modern, secular man has not freed himself from religion; he has simply replaced the living G-d with sterile gods of his own creation.

The problem with secular gods is that they eventually become tasteless and unsatisfying and must be replaced. What once lifted and excited becomes stale, and a steady diet of unsatisfying spiritual relationships has the same result as a string of unsatisfying romantic relationships: Pain.

This happens because just as our bodies need nourishment so do our souls. The former needs air, food and water to survive; if it doesn't get enough, it will be pained and debilitated. If the soul does not get enough truth and meaning, it will suffer the same fate. And just as a person will seek out relief when his body is in pain, he will need something to numb the pain in his soul.

When artificial meaning inevitably leaves us feeling empty, we turn to distractions such as sports, hobbies, entertainment or the pursuit of wealth or fame to deaden the pain. What does it say about modern society that the people who are the highest paid and most fawned over are the celebrities who provide a diversion and an escape from reality? To cope with all this emptiness, modern, secular society is in therapy and awash in drugs and diversions. A society without a spiritual component will need anesthesia.

This also explains the pain of boredom. It emanates from the soul. It is either the result of doing nothing or doing nothing meaningful. It is the antithesis of accomplishment. It is the soul that is in pain when we are bored because we are not fulfilling our purpose. It is literally a waste of life.

But the *yeitzer hara* tricks us. Though the pain we feel comes from the soul and must be dealt with on a spiritual level, we always respond physically. The cliché of the man having a midlife crisis is quite instructive here. He has reached a level of success and discovered it provides him no meaning. His false god has been exposed, his soul starved. Yet, instead of looking into the meaning of life, he responds in the worst possible way: He breaks up his marriage, buys a sports car and dates women half his age. He pursues thrills in order to feel alive—but they, too, will not suffice for long.

Every human being has, at one time, come face to face with the terrifying thought that there is no meaning to life. We have all thought, *Why bother with all this? Why not just end it?* These moments can be very scary, but they should be used to get in touch with what we really want out of life.

In this way, our existence is fundamentally different than all other types of life on this planet. The animal kingdom goes about its daily activities without ever wondering what it's all about, but a human being needs to understand his place in the cosmos. This is evidenced by the fact that every single culture and society, from the beginning, has needed to offer explanations of and theories about the origin of the world and mankind. Whether through myth, religion or modern cosmology, man needs to understand his place in it all or he feels lost. He needs more than "what"—he needs to know "why."

In addition to this, being in touch with our higher purpose creates an inherent joy and inner peace that translates into a more satisfying, healthier and longer life. Study after study on the correlation between religion and mental health shows that those with religious beliefs are happier in life, more fulfilled in marriage and far less likely to be depressed, suicidal or abusive of drugs and alcohol.

Orthodox Jews, not coincidentally, have higher birth rates and lower divorce rates, and suicide is almost nonexistent. Today, in Israel, the city with the highest life expectancy is Bnei Brak, a suburb of Tel Aviv that is home to approximately 100,000 Orthodox Jews. It is also one of Israel's poorest cities. Ironically, it's not a *kibbutz* or *moshav* in the Galilee or in the fertile valley along the coast, where men and women work outdoors on the land. Rather, it's an urban environment in the most congested part of the country.

So, to sum up, we have two parts—one spiritual and one physical. The spiritual is intended to be the more-powerful driving force while our physical side is meant to play a supporting role. The soul and the body have different desires, and we must constantly make freewill choices in favor of our souls.

By using our free will, we emulate G-d Himself, who chooses his actions independently and without compulsion. No one and nothing makes G-d do anything; He is completely independent. By choosing correctly and overcoming the attempts of the *yeitzer hara* to mislead us, by subjugating our animal drives and strengthening our spiritual drives, we create ourselves. With each correct moral decision, we become greater and greater—closer to G-d and more like G-d. Life is a journey of constant self-creation done solely and completely by each one of us.

This is the meaning of life.

Chapter Four

What Exactly Is the Torah?

How Come Nobody Ever Told Me?

You might have asked yourself a question while reading the end of the last chapter: How could the meaning of life be such a secret? How come nobody knows all of this? If this is really the way we are supposed to live and the Jews have known it for over 3300 years, shouldn't it be common knowledge throughout the world?

In other words, is it really possible that almost all human beings are living without the basic knowledge of what they are living for?

Unfortunately, yes.

And is it possible that most human beings will live out their entire lives without ever figuring out what they were here for in the first place?

Again, unfortunately, yes.

Another question that might have troubled you: If we are supposed to be constantly utilizing our free will to choose the right and moral choices, how are we to know what it is? How do we really know what G-d wants?

If these circumstances—people not knowing the purpose of their lives or knowing what G-d wants for them—seem like a contradiction to G-d's purpose, it is. But we need to remember that we have free will and that this state of affairs has been created by man's choices and behavior since the very beginning. Here's how it started:

Adam and Chava certainly knew why they were created and what they were supposed to accomplish. But the Torah recounts how subsequent generations began to change their orientations and how these slight changes took mankind way off course. In those generations, there were no doubts that there was a G-d; even when man defied G-d, he knew whom he was defying. When Adam's son, Kayin (Cain), murdered his brother, Hevel (Abel), he did so out of rage that G-d had rejected his offerings and accepted Hevel's.

Beginning in the third generation of mankind, some people, in an attempt to show reverence to G-d, began to show reverence to His celestial creations, just as one would honor the king's ministers as a way of showing honor to the king. Eventually, this reverence took on a life of its own and people began to worship the sun, moon and stars in earnest and attribute to them real powers; at first this was in conjunction with the true G-d, then as intermediaries, and finally as false gods who came to replace the real one. Soon, man wound up worshipping all kinds of power—fire, volcanoes, even powerful human beings. Every force of nature either became a deity or was assigned one.

This course continued until mankind was firmly entrenched in idol worship, which eventually led to widespread promiscuity and finally to a violent society. At this point in history—ten generations after Adam—mankind had passed the point of no return. There was no way that the purpose of creation could be realized. G-d would have to, so to speak, start over.

So, He instructed Noach (Noah), who was the most righteous man of his generation and who had not participated in the perversions of his society, to build an ark to house himself and his wife, their three sons and their wives, and representatives of all land-based animal life including birds. The rest of mankind He washed away. When Noach emerged from the ark exactly 365 days later, it was a fresh, clean, new world.

Remarkably, the flood did not change things as might have been expected because Noach's descendents still had the natural human desire to worship or serve *something* that is above him or more powerful than him and, being human, they were still susceptible to the cajoling of the *yeitzer hara*. Before long, mankind returned to the ways of the previous generations, serving the forces of nature or gods of their own making. It is very difficult, if not impossible, for a modern person to understand or relate to the seduction of idol worship. Until the destruction of the First Temple in 423 BC, human beings had a spiritual craving to worship that was akin to a physical desire. They *needed* to do it. But we have lived without this desire for almost 2,500 years and so today it seems very weird and very primitive.

Free will requires that there be a choice of what to worship, and so false gods were, at one time, a very compelling alternative to the true G-d. The Talmud relates how our Sages, at the beginning of the Second Temple period circa Jewish year 3408 or 353 BC, asked G-d to kill this desire. It had caused catastrophic problems for the Jewish people even while they had lived in the Land of Israel where they had been able to enjoy sublime spiritual experiences and witness open miracles in the First Temple. But now, most of the Jews lived in Babylon, prophecy had ended and the Second Temple did not emanate the same level of spiritual power as the first one. In this situation, how were we to survive the passions generated by this drive?

G-d complied, and our desire to worship false gods was taken away. Today, because our Sages went to battle for us, we feel no compulsion to bow down to statues; such an act even seems a little silly. However, free will requires a level playing field so, when we lost the burning desire for false gods, we also lost the burning desire for the real G-d. In other words, once the desire for idol worship was extinguished, the world saw the birth of secularism. Before that it was impossible not to have a desire to worship a god in the same way it is impossible not to have a libido.

This explains why, at that stage in history, there suddenly appeared a people—the Greeks—with ideas that were radically different from all that had preceded them. The Greeks were a unique people in the history of the world. They shared nothing philosophically with any people before them, and they created a template for all of Western civilization in the future. Until the Greeks, mankind questioned "Who or what is god?"; after the Greeks, mankind instead asked, "Is there a god?"

The Greeks certainly had a full roster of gods, all of whom they viewed as anthropomorphic reflections of themselves. However, by the time Alexander conquered the known world, the Greeks had become a bit casual about the whole idea of religion. Alexander did not care if the people he conquered continued to worship their local gods as long as they included the Greek gods. But the Jews maintained their allegiance to the truth and did not agree to add more gods to their lives. As a result, it was only Judaism that the Greeks saw as a threat. Not only were the Jews themselves stiff-necked but the Torah contradicted the Greek man-centered philosophy. Judaism was the only religion in the entire history of their empire against which they took up arms (the story of Chanukah).

So getting back to Noach and his family, when they walked off the ark, their inherent natures remained unchanged and the future of mankind still hinged on man's free will just as it had before the flood. And though all of mankind was and is descended from the three sons of Noach, and although the sons certainly passed on tales of life on the ark to subsequent generations, the moral lessons of past experiences will only have so much effect on future choices and actions. For the next ten generations, mankind continued to follow the same trajectory it had followed before the flood getting farther and farther from the whole point of creation until G-d was ready to restart the whole process. But at that juncture in history, one man stepped forward who would have a more profound effect on the human race than any other single person in the history of mankind.

Avraham

At the age of three, Avraham (Abraham) began to question the beliefs of his father's house and his father's society in Ur, a city located in Babylonia, in what today is Iraq. He did not see the logic and the efficacy of praying to wood and stone.

His transformation was not quick and easy. For years, Avraham grappled with fundamental philosophical and theological questions of life and existence until he arrived at the understanding of the nature of the One, loving, altruistic G-d, who transcends time and place; creator of all existence, both physical and spiritual, who continues to will it into existence every moment as an act of love in order to bestow good to His creations for their own benefit. This realization was a radical departure from the beliefs and practices of Avraham's time, when there were multiple gods who needed flattery and appeasement.

Avraham's father had a nice business making idols, and Avraham very easily could have bought into it like his brothers did. However, he did not. He was determined to spread the truth and so challenged the prevailing theology of his native land, which was a dangerous thing to do—think of someone challenging Islam in Saudi Arabia. He was jailed and eventually, the king of Babylon at the time, a man named Nimrod, decided to execute him for being a troublemaker. Miraculously, Avraham survived and left on a journey that would eventually take him to the Land of Israel.

A biography of Avraham would fill the remaining pages of this book. Suffice it to say that while the entire world believed in a menu of gods, Avraham was the only person to recognize the One G-d and so he is rightly considered the father of monotheism. But, that title is not completely accurate. Monotheism is not enough; one must also have the true picture of G-d. For example, the Moslems believe in one god, but their religion is not true and their characterization of G-d is incorrect. Avraham, in addition to bequeathing the concept of one god, gave the world the true picture of the one G-d. He set in motion the process that would produce the Jewish people, who would eventually receive the Torah and thereby maintain for the world not only monotheism but also the truth. He also set in motion events that are still unfolding today. (This will be explained in the last part of the book.)

Avraham's quest was the first time since creation that a human being went searching for the true G-d. And, for the first time, G-d had a partner through whom mankind could be taught and who could lead mankind to the fulfillment of its destiny.

By undertaking to teach the world about the one true G-d, Avraham took responsibility for insuring that G-d's purpose for the world would eventually be realized. Once he took that responsibility, there would never need to be another flood because there would never be another need to start over. Avraham was an advocate for truth in this world, G-d's representative who would always be a countermeasure to the insanity that would inevitably result from false gods, false religions, false ideologies and false ideas. There would always be a moral voice at the table. The Jewish people are his direct descendants both physically—his offspring—and spiritually—his mission and his message.

This was how the family tree grew: Avraham had two sons—Yitzchak (Isaac), who continued in the ways of his father, and Yishmael (Ishmael), whose progeny evolved into the Arab nation. Yitzchak then had twin sons, Yaakov (Jacob) and Eisav (Esau). Eisav's descendants were later called Edomites and eventually Romans. (This is explained in depth in chapter ten).

Yaakov was the only one who continued in the ways of his father and grandfather. He had twelve sons who sired what came to be known as the Twelve Tribes. Towards the end of Yaakov's life, his sons and their families settled in Egypt, where Yosef (Joseph) was viceroy to Pharaoh.

After Yaakov and his twelve sons died, the period of Egyptian slavery began and would last for 190 years until Moshe led us out of Egypt, through the Red Sea and into the Sinai desert. When we left Egypt, 500 years after the birth of Avraham, we were a nation of two to three million people, and we were ready to begin our mission. After seven weeks of travel we arrived at Mount Sinai, where we as a nation were given the Torah. Since then, the world has never been the same.

Instructions for Living

You might have heard the word "Torah" used in different ways. Many people view the Torah as a collection of stories—one part history, one part moral primer—but this definition only skims the surface.

In Hebrew the word "Torah" literally means "instructions" and in modern terms, the Torah could be compared to an owner's manual. Not only did G-d create us with a purpose, but He also gave us the instructions on how to achieve it.

This owner's manual comes complete with all the necessary instructions and guidelines to help us make the most of life—to gain the most happiness and fulfillment—as well as restrictions and prohibitions to steer us away from harm and misfortune. Without the manual, life is a random series of trials and errors during which we, in essence, attempt to compile our own manuals, based on our own ideas and experiences, in order to make sense of it all. A great deal of pain and damage can happen this way, and there are many who never quite figure it out.

Without our referring to the manual, life tends to be a little bewildering; We each have been given a remarkably rich and complex life full of potential, but we just don't know what we're supposed to do with it.

Jews view living as one would view a profession: It requires study, guidance and preparation. All parents intuitively understand this and would never allow their children to experiment with everything they wanted to nor act in any way they desired. Normal parents are always trying to instruct their children in any way they can; every parent would love to be able to give their children the ability to understand the meaning of life, how to love and be loved, how to be truly happy and the difference between right and wrong. These are the bases of life and without an understanding of them, everything else loses meaning. No amount of health, wealth or fame will mean anything if a person feels empty inside.

The Jewish people also see G-d's giving the Torah to us as an unequivocal demonstration of His love for us.

To illustrate, imagine that you are an athlete training for the Olympics, and your father is your coach. To help you, he compiles a training manual. Obviously, the purpose of this manual is to help you excel. What would such a manual contain? It would certainly include a litany of instructions to help you develop your skills as well as prohibitions to prevent you from hurting your chances of success. It would discuss your diet, sleep, attitude and frame of mind and would touch on many of your daily activities because, as your coach, your father understands that everything you do will affect your performance. He would also want you to maximize your time and be efficient.

Everything in the manual would be written with an eye on the eventual goal. It would include words of encouragement and inspiration and stress how capable you are of attaining the highest achievements. It would also include reminders from time to time of how much your father loves you, how highly he thinks of you and what you mean to him. It might also include stories that impart messages that can help make you the best that you can be.

This is the Torah.

Prophecy

A fundamental tenet of the Torah is that G-d speaks to human beings. Of course, this is perfectly logical. If we are created by Him to experience Him and have a real relationship with Him, it follows that there would be some sort of communication. In fact, it is logical to assume that G-d wants to speak to us.

This is the Jewish definition of prophecy—a crystal clear experience of hearing G-d communicate with you—and it is the result of a human being achieving such a high degree of spiritual perfection that he or she gains a unique bond with G-d. On this level, the person's existence will be one of significant discipline and enlightenment.

The Talmud states that during the 1,000 years in which the Jewish people experienced direct prophecy—from the exodus from Egypt to the destruction of the First Temple—we produced approximately 1,200,000 individual prophets, both men and women. Out of this number, only forty-eight are mentioned in the Bible and only fifteen had their prophecies redacted in books bearing their name; this was because their prophecies were intended for all of Jewish history and not just for the time in which they lived. During this time, there were actually academies for people who wanted to learn how to attain this prophetic level. Naturally, to be accepted, they had to be of sterling character and possess great wisdom.

Before the destruction of the First Temple, prophets helped deepen our relationship with G-d. If a person wanted to clarify his Torah learning, he would ask a prophet. If people were experiencing difficulty with business, with conceiving children or with raising difficult children, they would seek out the counsel of a prophet, who would instruct them on what measures to take or on what aspects of their character G-d wanted them to improve. Other prophets, the ones we know by name, were sent on missions to rebuke the people and told to speak in G-d's name. Our Torah was transmitted through the greatest prophet who ever lived, Moshe. He is considered to have reached the highest spiritual level of which a corporeal human being is capable.

After the First Temple's destruction, when we were forced into exile and made to live amongst the other nations of the world, the spiritual level of the Jewish people declined. Since that time, the majority of Jews have lived outside of the Land of Israel, and we have been unable to regain our previous lofty heights. When the Messiah gathers in the far-flung remnants of the Jewish nation and builds the Third Temple (see chapter thirteen), prophecy will return.

Written and Oral Torahs

The Torah is divided into two parts. One is referred to as the Written Torah and is also known as the Five Books of Moses: Bereshit (Genesis), Shmot (Exodus), Vayikra (Leviticus), BaMidbar (Numbers) and D'varim (Deuteronomy). This is what is written on scrolls of parchment and placed in the Ark in a synagogue. The Written Torah is only the skeleton of the body of Judaism, however; the second part, the living, breathing, pulsating, vibrant life force of our existence is the Oral Torah, which was given to Moshe on Mount Sinai along with the Written Torah.

Without the Oral Torah, we would have no idea how to perform any of the 613 commandments. In fact, from the text itself, there is no way to figure out how to do *anything*—not one commandment is explained in the Written Torah. For example, it tells us to keep the Shabbat, but you will not find any instructions on how to do so. We are told to wear *tefillin,* but good luck finding any definition of what that is (these are usually translated as "phylacteries" and will be discussed in chapter seven). In Deuteronomy 12:21, the Torah states, "You shall slaughter your cattle...as I have commanded you," but there is no such instruction in the text.

The Oral Torah is also referred to as the Oral Law, the Oral Tradition and the *Mesorah* (which translates to "the transmission" or the "the passing" from one generation to the next, similar to a baton in a relay race). For over 1,500 years, this Oral Law was never recorded in written form; it was G-d's intention that it be an interactive transmission requiring a teacher-student relationship. A human being is a much better teacher than a book and is much less likely to be misinterpreted.

The *Mesorah* can be explained as the bequeathing of a very rare and precious family heirloom from one generation to the next. Those receiving it are given care instructions and an explanation of what they are receiving—i.e., where it came from, what it means and what to do to safeguard it. If it requires maintenance, that will also be explained. But this is a far cry from a game of telephone, a one-time whisper done in jest from one person to another. The Torah is a lifetime of learning pursued by millions of people.

In fact all forms of knowledge require an oral transmission. One cannot become a doctor by reading texts alone; he needs to learn from another person as well. In fact, if you think about it, medical school is just an oral transmission of an accumulated body of knowledge. You wouldn't hire a contractor to build you a house if he had only read books about construction but never learned it from someone in the industry. Another benefit of an oral tradition is that knowledge that is in your mind becomes a part of you, but knowledge written in books does not.

In this way, the *Mesorah*, which ties every generation directly back to Mount Sinai, is so fundamental to Judaism that it is always the first target when someone wants to attack or change Judaism. Many times during the Middle Ages, the Catholic Church instigated disputations of the Talmud and would even put it on trial. Of course, the Talmud was always found guilty of being anti-Christian and bonfires were made of its volumes. Beginning with the Reform movement in Germany in the 1800s and continuing until today, "scholars" often have "proven" that much of Judaism actually developed, evolved or was created by different rabbinic leaders at different periods in Jewish history and that therefore they also have the right to "adapt" Judaism to modern times. (This is all explained in chapter eleven.)

This system of a strictly oral transmission lasted nearly 1,500 years. However, beginning in the period after the destruction of the Second Temple (68 AD), the Oral Law was in great danger of being forgotten or distorted. The Roman exile was taking us to the farthest points on the map, and the conditions necessary for the transmission of the Oral Law (lack of persecution, a settled life, close proximity to other communities, etc.) were not present. At this time, the first redaction of the Oral Law took place and the Mishnah was compiled. Written in terse, succinct sentences, it was intended almost as a shorthand version of the Oral Law that could be memorized but would still require a teacher to explain. Within a few hundred years, due to the continuing deterioration of our physical conditions, the Gemara, an elaboration of the Mishna, was compiled. Together, they are known as the Talmud which, even though it is in written form, still requires a teacher, or a Rebbe as he is called in Hebrew.

Another part of the Oral Law is called *midrash*. This term refers to commentaries on the Written Torah as well as the other nineteen books of the Bible. Sometimes it deals with Jewish law (*halacha*); other times it is written in homiletic fashion. The *midrashim* (plural of *midrash*) shed light on and explain and fill out aspects of the Written Torah. Like the other parts of the Oral Law, it is indispensable. The *midrashim* were also originally passed down orally from generation to generation until they were eventually compiled, for the same reasons as the Talmud and at the same time, in written form.

Over the last fifteen centuries, the Oral Law has been further expounded upon with each generation. Volumes have been written, but still nothing can take the place of a teacher. This ongoing elaboration is necessary because we view each subsequent generation as getting progressively smaller in spiritual stature and ability, and more in need of remedial assistance. These attenuating factors are a result of the amount of time that has passed since the giving of the Torah and especially since the last of the prophets. The event on Mount Sinai can be compared to an explosion: Those closest to it felt it more intensely; those farther away less so. Now, over 3,300 years from zero hour, things aren't as clear as they once were.

Additions and Subtractions

It is often claimed that during its long transmission process, many things were added to the Torah and that the Judaism we have today is very different from what the Jews practiced throughout history. It's true that Judaism has adapted to changing times and circumstances. Our history has produced holidays, like Chanukah and Purim, and numerous fast days that Moshe did not experience and earlier generations lacked.

But this is not what the detractors mean. They want to claim that the Torah we possess today has been altered throughout history in an ongoing, evolutionary process—but there is no way this could have occurred. First, the idea of a conspiracy to hide the truth about the "real" Torah is impossible. Millions of people throughout the world, over thousands of years, somehow would have had to conspire together. If you rented a movie with such a plotline, the stupidity of it would probably make you groan out loud. Besides, anyone who is even somewhat familiar with a Torah sage will know that his piety, honesty, wisdom and love of his fellow Jews would render such an idea beyond absurd.

Some people also propose that additions were later inserted into the Torah or that parts were removed from it—but such people are obviously unfamiliar with Jewish history and laws. The Talmud recounts how, before his death, Moshe wrote twelve Torah scrolls that were given, one each, to the high courts of each of the twelve tribes. These scrolls were to be used as the prototypes for every single Torah written in the future. Jewish law requires that the method of writing a Torah scroll is to copy it word for word from an existing scroll. A scribe cannot write it from memory—not even one word of it! In fact, he is also required to say each word out loud as he copies it. Not surprisingly, to write a complete Torah takes twelve months of full-time work.

This means that every Torah scroll in the world today has been copied from another one, going all the way back to those original twelve scrolls.

So, how would additions or deletions be accomplished once Torah scrolls proliferated throughout the nation? Could the number of scrolls have been restricted and controlled by some sort of cabal that was running the Jewish people? Not a chance. One of the 613 commandments is that every single, Jewish male should write his very own Torah scroll or, if he lacks the time or skills, pay to have one written on his behalf (even today this is required). The Torah reports that 600,000 men between the ages of twenty and sixty received the Torah at Mount Sinai. Even if only ten percent of them fulfilled this commandment, this cabal would very quickly lose control of the contents of the Torah.

Perhaps then, our detractors could say, some later regime confiscated all the Torahs and rewrote them. However, this is very farfetched and unreasonable. No regime has ever been able to successfully squash the truth; there are always dissidents. Some type of civil war would have broken out over such an attempt to change the religion. The Jewish people would have splintered and there would be many versions of the Torah in the world today.

The *Mitzvot* and Their Meanings

The Torah contains 613 *mitzvot*. Of these, 248 are positive or "do" *mitzvot* (like honoring your mother and father) and 365 are negative or "don't do" *mitzvot* (like not eating anything from a pig). They are all mentioned in the Written Torah and explained in the Oral Torah.

But what exactly is a *mitzvah*? Let's start by saying what it isn't. It isn't a good deed. Performing *shechita* (killing an animal by slitting its throat in a way that cuts the windpipe and esophagus in one fluid movement instead of, for example, shooting it in the head) is not the definition of a good deed. Nor is circumcising an eight-day-old baby boy (not that it's a bad deed, but if someone asked you what good deed you did today, you wouldn't answer that you circumcised a baby). In addition, many of the *mitzvot* don't involve any deed at all. They involve hearing, seeing, thinking or speaking. And the 365 negative *mitzvot* cannot be considered a deed at all since refraining from doing something is not defined as a deed.

The translation of the Hebrew word *mitzvah* is "commandment," and the *mitzvot* are, plain and simple, G-d's instructions on how we are to live our lives. The purpose of the *mitzvot* is to elevate us as individuals, as communities and as a people. Some *mitzvot* govern our actions between man and G-d (Shabbat, kosher laws, holidays, prayer, etc.) and some govern our actions between man and man (stealing, lying, murder, charity, etc.) These are not 613 unrelated laws to be applied in random situations. Rather, the *mitzvot* comprise an organized and practical system with an underlying theme: To create a deep and sincere relationship between each Jew and his creator by elevating him and giving him complete mastery over his physical self. And since they are the instructions of a loving parent, none of the *mitzvot* are harmful or dangerous in any way.

Understood this way, Judaism is not really a "religion" *per se*. It is not an arbitrary set of rules but an all-encompassing and permeating relationship with G-d that involves every aspect of our lives. To term Judaism a "religion" actually denigrates it. The *mitzvot* force us to live spiritual lives through our material, tangible beings. We take our senses of seeing, hearing, smelling and tasting and elevate them into spiritual experiences. We use our minds and hearts and limbs to fulfill the *mitzvot* that G-d has given to us.

This illuminates a basic tenet of Judaism—that it is a religion (for lack of a better word) of action, not faith. When Adam and Chava chose to disobey G-d and, as a result, imbued their bodies with a certain independence, the only way to rectify the situation was to force the body into a spiritually oriented existence and make it once again subservient to the soul. Actions, not faith, accomplish that goal because people are molded by their actions. If you don't want your children to be thieves you don't tell them, "It's not nice to steal" and hope they don't. You tell them, "You cannot steal", make sure they know the consequences and enforce the rules when necessary. Character is created by actions and experiences, not ideas or philosophy. Doctrines or abstract ideas can be misunderstood or even manipulated to satisfy someone's desires. Laws are ironclad.

No one person can fulfill all 613 *mitzvot*. Some are directed only toward a Kohan, a Levi, a king, a judge or a soldier. Some are incumbent on the courts or on the community. Some deal with money, some with marriage, and some with agriculture. Some only apply on specific days or at specific times. But there is no aspect of life that is untouched. Whatever we do or whatever occurs in our lives at any time, the *mitzvot* are there to elevate our actions and responses.

They also deal with life in its most brutal reality. The Torah has no impossible-to-keep laws or starry-eyed dictums. We are not enjoined to turn the other cheek (which no one can do and stay alive, which is why Christians never do it). We are instead commanded to defend ourselves even to the point of preempting an attack by going on the offensive when there is no other choice. In Judaism, there is no phoniness. The Western world seems to think that a truly religious person will be meek and soft, his face characterized by flaccid muscles and a vacuous smile, his nature so gentle that he will never exhibit anger or have a lustful thought. We do not subscribe to any of this nonsense. People are people and many are born with strong personalities and even hot tempers. Flashes of anger or lust are not evidence that a person is not really religious or, worse, a charlatan or a hypocrite. It's just evidence that this person slipped up, like all human beings will do from time to time. Self-refinement is a lifelong endeavor.

Though the *mitzvot* are, in essence, rules by which we should live our lives, to see the Torah as simply a rule book would be a tremendous mistake. It is not just a collection of laws accompanied by empty or symbolic rituals, and doing the *mitzvot* by rote will not fulfill their ultimate purpose. The Torah is a book of deep, meaningful lessons, and its ultimate fulfillment requires that both the head and the heart be engaged. Giving charity because one "has to" will certainly make one a better person. However, if a person is cognizant of all the meaning behind his actions when he reaches into his pocket and puts his hard-earned money into the hand of someone less fortunate, he has a real opportunity to grow as a human being.

Through their fulfillment, the lessons of the *mitzvot* become part of our basic nature.

To Life!

The Jewish people view the *mitzvot* as constant opportunities to grow and develop ourselves into great people and to deepen our relationship with G-d.

Because our time in this world is so infused with meaning and has so much potential for accomplishing great things, Jews cherish life itself. Other nations raise their glasses to "Cheers" or "To health." We raise our glasses and toast "*L'chaim*"—to life—because life is our most precious possession. In fact, we view every second as precious and meaningful. Wasted time is wasted opportunity. Most of the world, unfortunately, is either biding time, passing time or killing time. It doesn't seem to hold the same value to them.

Jews traditionally bless each other with the hope for long life. But we don't desire long life so we can eat, drink or shop a lot. We don't drink "to life" in the hope that we will have more years just to make more toasts and drink more *l'chaims*.

Jews wish for long lives so we can have many years to fulfill the purpose of our lives. The longer we live, the more *mitzvot* we fulfill and the more we accomplish; a Jew can do *mitzvot* right up until the very moment he dies. This is why Jews always consider death to be a terrible thing regardless of the circumstances. Even if a person is suffering and has no chance of survival, his death, though it might be a relief from pain, ends forever all opportunities for accomplishing his purpose. And that is a great loss.

Chukim

Because the 613 *mitzvot* cover the entire gamut of human life, they can be organized into categories to better understand their meaning. For example, one category called Mishpatim deals with legal statutes and financial laws and includes all the laws regarding stealing, paying workers, bodily injury, property damage, judges and the courts.

A unique category of *mitzvot* is called Chukim, which translates as "decrees." A *chok* (singular form of *chukim, rhymes with poke*) is a commandment of which there is no rational or logical understanding. **These laws never apply to our interactions with other people, only to our interactions with G-d.** While we utterly reject the idea of accepting a religion on blind faith, once we understand clearly that G-d gave us the Torah, we also understand that there will be much to it that will be beyond our ability to fathom.

A Jew is supposed to be humble enough to accept the fact that there are things he does not know or understand and never will. Much of the Torah is beyond human understanding or comprehension. The greatest genius toiling day and night for 120 years could not approach the knowledge of the infinite G-d who created all of existence.

This, of course, is perfectly logical since a finite being cannot conceive infinity. Just like we cannot see beyond a certain distance or hear or smell beyond a certain distance, we cannot understand beyond a certain point. In our corporeal state, we cannot comprehend infinite space or infinite time, nor infinite wisdom or intelligence. Logically, it is absurd to think that the finite mind of the creation could ever comprehend the infinite mind of the creator. And it is essential to know that there is no sense in trying to make rational sense of the Chukim because their reasons are hidden from the human mind.

Probably the most famous example of a *chok* is the laws of *kashrut* or keeping kosher. Many silly theories have been proffered to explain away the prohibition of swine or shellfish, such as their being more prone to dangerous bacteria and parasites and while true, the theories do not explain or even attempt to explain many other fundamental components of *kashrut*. For instance, why is *shechita*, or ritual slaughter, required? Why is a hunted deer unkosher while one that is slaughtered properly kosher? Why is a cow that is shot in the head unkosher but one slaughtered by *shechita* kosher? This makes no sense to the human mind. There is no rationale.

For a land animal to be kosher—permitted for consumption—it must have split hooves and chew its cud (regurgitant). Those requirements seem just a little insignificant don't they? Does it really matter what kind of foot it has? A cow is permitted but a horse is not. A giraffe is kosher but its elephant neighbor is not. A gazelle and a wildebeest are both kosher while their fellow grazer, the zebra, is not. All are herbivores, yet some are okay and some are not. And the personality seems to have no bearing. An African buffalo, which is a nasty, ornery and dangerous animal, is kosher while a cute, little bunny rabbit is not.

Sea creatures, in order to be kosher, need to have fins and scales. Tuna is fine, but swordfish is not, and poor Flipper is not welcome in kosher homes and restaurants. Shellfish might pose a health risk if not prepared properly, but does a whale or a marlin or a sturgeon? Regarding birds, all are kosher except for the ones listed in chapter eleven of Leviticus and chapter fourteen of Deuteronomy—no other reason is given.

Furthermore, one is forbidden to take kosher meat and kosher cheese and combine them. The meat is kosher, and the cheese is kosher, but together they become unkosher—not very logical.

Another example of a *chok* is the law prohibiting a man to shave his face with a straight-edged blade (although it is permitted to cut one's beard with a scissor or an electric shaver that cuts like a scissor to or remove it with a depilatory cream). This prohibition is one of the main reasons why Jewish men have traditionally worn beards. But, no reason is given for the prohibition of razor blades, and there is no rational reason for it. Perhaps G-d wants us to be highly visible in all situations.

Despite our lack of understanding of the Chukim, however, we can still learn from them and should try to do so. For example, there is a great deal to learn from the laws of *kashrut*. Jews do not eat predators, or animals that kill other animals in order to eat them. Nor do we eat scavengers, or animals that feast upon the carcasses of dead animals. The kosher animals do not use their limbs aggressively, only in self-defense. Even the birds fall into this category. The Talmud describes the use of talons to hold prey as a sign that a bird is unkosher.

Regarding the prohibition of mixing milk and meat, the Torah's literal wording is: "Do not cook the kid in its mother's milk." In other words, do not take the baby goat and cook its dead body in the milk that was supposed to nourish it and help it grow. Stated in that way, the act seems a bit sadistic. Understanding this can lead one to a greater sensitivity towards other living things.

Shechita is the domain of specifically trained men who make their living from it and so has traditionally been relegated to a specific place within the community. The result is that Jewish women never kill. In fact, Jewish women are the only women in the world who until recently did not go out to the barn and come back with a beheaded chicken or goose. This allowed them to avoid developing the inherent sense of cruelty that comes from killing another living thing, which in turn allowed Jewish women to remain solely life-giving beings. A woman who does not kill creates a different type of home and raises a different type of child than a woman who kills. Jewish women are only life givers and never life takers.

From these laws, we can certainly see that at the least, G-d is instructing us to develop moral sensitivity and avoid any form of cruelty. But regardless of what we can or cannot learn from a *mitzvah*, we must fulfill each of them to the last detail.

Trading Up

To an outside observer, a life of *mitzvot* can seem quite oppressive, and this leads to the common misconception that religious Jews give up pleasure in order to listen to G-d.

But this is not at all true, and it's based on superficial observations.

Firstly, what purpose would G-d have in prohibiting Jews from enjoying many of the physical pleasures that He created? Is it to see if we will be obedient? No, He doesn't need our obedience. In fact, He doesn't need anything from us. All of creation is for the benefit of mankind, there is no point to such a test.

Furthermore, there is no concept in the Torah of "sacrificing for G-d." A sacrifice is something that is given up without gain, and there is no sacrificing for G-d. He has no need for our sacrifices; He needs nothing from us at all. He only wants our good. Everything G-d has commanded us to do is for our ultimate benefit, not His. What normal parent would want his child to sacrifice something to demonstrate his love and loyalty?

And besides, whatever could we do for Him, anyway? Take the sheep He created and sacrifice them to Him? Take the money He has given us and donate in His honor? Use the mouth, tongue, lips, teeth and vocal cords He has given us to tell Him how wonderful He is? Do we really believe that G-d needs our prayers and sacrifices? Pagan gods, since they are human creations, conceived with all the foibles of human beings, needed to be appeased—but not the one true G-d.

Not only do we not sacrifice anything by fulfilling the *mitzvot,* but in fact we only gain. As we have seen, if G-d had created us to do only what He said, He would not have created us with the freewill ability to choose to disobey Him. Since He created us with this ability, it is clear that He did not create us for His benefit but for our own. It follows, then, that His commandments are not for His benefit but for ours as well. In this scenario, there is no such concept as sacrificing for G-d. It is illogical.

In fact, the concept of sacrificing pleasure in this world is decidedly un-Jewish. The reality is that Jews don't *give up* anything—we *trade up.* And trading up is always a good thing. Nobody complained when color television came out and people had to trade up from their black and white sets. This is because the color sets gave them more pleasure.

When we fulfill the mitzvot, we give up a lesser physical pleasure for a greater spiritual pleasure. For example, by not eating on Yom Kippur, we are not sacrificing our desires for food and drink to demonstrate to G-d our devotion. He has no need for such displays. Instead, on Yom Kippur, we forego mundane and distracting physical activities in order to spend the day in intense self-examination through which we shed the spiritual calluses that we have allowed to build up and that prevent us from having real relationships with G-d.

This embracing love of the spiritual side of life also manifests itself in the Orthodox approach to children. We love children and purposely have a lot of them. Anyone who has had exposure to Orthodox families knows that, on average, they are larger than similar families, Jewish and non-Jewish, in their socio-economic bracket. Only Orthodox Jews seem to defy the rule that economic success results in smaller families and a reduced population.

This is because we see children as a blessing and a source of incredible joy and we understand that raising them is a great honor and one of the most G-dlike things we can do in life. Except for extreme cases, financial considerations rarely affect the decision. We don't limit the number of children, i.e our most important possession, so that we can indulge in lesser important physical pleasures and luxuries. And less well-to-do families understand that limiting family size so that the one or two existing children can have "more" is disingenuous. Children would much rather have siblings than stuff.

So whereas most people today view birth control as the norm and pregnancies as the exception, a newly married Orthodox couple does not immediately run to the pharmacy. Instead, they eagerly pray for and look forward to starting and eventually building a large family.

(Regarding birth control, Jewish law does not sanction the casual, unfettered use of birth control as a normal way of living. We do not believe in preventing life from coming into being. But that being said, since the Torah is the product of a loving G-d, it certainly allows individual situations a great deal of leeway. Many Orthodox women are on birth control due to health reasons, mental health included. If a woman feels overwhelmed or incapable of being a good mother if she is pregnant or has a large family, these are considered completely valid reasons for limiting family size.)

Similarly, look at the *mitzvah* of *tzedakah,* which is generally translated as "charity" although its etymological roots are actually in the Hebrew word for righteousness. What happens when we give *tzedakah*? Are we sacrificing our hard-earned money in order to obey G-d? Or are we taking money that we would most likely spend superfluously and instead giving it to someone in need in order to help them make ends meet? Which is more important—another suit of clothing or another evening in a restaurant or giving another family a little happiness? The answer should be obvious. When G-d commands us to give *tzedakah,* it is for our own good. It helps us become better people, less self-centered and more caring. There is no sacrifice here, only gain.

And so not only is it completely untrue that religious Jews sacrifice the pleasures of this world for some reward in the next world, I would submit that Orthodox Jews even get more pleasure from the physical pleasures of this world than anyone else.

On the surface, it seems as though non-Orthodox Jews are free to do anything they want, go anywhere they want and eat anything they want while the Orthodox cannot, due to the restrictions on their lives. The missing element in this view, however, is the fact that once the meaning is removed from the experiences—the food, drink and good times, they become less tasty and less fulfilling over time.

A religious Jew knows this and lives accordingly. His goals are not physical; he does not look to physical pleasures and sensations to stimulate him and make him feel alive. His goals are spiritual, and he looks to spiritual experiences for stimulation. Thus, he is free to enjoy the physical world because he doesn't look to it for more than it is.

There is another basic reason why religious Jews enjoy the physical world more than secular Jews: They understand that it is all a gift of love and, as a result, they have a greater appreciation of each bite they take, each sunset they see and each flower they smell. The difference between seeing this world as a random accident and seeing it as a gift is immense. Try this test: Take your favorite fruit and having in mind that is just a fluke of millions of years of evolution, take a bite. Now, having in mind that this was made for you by a G-d that loves you and created it for the sole purpose of your enjoyment, take another bite. I've done this experiment with many people, and the second bite is always a different experience.

Obvious Results

The Jewish people have been molded by the *mitzvot,* and the results are clear to an unbiased eye.

In March of 1898, Mark Twain published an essay entitled "Concerning the Jews" in *Harper's Magazine.* He wrote this essay in response to a letter he had received from a reader asking him why Jews suffered from anti-Semitism. This is how his unbiased eyes viewed the Jews:

> The Jew is not a disturber of the peace of any country. Even his enemies will concede that. He is not a loafer, he is not a sot, he is not noisy, he is not a brawler nor a rioter, he is not quarrelsome. In the statistics of crime his presence is conspicuously rare—in all countries. With murder and other crimes of violence he has but little to do: he is a stranger to the hangman. In the police court's daily long roll of "assaults" and "drunk and disorderlies" his name seldom appears.
>
> That the Jewish home is a home in the truest sense is a fact which no one will dispute. The family is knitted together by the strongest affections; its members show each other every due respect; and reverence for the elders is an inviolate law of the house. The Jew is not a burden on

the charities of the state nor of the city; these could cease from their functions without affecting him.

When he is well enough, he works; when he is incapacitated, his own people take care of him. And not in a poor and stingy way, but with a fine and large benevolence. His race is entitled to be called the most benevolent of all the races of men. A Jewish beggar is not impossible, perhaps; such a thing may exist, but there are few men that can say they have seen that spectacle. The Jew has been staged in many uncomplimentary forms, but, so far as I know, no dramatist has done him the injustice to stage him as a beggar. Whenever a Jew has real need to beg, his people save him from the necessity of doing it. The charitable institutions of the Jews are supported by Jewish money, and amply. The Jews make no noise about it; it is done quietly; they do not nag and pester and harass us for contributions; they give us peace, and set us an example—an example which we have not found ourselves able to follow; for by nature we are not free givers, and have to be patiently and persistently hunted down in the interest of the unfortunate.

These facts are all on the credit side of the proposition that the Jew is a good and orderly citizen. Summed up, they certify that he is quiet, peaceable, industrious, unaddicted to high crimes and brutal dispositions; that his family life is commendable; that he is not a burden upon public charities; that he is not a beggar; that in benevolence he is above the reach of competition. These are the very quintessentials of good citizenship.

Other thinkers have clearly seen the difference between the Jewish people and the rest of the world. This is a direct result of the Torah and the 613 *mitzvot*. Some examples:

It would be a mistake, however, to ascribe to Roman legal conceptions an undivided sway over the development of law and institutions during the Middle Ages. The Teuton came under the influence, not of Rome only, but also of Christianity; and through the Church there entered into Europe a potent leaven of Jewish thought. The Laws of

Moses as well as the laws of Rome contributed suggestions and impulse to the men and institutions which were to prepare the modern world; and if we could have but eyes to see the subtle elements of thought which constitute the gross substance of our present habit, both as regards the sphere of private life and as regards the actions of the state, we should easily discover how very much besides religion we owe to the Jew.

—President Woodrow Wilson
in his book *The State*, published 1889

In spite of Bolingbroke and Voltaire, I will insist that the Hebrews have done more to civilize men than any other nation. If I were an atheist and believed in blind eternal fate, I should still believe that fate had ordained the Jews to be the most essential instrument for civilizing the nations. If I were an atheist of the other sect, who believe or pretend to believe that all is ordered by chance, I should believe that chance had ordered the Jews to preserve and propagate to all mankind the doctrine of a supreme, intelligent, wise, almighty Sovereign of the universe, which I believe to be the great essential principle of all morality, and consequently of all civilization... They are the most glorious nation that ever inhabited this Earth. The Romans and their empire were but a bauble in comparison to the Jews. They have given religion to three-quarters of the globe and have influenced the affairs of mankind more and more happily than any other nation, ancient or modern.

—President John Adams
in a letter to Francis Adriaan Van der Kemp,
February 16, 1808

The Jew is that sacred being who has brought down from heaven the everlasting fire, and has illumined with it the entire world. He is the religious source, spring, and fountain out of which all the rest of the peoples have drawn their beliefs and their religions. The Jew is the pioneer of

liberty… The Jew is the pioneer of civilization… The Jew
is the emblem of civil and religious toleration…
—Leo Tolstoy, "What Is a Jew?" 1891

What accounts for this significant difference? Only the Torah and its
mitzvot. When a Jew abandons his heritage, within three generations he is
indistinguishable from his surroundings. He loses his distinction and his
greatness. Our virtues, our morals and our very character come from the
613 *Mitzvot*.

Learning Torah

The most important of the 613 *mitzvot* in the Torah and the one described
as being equal to all the others combined is the *mitzvah* of the actual study
of Torah. All Jews must learn Torah from the time they are able to read
until their souls finally leaves their bodies. Every Jew is required to know
all of Torah and be able to know what is right in any situation, and anyone
can become the greatest scholar of the generation. Judaism is the world's
only true meritocracy. We are not a religion of elites who instruct the
unlearned.

Specifically, the term "learning Torah" refers to the Written Torah, the
Oral Law (Talmud), the Prophets and Writings that comprise the rest of
what we call "The Bible" and all the commentaries and rabbinic writings
that have been produced over the last 1,800 years.

But learning Torah is not an academic endeavor. It is a spiritual
experience that cannot be accurately described in words. To describe an
experience one needs to use references that the listener can understand.
To grasp a description of swimming under a waterfall, the listener needs
to have a familiarity with waterfalls and with the feeling of swimming in
water. It would be very difficult to understand the description without this
prior knowledge. The same goes for describing the taste of chocolate to
someone who has never eaten it, the sound of music to one who is deaf or
the beauty of color to one who is blind. It is simply not possible.

Similarly, a true description of the learning of Torah defies words. It
is an experience that is not felt by any of the five physical senses; it is felt
by the soul, and someone who is not accustomed to using his or her soul
will not be able to understand the description. A person who has never
learned Torah will not comprehend its sweetness, its brilliance, the inner

satisfaction and joy it provides or the sense of true meaning it radiates. One who has not drank from its waters cannot understand how grown men can spend hours a day and years of their lives dedicated purely to the study of Torah. (How many times have I been asked, "What *have* you been learning for so many years?")

The same Torah can be studied by a six-year-old and a ninety-six-year-old, and each will be able to find meaning in it. In fact, you will very often see fathers and grandfathers teaching it to their young children or grandchildren with excitement and passion. The same Torah speaks to all of them even with their different levels of intelligence and understanding.

In the Torah world, it is common to see groups of men in their teens and twenties following an octogenarian down the street, straining to hear his words. Those who learn Torah become part of a living chain that stretches back thousands of years. We refer to and quote sages from the present all the way back over 2,000 years. We know them by name and follow their discussions and arguments in the Talmud.

Jewish study halls where this learning takes place are rambunctious, roaring-fire environments wherein study partners passionately hash out the meanings of their studies as opposed to the eerie, morgue-like silence of libraries. To walk into a *beit medrash* ("house of study" in Hebrew) is to walk into an ongoing explosion.

There is obviously something very deep and meaningful about a "book" that can be studied constantly and in depth by an entire nation for thousands of years—so much so that we hug and kiss the Torah and dance with it out of sheer joy. I have never seen law students or medical students do this with their textbooks. In fact, I have never seen anyone kiss a book besides an Orthodox Jew.

―――――――

The first part of this book deals with the foundations of Orthodox Jewish thought and while the past four chapters have sort of flowed into each other, the next chapter is a slight departure. Up to this point we have seen why G-d created this world and, in particular, human beings and we have seen that everything is an act of love, especially the Torah and its *mitzvot*. For many sensitive people, however, human suffering acts a monumental confutation to any idea of a loving G-d but this is only due to a lack of understanding of the meaning of our suffering. The next chapter will hopefully clear this up.

Chapter Five
Reward, Punishment and Why Bad Things Happen to Good People

Suffering Hurts

Suffering, either our own or that of another person, bothers anyone with a heart. It causes us emotional pain and like all emotions, if we do not control and direct it, our feelings will overwhelm us and prevent us from thinking clearly. We need to keep this in mind as we discuss this issue.

As Jews, we have an innate sense of justice and want to see the world as a just place. And, even though free will requires us to have the potential for great evil and the ability to cause great suffering, we still have to answer the question of why a specific individual is affected when another person chooses to perpetrate evil. A drive-by shooting kills some and leaves others untouched. Some survived the Holocaust while the rest of their families were wiped out. There is also the question of natural disasters and illnesses that afflict some but spare others.

If you wonder why bad things happen to good people, you might be relieved to learn that you are in good company; even great men have grappled with the question. This chapter will hopefully explain the true Jewish view of suffering and the true Jewish view of reward and punishment.

My Father

On the afternoon of Monday, May 5, 1975, I sat down to do a homework assignment for my eighth-grade English class. I was thirteen years old. The assignment was to write a descriptive paragraph about someone's face. The local newspaper had a cartoon caricature of Frank Robinson in its sports section that day; he was in the news because he was in his first season as the player/manager of the Cleveland Indians and was the first black manager in Major League Baseball. I decided to use this drawing for my assignment.

I sat down at the desk in our den. Sitting at the desk, if one looked over his right shoulder, he would look up a flight of stairs into the kitchen. The

radio was playing "The No No Song" by Ringo Starr. My father was forty-five years old at the time and had been, until his first heart attack eight months earlier, a heavy smoker. After his heart attack, which occurred on a Friday night one week after my Bar Mitzvah, he had given up smoking. But his heart had sustained damage, and his doctors had told him that he could not engage in any strenuous activity. He had always loved working on our lawn but now he was prohibited from mowing it; from then on, it was to be my job.

However, on this spring afternoon, my father decided to mow the lawn. I offered to do it, but he told me that the first mowing of the season was tough—that he would do it and then I would take over the rest of the year. He was trying to help me but never anticipated what was about to occur.

As I began my assignment, my father had just finished dinner and was still sitting at the kitchen with a cold drink. He looked very tired. After I'd written a few lines, for no apparent reason, I looked up into the kitchen just in time to see him fall off his chair and crash onto the kitchen floor. His body was convulsing.

I ran upstairs and called to him, but he was unconscious. I screamed to my mother, who came running to the kitchen, grabbed the phone and called 911. Then, we waited. Within a minute or two, police cars with sirens wailing came tearing into the cul-de-sac where we lived and screeched to a halt in front of our house. The policemen ran in and instructed us to get a pillow, which one of them put under my father's head, and a blanket, which he laid over him. Seconds became minutes and then more minutes and then more minutes. The police were getting very agitated that no ambulance was coming.

My father stopped convulsing. One policeman started to scream into his walkie-talkie about an ambulance. I distinctly remember him saying "This isn't a joke, this is serious." Finally, the ambulance arrived and my father was taken out on a stretcher. By this time, the entire neighborhood was in front of my house, and someone instructed me to go find my little sister, who was out riding her bicycle with friends somewhere in the vicinity. Miraculously, I found her right away.

The ambulance took my father to the nearest hospital, which was only half a mile away, but it was a futile effort. He was dead on arrival.

Before long, a police car pulled up in front of our house again. My sister and I were waiting outside on our driveway along with the rest of the neighborhood. My mother got out of the police car and motioned for us to come over, her expression confirming what I had already known when the

ambulance had pulled away. I bolted the other way and in a mix of tears and rage, started walking laps around the house. I guess I wanted to get out of there, but I really had no place to go.

At that point, my memory gets foggy, although I have a few snapshots in my mind, such as my mother, sister and I meeting with the director of the funeral home. I vaguely remember the funeral.

At the ripe old age of thirteen, I had stood by helplessly and watched my father die on the kitchen floor. My sister was twelve; my mother was a widow at thirty-nine. I sat *shiva* for my father for a week, and my friends came over and we talked about everything except the fact that my father had just died. For many years, I was the only person I knew with one parent; this was the 1970s, and most people had two. I only knew two girls whose parents were divorced.

After that, I became the go-to guy when it came to death. When a friend lost her brother in high school, I went to pay a *shiva* call. Upon seeing me enter her house, she jumped up, literally grabbed me by the arm and pulled me into another room. "I've been waiting for you. You're the only person I can talk to about this who will understand," she told me. It was a dubious sort of honor, and one that I would have gladly passed up.

Still, today, when people find out that my father died when I was thirteen, they seem a little shocked.

Why do such tragedies happen to people? What did I do, at the age of thirteen, to "deserve" watching my father die on the kitchen floor? What did my mother do to "deserve" becoming a young widow? Or my little sister, burying her father before she could celebrate her Bat Mitzvah with him?

The short answer is that I didn't do anything to deserve such a tragedy, and neither did my mother or sister because the word "deserve" doesn't even belong in the equation. As I will explain, many things happen to people in their lifetimes that have nothing to do with deserving or not deserving.

But first, a few other points.

The Question Says a Lot

If the question of suffering bothers you, your discomfort reveals a great deal about how you envision G-d. Either consciously or subconsciously, you recognize that:

a. G-d is kind and just.
b. He runs the world.
c. Everything He does has meaning.
d. We were created for pleasure.

a. G-d is kind and just.

Why should suffering be an issue in the first place? Perhaps there is suffering in the world because G-d is angry or has a bad disposition? Or has not been properly appeased? Of course, a Jew cannot take these suggestions seriously. The only reason why you are bothered by suffering is because you believe in a kind and just G-d. If you didn't, you would have no expectations and there would be no question about suffering. Asking "why?" reveals that we are questioning the justice in it and that we cannot accept injustice.

This is not true of other religions and philosophies. Christian doctrine is based on suffering, and Islam seems to encourage it. And, in the rest of the Third World that is not Christian or Moslem, they don't even see a question.

When I was in high school, our English class had to read a sermon written in 1741 by a Calvinist preacher named Jonathan Edwards entitled "Sinners in the Hands of an Angry God." In it, he said:

> The bow of God's wrath is bent, and the arrow made ready on the string, and justice bends the arrow at your heart, and strains the bow, and it is nothing but the mere pleasure of God, and that of an angry God, without any promise or obligation at all, that keeps the arrow one moment from being made drunk with your blood.

And other goodies like:

> The God that holds you over the pit of hell, much as one holds a spider, or some loathsome insect over the fire, abhors you, and is dreadfully provoked: his wrath towards you burns like fire; he looks upon you as worthy of nothing else, but to be cast into the fire; he is of purer eyes than to bear to have you in his sight; you are ten thousand

> times more abominable in his eyes than the most hateful
> venomous serpent is in ours.

This philosophy, which, to a Jew is quite repulsive, was the tone of Christianity until very recently. European missionaries also discovered that this type of talk didn't go over that well in the Third World, and so the concepts of peace and love began to be emphasized over the suffering and damnation stuff.

I went to college in the late 1970s and roomed with two other guys in an ethnically stereotypical dorm room. I was the Jew from New York; one was an Irish Catholic from Pittsburgh and the other a Protestant from Philadelphia. When we had spare time, which was all of the time, we did what all college students are required to do—we hung out and drank beer, often with another Jewish student from Westchester County, New York. I did this even though I did not and still do not like beer, but there was simply no option—drinking beer is absolutely mandatory for college freshmen.

Interestingly, we three roommates were spiritually oriented; the guy from Westchester was much less so. I had always had a strong belief in G-d although I was not at all observant of ritual and could not have articulated a coherent philosophy. The Catholic was a believer and a churchgoer, and the Protestant was active in his church's youth group. Many times, we discussed G-d and the meaning of life.

Alcohol brings out an inner voice and the more beer that went in, the more secrets came out. And what I found was that the differences between the Jews and the Christians were astounding. The other Jew and I would offer up ideas about how the world is a good place, how G-d does everything for the best and how we are here to enjoy life. Not the Catholic, though—with each beer he consumed he grew darker and darker. To him, we were here to suffer for our sins, the one we were born with and the ones we did ourselves, and each of us had a cross to bear. We were all destined for hell if not for the grace of G-d. The Protestant, incredibly, had no opinion. He confessed that he really didn't know what to make of it all and it didn't bother him.

To me, all of this was a fascinating discovery. I knew that the hell and damnation stuff had once been the basis of Christian philosophy, but I thought that was a thing of the past. As I was to learn in more depth later in life, however, the views had not changed—only the marketing had. To a believing Christian, the issue of suffering is not an issue at all. It's the purpose of life.

But it isn't for us. How often have you heard someone say, "I can't believe in a G-d after the Holocaust"? Or, "How can there be a G-d if there is so much suffering?" In a Jew's universe, there cannot be a G-d who is mean or cruel.

But what bothers us is not suffering *per se* but suffering that seems unjust. Life is full of all types of pain. A trip to the dentist's office can cause great discomfort, but nobody leaves there questioning the existence of G-d. A death of a family member is very painful, but when an eighty-year-old woman passes away, there is not a collective shaking of heads and muttering about the lack of justice in the death of an innocent woman. And suffering that comes to those that seem to deserve it is never questioned—in fact, it's often welcomed by observers. Nobody laments the suffering of the German people during World War II—except, of course, the Germans. In fact, many people feel that they didn't suffer enough. A just G-d dispensing true justice is actually a happy event. We only get confused when the suffering seems unjust because we know that He is just.

b) He runs the world.

The question of suffering reveals that you acknowledge that G-d is actively running the world. If you didn't believe in G-d, you wouldn't ask the question at all—there would be no one to whom to pose the question. And if you believed in a G-d who created the world and then left it or has limited abilities, you also wouldn't ask the question because either G-d's not involved or He can't do anything about it. In either case, questioning Him about suffering would be akin to holding a weatherman personally responsible for the weather.

If we question the existence of suffering, it is only because we understand that there is a G-d to whom we can direct the question—one who is ultimately responsible for what occurs.

c) Everything He does has meaning.

When we ask "why?" it implies that we are looking for an answer that provides an underlying reason. When we suffer personally, this aspect of the question takes on an outsized significance. Very often you will hear someone voice the question, "Why me?" in one way or another. Asking this confirms that a person believes that there must be a reason for what they

are enduring. They understand that what is happening is not random but rather directed.

d) We were created for pleasure.

When we question suffering, we are clearly stating, "This shouldn't be." The question confirms that we understand that life is good and that G-d created us to give us pleasure, and suffering runs contrary to that under-standing. The proof of this is that the question is very rarely asked when things are going well—only when things are not going the way we'd like. It's almost as if we expect life to be good.

So, before tackling the issue of suffering directly, let's review. The question of suffering, whether it's ours ("why me?") or someone else's, reveals that we believe in a kind and just G-d who runs the world. It also reveals that we believe that what happens to us has meaning and that life is meant to be good and pleasurable. And it is this knowledge that causes us pain because, when bad things happen, it doesn't follow logically from what we intuit, and it seems like a contradiction. So, we ask questions like, "How can a loving G-d allow for this?" or, "How could G-d let this happen?"

The work is in reconciling what we know with what we feel.

Ground Rules

There are four essential points that we must understand in order to grasp any meaning behind suffering. Without these four, it can never make sense. They are:

1. Everything is a gift
2. There is no such thing as "fair"
3. If life has meaning, then the pain also has meaning
4. There is an afterlife

1. Everything Is a Gift

If we look at our lives and the myriad gifts we possess, we very quickly see that we don't deserve any of them. Why does a person deserve the gift

of sight or hearing? There are many blind and deaf people—why do they not deserve such gifts? Why does any person deserve the gift of a properly functioning digestive, nervous or reproductive system, or legs or teeth or children or food or brains or a house to live in or any number of the literally thousands of things that we take for granted?

We all know deep down that we have not earned any of the gifts we possess and that everything we have is a gift. Nevertheless, we go through life expecting everything to work out the way we want it to or, at least, not badly. And when there are setbacks or tragedies, suddenly we want to know, "Why me?"

But once we understand that since we do not deserve anything and that *everything* is a gift for our benefit, we can appreciate that suffering must also somehow be a gift. Once we realize that we are constantly receiving gifts of love, we view suffering quite differently.

Unfortunately I have a real life example that also sheds light on this: I have a cousin named Ann who once had three healthy children. One day, thirty years ago, her two-year-old was in the backyard, playing with her siblings and some other neighborhood children, when she wandered off. Nobody noticed how long she was missing and when they eventually found her, she was face down in a neighbor's in-ground birdbath which was full of water. She had been there a while, and her brain had been deprived of oxygen long enough to leave her severely retarded. She eventually died at the age of twenty-two, still wearing diapers.

Years later, a female relative of mine approached me about this, "Tell me what Ann did to deserve that" she demanded, "Ann is such a good person."

I answered her with the following: "If you can tell me what Ann did to deserve two healthy children, I will tell you what she did to deserve this."

This answer did not mean that I wasn't brokenhearted about what had happened. I was. I remembered when my cousin was born and I remembered holding her when she was a baby. But I wanted to show my relative that there is no answer because there is no question. We don't deserve the good and we don't "deserve" the bad. Everything is a gift—our eyes, our ears, our children, our food but also illnesses, deaths, disasters and tragedies.

But, we still need to understand how.

2. Life Is Not Fair

How often have we heard the expression "life is not fair" or "there is no justice in this world?" This is 100-percent true. Not only is life not fair, it is completely unfair. Where is the fairness in some being born rich and some being born poor, some beautiful and some plain, some seeing and some blind, some hearing and some deaf, some healthy and some sickly, some fertile and some barren, some intelligent and some simple, some mentally fit and some mentally ill, some musically talented and some tone deaf, some charismatic and some painfully shy?

Fairness is a very distorted concept. Its roots might be in our desire to see everybody have a wonderful life but in reality, when we complain that things are not fair, it only means that we are jealous of what someone else has. In fact the concept of "fair" is so foreign to Jewish thought that in the Hebrew language, there is no word for "fair." Modern Hebrew has adopted the word directly from English. If you want to complain in Hebrew you say, "*Ze lo fair.*"

To quote a cliché, life is a journey; there is no objective finish line to which we are all racing. We all die at different times and in different ways but it's not the end that matters, it's what we do while we are here, with what we are given. The proof of this is readily apparent. Just walk through any cemetery: Everyone there has the same net worth, is in the same state of health, owns the same amount of real estate and is as good-looking as the next.

We are each created with our own unique path in life. G-d desires the same end result for all of us, but our itineraries are personalized, each person's being different from the other. Therefore, G-d has equipped each of us with the custom-designed tools that we will need for our own individual journeys. It doesn't matter what your neighbor has because what he has is good for him but not for you, and vice versa. Everything you need, you have. Everything you will need, you will receive. Knowing that G-d has created each of us with our personal path to tread and with all the tools and skills that we need eliminates any basis to complain about the inequities of life.

Knowing this also obviates the need to be concerned with keeping up with the Joneses. People often create their own unhappiness by focusing on what they *don't* have. A person who appreciates what he has will not become unhappy when his neighbor pulls up in a new Mercedes. Sadly, if one does not believe in G-d, then one's lot in life is only the result of cruel and capricious fate, which only causes bitterness and fosters resentment against those perceived as being blessed by fate.

3. If Life Has Meaning, Then the Pain Also Has Meaning

If life itself has G-d-given meaning, then so must every aspect of it including the pain and the setbacks. Therefore, the pain of life is a part of the gift of life. A person whose life is focused on personal growth and eternal existence will understand that pain is part of the package and this knowledge enables a person to bear it. On the other hand, believing that there is no purpose to pain can be more painful than the pain itself. Meaning allows a person to endure suffering and become stronger. Meaninglessness prevents a person from even enjoying comforts.

On some level people do intuit that there is some ultimate plan and reason for what happens in their lives. If given a choice, a person who is suffering would still not prefer to be changed into, let's say, a horse or fish in order to escape his predicament, even if it were possible. This is because he intuitively knows that his life has meaning—even if he is suffering—and the life of an animal does not. He would rather be a human being with the pain than an animal without it.

4. There Is an Afterlife

If there is one thing that all Western Jews know for sure, it is that Jews don't believe in an afterlife—or, at least, in any concept of hell. In their minds, Heaven and Hell are purely Christian concepts.

However, nothing could be farther from the truth. Belief in the afterlife is one of the unequivocal foundations of Judaism, although our ideas of heaven and hell are fundamentally different than the Christian or Moslem concepts. The Jewish concepts of punishment and hell certainly have nothing in common with Christian beliefs or how they are portrayed in Western culture (which is basically Christian theology filtered through the arts).

In general, the concept of heaven and hell is very threatening to people when it concerns them personally but not when it's applied to evil people. Nobody would object to finding out that there is a hell but it's reserved only for Nazis; people just don't want to think that they might wind up there themselves.

In fact only the existence of an afterlife gives this life meaning. Since, as we have seen, this world is chock full of inequities and injustice, we are left with two choices: Either there is another place where true justice is meted out, where both the righteous and the evil receive their just rewards, or the world in which we live is just cruel and arbitrary, and people are either winners or losers. Believing the latter would mean that murder victims just had bad luck (wrong place, wrong time) and tyrants really do get away with mass murder; the little old lady who gets swindled out of her life's saving is just a poor sucker and her swindler will never face true justice if he's never caught.

Only an afterlife where a final accounting is made gives the trials and travails of this lifetime any ultimate purpose. So before explaining how a Jew views suffering, we need to first understand the Jewish view of the afterlife because as we will see they are intertwined.

Heaven and Hell

Many people, when discussing something they did wrong, will joke about G-d striking them with lightning. But let's be honest: If G-d was going to "get us" every time we did something wrong, not too many of us would be left. I certainly wouldn't.

G-d is not lurking in the bushes waiting to get us. He loves us like a parent loves a child, and good parents do not look to zap their children for the slightest transgression. Furthermore, if we are to have free will, G-d cannot strike us down when we do wrong. As I have mentioned, it would be impossible for G-d to interact with this world with a heavy hand since it would kill our ability to choose freely. That would be analogous to having a gun to our heads at all times and when there is a gun to your head you don't have much free choice. Free will and true justice cannot coexist in this world.

And so as we travel through life, we do good and we do bad. Sometimes our words are kind and sometimes our words are mean. Sometimes we are honest and sometimes we are not so honest. Sometimes we are generous and sometimes we take things that are not ours.

When we fulfill the *mitzvot* or violate the *mitzvot*, we actually affect our souls. We either strengthen it, like it's a muscle, or we weaken it. We easily understand this in extreme cases—a person who spends his life help-ing people will have a different soul at the end of his life than someone who has spent his life hurting people—but this law of spiritual cause and effect applies to everything we do. So even if during our lives we were ninety percent on target and ten percent off, that ten percent will create a variety of spiritual blocks that, unless removed, will prevent us from completely enjoying our eternity. On some level, our actions have erected a barrier between us and G-d. And since it is G-d's intention that we have eternal spiritual pleasure through a close relationship with Him, He needs to remove these blocks.

This is the Jewish concept of the afterlife. In Hebrew it is called "*Olam Haba*"—literally, "the world to come," which corresponds loosely to the common idea of heaven. *Olam Haba* is where all of our souls go after they leave the confines of the human body, where we bask in G-d's presence without any adulterating thoughts, concerns, confusions, desires or questions. If a person has led a properly directed life—identifying with the spiritual and not the physical, he will be able to enter this world without much of an adjustment.

But if he hasn't, he will have no way of relating to or enjoying *Olam Haba* until his blocks are eliminated, and this is the Jewish concept of "*Gehinom*", which corresponds very, very loosely to the generally accepted concept of hell. We all are familiar with medieval Christian imagery of fire and torture; some of that is based on Jewish theology that describes *Gehinom* as a place that burns and is painful. But we must remind ourselves that we are talking about a G-d who is completely altruistic and benevolent, who created us out of love only to bestow goodness and kindness upon us and who only wants our pleasure. So, where does hellfire fit into this picture?

The Jewish understanding of *Gehinom* is the following: After we die, we are shown our entire lives. Throughout this process we need to explain our thoughts, words and actions. This is not to crush or destroy us, like some kind of political tribunal; it is just the final chastisement from a gentle, loving father who, in order to help us rid ourselves of adulterating thoughts, concerns, confusions, desires or questions, must show us clearly where and why we erred. *Gehinom* is not a place where an angry god punishes sinners—because we have seen that He is not angry and that we are not sinners.

The Talmud describes the shame from this experience as more painful than anything we can experience on Earth. Given that I can think of quite a few unbearable situations, *Gehinom* sounds like somewhere to be avoided. Imagine if everything you ever thought, said or did was posted on a Web site for all to see. Or broadcast on a Jumbotron before a packed football stadium of everyone you ever knew. The shame and humiliation would burn. It is said that if we were to see *Gehinom* for even a moment, we would never do anything wrong again.

After we emerge from *Gehinom*, we can enter *Olam Haba* and enjoy our spiritual eternity. *Gehinom* is a cleansing; it removes the impediments to a true relationship with G-d that we have created during our lives on this Earth. Without this cleansing, we would be eternally handicapped and unable to have the pleasure for which we were created. Therefore, *Gehinom* is good for us and serves G-d's ultimate purpose which is to give us eternal spiritual pleasure. (This step can be avoided, as I will explain in a few pages.)

The Talmud describes one moment in *Olam Haba* as more pleasurable than a lifetime of all the pleasures of this world. And it never ends; it is our eternity. In Jewish theology, our physical lives are referred to as corridors that we pass through for a short but very meaningful time, during which we literally create ourselves using our free will. We create our eternity through our actions here and that is why, in Judaism, this world is the primary focus, not the next world. *The next world is only an extension of this one; it's not that we have to endure things here in order to be rewarded later, but rather that everything that happens later is a direct result of what we do here.*

The Customized Rule of Admission

While we are on the subject of heaven and hell, I think it is important to recognize a fact of human psychology. Most people, according to polls, believe in an afterlife. However, since people want to be able to do what they want without consequences, they always define heaven using what I call "the customized rule of admission." which is the following: People always define heaven in a way that guarantees they will get in. Ask the average person who will go to heaven and he or she will invariably answer, "Those who haven't hurt anybody." This seems like a pretty feeble test of character. Why should someone whose only great achievement is not hurting anyone get eternal reward? Aren't we expected on a basic level not to hurt others?

Imagine you come home from work and one of your children greets you at the door and says, "I want you to know that I have not hurt my little brother today nor have caused him harm in any way. May I please have a treat?" You would probably answer with something like, "You want a treat for not hurting him? I expect you to not hurt him. What have you *done* for him that I should reward you?"

Or, imagine that the president of the United Stated comes to your city on a campaign stop and announces that he wants to acknowledge the good citizens of your city. Holding up a presidential ribbon, he announces that he will award one to every citizen who…has not hurt anybody! Wouldn't you laugh at his remark? Wouldn't you be embarrassed to wear such a ribbon?

The reason why people define heaven in such a way is because it is comforting. In their minds, it guarantees their admission. How do you think people who actually have hurt someone, like thieves or murderers, define it? They will say that if a person is sorry and regrets his evil deed or really didn't mean to do it, he, too, will be able to enter the gates of heaven. The bottom line is that everybody wants in—but they want in on their own terms.

I only mention this because it is important to bear in mind that personalized definitions of heaven or hell will have no meaning at all when it becomes a practical issue.

Resurrection of the Dead

Olam Haba is not the last stop. When Adam and Chava were created, they were intended to live forever in physical form on this earth. Only after they ate the fruit from the Tree of Knowledge of Good and Evil did death come into the world. Since their bodies developed desires independent of their souls, two things resulted. Our time on Earth had to be limited in order to focus our attention, and our bodies had to rot so that we would clearly understand what a senseless waste of time it is to cater to its desires.

Just imagine if people lived forever. Nothing would get done. Nobody would work, and difficult projects would never be attempted because everything would be pushed off and postponed. There would be no urgency to get anything done beyond the most basic needs since there would always be plenty of time to do it later. Dying is painful for all involved, but it makes life more meaningful and more focused. In a sense, we are racing the clock. This compels us, hopefully, to be occupied with those matters that are most important. If we lived forever we would never get to any of them because we would be too busy partying and indulging.

In addition, because of Adam and Chava's choice which led to the body/soul dichotomy, it became necessary for the soul to witness the body's decay. The rotting of the body is described as painful to the soul but, again, it is a benefit to us; it reduces the pain of *Gehinom* by helping remove the spiritual blocks that come from identifying with the body during our physical life.

This is one of the reasons for the Torah's prohibition of cremation. When a body is cremated, the soul loses the very necessary opportunity to regain an understanding of its primacy. This lost opportunity only causes a person more pain in the long run because it is one of the ways that the spiritual blocks are removed. Cremation is also considered a disgraceful way to treat the body that has housed the soul and enabled the person to fulfill the *mitzvot*.

But cremation is more than an act. It is a statement that negates one of the foundations of Jewish belief: That there will be a resurrection of the dead that will restore mankind to *Gan Eden*, the intended state of the world. The reason why this is one of our fundamental beliefs is that it reaffirms the truth that our lives have meaning and that creation is working towards a goal. Cremation of the body expresses the opinion that all of existence is meaningless, and that the body will never have any use again.

In Judaism, burning is an act of utter and permanent annihilation—it vaporizes physical matter. We are commanded to burn idols and all forms of idol worship. Before Passover, we burn our leavened products. We burn things, like trash, that we want to be gone forever. But a human being should never be burned even after he or she has died. This natural aversion is evident in our reaction to the crematoria in the Nazi concentration camps. The fact that the Germans murdered millions of our brothers and sisters is painful beyond words, but mass graves do not invoke the same anathema that the ovens do. The fact that after murdering us, the Germans shoved millions of bodies into furnaces to be destroyed without a trace adds even more pain to an already unbearable situation.

At some unknown point in the future the good and righteous people will return to life. Their souls and bodies will be reunited, their bodies will return to their original states of holiness and they will dwell again in *Gan Eden*. Mankind as a whole will be back where it was on that fateful first day, and where it was supposed to be all along. The world will have finally reached its intended state of perfection.

Reward and Punishment

Now that we have an understanding of the bigger picture, we can begin to delve deeper into the mystery of human suffering.

The idea of reward and punishment is not very popular today. Nobody likes to be judged; it implies that are you are bad, and that's not good. We live in a world where every Little League team gets a trophy at the end of the season even if they didn't win a single game and every special-interest group is constantly offended and in need of an apology. Since our emotions now have the tensile strength of cotton candy, it's hard to discuss the topic without sounding downright mean or hurting someone's feeling.

In addition, the idea of G-d and punishment summons up all types of bad feelings in us because of the distorted and negative doctrines of other religions that incorrectly portray G-d as angry and vengeful. To a Jew, the whole idea reeks of Christianity.

So we need to understand the *Jewish* concept of punishment and the first obstacle we need to overcome is the word itself. The term "punishment" is so loaded. Why? Because who gets punished? Bad people, criminals, evildoers, maybe even wayward teens—but not good people and certainly not grown ups who go through life not doing evil and sometimes doing good. And since we Jews believe that people are inherently good, the idea of getting punished seems harsh and out of place.

And since, in today's world, punishment is usually meted out in anger and received with dejection (which makes sense—anger will cause dejection) it is hard to reconcile the idea with a loving G-d.

Yet, as parents, we punish our children. Are they bad? No, they are beautiful little beings that just need discipline and guidance. So, why do we punish them if they do not listen to us or if they misbehave? Because we love them and—here's the important part—we know it is for their ultimate good even if it's painful for them at the time. They need to learn that there are consequences to their choices and to their actions. Through properly administered punishment, a child learns about free will.

Conversely, a child who gets away with everything and is not punished is effectively destroyed. Even as an adult he will have no way of dealing with the concept of right and wrong. He will very likely mature into a selfish sociopath who will lead an unpleasant life and cause others pain and unhappiness.

Free will requires consequences, hence reward and punishment. As stated earlier, if there were no consequences to our actions, our decisions would have no meaning and life would be a cruel charade. Free will means that not only can we do good or evil but we are ultimately accountable for the choices we make. If we weren't accountable, we would be no different from a child who gets away with any type of behavior. And deep down, we don't want to get away with everything. We want our actions to have meaning.

Imagine for a minute that you have just died after reaching your one-hundred-twentieth birthday. You ascend to heaven (of course) and you are met with a surprise: After being ushered into paradise, you are informed that almost everyone who has ever lived is there. Not only good people, but even very evil people—tyrants, murderers, rapists, child molesters and so on. There are storm troopers there, Crusaders, agents of the Spanish Inquisition, secret policemen, and even Hitler himself, along with thousands of other Nazis of whom you've never even heard.

Naturally, you are shocked. So shocked in fact, that you decide to find out exactly what is going on. So, you walk up to G-d and you say, "Excuse me, G-d, I am confused. All my life I tried to be a good person so I could get into heaven, but now that I am here, it's not exactly the way it was described in the brochure. I mean, why are all these evil people here?"

And G-d answers you: "Anyone who believes in me, no matter what they did during their life, spends eternity with me after they die. How can I reject someone who believes in me? Aren't all people my children?"

Imagine your shock and disappointment. Just to imagine such a scene is demoralizing.

But why? Why should this illustration bother you? The obvious answer is that in this scenario, all your choices and actions throughout your life really didn't matter. Being good or moral had no more value than being vicious and cruel. If this scenario bothers you then not only do you believe in reward and punishment, but you actually desire it. Deep down, you want there to be consequences to your actions and you certainly don't want to see evildoers have the same eternal benefits as the good people.

The Jewish View

In the Torah (Deuteronomy 8:5), Moshe tells the Jewish people, "Just as a man chastises his son, so too G-d chastises you." We do not chastise our children because we hate them or because they are evil or because they deserve it or for any other wrong reason. And we should never discipline them because we are angry. We discipline our children because we love them and want the best for them. Discipline includes giving direction, warning against certain behavior and talking to them when they are not behaving properly, and it also includes drawing a line when needed and punishing them if they cross it. When G-d has to resort to discipline, it is a similar response to our actions, and it is only meant to educate us and guide us toward improvement.

We are used to hearing words like "sin," "repentance," "punishment," "heaven" and "hell," but these are gentile words representing gentile ideas. The Jewish approach to the concept of reward and punishment is radically different.

The Hebrew word for doing something wrong is "*cheit*" (rhymes with "hate"), and it literally means to veer off course or miss a target. If we do transgress, we rectify it by doing what is called "*tshuva*," which literally means "return." *Tshuva* involves three steps: 1) We have regret for what we did; 2) verbally acknowledge it to G-d and apologize for it; and finally, 3) resolve not to do it again. In the Jewish world, we do not sin and repent; we go off and we come back. When a child disobeys his parent he has veered from the proper path of behavior. When he regrets it, apologizes and resolves not to do it again, he has returned. Obviously, there are levels to the misdeeds, and a murderer will have a much harder time returning than someone who stole a candy bar. A hardened criminal is harder to rehabilitate because his behavior is much more a part of him. But the process is the same.

However, when we use our free will, we do more than just rack up points for either good or bad on that great scoreboard in the sky—we change ourselves and our essences. If we constantly choose to do good, we become great; if we constantly choose to do bad, we become evil. If we sometimes choose to do good and sometimes choose to do bad, we become mediocre.

A loving G-d, though, wants us all to be great and to this end he will tap us on the shoulder once and a while to get our attention or to wake us up.

Earlier I mentioned that the process of *Gehinom* can be avoided. The key to avoiding it is to do *tshuva* during one's lifetime. Through *tshuva* we remove the spiritual blocks and preempt the need for *Gehinom*. The more *tshuva* we do, the less *Gehinom*; the less *tshuva*, the more *Gehinom*. G-d does not want us to have to go through *Gehinom*. His desire is that we leave the world all ready for the next one. And suffering in this world works toward that goal in two ways.

Firstly, it acts as an alarm. Pain is an indication that something is amiss and an Orthodox Jew understands that when things go wrong, the first order of business is to do a personal spiritual accounting. "Going wrong" can mean anything from a flat tire to cancer. Many times, in response to setbacks and even to tragedies, we can find and correct things that would have gone overlooked without the introspection that was brought on by events.

Secondly, it can act as a sort of *Gehinom* on earth, meaning that it removes spiritual blocks while we are still alive, thereby allowing us to go straight to *Olam Haba* and avoid *Gehinom* entirely. This is called atonement and this is actually a blessing even though it can be miserable and excruciating. If *Gehinom* is worse than anything imaginable in this world, intellectually we can understand why suffering here would be preferable to suffering there.

Challenges in Order to Grow

The idea that suffering in this lifetime can be a means of waking us up or can act as atonement only satisfies part of the issue because it doesn't answer two fundamental questions: 1) Why do bad things happen to good people?; and 2) Why do good things happen to bad people? The righteous certainly do not need painful wake-up calls, and evil people do not wake up from good fortune. And if anyone needs atonement, it is the evil man and not the good one. The answers to these questions are not light and easy but they are understandable.

To understand why bad things happen to good people, we first must recognize the function adversity plays in our lives and how it is designed to make us greater. Westerners have a difficult time with this truth because of the society in which we live.

Let me pose a question, and please think of an answer before reading on: What is the opposite of pain?

Nine out of ten people will instinctively answer "pleasure." Unfortunately this only means that nine out of ten people are not correct. The opposite of pain is, simply, no pain—or in other words having no discomfort or having it easy. While it is certainly true that being comfortable will produce a pleasurable reaction in people, it is just as true that we find deeper pleasure in those things that have caused us pain in one way or another.

In fact, further thought on the matter reveals that *only* those things in life that require effort give us real pleasure. Accomplishments require effort and great accomplishments require great effort. These don't have to be acts of heroism; careers, degrees, families (especially raising children), projects we undertake or even simple vegetable gardens in our yards—anything that we have to work on—are sources of pleasure. In fact, the more difficult the effort made, the more the accomplishment is appreciated. Therefore, the more pain, the more pleasure.

A person whose life is focused on achievement will understand that pain is part of the package; a person whose life is focused on being comfortable will see pain as the one thing to be most avoided. This is why Western society has become so decadent and so unwilling to make hard choices or sacrifices. Its focus on physical comfort makes people soft. This decadence has affected our thinking and behavior regarding pain, suffering, setbacks and adversity. Decadence causes us to identify with our bodies and complain when things get uncomfortable. G-d, however, loves us too much to allow us to waste our lives. It has been said that calm seas do not produce great sailors. This is very true. Our souls want to achieve our full potential; our bodies want it easy. A life spent identifying and listening to the body does not produce greatness. Overcoming adversity does.

Sometimes, G-d will cause us to go through an ordeal simply to make us better—stronger, wiser, kinder, more compassionate, more resourceful or even more well known to others. How often have we seen someone go through adversity and come out of it a better person? This is because pain breaks the bonds to the physical world and strips away illusions about life. We are not so enamored with physical things when we are in pain—and that is why people in pain, whether it's physical, mental or emotional, very often turn to G-d.

In the secular world this is seen as a crutch and G-d is seen as something only for weaklings and losers. But the truth is that secular life is the illusion and pain shatters it. Once the illusions melt away, a person will inevitably turn to the spiritual. How often has something seemed tragic while it was happening but later on, in hindsight, was actually a blessing? How often do we read about tragedies that have produced amazing results or about people accomplishing wonderful things after their outlooks on life are completely changed?

It is a tenet of Jewish philosophy that G-d will never give us a challenge that we cannot pass. He will never set us up to fail—why would a loving parent do that? Challenges can bring out latent talents, strength and skills that would never have been forced to the surface in an easy life. Sometimes this is for the benefit of the person who is challenged; sometimes it is to make the person's innate greatness known to others. And this can apply to either spiritual or physical talents.

Challenges always entail a certain degree of pain. In this way the pain of life is also part of the gift of life but it takes emotional maturity to appreciate it. Imagine the following scene: You give your child a birthday present that is beautifully wrapped with a bow on top. He eagerly tears off the gift wrapping, opens his toy and begins playing with it. Later on, it is time for bed and you tell him that he needs to stop playing and clean up the box and wrapping paper that is still on the floor.

Now, imagine that he turns to you and says, "Why should I clean it up? I didn't ask for the wrapping paper, I only wanted the present. *You* decided to wrap it, so *you* clean it up." Or, worse, "I didn't even ask for the present, let alone the wrapping paper, so why should I have to clean it up?"

Similarly, when we complain about our lot, are we not really saying, "G-d, I didn't ask for this life. I was never asked if I wanted to be born. And even though I am enjoying the friends, good times and family that I have, I don't want any problems. I want everything to go easily and in the way I want it to, and I'll be very upset if it doesn't." It seems a little unscrupulous to be willing to accept the unearned good in life but then complain about the bad.

G-d has given us the strength, resiliency, tenacity, gumption and depth of character to cope with challenging situations, but someone bemoaning his fate will not be able to draw on these strengths. Only someone who understands the bigger picture will have that ability.

An answer to the second question—why do good things happen to bad people?—reveals much about G-d's kindness and tolerance. We have already seen that G-d must remain hidden in this world in order to allow human beings a complete range of free choice and that if only the good were rewarded and only the bad suffered, our free-will abilities would be severely hampered. To that end, the Talmud teaches us that the reward for the *mitzvot* that we do is given to us in the next world, not this one. However, this statement is only referring to someone who will be in the next world, i.e. *Olam Haba*. It is possible for a person to be so bad and to destroy his spiritual nature so extensively that he will not continue on from *Gehinom* to *Olam Haba*. This type of person, however, still must be rewarded for whatever good he has done and so G-d "pays" him, so to speak, in this lifetime. So when you see bad people living it up, don't be jealous; they're just depleting their treasury and when they die, their account will be empty.

Reincarnation

There is one last point to be made. Even though a child's sickness, disability or death can often bring out the best in its parents, siblings, friends and community, it doesn't answer why this specific child had to suffer or die. How did the child benefit from its ordeal? This requires us to discuss reincarnation, or what in Hebrew is called *gilgul neshamos*. I know it can be shocking to find out that Judaism contains many concepts that the average secular Jew always thought were Christian, but keep in mind that the Jewish people had been world-renowned for over 1,500 years before Christianity was even born, and that Christianity's founders simply plagiarized and repackaged much of the Torah. And, like everything else that they took, they distorted it.

Regarding *gilgul neshamos*, there are times when a soul needs to return to this world to finish or rectify or resolve something. This mission can be accomplished quickly, or it can take a lifetime. In cases of an infant or a child dying, the soul did what it had to do in short order. In cases of retardation or disabilities that prevent normal mental functioning, the soul needs more time. Given these tragedies, the soul accomplishes its mission by being a passive participant, not an active one. It accomplishes its mission by being a catalyst for change in other people.

A Real Relationship

A third reason we might endure suffering is to awaken in us spiritual wellsprings that will draw us even closer to G-d. In fact, many times things happen to us for the sole purpose of eliciting an awareness of G-d and initiating or developing some sort of communication with Him.

There is a very interesting statement in the Torah's account of creation in the Book of Breishit (Genesis). In chapter two it says that on the third day, a wet mist covered the ground but "G-d did not cause rain to fall on the land because there was no man to work the soil." Our sages teach us that G-d was waiting for Adam to recognize the need for rain and pray for it. But this is a seemingly strange statement. A lot of things were created for which man had not prayed. What is so significant about rain that it had to wait for man's prayers?

Rain is a direct relationship between man and G-d; without it, we die but we have no control over it. This means that we are completely dependent on G-d to provide the necessary water for our crops. (Even with modern irrigation methods, there would be terrible famines if it didn't rain for an extended period of time.) He created this structure to ensure that we call home on a regular basis, no different from a parent wanting to hear from his child. The parent knows his child needs money, but also knows that if he sends it on a regular basis, his child will hardly ever call. Given this, he might decide to send the money only when his child calls and asks for it. This way, he can have the pleasure of hearing his child's voice once in a while.

Most parents also know intuitively that it isn't good for a child's character to receive money without the courtesy of a phone call—they begin to think that everything is coming to them and that makes them selfish. Similarly, when people feel that they are self-sufficient and don't need G-d, it eventually leads to their downfall. This is why wealthy people tend to be less religious and why wealthy nations are more secular and hedonistic.

G-d, being altruistic and benevolent, only desires that we be in touch with Him for our own good. Man was created for pleasure and the spiritual pleasure of a relationship with G-d outweighs anything this world can offer. If G-d would let us drift off into a haze of misconceptions—such as that we are independent beings with no need for Him—we might be lost for good. Requiring us to be cognizant of Him and of our need to turn to Him helps us stay in touch with the truth.

There will be many times in life when G-d will cause us to undergo trials for the sole purpose of eliciting prayers or creating an awareness of His existence. My *rebbe*, Rabbi Noach Weinberg, of blessed memory, used to tell a story of a young man he met in Jerusalem years ago. The man had been bicycling across Europe before arriving in Israel. When he met Rabbi Weinberg, he announced to him, "Rabbi, there is no need to try to convince me. I already believe in G-d. In fact, He just saved my life by performing a miracle."

It seemed this fellow had been bicycling on a road that hugged the Mediterranean coast, along a mountainside that dropped off straight down to the ocean. As he was rounding a turn, a truck coming in the opposite direction took the turn too fast and swung wide, straight at him. He had an instant to make a choice: Get hit by the truck or go off the cliff. So, he flew off the cliff and plunged about fifty feet into the water, landing on his back on the rocks in the shallow surf.

And…he got up and walked away. "Rabbi," he said, "I felt G-d's hand catch me and lay me down on the rocks."

When Rabbi Weinberg heard that, he saw an opportunity to teach this young man something. "It's amazing that G-d caught you," he replied, "but tell me, friend, who do you think threw you *off* the cliff in the first place?"

Sometimes, G-d will throw us off a cliff and then catch us so that, while we are sailing through the air, we can remember that He is there—or discover Him for the first time. The opposite—G-d not wanting to hear from you—is considered a curse. When the snake convinced Adam and Chava to disobey G-d, G-d cursed it by having it crawl on its belly. At first glance, this doesn't seem so terrible; at least the snake's mouth is always near its food. But after learning how G-d desires communication, we can see that it *is* a curse: The snake will have everything it will ever need—G-d doesn't want anything to do with it. (The Talmud teaches that if everything goes perfectly for thirty days, you should start worrying.)

Ironically, the more righteous a person is, the more trying times G-d might put him through in order to draw him even closer. This can be compared to two people who are being coached in a gym. One is grossly overweight and out of shape. The other has gotten a little soft over the years but had once been active. What does the trainer do?

He begins the overweight man on a very light training regimen. He has him take walks to build up his stamina and to increase his metabolism, and maybe has him do some very light weight training to build some muscle. For the other fellow, he sets up a more strenuous and more ambitious regimen—running, sit-ups, push-ups, weight training and so on.

On the surface, this is strange and illogical. The first man who is in much greater need of physical fitness gets the lighter workout and the second man, who needs it less, gets the harder one. But with understanding, we see the wisdom in it. Yes, the first man needs more but in his condition, it would probably kill him. The second man can take it.

Sometimes, righteous people suffer, but it only makes them greater and greater. A lesser person would be broken by what they go through.

What Is Prayer?

One of the most basic components of a relationship is communication. We have seen in this chapter that G-d is always communicating with us, trying to encourage us to take the good path in life and helping us to excel. We also saw in the last chapter that G-d even desires to communicate directly with those who are more righteous, and this is called "prophecy."

But what is also true is that G-d desires to hear from us, and this we call "prayer" in English or "*tefillah*" in Hebrew. And because the Jewish people have been educating the world for the last 3,322 years about the true nature of G-d, the idea has caught on. If the polls are correct, close to seventy-five percent of people in the United States believe that G-d has answered their prayers at least once in their lifetime—though I surmise that a greater percentage of this book's readers would answer in the affirmative on that one.

So, if you are one of the seventy-five percent, please tell me, how did you get G-d to comply with your request? What did you give Him? What did you have to pay? Maybe a big, fat, juicy cow? Maybe your first born? Or was it just a lot of money?

We know, of course, that these are ridiculous suggestions and this shows, once again, that we Jews have a strong intuition about G-d's true nature. We know, deep down, that there is no way we can do anything for G-d, and we certainly can't bribe him.

But the question still remains: Why did He answer you? The only possible answer is that He responded to you because He loves you. But you knew that to begin with because if you didn't feel He loved you, you wouldn't have bothered asking Him for anything in the first place.

The Jewish approach to prayer is significantly different than any non-Jewish approach. When we speak to G-d, we are not trying to bribe him or appease him, and we know that there is no use trying to fool him. Instead, our prayers are real discussions, and they must be based on reality and an understanding of the following:

- G-d loves us more than anyone, including our parents, spouses and children.
- He is aware of everything—He knows our thoughts, feelings, desires and goals.
- He has all the power to give us everything; there are no other powers.
- He does more for us than we ask for (have you ever *asked* for your epiglottis to work properly?) and has been doing so since we were born.
- He gives without any strings attached. This is the hardest concept for Westerners, who are not used to unconditional love.
- He is looking to give to us even before we ask.
- He knows what is good for us.
- We must be willing to trust Him and listen to Him. Sometimes the answer will be "no," but it is not out of meanness or disinterest; rather it's out of concern for our best.

These are hard concepts to integrate, especially for someone not raised in an environment that acknowledged these truths. But if you do pray to G-d periodically, try formatting your mind on these bullet points first. I think you will find yourself more at peace and feeling closer to the One to whom you are speaking. And by the way, when you pray, expect results. Otherwise, you're not serious.

The entire structure of Jewish prayer is based on the premise that we have a real relationship with G-d. This is one of the reasons why Jewish law requires prayers to be said audibly, low enough for us to hear ourselves but not so loudly as to disturb anyone else. We need to hear ourselves speaking to G-d—it reinforces in our minds that someone is listening. Think about it: A person only speaks aloud to someone or something that is real; we seek professional help for adults who speak to imaginary friends. Because of the cynical influence of Western society, most people who walked in on someone speaking out loud to G-d would consider him crazy and back out of the room. An Orthodox Jew would apologize for interrupting.

Make the Appropriate Effort

But is prayer all that is required for success? How does it reconcile with our own efforts and ideas?

The Torah's emphasis on the real world is also reflected in another aspect of the Jewish understanding of prayer and that is the requirement to make a reasonable effort.

Again we turn to the farmer to provide the perfect metaphor. Making a living is really just another kind of farming —an area of life that reveals the need for a tremendous amount of what people refer to as "luck."

The farmer must prepare the soil by plowing it to aerate and loosen it. Then he seeds it, and he tends his crops by watering and fertilizing them. Through hoeing, weeding and pruning, he works to remove anything that could kill his crops or retard their growth. But that is all he can do. He can't make the seeds grow nor can he make the rain fall. He can create and maintain the proper initial environment but after that, there are many variables that are out of his control. He cannot determine the weather. He cannot stop blight or disease. He cannot prevent locusts or infestations. Those are in G-d's hands. A farmer's success is a result of his efforts and G-d's blessing. One without the other will have no effect. If he doesn't do his part, there will certainly be no crops. But his tasks alone do not ensure success; even after all his exertions, he could still wind up with dry dirt.

We are required to go to work and make a legitimate attempt to make a living, not empty, farcical or tokens displays. For example, trying to sell ice to an Eskimo would be considered foolish, and any person who did so would only have himself to blame when his ice store failed and he became impoverished. If we want to "win" with G-d's help, we must make true, valid and appropriate efforts to be successful in any given situation. Any less would be to rely on or expect a miracle, and the Talmud warns that we are *not* allowed to rely on miracles. However, once a person makes a legitimate effort, success or failure is in the hands of G-d. And that is when prayer is required.

A person who sits at home and expects G-d to send him money miraculously is not a believer—he is a fool. However, because of Christianity's fixation on miracles, many non-Orthodox Jews believe that religious Jews also live in this sort of fantasy world—that all we do is think about, talk about and wait for miracles. We do not. We merely realize that just as prayer doesn't work by itself, neither does human effort.

All breadwinners face the same trials as the farmer. They can earn the degrees, make the phone calls, do the research, meet the right people and buy the right goods but, in the end, success or failure will be determined by what G-d wants for us. That is why we pray for sustenance—because making the effort is only half the battle.

Most people who have created their own wealth will admit, though sometimes only in private, that they can clearly see a divine hand in their success. And no matter how rich or poor a person is, there is always an undercurrent of worry in the efforts to provide for one's family. Everyone knows that they can very easily find themselves out of a job or find their business in trouble and sinking.

This concept is illustrated in a joke that is deeply Jewish. There was a town situated next to a river and after many days of thunderstorms, the river broke it banks and flooded the town. Those who saw it coming evacuated before the levees broke; others had to be rescued by boat from the upper floors and roofs of their homes.

One man, in his mind a true believer, refused help. When the first motorboat pulled up in front of his house, he waved them off, calling out from his attic window, "The Lord will save me." When the waters forced him up onto the roof and another rescue boat came to get him, he was firm in his faith: "The Lord will save me," he assured them.

Finally, the surging waters forced the rescuers to switch to helicopter evacuation. By this time, the man was sitting on the top of his chimney, which was the only part of his house still above water. Hovering over him and dangling a rope ladder, the rescuers pleaded with him through a bull-horn to grab the ladder. "There is no need for the ladder," he told them, "the Lord will save me." Eventually, he drowned.

Soon, he found himself standing before a bright light, and he was very upset. "G-d," he said, "all my life I had complete faith in you. I tried to live a life that would please you. Even when danger threatened, I put my faith in you, yet you did not save me. You let me drown."

"What do you mean I did not save you?" G-d replied. "I tried! I sent two boats and a helicopter!"

Conclusion

The Talmud gives us the guidelines for evaluating our suffering. If we find ourselves in an uncomfortable situation, regardless of the degree, we are to go through three steps:

1. First, we must scrutinize our actions. Perhaps we are being chastised, for our own good, to improve ourselves or abandon negative traits or behaviors. Again, this is not punishment but rather the prodding of our loving coach who wants us to win.

2. Second, if we do a self-evaluation and it does not seem to us that this is the cause, we are to evaluate our time to see if we are wasting it instead of applying it to Torah study. This is the most sincere way to have a relationship with G-d and He desires us to study Torah above all else.

3. And lastly, if that too is not the cause, then the Talmud attributes the situation to suffering which is good for us even though we cannot understand it in this lifetime.

After all is said and done, there are many times when the underlying reason for our suffering remains unknowable.

G-d has a real relationship with us whether or not we acknowledge or reciprocate it and He is always readjusting our world in response to our freewill decisions. His goal is always the same—only the manner and the methods change. He reacts to our every choice and decision and constantly reshuffles the deck in order to deal us the best cards, given our choices.

He does this to guide and help us; everything is done with an eye on our eventual best.

Sometimes G-d is active and will intervene and frustrate our plans; other times He will be passive and allow our decisions to run their course. This applies to both good and evil plans.

Sometimes the only reason for suffering is to draw us closer to Him. Sometimes our suffering is designed to act like a big alarm clock by focusing us on what is truly important and preventing us from wasting our lives in a dull fog. It can be a wake-up call for an individual, a nation or the world as a whole.

Sometimes our suffering can be intended to remove negative traits.

Sometimes it is intended to prevent a greater evil or bring a greater good.

Sometimes its only purpose is to bring out our potential.

Sometimes the whole situation has to do with the next world and not this one. In these cases, when we can't see the big picture, the suffering will seem unjust.

The righteous might suffer in this world because their *mitzvot* are the most fundamental aspects of their beings, they are spiritually oriented and it would be a waste to reward them in this world, which doesn't mean that much to them. They are not interested in fame or expensive cars or big homes.

On the other hand, the evil who do some good and therefore must be paid, might get rewarded here in this world because their good deeds are the superficial part of their lives and not of great importance to them. Therefore, they get paid in this world in ways that matter to them. They would not be able to appreciate a spiritual reward.

G-d's decisions will always include the variable of how His actions will affect everything else in the cosmic equation. For example, Hitler could have gotten sick and died as a child. Clearly, the world would have been a better place if he had died. But an evil man like him might be kept alive even later in life when his demise would surely be an act of pure justice because of other factors. G-d has plans for humanity as well as individuals, and this is factored into every decision.

But for reasons that remain hidden, we are not entitled to know why we suffer even as we go through the pain. Perhaps knowing why a child is born with Down's syndrome, or why a husband dies as a young man leaving a widow and orphans, or why a person develops multiple sclerosis will negatively affect our free will.

We can understand the rules, but we cannot begin to fathom the calculations that go into G-d's interactions with us, balancing our eternal needs, the needs of our society and the needs of mankind. Since there are so many factors that are beyond our limited understanding, suffering often seems arbitrary and unfair. Yet it is neither.

We have to accept that everything is done for our good and that one day, we will understand the reasons for what happened to us in our lives on Earth. I once heard our lives compared to a tapestry: If one views the back, it's incomprehensible, full of all kinds of threads of different lengths, colors and thicknesses, seemingly thrown together haphazardly and arbitrarily. It's hard to make any sense of it all, and it's impossible to form any kind of picture from them. But, just turn the tapestry around and all of a sudden everything becomes clear. The messy back makes total sense in light of the front.

After we depart from this world and enter the world of truth, we will all come before G-d with our questions. The good news is that we will finally get answers. We will clearly see the reasons for every one of our lives' occurrences, from the most trivial to the most sublime. Not only will we have no further questions, but we will be grateful for what happened to us. And, regardless of how unpleasant our lives were while we passed through this world, it is still better for us to have gone through it than not to have been created at all. This is because, regardless of our suffering, we have a pleasurable eternity ahead of us (which gives, I think, new meaning to the old saying "better late than never.")

This future encounter can best be illustrated by a story that I once read back in 1988. I always remembered it because I found it to be such a perfect analogy to life. Unfortunately, I haven't been able to substantiate it so it might not be true but nevertheless, since it is so on the mark, it is worth retelling even with the disclaimer.

It happened in the men's room in London's Heathrow Airport on December 21, 1988. On that day, a man who had a ticket to fly on Pan Am 103 to New York, which was blown up in midair over Lockerbie, Scotland, by agents of the Libyan dictator, Muammar Gaddafi got locked in a toilet stall and missed his flight.

I don't know why he didn't climb over or crawl under the door (maybe he was physically unable to) but I can easily imagine his becoming increasingly unhinged as he came to realize that he might miss the flight. In fact, it is hard to imagine the average person not being upset or getting angry on some level. As time continued to tick away, I can see him screaming "help!" at the top of his lungs. And as he sat waiting for a maintenance man knowing that his flight was boarding, I can see him kicking the door with all his might while cursing the British "who can't even make a stupid door that works." Imagine how pleasant he must have been when he was finally freed—only to learn that the flight was closed and he would have to wait for the next one to New York. Imagine his sense of frustration while he sat for hours, waiting for the next flight, wondering the whole time about the fate of his luggage that was checked on that flight. How would he even explain this to people?

Now, imagine how completely his mood must have changed when the TVs in the airport's waiting areas broke into their regular programming to broadcast a news bulletin about the terrorist bombing of the flight. Imagine how his mood would have changed even more sharply as he learned that every person onboard that flight was now dead. Suddenly, his ordeal in the men's room takes on a totally different meaning. Not only is he no longer angry, but he is actually grateful that he'd gotten stuck there. He might even have said, "Thank you, G-d, for jamming the door." The same series of events is now seen entirely differently than it had been only a few moments before. His experience did not change—only his understanding of it. The same experience seen through a different lens now produces a much different reaction and in hindsight, what seemed like a bad thing turned out to actually be a good thing.

When we eventually stand before G-d and see our lives replayed, this will be our reaction to everything that has happened to us, both good and bad. We will see all things for what they truly are: Acts of love that were done on our behalf. And we will be thankful for everything—*everything*—that we endured during our short stay here in this world.

PART TWO

The Jew and His Society

Chapter Six

Integrity and Interpersonal Relationships

The Two Halves of the Whole

Probably the most famous sentence in the Torah, the one that is known throughout the world by Jews and non-Jews alike, is: "Love your neighbor as yourself." There is a delicious irony in the fact that most people who are unfamiliar with the Torah describe it as a book of religious laws that we must follow in service to G-d, and yet its most famous line deals with interactions between people.

The correct translation of the Hebrew is "Love your fellow as yourself" and this is what I will use in this chapter. The Hebrew word for "neighbor" is different from the word used in this verse. Either way, the sentence, however ironic it may seem, is a perfect example of the true essence of the Torah.

The 613 *mitzvot* of the Torah are divided into two groupings in the Talmud and all rabbinic writings. The first group of *mitzvot* guides the relationship between man and G-d and includes prayer, kosher food, Shabbat and the holidays. The second is the *mitzvot* that guide the relationships between man and his fellow man such as not stealing, loving each Jew and providing for orphans and widows.

Now, let me pose a question: Which category do you think G-d considers the more important of the two? To expand the question, which would G-d prefer—that we love each other and act as a harmonious family while eating ham and cheese sandwiches at the beach on Saturday, or that we hate each other and fight in synagogue on Shabbat?

If this question were posed to a Christian and a Moslem regarding their communities, what do you think their answers would be? They would probably answer that they need to get along, but obedience to G-d is paramount.

But the G-d of Israel sees things quite differently—which should not be a big surprise at this point. As we have seen, the G-d of Israel is not an angry tyrant who needs adulation and obedience. Rather, He is a loving parent who only wants to give us the greatest pleasure. And since there is no joy or pleasure in dissent and conflict, and since G-d created this world in order to bestow good upon it and give pleasure to His creations, He will be just as concerned about the interactions between people as He is about their interactions with Him. Both are essential for a full life.

In fact, it goes farther than that. The Christian and the Moslem are not completely wrong—obedience to G-d *is* paramount. But what they do not understand, and what no adherents to a man-made religion or philosophy can understand, is that being kind to one another is also a form of obedience to G-d. This is an idea that is uniquely Jewish. The Torah makes no distinction in importance between the *mitzvot* between man and G-d and the *mitzvot* between man and man. Both are obligations. Both are intrinsic parts of the Torah, and one cannot exist without the other.

In fact, one can correctly make the point that the way one treats other people is the true test of his religiosity. How you treat your friend's children is a direct reflection of how you feel about your friend; how you treat G-d's children is a direct reflection of how you feel about G-d. In Judaism, you cannot love G-d and dislike people. If you truly love G-d, you will naturally love his creations. Through our behavior towards others, we either acknowledge our belief that G-d runs the world or we reveal that deep down we do not believe it. A truly G-d-oriented person does not lie, manipulate, abuse or mistreat anyone.

The verse itself is written in the singular sense meaning that the *mitzvah* is to love every individual Jew. G-d does NOT say, "Love Jews" or, "Love the Jewish people" because we all know how easy it is to claim to "love" people in general yet hate individuals. Instead, we are told to love the person who lives next door to you or in your neighborhood, or someone with whom you work who gets on your nerves. Often the hardest person to love is the person to whom you are exposed with the greatest frequency. But if you can love the person sitting next to you by seeing the good in him regardless of some of his actions, you will be able to love everybody else and all of mankind.

The duality of the *mitzvot* between man and G-d and the *mitzvot* between man and man is demonstrated by the two tablets on which the Ten Commandments were inscribed and which were given to Moshe on Mount Sinai.

The first tablet held these five commandments:

> Know there is a G-d
> Have no other gods
> Do not use G-d's name in vain
> Remember the Shabbat
> Honor your father and mother

The second tablet held these five commandments:

> Do not murder
> Do not steal (a person i.e., kidnap)
> Do not commit adultery
> Do not be a false witness
> Do not covet

The first tablet contains *mitzvot* that affect the relationship between man and G-d; the second tablet contains *mitzvot* that affect the relationship between man and man. They are both equally intrinsic to a Jewish existence. (Why the *mitzvah* of honoring your father and mother is on the first tablet will be explained later.) This means that, according to the Torah, bearing a grudge against your neighbor is no different than eating a ham sandwich.

Why is this so? On the simplest level, it is because both are commandments, and we do not differentiate between or rank the *mitzvot*. A commandment is a commandment.

On another level, it is obvious that harmony is the prerequisite to a spiritual life. Without it, human beings are not free to focus on higher aspects but are instead mired in constant physical or emotional conflict. Whether the disharmony is between neighbors, groups or nations or simply within the individual, it is a destructive force that squanders time and resources and prevents us from being able to receive the blessings that He created us to receive.

But there is an even deeper meaning to these *mitzvot*. All societies require some type of civil behavior from their citizens. It is a way of maintaining order and allowing for the social and commercial interaction that is necessary for the functioning of any society. However, the *mitzvot* that G-d has given us that regulate our inter-personal conduct are far more than simply laws and manners. They are the tools for self-mastery, for putting the rider firmly in the saddle and subjugating our lower and more dangerous passions. A life spent living according to these *mitzvot* will create a wonderful, beautiful human being. In Judaism, this self-creation is considered the highest aspect of our lives and the main purpose of our existence.

Self-Love

The *mitzvah* to "love your fellow as yourself" is a commandment to love others as much as we love ourselves. Therefore, it is clear that we are commanded to love ourselves. In fact, to be able to love another person, we first need to love ourselves.

The Torah requires us to develop ourselves through three relationships—with G-d, with our fellow man and with ourselves. Clearly, we must have a healthy self-esteem before we will be able to get along with others but the Jewish concept of self-love is not the type that fills daytime television and trendy books. Instead, it focuses on recognizing that we are creations of a loving G-d who is constantly working on our behalf.

Just knowing that human beings were created in the image of G-d completely alters a person's self-image. It is what gives us inherent value.

Self-love is also a recognition of our strengths and gifts; since we know that they are gifts, self-aggrandizement is the height of absurdity. It is also an acceptance of our flaws and weaknesses because we know that no human being is perfect and we will all make mistakes at one time or another. Further, it is an exhortation to evaluate ourselves constantly with the goal of becoming greater.

The Torah also encourages us to recognize and cultivate our individuality. Adam alone was created as a singular being; all other animals and plants were created in large numbers—in groups and herds. From this we learn that each human being is considered a world unto himself or herself, evidenced by the Talmudic statement that "one who saves another person is as if he saved an entire world." We also learn this from the fact that each one of our faces—the expressions of our souls—is unique, even in cases of identical twins.

However, in a stark contrast to modern thought, the Torah understands that individuality can only be achieved when the outside world is defined. Where it is not, individuality is incorrectly defined as expressing oneself through clothing, hair and behavior. People who work on their self-definition through these external expressions and outward appearances ignore the deeper aspects of individuality. And since they do not develop true individuality, they tend very often to look uncannily similar, if not identical, to other self-expressing individuals.

Individuality is discovering our true inner selves. These are our souls, and that is where we find our individuality.

Be Great

I have listed below a sampling of some of the *mitzvot* that govern the way Jews are required to treat each other and what a Jewish society looks like. Most of these *mitzvot* will be explained briefly in this chapter.

1. Love each Jew
2. Do not hate another Jew in your heart
3. Judge each Jew favorably
4. Reprove another who is doing wrong (to dissuade him from continuing)
5. Do not embarrass another
6. Do not oppress the orphan or the widow
7. Do not speak derogatorily of others
8. Do not insult or harm another with words, directly or indirectly
9. Do not take revenge
10. Do not bear a grudge

11. Love converts
12. Do not cheat a convert (monetarily)
13. Do not harm a convert with words

14. Fulfill what you say you will do
15. Do not break oaths or vows
16. Do not testify falsely

17. Do not put a "stumbling block before the blind"— i.e., do not give misleading or deceptive advice
18. Do not fail to repay a debt

19. Do not covet another's possessions (do not pester or press him to give or sell something to you)

20. Do not desire another's possessions (in your heart)

21. Pay wages on the day they are due
22. Do not delay paying the wages
23. Allow a hired worker to eat from the crops in the field where he is working
24. The hired worker may not eat on hired time
25. The worker may not take more than he can eat

26. Do not overcharge or underpay for an article
27. Return a lost object
28. Do not ignore a lost object
29. Do not stand idly by if someone's life or possessions are in danger
30. Do not rob (forcibly)
31. Do not steal (stealthily)
32. Return stolen objects
33. Ensure that your weights and scales are accurate
34. Do not commit injustice with weights and scales
35. Do not own inaccurate weights and scales
36. Do not move a boundary marker to steal property

37. Respect your father and mother
38. Fear your mother and father
39. Honor those who know and teach the Torah

40. Give charity (*tzedekah*)
41. Do not withhold charity from the poor
42. Leave the edge of your field unharvested for the poor
43. Do not harvest it
44. Leave the dropped gleanings in the field for the poor
45. Do not gather the dropped gleanings
46. Leave the forgotten bundles for the poor
47. Do not retrieve them
48. Leave the edge of your vineyard unharvested for the poor
49. Do not harvest it

50. Leave the dropped gleanings in the vineyard for the poor
51. Do not gather the dropped gleanings
52. Leave the unformed clusters of grapes
53. Do not pick the unformed clusters

54. Lend to the poor
55. Do not press someone for payment if you know he cannot pay
56. Do not forcibly take collateral
57. Return the collateral if the other person needs it
58. Do not delay its return
59. Do not demand collateral from a widow (even if she is wealthy)
60. Do not take, as collateral, utensils that are needed for preparing food
61. Do not lend to Jews with interest
62. Do not borrow from Jews with interest
63. Do not intermediate or be involved at all with an interest-bearing loan to a Jew

64. A judge may not pity the attacker
65. A judge may not have mercy on the poor
66. A judge may not have respect for a great man
67. A judge must not have a bias against a repeat offender
68. A judge may not pervert justice
69. A judge may not pervert justice for an orphan or convert
70. A judge may not fear a violent man
71. A judge may not accept a bribe
72. A judge may not accept testimony unless both parties are present

You might question the practicality of some of these laws, but you cannot deny that following them would create a beautiful and righteous society.

Again, I want to stress that these *mitzvot* are part and parcel of Judaism, no more and no less than hearing the *shofar* on Rosh Hashanah or eating *matzah* on Pesach (Passover). This news often comes as a surprise to non-Orthodox Jews because it is an unknown fact that Judaism is very focused on individual human beings and the realization of one's ultimate potential. In fact, the entire purpose of our creation, the purpose of the Torah, our free will and the meaning behind everything that happens to us are all directed towards personal growth and development.

Therefore, you might ask, why didn't they teach me this in Hebrew school? And why have I never heard of most of these *mitzvot*?

The reason is very revealing. Modern-day secular Jewish life is almost completely focused on the concept of community and peoplehood—synagogues, community centers, charities and Israel. Farther to the left on the spectrum, the age-old Jewish concept of *tikkun olam* ("fixing the world") is also stressed but is mostly misdirected towards working on behalf of non-Jewish causes.

However, nowhere in the non-Orthodox Jewish establishment does anyone speak of the individual and his or her relationship with G-d. The reason for this silence is that—and this will be elaborated on in chapter eleven—all non-Orthodox movements, including Reform, Conservative, secular and so on, do not really believe in a G-d-given Torah and therefore don't subscribe to the idea that the point of life is to create ourselves and our eternities. In a secular life, there is no point to improving yourself or aspiring to be righteous unless you find some sort of personal satisfaction from it. But there certainly is no obligation. And that is why they are silent.

A man who believes that G-d created him for a purpose and for eternity understands that self-actualization—i.e., "creating" oneself—is the point of it all. Becoming a big person—kind, generous, magnanimous, positive, friendly, fair, honest, merciful, dependable, grateful, caring, responsible, trustworthy, reliable—is what each of us is here to accomplish. Who reading these words would not want to be described with such adjectives?

But why should we desire such a reputation? Why do we instinctively like the giver and not the taker, the kind person and not the cruel person, those who are friendly and not those who are bitter? The reason is that these people possess qualities of G-d and are therefore more like Him. And the more a person emulates G-d, the more he or she will elicit feelings of love and affection from others. At the same time, the more a person emulates G-d, the more he will be able to have a true relationship with Him.

Fortunately, one does not have to go to Barnes & Noble to find how-to books on personal growth or fulfillment in order to become a great person.

The original book was given to us by the original author a long time ago, and it is the inheritance and possession of every Jew.

Now, let's look at these *mitzvot* more closely and see what type of human beings they create, and what type of society they form.

One Large Family

- Love each Jew
- Do not hate another Jew in your heart
- Judge each Jew favorably
- Reprove another who is doing wrong (to dissuade him from continuing)
- Do not embarrass another
- Do not oppress the orphan or the widow
- Do not speak derogatorily of others
- Do not insult or harm another with words, directly or indirectly
- Do not take revenge
- Do not bear a grudge

- Love converts
- Do not cheat a convert (monetarily)
- Do not harm a convert with words

The Torah was given to a nation, not a group of individuals, and this is because the mission of the Jewish people requires a nation and not a group of individuals. It is through the unique and sublime manner in which we function as a society and as a nation that sets us up as a guiding light to the other nations of the world.

However our nation has a unique foundation. It started as a family; our forefather, Yaakov (Jacob), is the progenitor of the Jewish people. He was given the name Yaakov at birth but later in life, G-d gave him another name, Yisrael (Israel), which indicated his spiritual greatness.

After G-d changed his name, we became known as the Children of Israel, and we still are called this today. This means that despite our numbers or the distance separating us, we are still a family—cousins, really, and all the *mitzvot* that regulate our interactions are based on this fact. In fact, if, when you reread the list of *mitzvot*, you imagine that they are all referring to members of your immediate family whom you love dearly, they all make sense.

G-d, however, wants us to extend our family circle to include all Jews, which brings up another essential point about the Torah: It was not given to the world. It was given to the Jewish nation to be used internally, and is the guideline for a Jewish society so that when people of the world see us conducting ourselves in a certain manner, they will learn from us and change. They benefit from the Torah, though it is indirect.

You might protest and say, "I can't possibly love *everyone*—some people are just plain you-know-whats." It is definitely true that some people are much harder to love than others, but loving all of them is still possible. Think about it: *Somebody* loves that person whom you can't stand. Maybe it's a parent or spouse or friend. Either way, that person was once a little child who wanted his parents' love and approval. Somewhere in his life, something happened that changed his attitude for the worse, however, if you look past his obvious faults and focus instead on his good traits, it will evoke feelings of affection. You might even feel sorry for him.

"OK, OK," you're saying. "I can feel sorry for him and yes, I can see him in a different light, but LOVE him? How?"

It's not as difficult as it sounds.

Love is the emotion we feel when we identify someone by his or her virtues. When we do the opposite and identify a person by his or her faults, we feel antipathy and loathing. This is easy to demonstrate. Think of the qualities of someone you like. These attributes will be overwhelmingly positive. Now, think of someone you dislike. In your mind, this person's qualities will mostly be negative. This doesn't mean that the person has only good or bad traits; it just means that we identify the person only with either the good or the bad ones.

We all have met people who are incredibly positive, forgiving and happy and have a natural ability to look at the best in people. Then, there are the rest of us, who need to make an effort to do so. Finding the good in others is not always easy to do, but it is a commandment, and it is something we need to work on throughout our lives. Like everything else, with time and effort, it becomes easier and easier, and eventually it becomes second nature.

This outlook towards people makes all the *mitzvot* in this group much easier. Someone who loves other Jews will not embarrass them, oppress them or speak ill of them. He will not bear grudges or take revenge. And he will always give others the benefit of the doubt. Nevertheless, there will always be situations, even for the most positive thinker, that require extra effort.

Back on our list, you might have noted the additional *mitzvot* concerning converts. Every rule that applies to Jews applies equally to converts but G-d adds additional requirements and prohibitions when dealing with them. So, for example, if a storekeeper cheats a convert, he has transgressed two *mitzvot*—one regarding all Jews in general and the second regarding converts in particular. We are given these additional *mitzvot* regarding converts because converts are deserving of extra love and consideration since they will be more sensitive and easily embarrassed. In fact, we are commanded forty-eight different times in the Torah to love the convert.

And they are certainly deserving of additional respect. For a non-Jew to leave his society, religion and family and join the Jewish people—not the most popular group on Earth—takes remarkable strength and integrity and a burning desire for truth. There certainly aren't many practical benefits to making the move and at times, it has meant putting one's life in danger. A person who is willing to do this deserves the utmost admiration and regard. (I am referring here to converts of conscience, those who convert with the intention of keeping the *mitzvot* (which is the definition of conversion). A person who converts for any other reason—for example, to marry a Jew—but goes through the process without intending to begin fulfilling the *mitzvot* immediately, has not converted; his or her status is unchanged.

Integrity

- Fulfill what you say you will do
- Do not break oaths or vows
- Do not testify falsely

- Do not to put a "stumbling block before the blind"— i.e., do not give misleading or deceptive advice
- Do not fail to repay a debt

- Do not covet another's possessions (do not pester or press him to give or sell something to you)
- Do not desire another's possessions (in your heart)

- Pay wages on the day they are due
- Do not delay paying the wages
- Allow a hired worker to eat from the crops in the field where he is working
- The hired worker may not eat on hired time
- The worker may not take more than he can eat

- Do not overcharge or underpay for an article
- Return a lost object
- Do not ignore a lost object
- Do not stand idly by if someone's life or possessions are in danger
- Do not rob (forcibly)
- Do not steal (stealthily)
- Return stolen objects
- Ensure that your weights and scales are accurate
- Do not commit injustice with weights and scales
- Do not own inaccurate weights and scales
- Do not move a boundary marker to steal property

There was once a time when a man's word was his bond, but this is becoming increasingly rare. Today's headlines are filled with case after case of people in public service acting dishonestly and outrightly lying. Institutions that once were looked upon as bastions of integrity have little credibility today. Truth has become an endangered species. What has caused this fairly rapid deterioration? What happened to honor?

The short and simple answer is that integrity is based on morals which can only be based on a belief in G-d. And this could be demonstrated by looking at the situation from another angle. Having integrity means that there will be many times when a person will suffer a loss, financial or otherwise as a result of making the correct moral choice. Sometimes, this loss can even be one's very life. What would compel a person to disregard personal gain for an idea as ethereal as doing the right thing?

Only a belief in G-d.

As we have seen, we are composed of two elements—a body and a soul, each of which has a different agenda. The body sees no higher accomplishment than fulfilling its desires. The soul obviously sees many other accomplishments as supremely more important. Therefore, this can lead to many internal conflicts. How people respond to moral situations demonstrates the degree to which their souls control their bodies. If they act according to the dictates of their souls, they will show a great deal of integrity. If they act according to the dictates of their bodies, they will show a distinct lack of integrity.

Doing the right thing *because it is the right thing* means that there is something higher than personal gain and when a person acts this way he is demonstrating (whether he is aware of it or not) his belief in G-d and ultimate reward and punishment. He is identifying with his soul and rejecting the immature and vulgar demands of his body. Even when a person gives up his life, he is stating that there is something more important than even being alive. This obviously requires a belief in an ongoing transcendent existence.

The reason for the moral decline of the West is its secular nature. The more secular a society, the more immoral it will be.

For example, you are walking down Fifth Avenue in New York City when there is a sudden blackout. There are no streetlights, store lights or burglar alarms. You are now free to smash a storefront window and help yourself to some very fine presents. What do you do? This somewhat extreme case famously happened twice, in 1965 and 1977. In 1965, the citizens of New York came together and helped each other. There was very little looting and almost no crime or arson. In 1977, the city went berserk (to be fair, the poor sections of the city went berserk); 1,616 stores were damaged and looted, 1,037 fires were started and 3,776 people were arrested.

What happened in the intervening twelve years that produced such a radically different reaction? The answer can be summed up in two words "The Sixties", a time when vocal elements of society were encouraging people to do what they pleased if it felt good. Twelve years of being told to indulge their bodily desires had obvious effects on people's personal integrity.

Let's take a more subtle case. You enter a taxicab just as a bejeweled and obviously wealthy lady steps out. On the seat you find a diamond bracelet, which from the looks of it is probably worth $15,000 to $20,000. Your body wants to keep it; your soul wants to return it. Your *yeitzer hara*, always present, starts to chime in with a litany of rationalizations and justifications: She's so rich, she won't even miss it; she can afford to lose it; she probably wouldn't even return it herself; even if I return it, she won't give me the reward I deserve.

The *yeitzer hara* will try to twist your emotions so you feel good or justified about doing the wrong thing. But one fact doesn't change: It's not yours. It's hers. And you have no right to it.

An Orthodox Jew might face the same conundrum, but probably not. He has been trained from the time he was a toddler not to steal, not to touch what isn't his and to return lost objects. And if the Orthodox Jew in the taxicab had been paying attention throughout school, he would know that if G-d wanted him to have wealth, he would have it without having to resort to stealing. He also would know that the reward in the next world for fulfilling the *mitzvah* is far greater than all the money in this world.

Thanks to a proper education, the dilemma is quickly resolved to the benefit of all parties. Proper moral training leads to integrity. There will always be a few bad apples but nevertheless, if you are planning to lose something of value, I recommend doing it in an Orthodox Jewish neighborhood.

Unflinching Honesty

Our inner sense of integrity is very closely tied to our words and speech. A Jew is not allowed to lie. Deception is a type of theft—liars are thieves and thieves are liars.

And a closer look shows that truth is an inherent part of the Torah itself.

Although I enumerated only four PERLs in chapter two, there are other, more subtle, facts that indicate that the Torah is not a product of human hands and one of them is its brutal honesty. Not only are the Jews not praised very often in the Torah, but they seem to be criticized constantly and every skeleton in their national closet is exposed. An uninformed reader can easily come away with the wrong impression—that the Torah is basically hundreds of laws interspersed with accounts of the Jewish people's mistakes and errors. In fact, if you didn't know better, you would think that the Torah was written by an anti-Semite.

In the Torah, we learn that:

Regarding our forefathers:

- Avraham (Abraham) did not recognize the bad nature of his son, Yishmael (Ishmael). Only his wife, Sarah, saw it and G-d himself came to Avraham to tell him that she was right and to listen to her (Gen. 21:9-13).
- Yitzchak (Isaac) did not see Eisav's (Esau's) true nature and wanted to give him a significant blessing, which would have been disastrous for Yaakov (Jacob) (Gen. 27:5-13).

- Only Yitzchak's wife, Rivkah (Rebecca), saw the true picture and instructed Yaakov to fool Yitzchak (Isaac) so he could receive the blessing (Gen. 27:5-13).
- Ten of Yosef's (Joseph's) brothers conspired to kill him (Gen. 37:18).
- After further consultation, they decided to sell him into slavery in Egypt instead (Gen. 37:27-28).

Regarding the Jewish people:

- While still in Egypt, they complained to Moshe about coming and starting up with Pharaoh after Pharaoh increased their workload (Ex. 5:21).
- At the Red Sea, they accused Moshe of trying to get them killed (Ex. 14:11).
- Forty days after receiving the Torah, they built the Golden Calf (Ex. 32:1-6).
- They complained to Moshe about the lack of food and water (Ex. 15:24, 16:3, 17:2-3).
- They talked of returning to Egypt (Num. 14:3-4).
- They mourned when the twelve spies came back with negative reports about the Land of Israel (Num. 14:1) and, as a result, had to spend forty years in the Sinai Desert until that entire generation had died out (Num. 14:26-34).

Regarding Moshe:

- Moshe had a speech impediment that required his brother, Aharon (Aaron), to act as an intermediary when Moshe spoke to Pharaoh (Ex. 4:10).
- When, after his first meeting with Pharaoh, the Jews were given additional burdens, Moshe turned back to G-d and questioned why he had been sent, since things only got worse (Ex. 5:22).
- On one occasion he was accused by the Jewish people of being a murderer (Num. 17:6).

- He was publicly questioned by five sisters regarding a law of inheritance and was unsure of the correct ruling until G-d told him the sisters were correct (Num. 27:1-11).
- He was forbidden to enter the Land of Israel with the Jewish people. Instead, G-d chose his disciple, Yehoshua (Joshua), to take over and lead them in (Num. 27:12-20).
- The reason for this was that Moshe did not carefully listen to G-d's instructions on one occasion and therefore, G-d declared that Moshe "didn't believe in Me" (Num. 20:12).

After reading this list, you might have a sour feeling and be wondering why we consider any of these people great. But they were, in fact, great and that becomes apparent if you look at every event on this list in context and with the proper understanding of what truly happened.

Those with a more cynical bent will no doubt shout, "Cover-up!" They will accuse Orthodox Jews of making excuses and explaining away all the blemishes in our history with dishonest apologies and sugar coating. But this is exactly the point. The Torah is the only one amongst many religious "holy books" to speak honestly. The very fact that we are discussing the blacker marks in our history shows that first, the Torah was not written by human beings and second, it values truth and honesty. The Torah is not only honest—it is excruciatingly honest.

All man-written histories are biased. You will not find anything negative about Jesus in the New Testament, nor will you find anything negative about Mohammed in the Koran. No two sides of a conflict, even if they are democracies, will have the same account of history. The American Revolution is understood differently in the United States and Great Britain. The history of the American Civil war will vary by state. Human beings will always recollect in ways that are complimentary to their sides or causes. If the Torah had been written by a man who was trying to convince a people to accept it, including anything negative would be very counterproductive. And even if all of it did happen, still, no nation would want any distasteful episodes recorded in their national book.

If the Torah were a human creation, all the great figures of our founding would have been perfect in every way. Moshe would have been perfectly eloquent, and the Jewish people would have been absolutely obedient. Moshe would have conquered the Land of Israel riding on a white horse at the head of his triumphant armies, and what would have happened at the end of his life? Resurrection? Flying up to heaven alive? Certainly, he would not have died and been buried in an unknown location because G-d did not allow him to enter Israel—which is exactly what the Torah describes.

Even in today's modern, scientific world, there is not much objectivity. To be sure, a totalitarian regime has no regard for truth and will record, rewrite or fabricate history to its advantage. But even among democracies there will be half truths and omissions that will portray the country in a good light. The national histories of France, Spain and Poland will not include the barbaric brutalities they perpetrated against the Jews over the last 1,000 years because that reveals a sickness in their souls, and they don't want to be stigmatized. Frankly, it would be embarrassing.

Yet, the Torah is very open about the mistakes made by our great figures. Why?

Because the Torah is neither a history book nor a new-age self-help book. It is a book of instructions for living, and we can learn from the mistakes of our great forefathers. We know they weren't perfect because no human being is perfect. Only a fool claims to never make mistakes, and it's silly when religions claim perfection in their founders or leaders. But there is much to learn from a great man who does the right thing ninety-nine percent of the time. *Because* he is great, even his errors are meaningful.

An average person is not a role model and the reasons for his mistakes are not very profound. But a great person can enlighten us even through his errors. Imagine a great general who won many epic battles for his country, a man whose exploits would be studied by historians and military strategists for all time. Now, imagine that during his career, he lost a battle or two. This, too, would be studied in military colleges because if such a great military leader could make the mistakes he did, all the more so could the average person, and soldiers coming up through the ranks would learn to be better soldiers through his few mistakes.

Similarly, since the Torah is a training manual for a great life, we learn from the great lives of our great figures and from the few mistakes they made. This commitment to truth permeates a Torah society. But—and this is extremely important to know—it is not the insincere, supposed ongoing search for the truth that the Western world has glamorized; the concept of the noble seeker who is always questioning and never certain, who Hamlet-like is constantly weighing both sides of a moral dilemma and is always in doubt if he is doing right.

If you met someone who told you that he has spent his life searching for the truth, that he has traveled the globe, read widely and sought out wise men, you would be full of admiration. Unfortunately, this romanticized image, like so many other concepts in modern Western thought, is very much off the mark. The life of such a man has never started. He is no different from the man who spends his life deciding what to wear and never dressing or a man deciding what to eat and never eating. This man never really lived because living is defined as spiritual growth (as opposed to just existing), and he never really grew. He just had a lot of exotic experiences. A life spent in such activity is wasted because the truth is the starting point, not the end point.

In addition, a strong case can be made that his "search" was never sincere. "The truth" of the meaning of life is not a secret known only to a privy few on a remote mountaintop. A true seeker will find his answers right under his nose, if he truly wants to. **The purpose of life is not the search for truth; it is the application of the truth**—perfecting ourselves and drawing closer to G-d. Truth is the starting point, and it is as necessary to life as oxygen. A human being will wither in an environment where there is no truth. Alexander Solzhenitsyn wrote that the worst part of living in the Soviet Union was the constant lies that were relentlessly foisted on the population by the government.

The *mitzvot* are the means for the ***application*** of the truth since they are all acts of doing or feeling. There is no commandment to seek out truth because the *mitzvot* are predicated on it. Nor is there a *mitzvah* to continuously question what you already know to be true because after a certain point, further questioning is only counterproductive and a method of avoidance.

We build our lives on the truth. Optimally, we should receive the truth from our parents and then spend our lives engaged in the *mitzvot*, which mold us. The most basic truths about life are quite simple and it would follow logically that a loving G-d would want all of us to understand our lives. It is the application of the truth that is difficult; it requires lifelong effort but through that effort, we attain greatness.

Regardless of the challenge, truth is invigorating and inspiring. Lies and falsehood, on the other hand, sap our energy and depress our spirit. Inner peace comes from being in touch with the truth; a Jewish refusenik and prisoner of conscience in the former Soviet Union could feel satisfied about his choice even if the result of his choice was an unheated, concrete cell in a Siberian prison.

Gratitude

- Respect your father and mother
- Fear your mother and father
- Honor those who know and teach the Torah

While we are on the subject of truth, let's look at the Jewish view of gratitude.

The Hebrew word for "thank you"—*todah*—has the same etymological roots as *modah,* or "admission." So, *"todah"* can also be translated as an admission of the truth.

Saying "thank you" can be difficult and for those with less-refined characters, almost impossible. By saying "thank you" to someone, we admit that we needed him and that we owe him. The degree of the assistance you received affects the degree of your gratitude. If someone holds the door open for you, you do not owe him your life. If he pulled you out of a burning building, you might.

G-d requires us to demonstrate our gratitude to our parents and teachers of Torah—those who have helped us the most and asked for the least in return—with visible acts of esteem and deference. Besides the fact that these are precisely the people whose kindnesses can be so easily taken for granted and not acknowledged, showing honor to our parents and teachers of Torah reveals our deepest beliefs and values.

Honoring our parents is a demonstration that we are grateful for our existence. Regardless of what transpired after you were born, you owe your parents gratitude for simply being here at all. Without them, you would not have been brought into the world. And, since we know that we are here to achieve greatness and enjoy a wonderful, eternal life, there is very much for which to be thankful. Our lives are the greatest gift we receive.

This is why this *mitzvah* was engraved on the first tablet of the Ten Commandments, not the second: How you treat your parents has everything to do with your relationship with and attitude towards G-d. The Torah defines "honoring" as sustaining them, if needed, by providing them with food, clothing and shelter, taking them out of the house for their errands and for pleasure and always speaking to them in a pleasant manner. "Fearing" is defined as not sitting in their place, not contradicting them and not calling them by name.

Regarding the *mitzvah* to honor those who know and teach Torah, this touches on a much deeper issue. Who truly deserves to be honored? As I mentioned earlier, who we choose to honor reveals our true values. For example, America lavished praise on Charles Lindbergh for being the first to fly solo across the Atlantic. He was given parades and a medal from President Calvin Coolidge. He was considered a hero. Why? Because he was foolish enough to put his life at risk for an accomplishment of dubious value? Would you want your child to risk his life to do something similar? A Jewish society would not honor such a man, nor would it honor the man who risked his life to be the first to reach the North Pole. We would consider them to be *meshuga*.

A Torah society possesses a unique roster of heroes. Non-Jewish societies elevate and honor the warrior, the entertainer and the athlete—those who take people out of reality or create illusions. A Jewish society does the opposite and honors only those who bring its people *into* reality—the wise man, the teacher, the righteous. A child in a Torah school system has truly great men and women to admire and emulate and has no need to look for role models in tattooed athletes and drug-addled celebrities.

Because the Jewish people value reality and honor the wise man, the teacher and the righteous, and because our history is replete with real-life heroes, there are remarkably no fictional characters in our literary history. The non-Jewish world has been inventing fictional characters and stories since the earliest days; fables, myths and tales occupy the highest positions in national histories and cultures throughout the world. The world is awash in all types of unreality and people who never existed: Jason, Macbeth, Captain Ahab, Tom Sawyer or even Harry Potter are objects of study and sometimes even devotion. They are all creations of fantasy who become almost as real as the true characters of history. Similarly, actors and actresses, when discussing their roles, often refer to their characters as if they were discussing real people. The truth is that fictional characters have as much reality to them as Santa Claus or the Tooth Fairy and, if society did not bestow a value to such illusion, we would realize that it is no different than a three-year-old talking about her imaginary friend. (Giuseppe Verdi once said, "It may be a good thing to copy reality, but to invent reality is much, much better.")

Because we know that life has incredible meaning and limitless potential, we are only concerned with people who enhance our lives not distract us.

Economics

- Give charity (*tzedekah*)
- Do not withhold charity from the poor
- Leave the edge of your field unharvested for the poor
- Do not harvest it
- Leave the dropped gleanings in the field for the poor
- Do not gather the dropped gleanings
- Leave the forgotten bundles for the poor
- Do not retrieve them
- Leave the edge of your vineyard unharvested for the poor
- Do not harvest it
- Leave the dropped gleanings in the vineyard for the poor
- Do not gather the dropped gleanings
- Leave the unformed clusters of grapes
- Do not pick the unformed clusters

- Lend to the poor
- Do not press someone for payment if you know he cannot pay
- Do not forcibly take collateral
- Return the collateral if the other person needs it
- Do not delay its return
- Do not demand collateral from a widow (even if she is wealthy)
- Do not take, as collateral, utensils that are needed for preparing food
- Do not lend to Jews with interest
- Do not borrow from Jews with interest
- Do not intermediate or be involved at all with an interest-bearing loan to a Jew

The Talmud says that there are three ways in which to gauge a person's true nature: When he is drunk, when he is angry and how he deals with money. What do these three have in common? They arouse our animal passions like nothing else does and demonstrate the extent to which our bodies are under the control of our souls—or not. Most people's souls will be able to control their bodies most of the time. But unless that horse is thoroughly trained, if it gets riled, you might have a runaway stallion on your hands.

What is the Torah's view of money? Needless to say, it's fundamentally different from the Western view, which is based on what has come to be termed "economics." This is actually a philosophy with very specific views on the nature of man, and the Torah's philosophy disagrees with many of those assumptions.

It is interesting to note that there was no such thing as economics before the late 1700s. All types of scientific disciplines—medicine, mathematics, astronomy, animal husbandry, botany—have roots all the way back to the beginning of human civilization. However there are no Greek or Roman economists; in fact, the science of economics did not exist in any form in the ancient world nor even into the Middle Ages.

This is puzzling because there was always commerce, and there were always markets. From the earliest times, sea vessels plied the oceans and caravans crossed the deserts but until 1776, no one thought to formulate scientific theories about the value of goods or the organization of resources.

Why not? Because until then, human beings had a fundamentally different view of themselves. Only the gradual secularization of the Western world, beginning with the Renaissance and continuing through the Age of Reason, led to the completely new field of science called economics.

When Adam Smith, who is considered the father of modern economics, published *The Wealth of Nations* in 1776 he only formalized an image of man that had already begun to take root as a result of the decline of religion. Without religion and its accompanying focus on the spiritual, human beings were left with only their physical needs and desires on which to focus. After time, these needs took on an exaggerated importance and their fulfillment became become a lofty pursuit. Where man once saw himself as primarily a soul, he came to see himself as primarily a body.

Economics, which the Merriam-Webster Dictionary defines as "a branch of knowledge dealing with the production, distribution and consumption of goods and services," essentially makes a science of satisfying the body's desires. Before the modern age, this would have been seen as a perversion. That a person would use his infinite and transcendental mind, the loftiest aspect of his being, merely to satisfy his base needs as opposed to using it for higher understanding was viewed as denigration. The mind was meant for serious thought, higher purposes and more meaningful endeavors. Using it for base human needs would have been a statement that a person was no more than an animal, a body without a soul.

Other distortions were built into the science of economics as well.

Instead of being defined as souls, human beings were redefined as "consumers," as if to say that this was their essence. But this is not true. Cockroaches are consumers. People consume but are not consumers any more than they are breathers, sleepers or digesters.

Modern economics is also based on the concept that humans are only motivated by personal financial gain. In economic science there is no concept of mercy, compassion or kindness; man's basic humanity is not seen as a motivation unless he can make a buck doing it.

But none of this is true. Human beings are infinitely more complicated than economic theory acknowledges. The enormous amount of charity that is given in the United States is testimony to the fact that people will choose to lose monetarily in order to gain in other ways. In a way, economics ignores the best in people; it assumes a self-centered outlook on life and elevates unbridled greed, generally considered a character flaw, to a noble pursuit. It rationalizes the acting-out of a human being's lower drives.

It also distorts our aspirations. Adam Smith was not totally wrong—a human being does have insatiable desires, but they are spiritual, not physical. In a society where wealth is not considered a value worthy of lifelong dedication, a person's drive to succeed and excel would be directed towards knowledge, wisdom, understanding and, ultimately, G-d and the meaning of life. In the modern world, where wealth is often considered the prime benchmark of success, it is directed instead towards the accumulation of wealth far beyond what a human being could ever use in his lifetime. Profit and gain are seen as worthy of intellectual pursuit, time and sacrifice, but this is really just a different type of gluttony, and it creates sicknesses.

In our age, this distortion has led to the overvaluing of money as a goal in its own right. People work for money they do not need and this is seen as normal even though it could just as easily be defined as crazy. Imagine someone who is financially comfortable and can choose how to spend his day—either helping other people, learning something new or making money. In this case there is almost no reason to spend the day making money, and yet we all know many people who would make that choice. In fact, there are many who would not even see a choice at all. What we don't realize is that this attitude is a relatively new one. It did not always exist and there are many parts of the world where it is still not the basis of society.

In modern society, a rich person is considered "successful" even if he is obnoxious, on his fourth marriage and not on speaking terms with his resentful children. Everyone aspires to be millionaires even though they don't know what they would do with the money except indulge their desires. Money is a means that has become an end, a twisted philosophy that began, not coincidentally, around the start of the Industrial Revolution and became more accepted as mechanized processing created way more product than people really needed. In such a situation, a spiritual society simply would have reduced the workday and focused on other pursuits. Instead, new industries emerged, such as advertising and sales (of other's people products) to convince people to buy more than they needed. More sales translated into more money. And whereas products were once made to last as long as possible, the new buzzword became "planned obsolescence."

All of this creates an unending cycle. The accumulation of wealth leads directly to consumerism, which in turn leads to the need for more money. Today, a healthy economy is dependent on people buying new homes, new cars and more and more stuff for which they have no need. Accumulating wealth is now the standard underpinning of modern society, a phenomenon that has had disastrous effects on people's self-images, their day-to-day lives and their family structure. The pursuit of a high standard of living often leads to a low quality of life.

Charity

A Jewish society, however, does not reflect the attitudes and viewpoints of Adam Smith and modern economic thought. We believe that human beings are souls, not consumers, and that money is only a means and never an end; but it is a good thing, and we value it. In fact, in our daily prayers we ask for financial success and at the beginning of each month, in a list of requests for the coming month, we specifically ask G-d for wealth—not daily bread, but actual wealth. On Rosh Hashanah, we ask for a year of wealth that can be earned without extreme effort or great stress. Why do we do this? Because we know that wealth provides independence and opportunity. With it, we can bestow good upon others, therefore allowing us to emulate G-d on a deeper level.

There are no vows of poverty in Judaism, but we do not desire wealth in order to live fancy lifestyles. In fact, the Torah views any obsession with material goods as immature. As infants, we are preoccupied with our own needs and desires, which are entirely physical and emotional. As we mature into children, we are taught to control our passions—not to push to the front, not to grab food from the serving dish, to share with our siblings, to wait our turn, to share our belongings with friends. This process of maturation is supposed to instruct us that our needs and desires are not the axis on which the Earth turns and in the larger picture aren't that important at all. If these lessons are not learned, the result very often is an overgrown child.

The process of maturation also teaches us that there are things much more important than possessions. Growing up means that we shed our childish view of life revolving around our toys and our stuff. Sharing, giving and kindness are spiritual values whose importance far outweighs going first or having the bigger piece. When this outcome is not achieved, the result is a self-absorbed adult who still places an inordinate value on his material possessions and personal desires. Although he is no longer little, he is still small. The Jewish view of raising children is to create giving, generous, caring, concerned people who will be able to emulate G-d and relate to Him with a sense of inner peace. Anything short of the outcome will require remedial work as an adult. Many adults are grappling with issues that should have been left behind in grade school.

Material wealth is also short lived—we cannot take it with us and therefore, it is not worthy of extended effort. The common expression is "time is money," (again, reflecting the idea that money is supremely important). But to a Jew, the inverse is true—money is time, the most precious commodity. Money can be replaced; time cannot and so a Jew who understands his place in the cosmos does not overemphasis the accumulation of material possessions.

And since Jews understand that money is a G-d-given blessing we have few qualms about sharing it. This is why Jews are internationally renowned for being, far and away, the most generous people on Earth.

Doing the right thing with money will never jeopardize a person's financial situation. It's silly to fear sharing your wealth when the same G-d who blessed you with the wealth commands you to apportion a part of it to those less blessed.

This is why, even today, places that are not Christian or Moslem (again, using our ideas) such as the Far East and Africa, are notorious for their lack of societal kindness. China, India, Japan and Korea might have strong economies but they have yet to learn the higher aspects of civilization. Not surprisingly, it is the missionaries in these countries who have introduced the concept of charity. Without a transcendental, loving G-d, the world is inevitably viewed as a jungle where everyone must compete for limited resources of the finite pie. (Polls in the United States show a strong correlation between religion and charitable giving. Popular spin would have you believe that liberals are much more generous than conservatives but this is not the case. The "red" states are far more charitable than the "blue" states. And, interestingly, they also have higher birthrates than the "blue" states.)

Jews do not view wealth as a pie with a limited number of slices; we understand that our loving, all-knowing, all-powerful G-d has commanded us to share and that when we look at the pie, we are seeing only part of the picture. G-d can just bake another pie if He wants to. In fact, we know that He has a entire bakery full of them, and that if we finish the one we have, He has plenty more for us.

It's interesting to note that modern economic theory has come around to see what Jews have believed and practiced for thousands of years—that the more money moves around, the more wealth it creates, and that charity actually leads to wealth creation. This is evident in the fact that in today's world, nations with restrictive economies are the poorest. Jews, however, with their charity and confidence in G-d's support, have always been mercantile and the economic engines for societies in which they lived.

Community

The Torah does not teach that charity is something that is only practiced towards those less fortunate. A truly charitable person does what he can to help everyone, rich and poor because charity is not a financial tax; rather it is a philosophical outlook.

Suppose a person helps the poor and sick with money and personal assistance but harbors resentment against those he views as rich. This man is not fulfilling the *mitzvah* of loving his fellow; he is doing kind acts, but there are obviously impure psychological motives behind them. Sometimes people do things not because they are compassionate but because there are limits to their insensitivity—because someone else's pain and suffering is so blatant, it causes *him* pain, and then he must act to alleviate it. Or, perhaps, he helps simply to show how magnanimous he is or to show how much better he is than "those people."

When G-d commands you to "love your fellow" it means that you should wholeheartedly wish the best for everyone and wish it were in your power to increase everyone's success and happiness. We help out of our love for our fellow man, not to feel good or superior or for honor. Our motivations are pure, and we rejoice in others' successes and good fortunes. Everything we have has been given to us by G-d and is for our best, so why be jealous of what someone else has?

The Christian West has not fully assimilated this idea. Because of the intellectual detritus of socialism and the nonsense of class struggle, modern society has a schizophrenic relationship with the rich: Everyone wants to be one of them and yet resents them for what they have, harboring suspicions that they resorted to cheating and exploitation of "the little guy" to acquire their wealth. Much of this dates back to feudal Europe where the nobility actually did get rich off the backs of the poor, and much of it is rooted in plain jealousy.

But in a free society with a free economy, wealth is not created at the expense of others. In fact free markets lead to wealth creation for rich and poor alike. The rich have nothing to "give back" because they have not taken anything; they have, in fact, created wealth for others. Bill Gates, for example, does not owe me or anyone else anything. He had a good idea and worked hard and now he's fabulously wealthy. Good for him, I'm happy for him, and if anything, *I* owe *him*. Certainly the thousands of people who became rich as a result of working for or investing in Microsoft do, and maybe even society itself—he created jobs and wealth and provided needed goods and services. He earned his wealth honestly and has nothing to apologize for, nor any debt to pay back to society.

This is what we believe in a Torah society, and this philosophy is most apparent through the existence of what is called a *gemach*. The word is an acronym of a Hebrew phrase—**gemillut chasadim**—that translates to "doing acts of kindness." In English, a *gemach* is sometimes called a "free-loan fund" and it is a means of helping people who cannot afford their needs or helping people avoid purchasing costly items that will not be used very often. Basically, a *gemach* is an interest-free, cost-free loan operation set up by an individual on his own initiative.

In my community there are no less than fifteen *gemachs* that offer a huge array of goods and services ranging from business loans to diapers. At least three that I know of loan money interest free and distribute hundreds of thousands of dollars every year. If you are having a party or making a celebration you can borrow chairs, folding tables, coat racks, crystal bowls, vases, fruit trays, cake trays, three-tier servers, candy dishes and mirrored display trays. There is even one that provides liquor. There are *gemachs* for bridal gowns, headpieces, and ladies' and children's wedding attire and if you're pregnant, there's one for maternity formalwear. A medical *gemach* loans wheelchairs, crutches, canes, walkers and pumps for nursing mothers, and there are two that deal only with baby items—one loans out portable cribs, heaters, folding beds and high chairs and the other gives away formula, diapers, cribs, strollers, car seats and toys as well as children's furniture and clothing, including school uniforms.

There are also *gemachs* that loan out leaf blowers, Jewish books that cannot be found in the town's public library, Rubbermaid boxes for moving and *mezuzahs* for those who have just moved into new homes and haven't had the time to buy them. All people, rich and poor, are invited to use the *gemachs*—and all of them do. At no time does anyone prevent a rich person from using any of these resources or complain that they can afford to buy it, so why don't they? A person's economic situation is beside the point. The point that matters is giving.

This underscores a pillar of Jewish life—the community or *kehilla* in Hebrew. G-d created a world in which no man can exist in isolation; the continuity of mankind depends on each person producing for others. In fact, every day our basic needs such as food and clothing are provided through a staggering level of coordination among thousands of people. True, a man can take to the hills and live alone, hunting and gathering his own food, chopping his own wood, making his own clothes from animal hides but, in doing so, will live the life of an animal, existing from meal to meal. His accomplishments will be few; his greatest one will be his mere survival.

But we are here for more than that. And just as people need each other physically, we also need one another spiritually. The more a person is engaged with his fellow man, the more opportunities he has to emulate G-d. Every healthy human being has a spiritual need to give and share, most often manifested in the desire for children, and isolation deprives a human being of this essential need. Mankind's greatness and accomplishments come through cooperation.

True Wealth

Given the Jewish view of wealth, it should not come as a shock that the rabbis of the Talmud defined a rich man not as someone with a certain net worth but as someone who is happy with what he has. The Western world sees wealth in material terms but that is very limited; a person who has material wealth but is sickly or has buried his children cannot appreciate the benefits of his fortune.

The Torah instructs us to understand that what we have is exactly what G-d wants us to have, that it is for our best and—this is crucial—that our happiness is not dependent on our possessions. By appreciating what we have been given and not focusing on what we don't have, we are guaranteed to be happy. The inverse—a lack of appreciation and a yearning for what we do not own—is guaranteed to create deep unhappiness. This is why societies that become increasingly materialistic become increasingly mentally ill—because their happiness becomes defined as a result of achieving wealth or status. Once that the goal is achieved and the expected happiness does not materialize, it only causes stress, anxiety and even more unhappiness.

Happiness is no laughing matter. It is unbelievably serious and it all depends not on external circumstances but on our attitudes and outlooks. Happiness never "happens"; it is always created. It comes from the inside not the outside.

Unhappiness stems from identifying with the body. This leads to a distorted view of true significance and a skewed understanding of our real desires. Freedom from the shackles of the body's desires is only achieved through identification with the soul and if a person is truly free in the Jewish sense, he will never pin his happiness on external occurrences. He will never say, "If only..." because he knows that once that desire is satisfied, another will pop up to take its place.

Justice

- A judge may not pity the attacker
- A judge may not have mercy on the poor
- A judge may not have respect for a great man
- A judge must not have a bias against a repeat offender
- A judge may not pervert justice
- A judge may not pervert justice for an orphan or convert
- A judge may not fear a violent man
- A judge may not accept a bribe
- A judge may not accept testimony unless both parties are present

I have included these *mitzvot* because I have always believed that justice is a combination of truth and integrity, and it certainly is the foundation of any enlightened civilization. Therefore it falls somewhat within the subject of this chapter.

It is clear that G-d demands justice. But Jewish justice is significantly different from what passes for justice in other societies. We do not judge people; we judge actions. The circumstances of the perpetrator's life matter not. The only thing that matters is what he did. This viewpoint allows for a dispassionate, "blind" system with no lawyers spinning the so-called truth to gullible juries or to the press on the courthouse steps. There are no statements, no pleas for mercy, no sobbing to the judge. Those are all parts of a game in which those with the money to hire a better or more manipulative lawyer win.

In a Jewish court, the defendants and witnesses stand only before a panel of wise men who question them in detail to ascertain the truth. This method precludes our judges from activism and from perverting their opinions for social reasons. It is not uncommon in a Jewish court to see a rich person win a monetary case against someone who is not rich. This is because one's wealth has absolutely no bearing on the truth. The facts of the case are all that matter.

A New Look

Now that I have expounded on some of the ideas inherent in these *mitzvot*, it is worthwhile to reread the list with this new understanding. As you do, keep in mind that G-d wants us to be a warm, loving family wherein each of us has complete trust in His benevolent administration of the world and sincere concern for our fellow Jew. This state of mind allows us to act with perfect integrity. And it allows us to treat others with kindness, generosity and magnanimity. In short, G-d wants each of us to be a great person.

- Love each Jew
- Do not hate another Jew in your heart
- Judge each Jew favorably
- Reprove another who is doing wrong (to dissuade him from continuing)
- Do not embarrass another
- Do not oppress the orphan or the widow
- Do not speak derogatorily of others
- Do not insult or harm another with words, directly or indirectly
- Do not take revenge
- Do not bear a grudge

- Love converts
- Do not cheat a convert (monetarily)
- Do not harm a convert with words

- Fulfill what you say you will do
- Do not break oaths or vows
- Do not testify falsely

- Do not put a "stumbling block before the blind"—i.e., do not give misleading or deceptive advice
- Do not fail to repay a debt

- Do not covet another's possessions (do not pester or press him to give or sell something to you)
- Do not desire another's possessions (in your heart)

- Pay wages on the day they are due
- Do not delay paying the wages
- Allow a hired worker to eat from the crops in the field where he is working
- The hired worker may not eat on hired time
- The worker may not take more than he can eat

- Do not overcharge or underpay for an article
- Return a lost object
- Do not ignore a lost object
- Do not stand idly by if someone's life or possessions are in danger
- Do not rob (forcibly)
- Do not steal (stealthily)
- Return stolen objects
- Ensure that your weights and scales are accurate
- Do not commit injustice with weights and scales
- Do not own inaccurate weights and scales
- Do not move a boundary marker to steal property

- Respect your father and mother
- Fear your mother and father
- Honor those who know and teach the Torah

- Give charity (*tzedekah*)
- Do not withhold charity from the poor
- Leave the edge of your field unharvested for the poor
- Do not harvest it

- Leave the dropped gleanings in the field for the poor
- Do not gather the dropped gleanings
- Leave the forgotten bundles for the poor
- Do not retrieve them
- Leave the edge of your vineyard unharvested for the poor
- Do not harvest it
- Leave the dropped gleanings in the vineyard for the poor
- Do not gather the dropped gleanings
- Leave the unformed clusters of grapes
- Do not pick the unformed clusters

- Lend to the poor
- Do not press someone for payment if you know he cannot pay
- Do not forcibly take collateral
- Return the collateral if the other person needs it
- Do not delay its return
- Do not demand collateral from a widow (even if she is wealthy)
- Do not take, as collateral, utensils that are needed for preparing food
- Do not lend to Jews with interest
- Do not borrow from Jews with interest
- Do not intermediate or be involved at all with an interest-bearing loan to a Jew

- A judge may not pity the attacker
- A judge may not have mercy on the poor
- A judge may not have respect for a great man
- A judge must not have a bias against a repeat offender
- A judge may not pervert justice
- A judge may not pervert justice for an orphan or convert
- A judge may not fear a violent man
- A judge may not accept a bribe
- A judge may not accept testimony unless both parties are present

Chapter Seven

Men and Women

The Poisoned Well

Having demonstrated that G-d requires us to treat our fellows in a kind, generous and ethical manner, it follows logically that the next discussion should be about the most intense, emotional, significant and essential relationship that exists: The relationship between a man and a woman.

Of all the hard-to-discuss subjects, this is undoubtedly the hardest; few topics arouse more passion. Unfortunately, in our modern world, the well from which we drink has been poisoned and the water makes us all sick. So many untrue and distorted definitions enter the conversation that it is hard to have a real discussion about men, women and their relationships without someone misunderstanding, misinterpreting or getting insulted. This situation hurts both men and women.

I intend to shatter every misconception I can. Which means that not only am I going to enter the minefield, but I'm about to run through it full bore.

But as I do I will hew to the path of the Torah and the wise and open-minded reader will discover a brand-new approach to the whole issue. I urge you to leave all opinions, prejudices and biases at the door and sit back and learn about a philosophy and way of life that has produced loving, harmonious family relations for over 3,000 years and continues to do so even in today's modern, dysfunctional society. In fact, many of today's social ills would disappear if the world learned a thing or two from us.

The Torah's approach to men and women and the Western world's approach are not just dissimilar; they are completely different, as disparate as a Mac and a PC. Sure, they kind of look alike, and they're both computers, but there are two different worlds operating inside them. Similarly, Western terms, attitudes and assumptions just do not transfer to the Torah's world.

First we must understand how the whole subject came to be framed as it is, starting with how many of the ideas of Feminism became mainstream and how it has changed the assumptions and the definitions we use. Many women have a knee-jerk defense mechanism that kicks in when someone criticizes the Women's Movement but they also have very little knowledge of its history and philosophy. If this applies to you, I again ask you to be a fearless truth seeker here and look at the subject with complete detachment.

Disagreeing with the underlying philosophies and assumptions of Feminism does not make one a misogynist. Many people, including a great many women, do not subscribe to these beliefs. The Orthodox Jewish world certainly does not. But the reasons why are quite different from the usual labels that are affixed to religious Christians and Moslems—that they are cavemen, that their ideas are medieval and so on. Once the underlying philosophy of feminism is explained, the reasons why millions of women just don't buy into it will be clear.

A Short History of Feminism

In 1949 the French writer Simone de Beauvoir published a book entitled *The Second Sex.* In it she claimed that men and women were not different by nature, but only by history. She argued for a gender-neutral society without any distinctions. Needless to say, at the time her ideas were viewed as extremely radical and were not accepted into the mainstream.

One person who did read *The Second Sex* and later quoted it in her writings was a young Jewish woman from Peoria, Illinois named Betty Goldstein, whom we know by her married name: Betty Friedan. In 1963 she published a book called *The Feminine Mystique,* which launched what came to be known as the Women's Liberation Movement.

In the official version of Friedan's life story, she was a typical suburban housewife who felt that she and other women like her were wasting away by being "just" housewives and she just couldn't take it anymore. She claimed to have come to this conclusion after conducting a survey of her Smith College graduating class, which was prompted by the unhappiness she saw in them at their fifteen-year reunion. In their responses she found her classmates to be suffering deep unease with their lives and senses of loss for their potentials and even their identities.

This story was sold to American women so they would be sympathetic to her views, but the truth was very different. Betty Goldstein was from her college days, and until her mid-30s, a Marxist. She had been a radical and political activist in college and had worked for labor and union publications for ten years after graduation. She had a hostile view of American society even before she entered her marriage, let alone wrote her book.

Throughout Friedan's life she perpetuated the myth that she had no interest in the condition of women prior to the revelation that lead to her book, but this is not true. In fact, she was thoroughly imbued with Marxist philosophy and its view of the world as a struggle between the oppressors and the oppressed. Her marriage was never happy and she accused her husband, Carl—a fellow leftist who shortened his name from Friedman to sound less Jewish—of being physically abusive, but then later recanted. They divorced in 1969 after twenty-two years of marriage. She never remarried. (In 1981, she published a book entitled, "The Second Stage" in which she described her marriage as "self-destructive.")

In *The Feminine Mystique* Friedan simply took the Marxist view of class struggle and substituted women for the masses, the workers and peasants. If one reads her book and substitutes the idea of class for gender, it is easy to see the Marxist influence on her thinking. Women were, in her view, sleeping with the enemy that oppressed them, enslaved them and viewed them with contempt.

These were not original ideas. Marxist doctrine had always been disdainful of the idea of the family seeing it as a construct of the bourgeoisie and tool of the capitalist oppressors. Karl Marx and Friedrich Engels both wrote that sex roles needed to be redefined, divorce be made free and easy, the stigma of illegitimacy be eliminated and unrestrained sexual activity be accepted. They also saw the destruction of the family as the first step in the achievement of their revolutionary goals since it is the family that is the conduit for passing the social, cultural, and religious ideals of the established order on to the next generation.

Friedan's views, as expounded in the book, were the following: Women had bought into the big lie that they would find fulfillment through the lives of their husbands and children and, in doing so had negated their own sense of self and their own identities; what they needed was to be "liberated."

Her description of the lives of women was savage. She disparaged housework, which she stated was only for feeble-minded girls and eight-year-olds, and referred to the home as a "comfortable concentration camp"—strong words coming from a Jew only twenty-two years after the Holocaust. That she would use such a term before the ovens were even cold reveals a great deal about her.

The only way a woman could know herself, Friedan proposed, was through "creative work", implying that raising children and caring for a husband and family was somehow not creative and that a career outside the home was the only path to an identity and self fulfillment. In her world-view, a stay-at-home mother could never feel fulfilled. She also disparaged femininity as weakness, citing it as a male creation that was imposed upon women and which holds them captive in a second-class status.

If one looks at the Women's Movement with complete detachment, it is easy to see that it is not a general movement for the betterment of all women; it is a narrow ideology that promotes a specific vision of society. And just like all movements of the left, it meant to shatter traditional society, in this case the roles of men and women as well as sexuality and family.

What Friedan did not know or did not want to know was that if she had queried men, she would have found the same existential problems—this was, after all, the era of "The Man in the Gray-Flannel Suit." Society in the 1950s was undergoing great changes and there is no doubt that anyone without spiritual goals and activities was going to feel a little lost.

First, society was changing from an urban to a suburban culture; in the cities, women lived in close proximity to each other in apartment build-ings and socialized in neighborhood parks and on main avenues. In the suburbs, with fewer people and homes set farther apart, women felt more isolated. They might have used the telephone but that is very different from being surrounded by warm bodies.

In addition, technology had freed up a great deal of a woman's day. With the advent of in-home washing machines, a woman could just throw in a load and come back later to take it out, which was not the same as spend-ing time with her friends at the laundromat or in the apartment building's laundry room. Vacuum cleaners meant that homes could be cleaned in much less time and refrigerators meant that women did not need to go to the market as often. Suddenly, women had a lot of free time and they were spending more and more of it by themselves.

Nor was there anything very meaningful to fill the time. Mindless activities such as car pools, unique to suburbia since city children walked to school or rode public transportation, and errands that required more time since a woman had to drive to many different locations rather than just go to the avenue, only made the situation worse. Women did not feel as vital to the lives of their families as they once did and therefore felt real emptiness. But Friedan's suggestion that women assume men's roles and personalities in order to attain fulfillment was not the solution.

Very quickly, the radical roots of the Women's Movement came into full view. Certain terms and attitudes entered the discourse. Sexual differ-ences meant inequality. Marriage was a jail sentence, home life was hell, marital sex was forced rape, children were millstones around the neck, and femininity was a weakness that allowed women to become entrapped in the bonds of marriage.

The inevitable result was a spewing of hatred for marriage, family and children that seeped into the culture through the arts and entertainment. The desire to be a loving, nurturing mother whose primary interest in life was to care for her family was portrayed as stupidity and weakness. Today, it is generally accepted, even by those who would not define themselves as feminists, that a woman who aspires only to that is considered to be wasting her potential. Why would an intelligent woman want to devote her life to her family when she could become a doctor or an engineer or *something*? In other words, being a wife and mother is not being "something." However the woman who foregoes a family to devote herself to her career is never considered to have wasted anything, let alone her potential.

As a result of the Women's Movement Friedan launched and the fawning adoration it received from the liberal media, there are three givens that frame the discussion:

1. Besides anatomy, men and women are no different
2. Men have always oppressed and subjugated women
3. Women can only find fulfillment outside of their homes and families

But all of this is utter nonsense. Friedan's rewriting of history as a gender struggle was just as incorrect and concocted as Karl Marx's making everything about class struggle. And the idea that a woman can *only* find fulfillment outside of home and family is belied by millions of women's own experiences.

But it didn't matter. The pursuit of gender "equality" quickly became the mantra of enlightened society and the goal of legislation, lobbying and social agitation. Henceforth, the goal would be to ensure that women had access to the same professions and opportunities as men. Of course, this all implied that men had it better than women and that to be a real person, a woman had to live and act like a man. Young women were told, in essence, to emulate their fathers and not their mothers.

But the hard truth is that men and women not only are not the same, but they have almost no similarities. In fact, if you had to explain the characteristics of a man and a woman to someone who had no prior knowledge of either, he would probably conclude that you were describing two different species. It is clear that men and women have different interests and values; they react to different stimuli and react differently to the same stimuli. Of course, each human being is unique and many of the distinctions between the genders do not apply in every case, but there are certainly generalities that are hard to deny.

In fact, many of our distinctions have been clinically proven. Women have been proven to have better hearing and more sensitivity to taste and smell. Men, on the other hand, have keener eyesight and are better able to detect movement in their field of vision. Women are stronger in almost all aspects of speech and communication; men are physically stronger. Women have also proven better at interpreting nonverbal communication such as gestures, facial expressions and tones of voice. They have a greater ability to look at photographs and view videos without sound and intuit how the subjects are feeling.

Men are more abstract in their thinking and much stronger in spatial thinking, such as rotating three-dimensional objects in their minds; women are more practical and people-oriented. For example, a man approaches an accident scene and asks himself, "What happened here?"—an abstract question. A woman's first thought is concern for the people involved

Men and women also interact with the world differently. Men are more aggressive in behavior, woman more conciliatory. Women have been shown to have more moderate physiological reactions to stress; heart disease strikes men at younger ages. Men naturally organize themselves into rigid, hierarchal structures and are more analytical while women are more intuitive and prefer operating by consensus through open and free-flowing interaction.

Most of this research has only been conducted over the last twenty years because before that it had been taboo in the scientific community to investigate the idea of natural differences between the sexes. This academic censorship protected the dogma that there were no differences. Feminists feared that if real differences were discovered, it would be used against women's struggle for "equality", but by the 1980s this fear was no longer strong enough to prevent some scientists from pursuing the legitimate study of the brains of men and women. And once that began, very real differences were discovered.

Other changes to society soon followed. Men were discouraged from acting like gentlemen because that type of behavior implied that women were weak or incapable. Why should they have been polite when women were perfectly capable of opening their own doors or pulling out their own chairs? Once, men had been taught to offer their seats on buses or trains to women, but this is no longer taught and rarely practiced.

To further complicate matters, women were encouraged to take jobs that required a great deal of testosterone. Today we see women as soldiers, state troopers, weight lifters, construction workers and even boxers. It is *de rigueur* to see knockdown fistfights between men and women in all types of entertainment. (I'm not sure why watching a man hit a woman the way Ali hit Frazier is entertaining, but I believe that this phenomenon has a lot to do with the increase in domestic violence.)

The dogma that women are suppressed and need liberation and equality continues to be hailed as absolute truth in the media and on university campuses. "Inequality" in every form must end, we are told. The idea of women in combat units is a perfect example of this myopia. Despite the overwhelming evidence that women in army units undermine efficiency and discipline, and despite the official opposition of the armed forces, many still push to allow them into combat. The facts that women do not have the same physical strength and cannot be relied upon for digging bunkers, hauling gear, marching long distances, scaling barriers or carrying weaponry are ignored. Tests that highlight these differences are scrapped or altered to avoid the obvious conclusion.

The muddling of gender roles has created a litany of social problems, including:

- **The crisis of single women**. The more intelligent or successful the woman, the harder time she has finding a mate. Feminists will ascribe this problem to fragile male egos that see independent women as too threatening. Female power, they say, is a turn off because men want soft, malleable women.

  There is only one big hole in this self-serving explanation: A generation ago, intelligent, successful women did get married. That was because they were partners in their relationships, not competitors. The crisis of single women only developed after they were "liberated" and gained "equality"; only then did they find that men are not interested in "intelligent, successful" women and this is because a man does not want to marry a woman who thinks and acts like a man. He finds that very unattractive. What he wants and needs is someone who will complement his strengths with her own. He would prefer that she not be needed to provide for the family; he wants her to nurture and raise the family for which he will provide. Men are not interested in women who want to mimic them, but it has nothing to do with control or superiority; it has everything to do with not seeing femininity as weakness.

Part of the problem is that it is fashionable to mock men as dumb, insensitive, immature and unnecessary. This image pervades mainstream entertainment, where mothers or women are portrayed as all-wise and the fathers or men as overgrown children. This does not encourage men to commit to a relationship.

- **The social pressure on women to act in a morally loose way**. The feminist mindset requires women to abandon their natural approaches to sex and adopt the male approach, which is to view sex in a casual and promiscuous way. This calamitous idea has succeeded fabulously in destroying the lives of a great many women because it ignores three truths: Women are more prone to suffer emotionally from sexual encounters, are more susceptible to venereal diseases and, of course, it is women that get pregnant. What the feminists succeeded in doing was throwing meat to the wolves. Sexual freedom for a woman is not self-discovery. The more women imitate men sexually, the more pain they experience. One very telling fact in all of this is that, in a world where you can find a study to bolster any conceivable opinion or viewpoint, there are no studies—not one—that shows that sexually active girls are either happier, more fulfilled, more content or possessing better self-images than their inactive counterparts. In fact, all studies show the contrary. But women should have seen the problem right away. If Hugh Hefner was agreeing with the feminists and encouraging sexual freedom, someone should have seen the red flags. This is why what became known as the "Sexual Revolution" was so quick and bloodless. There was real no opposition. The Women's Movement endorsed it as part of liberation and equality.

And men wanted it because—why not? Men are game for anything sexual and if women wanted to shed their Victorian hang-ups about things like modesty, virginity and virtue, well, who were they to object? Men definitely believed that it made their own lives better.

- **The psychological pressure on young women.** The shapers of opinion in today's society—the media and academia—continue to churn out the upside-down message that the good girl is repressed and the bad girl is empowered and liberated. They instruct young women that being modern means being sexually assertive and active and that all women throughout history were repressed since they could not act out sexually. This indoctrination begins at a very early age as girls absorb the images and innuendos that saturate modern entertainment. But it explodes as they enter college. Colleges, with coed dorms and bathrooms, are breeding grounds for anxiety and depression for many young girls. They are thrown into an environment run by people on the far-left fringe of society, which encourages license and experimentation. University health departments are faced with hordes of young women suffering from depression and other psychological problems stemming from their sexual decisions. These same university health departments will schedule abortions, hand out birth control and prescribe medications for venereal diseases but never utter a word of advice to these young women about perhaps conducting themselves differently. Think of how crazy this sounds: A young woman who abstains from unhealthy food, smoking, drinking and drugs will be described as mature, sensitive, health-conscious and responsible. But if she abstains from sex she is simply "not sexually active" or worse, repressed or prudish. There is no praise for her abstention. How could there be? If that is praiseworthy it follows that the activity from which she abstains might be wrong or bad for her. Doctors will urge low-fat diets and exercise; pediatricians recommend bicycle helmets and healthy snacks. Drugs and alcohol are discouraged in every public service ad aimed at teenagers. And smoking is public enemy number one. But doctors or public health officials cannot counsel abstinence.

- **The collapse of the institution of marriage.** It's not coincidental that the divorce rate surged after the Women's "Liberation" movement found acceptance. If marriage is bondage, it logically follows that not being married is liberation. Why else would someone advise a young man or woman to have some "fun" before settling down? This, of course, implies that marriage is not fun or enjoyable. Why rush into a situation that will tie a person down and restrict hedonistic pleasure for the rest of one's life?

  However women seem to suffer much more from this "freedom" than do men. There is a phenomenon known as "the feminization of poverty"—women, and especially single mothers, are disproportionately represented below the poverty line. Moreover, fatherless families are a sociological disaster. Every single study done on the subject proves that children do overwhelmingly better in homes with fathers. They are less likely to get involved in drugs and alcohol, become teen parents, drop out of school, get involved with crime or be poor later in life. A man provides order and structure which is essential for character development. There is a very basic message in marriage—*I am not the most important person in the universe.* Simply living together without being married does not provide that message to children and actually reinforces negative traits since there is no real commitment. Boys who grow up in fatherless homes rarely learn the discipline and self-negation needed to function as the head of a family.

- **Women's increasingly common discovery, once way down the path of life, that they might have taken a wrong turn.** They are coming around to the fact that a career is just not that fulfilling and that the empty pursuit of success took a heavy toll. Either they are in their late thirties and facing a biological deadline that they were previously too busy to notice or they have children but now realize that by dropping them off at daycare during their formative years, they missed out on their greatest pleasure. The children certainly didn't gain anything. Working women know that is impossible to be a great mother and a great career woman. You can juggle them both but you cannot excel at both. And careers always seem to win, and children always seem to lose.

Feminism, by denying the inherent differences (read: strengths and weaknesses) between men and women, strips both of their value. It promotes a disdain of femininity among women and the adoption of masculine attributes. In reality there is no greater disparagement of women than this—to imply they have no worth unless they mimic men. In such a situation, no one really wins.

For forty years women have been absorbing these messages, which are untrue and diametrically opposed to a woman's true nature, and this has caused great stress and confusion. Women intuit that there is a great difference between what men and women want in life but are afraid that if they come out and say it, they will be confessing to being shallow and inferior.

Why should that be the case? As I once read a (female) psychology professor describe it, "There are things that men, on average, excel at and things that women, on average, excel at. But the fact that there are differences doesn't mean one is good and one is bad or that there's a winner or a loser."

As a result of this confusion, there is a vast disconnect between what women profess to believe and their actions. On one hand many women will mouth the party line that they are no different than men even though they don't really believe it or live that way. On the other hand discussions with women often reveal huge gaps between what they claim are their priorities and what they are doing with their lives.

However, many women never bought into this philosophy. They never believed that men were superior or had it better. In fact, I have never met a woman who truly would want to be a man if given the choice. Women generally see men as animalistic, shallow, out of touch, unemotional, uncaring and uninterested in what's important. They don't understand why, when a group of men get together, they need to posture and one-up each other.

They don't even see men as having conversations since, in a woman's mind, men aren't even listening to each other anyway, but just waiting for one to stop talking so another can give his opinion.

Most women do not envy anything about a man's life. They are not enamored of the idea of having to spend their days in office buildings, shops or factories and don't see the glamour of the daily grind. They clearly see the toll that the exhausting drudgery takes on their husbands and appreciate their sacrifices. The reason why the cliché arose about the man coming home from work and wanting a drink before collapsing into an easy chair to watch TV is that most men spend their days in efforts that are only meaningful in their outcomes. In other words, they are toiling to provide for their families but, with few exceptions, it doesn't really matter what they do as long as it pays. This fellow is a lawyer and this one owns shoe stores and this one is a claims adjuster. Who cares? No one lays on his deathbed and thinks about his job.

In a way, a woman's life is more directly satisfying because everything she does on behalf of her family has meaning and at the end of each day she can take pleasure and spiritual satisfaction in what she did. A man who sells plate glass or trades municipal bonds cannot.

The Orthodox Jewish approach to the whole subject is radically different from this radical orthodoxy (every pun intended). There is no concept of sexism. Concepts like equal rights, liberation, discrimination, equality and oppression have no translations in a Torah life because they are untrue and the Torah only deals with truth and reality. Women are not considered inferior or second-class citizens, nor do they feel they are treated that way. They do not consider themselves exploited or subjugated, so they don't have the anti-male biases that underlie such terms. Orthodox women do not and have never lacked spiritual fulfillment and they have never harbored feelings of doubt about their own value and worth, not even in today's modern world. They never felt enslaved and therefore never felt the need to be liberated. They never felt unequal, and therefore never felt the need to fight for equality. They never saw careers as fulfilling any real yearning and therefore never felt the need to agitate for them. In fact, they saw careers as taking them away from where they were crucially needed and from where their true happiness and fulfillment came.

This understanding should explain why feminism is an unwelcome stranger in a Jewish home. Orthodox women view their feminist sisters with bewilderment and a little sadness because they see that those women are at war with themselves. Feminism arose because women did not feel fulfilled in life and felt their efforts, talents and achievements were unappreciated.

Orthodox Jewish women, on the other hand, know they are appreciated by their husbands, their children and their society and, most importantly, they know their efforts are appreciated by G-d.

Adam and Chava (Eve)

The Torah's account of creation sheds a great deal of light on the true nature of men and women and what they should mean to each other.

When G-d originally created Adam, he was created as one being comprised of both a male and female aspect. Had nothing changed, he would have been able to reproduce by himself without a partner. Only Adam was created like that; the rest of the animal kingdom was created as males and females. Once Adam saw that all of creation had these counterparts, he desired to have one as well. And at that point, G-d removed half of Adam (a "side" in Hebrew, not a rib as it is usually translated) and using this as a base, built Chava.

This account raises many obvious questions. Why did G-d not create human beings as male and female at the outset? Why did He wait until Adam desired a mate to create one for him? Why did Adam desire it? What was he missing? And once Adam desired a mate, why didn't G-d pair him up with one of the animals that were already created? Or create a whole new being for him? Why did He need to take part of Adam? And, why didn't He make the second being identical to the first?

The answer to all of these questions lies in the purpose of life itself: We are here to create ourselves by emulating G-d in order to draw close to Him. If men and women did not need one another, we could very easily begin to feel that we are completely independent, which would lead us away from G-d, not towards Him. Had G-d left us in that state, His purpose in creation would never have been realized.

So why did Adam desire a mate once he saw that the rest of creation lived in pairs? It's hard to imagine Adam, who was created by the hand of G-d and lived in *Gan Eden*, being jealous of a giraffe or a squirrel. No, what he saw was that all of G-d's creations had interactive relationships, each giving to and caring for the other, and that he was alone. To emulate G-d and to fulfill his purpose, he needed to be a giver, but he had no one to give to. Once he realized that, he longed for a mate.

What was missing from the selection of animals before him that he could not find a mate? When G-d created man he gave him dominion over the "fish of the sea, the birds of the sky and every living thing that moves on the earth" (Gen. 1:28). A relationship with a subordinate being would not be a real one; to achieve its purpose the relationship between a man and a woman must be of mutual benefit. Each party must be able to develop an emotional intimacy with the other and be able to give to the other in a substantial way. This can only be done amongst peers.

This fact also alludes to the position of women in Jewish thought. Chava is not subordinate—why would G-d create a subordinate being for Adam after he had rejected all the animals for that very reason? Also, Chava was not created from his back or his foot. She was created from his side; therefore her place is at his side.

Now that we understand why human beings need a mate, why did G-d not create man from the outset as two beings? Because, again, that relationship would not fulfill G-d's intention for us. Our freewill requires that we choose our path, not have it thrust upon us. Adam had to consciously want a mate in order for him to be able to fulfill his purpose.

So once Adam desired a mate, why did G-d not just create a female from the earth in the same way He had made Adam? Because the female side had already been created—it was part of Adam, who was not considered male until his female side was removed. (Before Chava's creation, the Torah actually refers to Adam in the plural.) Had another being been created anew, Adam would still have viewed himself as an entirely autonomous being and could have fallen prey to the same problems he would have had had he stayed alone. By splitting Adam in two, G-d demonstrated that both men and women are incomplete and that we need the other half in order to be whole, that we are mutually dependent. This is why there are only two genders, not three or four or even more: The purpose is achieved with two.

This knowledge of our incompleteness is fundamental to understanding life. That is why the Torah goes to lengths to describe the creation of male and female but makes no mention of skin color, hair color or height and weight—because they are not important. For the same reason, it does not describe the creation of male and female in the animal kingdom.

Lastly, G-d created the female wholly unlike the male in order to force each of us to be true givers—i.e., to be sensitive to one another's needs. If man and woman were identical, the relationship would require almost no effort and neither would be much of a giver.

Judaism considers a single person to be incomplete: A man without a woman is only half a person and a woman without a man is only half a person. Alone, neither are able to reach the heights for which they were created. Without a good relationship with the other, neither are able to lead a full, happy life or have inner peace. The underlying truth is that each of us is one being that has been torn in half, and I mean that literally; the Torah goes out of its way to mention that G-d had to close up Adam's wound after taking the side of him that would form the foundation of Chava. It seems there was a gaping hole that would have killed him if not for the surgery.

Further, the Talmud states that ever since G-d took the side from Adam, man has been pursuing it. Obviously we need it, which explains why a man can be lonely in a crowd and yet at peace once he has a woman in his life. A man's loneliness is not satisfied by a group of friends because G-d didn't create a friend for Adam, he created a mate. Without her, he is always alone and always missing something, regardless of the size of the party.

One of the most unique aspects of human relations is that we each expect to find a soul mate for life. Imagine being told by a couple that they are getting married but for only three years, and then they'll be splitting up to go their separate ways, or asking a woman to marry you for a specific number of years. Imagine responding to your friend's excited announcement of her engagement with the question, "How long do you guys plan to stay married?"

Since marriage is basically a reattaching of a part of ourselves, our natural attitude towards it is the same we have towards any part of ourselves: We intend to keep it forever. Given the choice, each of us would always prefer to keep all of our body parts, even our tonsils and appendix. (There is no prohibition of divorce in Judaism but it is supposed to be an option of last resort. It is a tragedy when a family breaks up and so the option of divorce is usually exercised only in really unsustainable situations.)

Animals, however, do not share this attitude because their males and females were created separately, as separate beings. They were not created originally as one and then divided. For them, mating is simply a way to perpetuate the species, nothing more. They do not find lifelong relationships; they find breeding partners.

The Real Definition of the Relationship

While it is clear that men and women are different, it is not as clear that we are actually the inverse of each other.

In general terms, the man lives an external life and the woman an internal life. This means that a man's interests, way of thinking, and approach to almost everything is "outside" while a woman's interests, way of thinking, and approach to almost everything is "inside."

A man's way of life is to go "out into the world." Regardless of what he does for a living he still conquers, hunts, overcomes and strives. Men are constantly ambitious and perpetually dissatisfied. There is never enough; there is always more. Men are not happy unless they are striving. In situations where they cannot strive, they will become disinterested and withdrawn. It is women who seek contentment; men don't want it and they find it suffocating. A man must succeed to feel alive. And even though striving may often lead to failures, these failures are good for men because through them they learn how to pick themselves up and persevere. Teaching boys to avoid risk is to emasculate them. And this frame of mind does not just affect a man's approach to making a living; he will think and act this way in everything he does, even in his leisure activities.

There is no better way to illustrate this point than to use the "man with a remote" cliché. A woman is content to search until she finds a program she likes and stay with it even through the commercials, but a man feels compelled to surf the entire menu of choices until he can narrow it down to only two or three programs that he will watch that hour. And if, by cruel fate, all of those channels run commercials at the same time and he doesn't need to use the bathroom or replenish his snacks, he will use the break to check out "just a few" other channels.

Why is it that the overwhelming majority of history's explorers and discoverers have been men? It has nothing to do with the feminist accusation that men have dominated society and suppressed women. It's just that if you ask most women if they would like to go on an expedition to an unknown place and mention that they might not return alive, they will most likely look at you as if you were crazy.

Even today, when women have access to any profession, the leaders in all fields are predominantly men. This has nothing to do with intelligence. Women are just as smart as men. It has to do with the difference in the natures of men and women and their different needs. A man is simply not content with a comfortable, familiar life. He needs to explore, tinker, experiment, examine, probe, test and investigate. A woman might enjoy this as well but for her it is an activity, not an existential need. A man's mind is always "out there"—for better or worse.

A woman's life revolves around relationships, which are basically inner connections with other people. To a man, relationships are much less important. A man can actually have a long conversation with another man without knowing his name. This external/internal dichotomy explains other phenomena:

- Men speak more in public and less in private and women do the opposite. For a man, conversation has much less to do with creating relationships and much more to do with accomplishing a goal. Women will speak more in private because that is where relationships are made.
- Men judge people and things from the outside, women from the inside. This is why pornography is a male vice and not a female one. Women, in general, are much less judgmental about a man's physical appearance than men are about a woman's.
- Women want to be mysterious to men because it acknowledges the existence of a private, inner world that men cannot see. Men have no need or desire to be mysterious and think it's weird even to talk about it. They also have no means to truly understand a woman's inner world. (Men don't understand women and they know it; women don't understand men but think they do.)
- Men work from the outside in while women work from the inside out. For example, a man needs to do good to feel good; his self-image is tied to what he does. A woman needs to feel good to do good; her actions are a reflection of what is happening inside her.
- Women make up the majority of library patrons and books buyers while men prefer to go to the movies or watch TV. Books create an inner world that TV and movies do not.
- Women's mental disorders—depression, eating disorders and self-mutilation—tend to focus inward while men's tend to manifest themselves in anti-social behavior, such as alcoholism and violence.

By understanding this concept, it is easy to see how each complements the other in ways that cannot be done by a proxy. Since there is no way for either a man or a woman to thrive without the other, it is apparent that the

Torah could in no way use the words *superior, inferior* or *equal* with regard to the genders. Each is unique but vital to the success of the other and each has superiorities and inferiorities when compared to the other.

Without a woman to anchor him, a man will travel through life going from point to point until his life eventually ends. He will have no safe harbor from which to evaluate his journey or his options for the future. He will have no system of checks and balances. Without a woman he can wind up almost anywhere, his final destination the result of a string of happenings or a convergence of coincidences. He could easily finish his life confused as to how he got there.

A woman without a man is more stable and more grounded, but her world will not expand past a certain limit. It is man's abstract mind that pushes the boundaries not only of knowledge, science and exploration but of everyday life. Most big innovations and changes in life are usually made or initiated by men.

There are many types of relationships where the partners are dissimilar yet each is an essential member of the team and crucial to its success. Take a business partnership as an example. One partner is the salesman and the rainmaker, the other is the operations man who runs the business and takes care of all of its financial aspects. Which is more important? The question is not really a question—neither is more important, each is needed in his own way. Without one, the other would not succeed.

Similarly, in a soccer game, who is more important, the forward or the goalie? Try playing without one of them and see how well your team does. What about an army and its various positions? Which one is dispensable? Or in a stage production, who is more important, the lighting man, the soundman, the actor or the set designer? Which is the more important part of an automobile, the chassis or the engine?

A man and a woman, both created by G-d with their unique qualities, are two halves of a whole. They need each other and cannot thrive without the other. They complement and complete each other. The concepts and terms introduced into modern society only do damage to the relationship.

Spiritual Advantage

A woman's inner life gives her the distinct advantage in the realm of inherent spirituality. Since she is oriented inward, she is more in touch with her soul and with spiritual truths. The rabbis explain that a woman possesses greater spirituality because she was not created from the earth, as were man and the other animals. She was created from a part of an already-formed being, meaning that she started a step higher off the ground.

In fact, women are considered to be born already completed; they need no "fixing." Men, however, are born with an impurity that needs to be cut off—a foreskin. This teaches us that generally, men need to work harder on their spirituality than do women, for whom it is more natural.

The Torah repeatedly stresses the greatness of women in this regard and the eternal debt of gratitude the Jewish people have towards them for their actions in many historical crises. The Talmud and Midrashim are full of examples. Some of the more well known are:

- Sarah was a greater prophet than Avraham and was correct about the bad influence of Yishmael (Ishmael). G-d himself told Avraham that she was right and that Yishmael had to go.
- Rivkah (Rebecca) saw the truth about Eisav (Esau) when Yitzchak (Isaac) did not, and forced Yaakov (Jacob) to take the blessing Yitzchak was planning to give to Eisav (which would have been disastrous for the Jewish people).
- When the Egyptians began killing Jewish male babies during our bondage, the Jewish leaders decreed that men should separate from their wives lest they become pregnant, which would only result in infanticide. Miriam, the sister of Moshe and Aharon and the daughter of the pre-eminent Jewish leader at the time, Amram, argued with her father that while the Egyptians were killing boys, the decree was also preventing Jewish girls from being born, therefore furthering Pharaoh's evil designs. He agreed and the decree was reversed.
- During the era of the Egyptian bondage, the Jewish men would return home broken from the sadistic physical labor and torment the Egyptians put them through. As a result, the number of births dropped dramatically. The women realized that the future of the nation was at stake and made extra efforts to entice their husbands so that there would be a next generation. The Talmud states that the Jews were redeemed from Egypt in the merit of these women. In addition, the Talmud states that the future redemption, which

will come during the Era of the Messiah, will be due to the righteousness of the women.

- When the Jews built the Golden Calf, the women absolutely refused to participate, even refusing to contribute gold. The Golden Calf was built entirely of the men's gold.
- When the twelve spies returned from reconnoitering the Land of Israel with a negative assessment of their chances of conquering it, the men became distraught. The women, however, did not give the report any credence and remained one-hundred-percent confident in G-d.

This inherent spirituality provides women with a deeper sense of understanding. The Talmud, very wisely, repeatedly advises men to value and give deference to their wife's counsel.

Tzniut

The combination of a woman's inherent spiritually and her inner-oriented view of life strongly affects the way she presents herself to the outside world.

A common question is why Orthodox women wear the type of clothing they do. Why the long sleeves and long skirts in the summer? Why the head coverings?

These are very legitimate questions but, again, it is important not to see this issue through Moslem eyes. Our women don't wear *burkas* or veils. Orthodox women are free to wear the latest styles, wear makeup, paint their nails and walk the streets as human beings on a par with any man. We don't have police units that beat women if they show their ankles (as they do in Afghanistan), nor do we force young girls back into a burning building to die rather than allow them into the street without the proper attire (as happened in Saudi Arabia).

In fact, Jewish law does not require a woman to cover her face because this infringes on her dignity. In Hebrew the word for face—*panim*—and the word for inside—*p'nim*—share the same root. To require that a woman's face be covered is, in a sense, to deny her existence.

Unfortunately, due to the onerous and sometimes cruel dress codes practiced by other nations, Orthodox women are also seen as victims of

a) a dress code that b) is entirely for women and c) is imposed on them by men so that men will not be tempted. But this is wrong, wrong and wrong. It is not just a dress code. It applies equally to men and women. And its purpose is not simply to keep the beasts at bay. It is maddeningly ironic that Orthodox Judaism is called sexist by those who live in a society wherein women are commoditized and their bodies used to sell everything from chewing gum to motorcycles.

Let's recognize a fact—we all practice some sort of dress code. We intuitively understand that all modes of dress are not appropriate in all situations—which is why we get more dressed up for weddings and holidays than for the usual workday. The same woman who feels beautiful in a bathing suit at the beach would feel very uncomfortable walking down a city street wearing it. If you went to see a doctor and he met you in cut-offs and a tie-dyed T-shirt, would you feel comfortable having him perform open-heart surgery on you? Women are advised to wear certain types of clothing to job interviews in order to be considered seriously. Many restaurants and retail establishments require shirts and shoes in order to be admitted.

Traditionally, the more important a person was, the more elaborate the clothing; the less important the person, the more plain the clothing. Hence kings and queens were enrobed in velvet and ermine while the farmer and the worker toiled in simple garb. Today designer labels determine a garment's values and, by a perverted extension, the value of the person wearing it. (This explains why, very often, the poor and minorities insist on wearing name brands and labels. It is artificial self-esteem.)

Dress matters because it is how we present ourselves to the outside world. This rule would apply to all areas of deportment, including combed hair, a clean face and a pleasant scent (or at least a lack of odor). The way people present themselves to the world defines the way they view themselves. And since looks set the first impression, they are usually the basis for how we evaluate a person.

The manner of Orthodox dress is part of a concept called *tzniut*, a Hebrew word most commonly translated as "modesty," and it is a much deeper concept than simply a dress code. *Tzniut* is a state of mind that manifests itself in outward behavior. The true definition of *tzniut* is a manner of behavior that does not involve grabbing attention or imposing oneself on others. The prophet Micha (Micah) urges every Jew to "walk with *tzniut* before G-d." In the Talmud, men who acted with reserve and a lack of brazenness were described as having *tzniut*.

Tzniut means acting in an unassuming way and without presumption and boastfulness. People who conduct themselves in such a manner demonstrate a very strong self-image and true inner strength because they know that their worth is not dependent on how they affect others. Shallow waters make noise; deep waters do not.

Tzniut is comprised of two aspects. The first is the recognition of the ludicrousness of arrogance. Since everything we have, including life itself, is a gift, what exactly are we being arrogant about? Every strength, talent, ability and opportunity is a gift, as is every morsel of food, every breath, every idea and every success. How can a person who is constantly receiving blessings feel arrogant about what he receives? How can people with good looks, brains, physical strength, wealth or charisma flaunt their gifts and aggrandize themselves because of them? It's ridiculous.

The second aspect is the recognition that one cannot be focused on both the external (the body) and the internal (the soul). The Torah tells us not to focus on the body, which is temporary and will soon be dropped into a grave, but rather on the soul, which is eternal and meaningful. Therefore, both men and women are charged with conducting themselves with a certain deportment in order to focus their minds and their efforts correctly.

How this applies to men and women differs because of their inherent differences. For Orthodox men this has little bearing on their manner of dress because a lack of clothing does not get them attention. However, there are still applications. Orthodox men do not wear undershirts or tank tops on the street, nor do they wear their shirts open to the navel in order to demonstrate to passersby that yes, they do have chest hair. You will never see an Orthodox man go shirtless.

There is also a strong requirement for men to act humbly. They should not flaunt their wealth, good fortune or power. A man who dresses in an ostentatious way, drives needlessly expensive cars and wears outrageously priced designer clothes is not acting with the proper *tzniut*. A boastful man is not walking humbly before G-d.

For a woman, dress takes on a larger importance because she can easily assert herself by exposing herself. Because exposed skin has a profound effect on men, it is very easy for a woman to get attention and even affection by wearing (or not wearing) certain styles of clothing. But this is the wrong type of attention, and it is not real affection. If a woman does not have a healthy self-image and needs acceptance or approval, she will first turn to her looks to get attention. A woman who is not dressed properly will always get attention that is absolutely disproportionate to her real value.

There is no doubt that the specifics of a woman's modest manner of dressing take into consideration the overactive male libido. However, if the only point of *tzniut* were to eliminate men's temptation, a Jewish woman would look like her Arab counterparts. And this is obviously not the case. Orthodox women are not required to cover their faces, hands, forearms or calves, all of which could be erogenous. A man can be a sucker for a pretty face and can make himself sick with infatuation to the point of not functioning, but that is his problem, not the woman's.

There is a fine line between wanting to look good as a reflection of self-esteem and the need to look good in order to gain the approval of others. The Torah instructs Jewish women to carry themselves with dignity and self-respect. This means clean clothes and a clean body. It also means dressing in a manner that will not be debasing but rather in a way that states, "I am valuable."

Truly important women do not go about scantily dressed and women who habitually wear flirtatious clothing are not taken seriously. That is because by emphasizing their bodies, they announce that they do not take themselves seriously.

The emphasis on the superficial sells women short and this is not what G-d wants. Women are no less important in His eyes than men, and He wants a woman to develop a sense of self as a being created in His image. He does not want women to act in ways that debase them and reduce them to objects.

The Torah loudly declares for all to hear that a woman is not the merely the sum of her hair, face and figure. Instead, it requires her to dress in a manner that will safeguard her integrity and self-esteem. From the time she is little, an Orthodox girl is taught that she has an inherent value independent of her looks or what others, especially the opposite sex, think of them. In an Orthodox Jewish society, there is no pressure on women to act or dress in an inappropriate manner. Girls growing up in this environment do not experience the crushing pressure that literally mutilates the self-image of so many young girls today. Instead, their role models are spiritual and righteous women, not entertainers who dress like streetwalkers.

There is something fascinating about clothing: It is only for humans. Of all the species on Earth, only man clothes himself; no other species even considers it. Why do we wear clothing at all?

The answer is found in the Torah, in the account of Adam and Chava's mistake in *Gan Eden*. Initially they were naked and unashamed—until they ate from the Tree of Knowledge of Good and Evil and their bodies were no longer in harmony with their souls. Once the body was acting independently of the soul, it had to be reined in and controlled. By covering the body with clothing, we de-emphasize it and remove the lures that arouse its passions. It's as if we lock it away and only take it out at certain times. Human beings wear clothes because they have souls. If you don't have a soul, there is no need to cover up the animal side.

G-d himself made the first sets of clothing and gave them to Adam and Chava (Gen. 3:21). Ever since then, clothing has held deep meaning. The more civilized the society, the more covering; the less civilized, the less covering. There is an intuitive understanding that the more we expose our flesh, the more animalistic we are behaving.

Therefore, Orthodox Jews do not expose themselves in the summer months any more than they do in the winter months. Is it hot in the summer? Sure, but until the 1960s almost everyone dressed in a somewhat modest fashion. Look at old photos from the turn of the century and you'll see people at the beach fully clothed. As late as the 1950s men went to baseball games in jackets, ties and hats. And most homes and apartments were not air conditioned.

Society underwent a sea change after the Woodstock Nation began disrobing in public. It makes perfect sense that they would want to shed their clothing—the more one indulges his animal passions, the more he will come to identify himself with those passions. After a time, he will see himself as just a different type of animal rather than a being created in G-d's image. And animals don't wear clothing. Public nakedness de-emphasizes the spirituality of life and since it is in our spirituality that we are "in the image of G-d," it behooves us to strengthen that part of our existence and weaken the part that contradicts it. A physically oriented life, a life focused on food, sex and money, is neither elevated nor inspiring.

A woman's hair also falls under the laws of *tzniut*. Once she is married, she is required to cover her hair; to fully understand the reasoning behind this, we have to understand some deeper ideas about hair and the ways we relate to it, specifically the hair on one's head.

Hair is an unusual part of the human body. While we share this characteristic with all other mammals, only on human beings is hair completely superfluous. If we didn't have hair, it wouldn't have any detrimental effect on us. Many people are naturally bald or shave their heads or suffer from alopecia. Competitive swimmers remove all their body hair to reduce drag. Men from the Far East are almost hairless, while Mediterranean men are known for being hirsute and love their bushy chests. Still, aside from aesthetics, there is no benefit or detriment either way.

Another quality specific to human beings is that the hair on our heads continues to grow and requires trimming. On all other mammals head hair is no different than the hair on any other part of the body, it grows in and once fully grown, it stops.

In Jewish thought, the brain is considered the highest and most important organ because it both houses the soul and is the residence of the mind. Ironically, surrounding the skull which protects this most vital organ is the most superfluous part of the human body and the part that represents the wild animal: the hair. In fact, when society starts to loosen its morals (or has none), hair is always the first indication. It gets longer and freer, almost as if how things look on the outside of the head indicate what is happening on the inside.

A person's hairstyle will reflect his or her attitudes and lifestyle. For men, short hair is a sign of discipline; long hair a marker of rebellion and the rejection of control. The military and the hippies can be viewed as the two extremes. Because hair represents the wild, untamed side of a human being, G-d created it in a way that requires constant grooming, i.e. taming. We cannot let even one day pass without combing our hair. Unkempt hair is often a sign of mental illness.

Women have a somewhat different relationship with their hair than men do. When women want to be taken seriously or are functioning in formal or business roles (think nurses or corporate executives), they wear their hair either short or up. Long hair, on the other hand, represents informality and even an intimacy. The expression "let one's hair down," implies getting personal. When a woman undoes her hair in front of a man, she is sending an invitation, for hair is alluring to him. It's common for a man to see a woman from behind and think that she will be beautiful simply because of her hair.

For this reason, the Torah requires that once a woman is married, her informal, intimate and even wild side, as embodied by her hair, is to be reserved only for her husband and doesn't belong on the street.

There is one last but terribly important point regarding the issue of *tzniut*: Sex has an outsized determining influence on the building and maintenance of a society and a society's greatness is directly linked to the modesty of its women. Never in history did a society become great or powerful if it was licentious but all great societies eventually fell because of their increased level of decadence. This is because licentiousness reinforces the animal within us and creates self-centered people preoccupied with fulfilling their physical desires. In such a society, lives become redefined as endless quests to acquire, experience and satisfy. A licentious person will not put another before himself or someone else's needs before his own; he will view others only as means to help him accomplish his base goals. Such people will not sacrifice for the common good and will only cooperate when absolutely necessary for a specific reason. When a society is inhabited by such people, social strictures come apart, and the society collapses.

The Synagogue

Another common question regarding Orthodox women is—why don't they participate in public ritual? This includes being called up to the Torah, being counted in a *minyan* (a quorum of ten, required for some prayers), being ordained as rabbis and sitting behind a *mechitza*, the physical separation of men and women, in synagogue.

This question is almost always asked in an accusatory manner, implying that Orthodox Judaism is discriminatory. But it is not. As we have seen, Orthodox Judaism, which is based on the Torah and 3,300 years of unbroken transmission, is predicated on the fact that men and women are different physically, emotionally and spiritually. Therefore just as the physical and emotional needs of men and women are not identical, the spiritual needs of men and women are not identical. What a man requires in order to grow spiritually is not necessarily relevant to a woman and vice versa. Therefore, even though the majority of the 613 *mitzvot* apply equally, since the purpose of the Torah and of life is to grow spiritually, the paths that men and women need to take will differ.

That said, there is another important point to consider here. Christianity revolves around the church—a devout Christian is described as a "churchgoer"—and Islam revolves around the mosque. Non-Orthodox Judaism is similarly centered on the synagogue—a Conservative or Reform Jew will define himself as such by the synagogue to which he belongs. A Jew who does not belong to a synagogue will describe himself as "nothing" or "unaffiliated." To the overwhelming majority of non-Orthodox Jews who do belong to a synagogue, their Judaism will take place within its walls. Their homes might have nothing Jewish to them at all, and therefore non-Orthodox women see their participation in synagogue life as their fundamental, if not only, relationship to Judaism.

However, Orthodox Judaism does not revolve around the synagogue; it revolves around the home, which is the center of life. An Orthodox Jew who does not attend synagogue is doing wrong with regard to the *mitzvah* of prayer, but he can still be pious and devout in every other part of his life and be *mitzvah* observant. And whether a Jew keeps Shabbat or has a kosher home is much more essential to his life than attending synagogue.

Therefore, the issues that might offend non-Orthodox women do not bother Orthodox women. The fact that men play the central roles at the synagogue has no bearing on their sense of worth or their relationships with G-d. To them, synagogue is only one part of a very big picture. Orthodox men might go to synagogue on Shabbat morning but then they come home and have a festive meal with the family.

To non-Orthodox Jews, to whom synagogue attendance and participation is the definition of Judaism, not being allowed to participate is disenfranchising. Ironically, Reform, Conservative or unaffiliated women who attend synagogue infrequently are opposed to a *mechitza* while Orthodox women, who attend synagogue much more frequently, have no problem with it at all. Shouldn't it be the other way around? Shouldn't the women who come maybe twice a year have very little issue with it since it is so irrelevant to their lives? Logically, the ones who are faced with it all the time should be offended by the constant indignity and be firmly opposed to it.

However, a *mechitza* simply recognizes a truth: Men are attracted to women. Since women are not required to be at synagogue and men are, if women want to come, it must be in a context wherein they do not constitute a distraction to the men who are performing their duties. Orthodox women, understanding this truth and knowing that the men are involved in speaking to their Creator, do not want to be distractions. It is plain common sense.

But why are only men obligated in public prayer and not women? The answer, again, lies in the inherent spiritual differences between men and women. A man's religious observance involves many outward signs and actions that will influence his mind; he needs to see, do and say things out loud to reinforce many ideas and concepts that women, who are internally focused, inherently know. For example, since a man is an explorer and conqueror by nature, he more easily falls into the trap of believing in his omnipotence. Therefore he must do many things that will reinforce for him the truth that there is a G-d and that he is a mere mortal. This includes going to public prayer three times a day

It also includes other daily activities such as wearing a head covering, wearing *tzitzit* and donning *tefillin*. The traditional head covering or skullcap, called a *yarmulke* in Yiddish or *kipah* in Hebrew, is worn by Jewish men as a constant reminder of their subservience to a greater being.

Tzitzit are the knotted strings that must be affixed to any garment with at least four corners. Since we don't wear such garments anymore, Orthodox Jewish men purposely wear a four-cornered garment in order to fulfill the *mitzvah*. The strings are a constant reminder of the 613 *mitzvot*.

Tefillin are the square, black leather boxes that men are commanded to strap onto to their heads and arms each day. These boxes contain certain verses from the Torah written on parchment. When we don the *Tefillin*, it's as if we are strapping G-d's name itself onto our bodies. As you can see from these examples, as well as the *Brit Milah*, men's bodies need to be constantly subjugated in order for us to excel.

A woman, on the other hand, has no spiritual need for any of these things and, if obligated to do them, would find them insufferable. Today many women might claim the need to participate and express themselves Jewishly, but the source of the need is not pure. When women desire to perform the *mitzvot* that are required of men, they do not do so out of a longing to be close to G-d because that is not a path that a woman would naturally take. They do so out of a desire to be "equal" to men.

Man-made situations that are denied to women might very well be discriminatory, but G-d-given requirements are not. The *mitzvot* are given to us so we can grow spiritually and women are not required to do all of them because they don't *need* all of them. If a woman understands this, she does not have an issue with this but if she is not in touch with the deeper meaning of the *mitzvot*, she will see her reduced role as having to sit at the back of the bus. The push to include women in public Jewish rituals and ceremonies is the unfortunate introduction of these very distorted feminist ideas and concepts into Jewish life. It does not spring from a deep-seated desire to come closer to G-d.

Women can find private prayer constructive because of their strong inner spiritual lives. Men cannot, and are obligated to join with ten others *who have the same requirement* for public prayer because it is essential for their spiritual development. They need the group as an external reinforcement. A woman does not have this need and so her presence in this situation would be superfluous. The same reasoning applies to boys under the age of thirteen, who have no requirement to be there and so cannot be counted as one of the ten.

The internal/external dichotomy also explains the many public aspects of Judaism in which a woman does not participate, such as being called to the Torah and officiating as a rabbi. There is no true internal need for any of it. The introduction of "equality" into Reform and Conservative synagogue life was the result of feminism being grafted onto an already gutted religion.

Despite their differences, men and women are each equally tasked with carrying the Jewish banner. Each must develop himself or herself and each must develop a relationship with G-d. But it would be foolish to assume or require that two distinct beings take the same path. Each, using his or her unique abilities, strengths and modes of thinking and relating to the world, will arrive, hopefully, at the same destination. But to assume that men have it better or easier is to have no idea what you are talking about. The only people who feel that Orthodox women are victims of a sexist patriarchy are those looking in from the outside.

So you can see for yourself just how "suppressed" Orthodox Jewish women truly are, let me share with you something that one of my teenage daughters recently told me. She approached me with an ear-to-ear grin and asked if I wanted to hear a joke. "Uh oh," I said, sensing trouble. "Go ahead."

Three men were walking on a beach when they discovered an ancient-looking bottle. They opened it and a genie emerged in a wisp of smoke.

"Because you have released me, I can grant each of you one wish," the genie said.

This being an intellectual group, the first man asked for twice the average man's intelligence, and his wish was granted. His friend, seeing that it worked, asked for three times the average man's intelligence, and his wish, too, was granted. The last man, unable to accept anything less than what his friends received, asked the genie for *four* times the average man's intelligence. The genie cautioned him, "I don't think you should ask for that. I don't think you will like the result."

The man insisted, and the reluctant genie granted his wish.

Instantly, the man was turned into a woman.

Chapter Eight
Truth and Morality

Logically, this chapter should be about marriage and intimacy since it segues perfectly from the discussion of men and women. However, since it will deal with the topic of sex, which inevitably becomes a discussion of morality, it seemed more expedient to turn first to the subject of right and wrong.

This chapter and the next will cover many issues—right and wrong, absolute truth, abortion, homosexuality, evolution, the role of science, the separation of church and state—that can very easily raise hackles and send chairs flying. Because of the pervasiveness of the media in our society, I feel compelled to urge you once again not to view the discussions in this chapter through foreign eyes.

As you hopefully have come to see, the Torah is an entire system of thought that is based on ethics and principles that were created and designed by a loving G-d solely for our ultimate good. The positions of the Catholic Church and the various Protestant denominations are not our positions. There might be overlap but that is only because their religions are somewhat based on our truth. But like everything else that they have pirated, the principles have become bastardized and distorted because they lack an anchoring in the Oral Law—the true source of our beliefs.

Therefore, it must be understood at the outset that the Popes and the preachers do not speak for us.

And since this book is subtitled *Why We Do What We Do, Wear What We Wear and Think What We Think*, I need to explain why Orthodox Jews very often wind up on the other side of today's moral issues from secular Jews.

Absolute Truth

The first point that needs to be made is that the concept of right and wrong is predicated on the fact that there exists an absolute truth. To anyone who has attended college in the last forty years, this will be shocking since it has become an article of faith for any educated person that there is no such thing as absolute truth. All truth, we are told, is relative; what is true for you might not be true for me. Or, as Reuters defines it, one man's terrorist is another man's freedom fighter.

It doesn't take much of an imagination to see how relative morality can very easily spin out of control. But let's leave that idea for now. What is important for our discussion is to see just how inherently ludicrous this idea really is. Not only is there an absolute truth but *all truth by definition is absolute.*

To begin, we must realize that if there is no truth then there are only opinions. You might think that something is wrong, but that is only your opinion. I might think that the same thing is right. In such a case, the words "right" and "wrong" lose all meaning. All you can say is that you don't like what I am doing; you can't say it's "wrong" because, to me, it's "right." And you cannot even claim that your definition is right and mine is wrong since there are no such things as absolute right and wrong in the first place.

The joke that I like to play on someone who tells me that he or she believes that there is no such thing as absolute truth is to ask them, "Are you absolutely sure?" If you think about it, "there is no such thing as absolute truth" is a statement of absolute truth. If a person does not believe in absolute truth, they can't even make the statement at all.

Furthermore, not only is all truth by definition absolute truth, but every person believes in an absolute truth—they just redefine it to fit their needs. For example, ask the person insisting that there is no such thing as absolute truth about racial discrimination or pollution or religious coercion and suddenly he will begin speaking in absolutes.

Is it wrong to forcibly enslave another human being? Well, for most of human history it was considered perfectly okay and practiced throughout the world by all races. (The word "slave" actually comes from the word, "Slav," and was introduced into the English language through the Vikings, who used to sail down the Dnieper River capturing Slavs to sell in Constantinople.) Only in the last 200 years has it been considered, first by a few and later by a majority, to be wrong. But why? Maybe we are wrong and the earlier generations were right. Or maybe it's right for some and wrong for others. Who is to say?

When there is no acknowledgement of absolute truth, all morality becomes relative and with relative morality no issue can be said to be wrong or immoral. One can only say that they do not like it or that "we don't do that." And to say that "everybody knows that that is wrong" is a ridiculous comment. First of all, "everybody" doesn't know anything and secondly, they only "know" it until they change their minds. It is also very possible for "everyone" to "know" something to be right when it is in fact very wrong. History is full of examples.

Every human being who possesses any deeply felt moral opinion is referring to an absolute truth when stating his or her belief. Unfortunately that butts up against the modern notion of "tolerance" which is really predicated on the idea that there is no such thing as absolute truth. What exactly is tolerance? The Merriam-Webster dictionary defines it as "sympathy or indulgence for beliefs or practices differing from one's own." What the dictionary does not state is that the "beliefs or practices differing from one's own" must fall within the parameters of what a person considers moral. No one has the capacity to tolerate what he considers immoral. How many people do you know who would be tolerant of a group that believed in human sacrifice, even if those being sacrificed were volunteers? Or of a group advocating the re-enslavement of the black population of the United States?

The uncomfortable reality is that if a person has a position on a *moral* issue or sees it in the context of right and wrong, he or she cannot suffer another point of view. When people call for tolerance on a moral issue, what they really are saying is, "None of this really matters anyway." They are quick to call for tolerance except when the issue at hand is important to them, at which point they become very intolerant.

Morality

There is a *Midrash* that states that before G-d offered the Torah to the Jewish people he first went to all the other nations and offered it to them. He approached three nations that were also related to Avraham: Edom (another name for Eisav (Esau), grandson of Avraham and twin brother of Yaakov), Yishmael (Ishmael, the son of Avraham and another wife named Hagar) and Moav (Moab, the son of Lot, the nephew of Avraham).

First He approached Edom and asked, "I have a Torah for you; do you want it?"

Edom's response was, "What is written in it?"

To Edom's question, G-d replied, "You cannot murder."

Edom said, "No, thank you."

G-d then approached Yishmael, the father of the Arab nation, and asked, "I have a Torah for you; do you want it?"

Yishmael's response was, "What is written in it?"

To Yishmael's question, G-d replied, "You cannot kidnap (take hostages)."

Yishmael also said, "No, thank you."

G-d then approached Moav, a nation born of an incestuous relationship, and asked, "I have a Torah for you; do you want it?"

Moav's response was, "What is written in it?"

To Moav's question, G-d replied, "You cannot commit adultery."

Moav, too, declined the offer.

Then, G-d approached the nation of Israel and asked, "I have a Torah for you; do you want it?"

The nation of Israel answered, "We will do what it says to do and we will learn its laws."

And so the Jews were given the Torah.

There are three general questions that jump out from such a *Midrash*—which is written precisely so these questions will be asked:

1. Since G-d knows what will happen and therefore knew how they would respond, why did He bother with the whole exercise?
2. Why were the other nations offered the Torah before the Jews? If one of them had accepted, what would have happened to us?
3. Why did G-d answer the nations with the *mitzvah* that would be the hardest for them to keep? Why didn't He begin by explaining to these nations the easier and more pleasurable *mitzvot* and then lead into the more difficult ones? What was the point of knocking them out with the first punch?

The first two questions can be answered as one: Of course, G-d knew that the other nations would reject the Torah and that the Jews would accept it. There was no risk in asking the other nations first. G-d was not doing a road show to peddle his Torah. He offered it so that, in the future, the nations of the world would not be able to protest that, had they been offered a Torah from G-d Himself, they would have gladly accepted it. They'd had the chance and they said no. They were not interested.

The answer to the last question is very telling and its lesson applies to each one of us. Clearly G-d could have responded to the nations' questions with more enticing proposals. He could have begun with flowery descriptions of the benefits in this life of keeping the *mitzvot* and then lead into a description of the eternal benefits of living a moral, G-d-oriented life. Then he could have begun with the simplest, least-expensive and most-pleasurable *mitzvot*, like sitting in a *succah*, before getting into the more difficult or restrictive *mitzvot*. Why did he use a *mitzvah* that would be the most difficult to accept?

Because the asking of the question was the rejection. When the nations asked, "What is written in it?" that was a rejection of a concept of a Torah. If G-d comes to you and offers you a Torah, you don't ask what is in it. If you do, you are stating outright that you will only be willing to accept it if the Torah being offered does not conflict with any of your beliefs or practices. Once the nations had rejected the offer in this way, by in essence saying that they would take the Torah but only on their own terms, G-d was polite and still answered them, but made the outcome a *fait accompli.*

The Jews' answer, on the other hand, showed their unconditional acceptance, which is the only way one can accept a Torah from G-d. Acceptance of the Torah depends on its inherent truth and not on what it contains.

In fact, the challenge of accepting G-d's better judgment has been man's challenge from day one (actually day six). Adam and Chava's only commandment was to deny themselves something they desired. This represents the quintessential struggle of man. Here, G-d gave them a commandment that had no rational understanding, nor was any reason given. The prohibition involved food, which is a basic need, meaning that Adam and Chava would have to struggle with a basic, universal desire. The tree itself appealed to their sight, sense of taste and imagination.

Each one of us is faced daily with the same choice that Adam and Chava had to make in *Gan Eden.* We are all standing before the tree of the knowledge of good and evil and eyeing the luscious fruit that beckons us to bite into it. Do we obey the higher calling of G-d's laws and His ambition for us? Or do we obey our bodies' lusts and hungers, assisted by the yeitzer hara's rationalizations and justifications?

It stands to reason that morality must be a set of transcendent principles—meaning that it is not dependent on circumstances, opinions or politics. It must be a system to which man adjusts his behavior and not a system that man creates around his behavior. People very rarely see their actions or opinions as wrong. Only a transcendental, impartial set of values can be considered "morality." Morality is really just another word used to describe the G-d-given concepts of right and wrong.

What passes for secular morality today is only the prevailing opinion of the dominant group, and that can be easily changed or overthrown. But the slope is not just slippery—it is greased. A person might have no choice but to act according to society's whims but, unless those whims are tethered to a G-d given morality, they will bend and turn and be reshaped as pressure is applied.

We all have an intuitive sense that the word "moral" has a lofty, transcendental meaning. Similarly, when we say something is immoral, we assign the word a sacred inviolability. We know that if something is considered immoral, there can be no argument or further discussion about it.

Yet, because of the secularization of society, the use of the word "morality" is rarely applied to anything that does not involve having sex with children. In fact, one glaring characteristic of today's media is the almost total absence of moral outrage. Adultery, once considered a highly immoral act, is now celebrated in popular culture and the poor fool who uses the term "immoral" to describe it is immediately branded a fundamentalist and written off. Is stealing immoral? Is lying? There was a time, not too long ago, when they were. Why does the term no longer seem fitting?

In the end, there can be only one definition of right and wrong: Right is in accord with G-d's will, wrong is in conflict with G-d's will. This, of course, sets many people on edge because they assume that the next step is the reestablishment of the Spanish Inquisition. But again, we need to approach the issue through Jewish eyes. We don't have inquisitions or ayatollahs issuing *fatwas* condemning people to death. And this image of a theocratic reign of terror—which is more than a little hysterical—is fostered by the one side of the debate that is antireligious.

If morality is not transcendent but only relative—or, to put it another way, adjustable according to the circumstances—any evil is possible under the right conditions. Without a G-d-given system of morals, we are left with only a set of opinions. What's right for you might not be right for me. Is the only thing wrong about cruelty or oppression the fact that you just don't like it?

In such a relative world, good and evil become simply matters of preference. Good merely reflects what feels good and evil what feels bad. In other words, good and bad become only explanations of feelings, and feelings become the sole judge of right and wrong. This is as dangerous as it sounds.

Since human beings must feel as though they are doing the right thing at all times, they always will justify their actions, even the deepest barbarism. And since a secular society is free to redefine good and bad without any interference from a higher authority, the results will be horrendous. As the twentieth century proved with its totalitarian regimes and world wars, a godless society aided by the latest technology is hell on Earth. Sure, there had been bloodshed, and a lot of it, throughout history but not since the Romans had such barbarism been the policy of the state. Europe's descent into madness was the direct result of its throwing off the yoke of G-d and His morality. (This will be explained.)

This also explains why secular societies do not hate evil and, in fact, don't like to use the word: They don't believe such a thing exists. Subconsciously every person knows that without G-d there can be no such thing as right and wrong, so why get worked up over it?

Homosexuality, adultery, premarital sex and abortion are clear examples of the shifting guideposts of modern society. Not too long ago these were considered immoral acts. They might have been practiced behind closed doors but society held the moral view that these actions were wrong. It took only twenty years to transform them into perfectly legitimate acts and even elevate them to the status of rights that people marched in the street to defend.

Twenty years is an unbelievably short period of time for such a monumental shift in values. But, in truth, the shift had been underway for over a century. It had begun in 1831 with Charles Darwin's voyage to the Galapagos Islands and culminated in 1959 in Worchester, Massachusetts when a scientist named Gregory Pincus developed the birth control pill. The reason I cite these two events is because beginning with Darwin's theory of evolution, a new self-image of man was introduced and with the birth control pill, it was put into practice.

Conflict? What Conflict?

The ramifications of the philosophy that resulted from Darwin's writings —man being simply the most advanced mammal on the evolutionary chart and *nothing more*—cannot be understated. Until this idea caught on, Western man saw himself as a unique being with a G-d-given soul who was given dominion over the Earth and its creatures. This new Darwinian definition of man was the biggest influence on society in the twentieth century; in fact, almost every social and scientific movement in those years was secular in belief and practice. Karl Marx and Sigmund Freud, two thinkers who also proposed new definitions of human beings and their society, had no use for G-d and spoke of religion in the most degrading terms. (Freud rejected the existence of a soul and attempted to portray the entire essence of a human being in terms of sexual and hedonistic urges. He viewed religious faith as a type of mental illness and assumed that religion would die off as mankind developed scientifically.) Political movements such as fascism and Soviet-style communism either prohibited religion or controlled it with a heavy hand.

The idea of man as advanced primate also deeply affected and continues to affect the definition of personal morality. Today the fault lines on moral issues are generally defined by religious belief. Those who are religious fall on one side; those who are not fall on the other. The reason for this divide is based on an age-old conflict between science and the Roman Catholic Church. This will be expounded upon, but there is one point that first must be established: **Judaism has never had a conflict with science**.

How could there be? Science is the study of the physical world. If G-d made the physical world, where's the problem? A conflict only arises when certain parties use science to promote an agenda or suppress science to promote an agenda.

Because Judaism is incorrectly seen as just another religion, we get lumped into a conflict between science and the Catholic Church that pre-dated Darwin by about 500 years. For hundreds of years, the Church had kept Europe intellectually stagnant as a means of maintaining power. The Church felt, with justification, that if its doctrines were exposed to the light of day, they would be seen as intellectually flawed and indefensible. Beginning in the late 1300s Europe began to stir, and in a period of rebirth—a *renaissance,* in French—began to emerge from the intellectual coma that the Church had imposed on it. The Church had stifled free inquiry and intellectual questioning and opposed many scientific discoveries, viewing them as heretical to official dogma. So, science responded by becoming strongly anticlerical.

The persecutions of Galileo Galilei and Johannes Kepler are famous examples of how the Church responded to what it saw as challenges. Making someone recant a scientific fact is ludicrous. But in those two cases, the Church was very afraid. Galileo was a threat because the Church had always claimed that the sun revolved around the Earth, since Man was the center of creation. In the Church's view, a heliocentric (sun-centered) system would only trivialize man's place in the cosmos. (Ironically, this argument is used by those who loudly postulate that we are only passengers on a remote glob of space dust and therefore no better than any other element in the universe.) Kepler's crime of discovering that the Earth's orbit was elliptical and not perfectly round was also seen as a threat because it somehow contravened the idea that creation was perfect.

But to an Orthodox Jew, both these arguments miss the point. Whether the Earth revolves around the sun or the sun around the Earth, or whether the orbit is round or elliptical, does not change our understanding that the universe was created for man and our lives have purpose. None of that is determined by what lies at the center of the solar system or the shape of orbits. The vastness of space is meant to inspire awe in us; it in no way demotes or relegates us to anything we are not, nor does it change the meaning of our lives.

In fact, not only have the Jewish people always been intellectually curious and never theologically intimidated by anything found in creation but many of our greatest Torah sages were also leading doctors, scientists and astronomers. There are no less than three craters on the moon that are named after great Jewish sages—learned Rabbis from the Middle Ages who were also great astronomers. The Abenezer crater was named for the great twelfth-century Rabbi Abraham Ibn Ezra. A Spanish scholar, he is best known for his commentary on the Torah, which is still studied on a daily basis by Jews throughout the world. The Rabbi Levi crater was named in honor of the fourteenth-century sage Rabbi Levi ben Gershon, sometimes known as the Ralbag (an acronym of his name) or Gersonides. And the Zagut crater is named for Rabbi Abraham Zacuto, an astronomer, mathematician and historian who, in the fifteenth century, was the royal astronomer in the court of King John II of Portugal.

Nevertheless, the enduring result of the Catholic Church's efforts to squash man's natural and G-d-given curiosity was that science and religion became "sides" and battle lines were drawn. But none of this applies to Judaism at all, in any way, because in Torah Judaism *there is no scientific dogma*. As shocking as it might seem, neither a belief in an evolutionary process, dating the age of the universe in billions of years or the existence of dinosaur fossils contradict anything in the Torah. (These three subjects are the ones generally raised in discussions of the supposed conflict between science and the Torah.)

As we have seen, the Jews possess a Written Torah (the Five Books of Moshe) and an Oral Torah (the Oral Law). The Written Torah is just the starting point; the Oral Law is infinitely deep and expansive, containing the secrets of life and the answers to the mysteries of creation. Every Orthodox schoolchild knows that the seven-day account of creation in Genesis is shrouded in mystery and contains infinitely more information than is revealed in the text. In fact, the sages of the Talmud consider it one of the most esoteric subject matters within the Torah. Just as with every other aspect of Torah, the text alone cannot be used to fully grasp or understand the subject.

Both the Catholic Church and the fundamental Protestant denominations use the literal text of the Bible as their fact sheet but they are as much in the dark as to the meaning of the literal text as the scientists who mock it.

I reiterate, the Popes and the preachers do not speak for us.

A simple reading of the Torah text clearly shows that there must be more to it than meets the eye. Even before the Torah's narrative of the six days of creation there are two cryptic verses that describe something but remain enigmatic and murky to any Jew who has not reached the highest levels of Jewish scholarship.

The Torah describes six days of creation, each ending with the statement, "It was evening and it was morning..."—yet the sun was not created until the fourth day. How do you have an evening or a morning without a sun? There are many different understandings in rabbinical writings of what exactly the six days of creation in the Torah actually mean. They range from six twenty-four-hour periods (even without the sun) to six "days" with a definition of time that is different from ours. A Christian with only a Bible will find himself in an uncomfortable quandary in this discussion. But Jews who are endowed with an oral tradition find nothing to be defensive about and everything to be fascinated about.

Throughout the Talmud, the *Midrashim* and the rabbinical writings —all of which predate Darwin and modern science by centuries—there are references and discussion of ideas that non-Jews did not contemplate until recently. There are allusions to generations that might have lived before Adam and worlds that were created and destroyed before ours.

None of the modern notions are new to us. Jews were pondering the origins of life and the meaning of the Torah's account of creation while, to paraphrase Benjamin Disraeli, Darwin's ancestors were still swinging from the trees.

Regarding the age of the universe, it has always been understood in our tradition that the physical laws during the period of creation did not resemble the physical laws that exist today. This means that what occurred during the period of creation cannot be duplicated or measured accurately using post-creation laws of science. This view is now shared by quantum physicists who hypothesize that the physical laws of nature and time itself functioned differently in the early stages of the creation of the universe. That would seriously alter our ability to accurately gauge what happened when.

As to how the existence of dinosaurs can be reconciled with the biblical account of creation, there is no one answer and most of the answers are speculative. The Torah does mention the creation of great lizards or reptiles on the fifth day. It is possible that these are dinosaurs but I have no idea why G-d would specifically mention their creation if they are extinct and were completely unknown to mankind until the 1800s.

Of course, if the six days are not days as we know them today, the dinosaurs could have lived and died on the fifth "day." This would also explain the onetime existence of animals like the wooly mammoth and the saber-toothed tiger, which could have lived and died on the sixth "day."

I feel very comfortable saying that I just don't know how dinosaurs fit into the big picture. But not knowing does not in any way imply that the Torah is somehow untrue or that science has disproved it. Maybe the universe *is* billions of years old; maybe other species once lived on this planet and man was somehow developed from a lower primate until he was ready for G-d to endow him with a soul. Or, maybe not. To an Orthodox Jew, this is all very intriguing. To an unbiased listener, this only sounds like a lot of interesting questions for which there are still no answers. An unbiased listener would not have heard anything remotely resembling disproof of the existence of G-d or His hand in creation.

But many modern Jews still feel very uncomfortable discussing all of this.

This is because the Western world now "officially" adopts the view that the universe in general and life on this planet specifically began as a chemical incident. This is the party line that we are taught in school and hear repeatedly in the media. I put the word "officially" in quotes because, despite the constant repetition that life is accidental, most people still harbor some belief that G-d was somehow involved. They just don't know how to reconcile it with what they believe is the scientific truth.

That being said, let's be honest—99.99 percent of humanity couldn't care less how old the world is or if and when dinosaurs walked the Earth. The average non-paleontologist will go through life never giving any of these matters more than twenty seconds of real contemplation. They don't affect the stock market, any team's pitching rotation, the latest fashions or anyone's quest for true love and happiness. They are completely meaningless in the big picture of life.

But evolution strikes a deeper chord and must be explained in greater depth.

On the surface, evolution represents intellectualism. Even though the average Jewish person is unfamiliar with how the scientific community understands the process today, he has heard it spoken of in such absolute terms that he has come to believe that it is solid science. In his mind, to reject evolution would be to join the *imams* and the Sunday-morning preachers—not a very attractive option. Jews see themselves as intellectuals, not simpletons, so why should they choose faith over facts? In their minds the issue has been decided. If the Bible would state that there is no such thing as a moose and I am standing in the zoo looking at one, the Bible would be wrong. The same goes for evolution. The Bible speaks of six days of creation but science has evidence of billions of years. End of discussion. And those who don't accept it are seen as Luddites who ignore reality.

But there is something else going on below the surface; how else can we explain why people who do not understand the theory of evolution, who have never read about it in any depth and cannot even articulate it, become very angry when it is challenged? Most people, it seems, have an interesting relationship with the subject—they aren't familiar with it yet will defend it vigorously. I have had people scream at me, red in the face, that the theory is 100-percent true but could not support their rants with any logic or information.

Why does this subject evoke such raw emotions and arouse such passion? What causes otherwise reasonable people to go ballistic? And why is the theory of evolution accepted as absolute truth even by those who don't believe in absolute truth?

Evolution

Charles Darwin was raised in a religious environment, studied for the clergy at Cambridge and counted as his teachers and mentors a number of faculty members who were also practicing reverends. He was particularly interested in botany and the natural sciences. After graduating in 1831, he was recommended by his botany professor and mentor, Reverend John Henslow, to join a scientific expedition aboard the HMS Beagle, which was leaving to chart the coastline of South America.

The voyage took five years to complete and throughout that time Darwin collected an enormous amount of fossils and specimens, which he sent back to London for categorization. Henslow circulated Darwin's growing collection and promoted the work of his star pupil. By the time the HMS Beagle returned to London in 1836, Darwin, at the age of twenty-five, was a celebrity in scientific circles.

Darwin won many awards and titles and published many works over the course of the next forty-six years but he is not famous for his extensive work on plants, earthworms and coral reefs. Rather, he is known for a theory that human beings somehow evolved from lower forms of life, and that those lower forms evolved from even lower forms all the way back to a beginning. He hypothesized that the strongest species and the strongest elements within the species are the ones that have survived to this day. This philosophy, which was dubbed "evolution," was developed over his lifetime in works such as *On the Origin of the Species* (1851), *The Descent of Man* (1871) and *The Expression of the Emotions in Man and Animals* (1872).

At the beginning of his career, Darwin did not concern himself with whether or not G-d was involved in the process of natural selection. He was not as devout as he had been in his youth but still believed in G-d as the source of moral law. Eventually he described himself as an agnostic. Later in life, Darwin lost his belief in a just and beneficent god when his daughter, Annie, died at the age of eleven.

His final comprehensive belief was that everything—ideas, cultures, differences between races, gender roles and even morality—was the result of natural selection, or evolution. In *The Descent of Man*, Darwin even went so far as to write, "We may, therefore, reject the belief...that the abhorrence of incest is due to our possessing a special God-implanted conscience." It does not take a rocket scientist to see how the acceptance of Darwin's theory would affect moral issues. And it also does not take a rocket scientist to see why Darwin's theory would be attractive to those with certain agendas.

Darwin based his theory of evolution on the similarities that humans share with other mammals. But even Darwin's co-theorist of evolution by natural selection, a scientist named Alfred Wallace, believed that the human mind was too unique and too complex to have evolved from a lower primate. As a result, he felt, the theory of evolution was incomplete and not entirely accurate. Darwin bitterly disagreed and tried to prove him wrong by demonstrating that many of the unique human attributes can also be found in other mammals.

But Darwin could not conclusively prove his point since it was based on circular logic—the conclusion depends on the opinion with which the observer begins. If all things are created by G-d, similarities do not demand a common ancestor; they are simply interesting and probably exist for us to learn from. But if you begin with the idea of natural selection, the similarities can be used as evidence of a common ancestor.

Even Darwin had his doubts. When he wrote *Origins,* his theory was just that: a scientific theory that needed to be substantiated by facts. In *Origins,* he repeatedly asked his readers to ignore the lack of physical evidence for his theory. At the time paleontology was in its infancy and the lack of fossil evidence was not considered a refutation of his theory; it was assumed that the proofs would eventually be dug up. In fact, Darwin himself was of the opinion that if the fossil records were not found, his theory would be proven false.

But what kind of fossil record would be needed to prove Darwin's theory that species mutated from one form into another? Fossil evidence of intermediate species. If all species gradually mutated into other species there would be ample fossil remains of all or some of the in-between stages because it would have occurred slowly over millions of years. For example, if a fish developed legs and walked onto the land and gradually mutated into a lizard, there should be an ample number of fossils of fish with legs, fish with lungs, lizards with gills and so on, as well as everything in between those stages.

However, there aren't any, and here is where ideology seeped into the mix. There are absolutely no fossils whatsoever of any in-between stage of any proposed link in the chain of evolution—that is an indisputable fact. There are none. Not one. After 120 years of intense digging, not one link has been established. There are over 200 million cataloged specimens from all over the world containing the fossilized remains of about 250,000 species but none shows any transitional evidence. In fact, most fossils show consistency—i.e., no significant change over millions of years.

The absence of fossil evidence created an obvious problem for scientists and by Darwin's own criteria, he was proven wrong. There was not a shred of evidence to support his theory of evolution but, as many scientists have openly written, the alternative to evolution was unacceptable. And this is where science really began to veer off its own track.

In 1972 two paleontologists, Niles Eldredge, the curator of the Department of Invertebrates of the American Museum of Natural History, and Steven Gould, a Harvard professor of biology, formulated an idea called "punctuated equilibrium." This fancy term translates into the fantastic idea that species spontaneously mutated in bursts at specific intervals. This not only explains away the lack of fossil evidence for Darwin's theory of gradual evolution but also explains why fossils show that fully evolved species appear suddenly at different intervals in history. (Years later, in an article in *Natural History* magazine, Gould coined what would become a famous remark: "What good," he asked, "is half a jaw or half a wing?"

The problem with punctuated equilibrium, besides the fact that it enters the realm of fantasy, is that it cannot be proven one way or the other. The fact that nothing of the sort is happening today is answered with the explanation that it might not occur for another few million years—and that we never know when or why it will occur.

This theory contradicts Darwin himself. In *Origins,* he wrote:

> He who believes that some ancient form was transformed suddenly through an internal force or tendency into, for instance, one furnished with wings, will be almost compelled to assume, in opposition to all analogy, that many individuals varied simultaneously... He will further be compelled to believe that many structures beautifully adapted to all the other parts of the same creature and to the surrounding conditions, have been suddenly produced; and of such complex and wonderful co-adaptations, he will not be able to assign a shadow of an explanation... To admit all this is, as it seems to me, to enter into the realms of miracle, and to leave those of science.

In any other context, punctuated equilibrium would be considered science fiction. In fact there is a popular comic-book series called The *X-Men,* which has been made into a few full-length movies. In it, people have spontaneously mutated into superpeople with different or extraordinary powers. Their parents are normal but the mutants were just born with different genetics.—i.e. punctuated equilibrium. How many sane adults view such a concept as serious science? On the other hand, maybe it's all true; maybe people really are being born with wings or telepathic powers or the ability to walk through walls. And if such people are not being born today, if you accept the punctuated equilibrium theory of evolution, you must, for the sake of consistency, believe that the comic books and the movies are completely valid and need to be taken as seriously as any science.

Besides the utter lack of fossil support for Darwin's theory, there are other problems with the current explanation of how evolution took place. Evolution allegedly began with what has been termed the "primordial soup," the nutrient-rich, ancient oceans. They purportedly teemed with organic compounds that somehow assembled themselves into proteins and nucleic acids and eventually into molecules, which then assembled themselves into cells and so on. When looking at this idea, some obvious common-sense questions jump up, none of which are answered by science. For example: How does inorganic (non-living) matter suddenly spring to life? What drove the building process? What would compel an amino acid, for example, to build itself into an enzyme? And once an enzyme, why move on from there?

But there is another more-basic problem with the "primordial soup" theory: There is absolutely no geological evidence that this potent environment ever existed. If it had been sitting on the Earth's surface for millions of years, exerting millions of pounds of pressure there would some geological trace of it in the Earth's lower strata. Yet even the oldest rocks on the planet show no trace of it. It seems that these oceans evaporated without a trace—something that doesn't happen in real life.

Mutations

The theory of evolution, whether qualified by the theory of punctuated equilibrium or not, is predicated on the concept of mutations occurring either gradually or spontaneously. It behooves any intelligent person to understand what this means because it is the foundation of the philosophy that affects society's moral code.

There are two problems with this foundation. One is the truth about mutations and the second is their probability.

How beneficial are mutations? What do they achieve? Evolutionists will have you believe that mutations made the various species stronger, faster and more capable—in short, more fit to survive. But are mutants really the fittest or the least fit? Mutations in humans and animals produce deformities, diseases and monstrosities: They are mistakes. How can mistakes, compounded over generations, produce better, more-advanced beings? Nature repeatedly proves just the opposite—that mutations do not enhance organisms but hinder them. For example, we see that in humans, inbreeding, even amongst the greatest geniuses, will not produce even more brilliant offspring. It only produces retardation. Similarly, in the animal world, frogs born with extra legs fare no better than those with only four. They don't jump higher or farther; in fact, they are less mobile.

In all species, deformities lead to hard lives and early deaths. So, is it reasonable to believe that these anomalies became the norm and were the building blocks of all the species? Is it reasonable to believe that this "beneficial" process occurred continuously and gradually over millions of years, but then suddenly became a negative occurrence? Can we accept that mutations were once good but now are bad? When was the last time you read about a mutation—in essence, a birth defect—that somehow improved its owner?

Proponents also want you to believe that species spontaneously mutated at one or more times in the past and that these mutations became permanently embedded in the species' genetic codes—something that has never happened in human history. Retarded people will not inevitably produce retarded children. What would cause DNA to spontaneously mutate over and over again in thousands of species over millions of years?

And although we are told that these enormous changes happened for no apparent reason, evolutionists fail to explain why a species with everything it needed in its environment would suddenly change. They can't explain why a sea creature ever needed to evolve into a land animal—or why, according to the theory itself, only some evolved. The rest remained where they were and are still there today. They seem to be doing fine.

Additionally, if an organism (or a system within an organism) needs all of its parts to function, how can it evolve bit by bit? Until all organs within the animals of the various species fully evolved, the intermediary stages would have had no value whatsoever—just like buying a radio one part at a time gives you nothing until you have all the parts needed to receive a signal. Only when they are all assembled do any of the parts have any function.

Evolutionary science today is considered post-Darwinian meaning that no one accepts the notion of gradual evolution due to its inherent problems. Punctuated Equilibrium has won the day; however, in reality this idea is, in some ways, more preposterous.

Biological systems are highly complex and interdependent. For example, the human eye is so complex that Darwin himself stated in a letter to an American colleague that it "gives me a cold shudder" because there was no way to reconcile its existence and functioning within his theory.

A human being sees out of an eye that is comprised of various parts that must interact perfectly in order to see properly. If any one of the eye's components is not functioning correctly, vision will be impaired or worse.

This is how vision works: Light rays bounce off the object that we are viewing and pass through six layers within the eye—the cornea (a type of transparent tissue overlaying the iris and pupil), a clear, watery fluid called the aqueous humor, the pupil, the crystalline lens, more watery fluid called the vitreous humor and then, finally, the retina, which makes up eighty percent of the eye. The retina is the home of the nerve cells and light-sensitive cells that produce the images our minds see.

There are two types of light-sensitive cells in the retina—long, thin rods that lie towards the edges of the retina and allow us to see in dim light and wide cones, which lie in the center of the retina and allow us to see colors and sharp details in bright light. Nerve fibers attached to the rods and cones come together from all over the retina to form the optic nerve, which carries the image to a section of the brain called the visual cortex, which "reads" the image information. All of this is happening right now as you read these words.

If you want to believe that life began as a single-celled organism and evolved to where we are today, how exactly did the eye—an unbelievably complex and interdependent organ—evolve? Which part of it came first? Since a cornea without a retina would be worthless, why would one develop without the other? In fact, to be useful, every single part of the eye would need to evolve at exactly the same instant since without even one part, there could be no sight.

And if, as the punctuated equilibrium school claims, every single part of the eye popped into existence at exactly the same instant, the brain's visual cortex would have had to evolve at the same rate and would have had to "come online" at exactly the same time as the eye. What a waste it would have been if the eye had evolved perfectly but there was no visual cortex, and the optic nerve just hung there in the air. Or what if there had been no brain at all?

This short explanation does not even take into consideration other necessary parts of a functioning eye—such as eyelids, eyelashes and eyebrows, or the tear ducts and the ocular muscles that allow us to move our eyes around in their sockets or adjust to different lighting and distances. It also does not touch upon the fact that somehow both eyes developed identically. And, not only did they evolve identically but they work in tandem. You need both eyes working properly to have correct depth perception. One eye is not enough.

And there is still one basic overriding problem. We are viewing evolution from the end result—our finished world. But according to the evolutionary theorists, until recently, the world would have been populated by all types of grotesque, suffering creatures full of mutations of no value. In fact, no single mutation has any inherent value unless its end goal is clear. Since the eye, for example, is of no use until it is in its final, complete form with all of its functioning parts, how could any organism have functioned in those intermediate stages of the eye's evolution, when each stage provided no possible survival value and even acted as a hindrance? No single change had any value in and of itself.

Since natural selection presumes no knowledge of the ultimate end or purpose of the organ—in other words, it is an ongoing work in progress with no defined goal—it makes no sense. Why would there be a selection of organs or species in the intermediate stages when no function was served and when, in fact, they would need another few million years before they fulfilled their functions? This means that for millions of years the eyes were evolving even though, until they were finished, they were just worthless hunks of tissue.

So much can be written about the human body and the amazing way in which it functions. The circulatory system, the nervous system, the ear and the sense of hearing, the taste buds and the sense of taste, the nose and the sense of smell, the brain, the skeletal system, the muscular system, the immune system, the lymphatic system, the gastro-intestinal system, the endocrine system—all require fantastic coordination within the system to perform their purposes.

For example, to digest solid food requires no less than ten different parts of the body to work properly and collaboratively: The teeth begin the process by chewing; the digestion of food then is affected by the salivary glands, the esophagus, the stomach, the liver, the pancreas, the gall bladder, the duodenum, the small intestine and the large intestine. Working together, these parts use everything that is beneficial and expel everything detrimental. So, which one of them came into existence first, or did they all miraculously appear simultaneously?

Let's say the stomach came first. What would it have done? Just hang around until an esophagus evolved on its upper end? The punctuated equilibrium school of thought admits that this could not have happened. But, as we saw, instead of discarding Darwin's theory, they took a leap of faith and postulated that evolution happened in spurts. This means that the human eye, suddenly and with no prior development, materialized one day in the head of an organism. One day it wasn't there and the next day it was, along with some pre-arranged cavities in the facial bones to house the eyeballs and a brain ready to process the data from the optic nerve. And the proponents of evolution are completely serious about this.

But forgetting vision and digestion for a minute, how did any organism survive its sudden mutations?

The theory goes that fish developed lungs and legs instead of gills and fins and walked out of the water onto land. Of course, they needed to develop these lungs and legs at exactly the same second because one without the other would have killed it. A fish born with lungs but without legs would have blacked out in a few seconds from lack of oxygen, sinking to the bottom and drowning. A fish born with legs but without lungs would have been eaten by a predator very quickly since it wouldn't have been able to swim very well. Also, this sudden evolution would have had to happen close to shore because such a fish, if born in the deep sea, would have had the same chance of survival as a person afloat in the deep sea.

Alternatively, the little fish would have had to have some type of air-breathing system while it was still underwater because once it emerged from the water its gills would have had to shut down and its lungs would have had to kick in. If there had been a delay of even a few minutes, the poor creature would have been a goner.

But there would also need to be other instant mutations. For instance, its skeleton would have to be strengthened in order to support its body weight, something it did not have to do in the water.

Finally, there is the small problem of probability. We speak of mutations as if their occurrences are possible but rare. However, this is not the case. Mathematicians and statisticians have most vocally opposed any type of evolutionary theory based on genetic mutations. This is because, working strictly with the numbers, they know that the theories are impossible. Not improbable or extremely rare—100% absolutely impossible.

The problems begin at the most fundamental level. The odds of getting the right amino acids together at the right time and place to form a single enzyme has been estimated to be less than one in ten to the forty-thousandth power. And that's just the first step of the evolutionary process. The theory of evolution posits that *millions* of mutations occurred over *billions* of years to produce everything that we see in the world—people, animals, birds, fish, insects, plants, amoeba, viruses, microscopic life and so on. Each life form would require millions of mutations within its formation.

Since it is mathematically impossible for even one enzyme to have formed on its own, how can a scientist take this all seriously? One proponent of evolution even admitted that the odds of a horse evolving is one in one thousand to the millionth power—that's a one followed by three million zeros. How is this "science?"

The Genius of Creation

Science is the study of the physical world. In this role, it informs and demonstrates the marvels of creation. But it cannot do more than that. It does not provide wisdom or understanding. Science can explain how a sheep that eats only grass and drinks only water can produce milk, meat, wool and leather. But it cannot explain why. Science only describes the processes, not the reasons.

An unbiased look at the wonders of creation will inevitably lead one to conclude that a godless process of evolution is out of the question. Our natural world is so infinitely interconnected and interdependent, between the different species and even within single life forms, that it must be the work of intelligence and based on a plan. The design and order of the natural world also indicate there is a purpose to it.

Imagine that you are on a tour of Europe and, while in Florence, you go to the Uffizi Gallery to view Michelangelo's statue of David. Overlooking the fact that all of the details are wrong—his uncovered head, his nudity, his lack of circumcision—you can't help but be amazed by the genius that created such a masterpiece. Overcome, you blurt out at the fellow standing next to you, "Michelangelo was amazing!"

The man looks at you as if you're strange and says, "What are you talking about? This statue came about totally by chance. They were blasting in a quarry north of the city and this was dislodged from the mountain."

What would your reaction be?

You then head up to Vienna, where you attend a concert in the famous Musikverein. The Viennese Philharmonic Orchestra is performing Beethoven's Ninth Symphony. The hall is magnificent, the performance is wonderful and you leave the concert hall feeling elated.

On the way out you overhear two people discussing how amazing it is that such beautiful music could be created completely by chance by a group of monkeys with various instruments. You think to yourself, *Wow, there are a lot of weird people in Europe!*

Then, it's over to the Louvre in Paris. After waiting on the long line to see the Mona Lisa, you finally get your turn to view of one da Vinci's most famous works. While you study the painting, the fellow next to you comments, "You know what the most amazing fact about this painting is? It was unintended. You see, this was the drop cloth that lay on the floor in da Vinci's studio, where he painted his other masterpieces. The man was such an artistic genius that even his accidental pictures are beautiful!"

At this point you think to yourself, *Has the entire continent gone mad? No, somebody must be putting me on. OK, where's the hidden camera?*

In fact, for an organism to do anything requires coordination and cooperation between different systems. For a human being to pick up an apple, he first needs to see it with his eyes. Then, the nervous system needs to process the information and send a signal to the muscular system to extend the arm and get the hand to grasp the fruit and bring it to the mouth, where the digestive system takes over. Is it reasonable to believe that all of this just somehow came together?

A respiratory system would have needed to evolve on exactly the same schedule as a circulatory system because, without the circulatory system bringing oxygen to the cells of the body, what purpose would the respiratory system play? And vice versa. In fact, just to live for a few minutes requires these two systems to operate in perfect partnership.

When you take a breath the air enters through your nose or mouth and travels through the pharynx, larynx and trachea and into the two bronchial tubes, one of which veers into the left lung, the other into the right. From there the air travels through smaller and smaller tubes, called bronchioles, which resemble the root system of a tree, until the air finally dead-ends in tiny, cup-shaped hollows called "air sacs" or "alveoli." Scientists estimate that there are more than 600 million of these in the average lung.

In these sacs the oxygen is extracted from the air and enters the bloodstream by seeping through the sacs' thin walls into a network of blood cells called "capillaries." The formerly oxygen-depleted blood, which was blue in color, now becomes oxygen-rich and red in color and continues its round-trip journey through the circulatory system, carrying its oxygen to the cells of the body until it runs out and heads back to the lungs for a refill. These two independent systems must coordinate perfectly for us to be able to live.

Many of us haven't given this information a second of thought since being forced to memorize it in school, but it is worth revisiting. And if you are in a field of science or medicine that deals with this information, you probably learned it in a way that discouraged philosophical musings on the meaning of it all. But try to see it through new lenses now.

One last example, and really the most counterintuitive for those who subscribe to any permutation of a random, godless evolution, is the way we make babies. The human reproductive system (and, for that matter, all sexual reproduction), unlike our other systems, does not serve any purpose unless it works in partnership with a foreign system in another completely autonomous organism—in our case the opposite sex.

Think about it, the two reproductive systems contain four distinct components—the male genitals, the female genitals, the sperm and the egg. This means that the theory of evolution requires you to believe that no less than four independent evolutions all emerged independently but nevertheless work perfectly with each other. (If only one of the four were missing, there'd be nothing doing.)

Isn't it more than a little unbelievable that this would happen? That the reproductive systems in both the male and the female of the species would evolve independently yet be perfect anatomical fits for their counterparts? What if two types of genitals "evolved" but were incompatible?

Remember, this would have had only one generation to work. If everything hadn't been perfect the first time, the species would have died out. It is obvious that one of the reproductive systems without the other would have served no purpose. Imagine what would have happened if they had both evolved but at different rates—for example, if the woman had been ready one day with her eggs but the male had needed another few thousand years to get his act together (it's possible; everyone knows that men take longer to mature). We wouldn't be here today.

So, how were these two independent systems able to coordinate? How were the male and female organisms able to know what was going on in the other? Why did the female evolve with only unfertilized eggs if there was no counterpart to fertilize them? Why did the male species only evolve a fertilizing agent and nothing else? And, how could it have happened that the partnership of the egg and sperm evolved simultaneously with the partnership of the male and female genitals? This scenario requires the coordination of four distinct factors evolving together—two internally and two externally!

A further question: If "nature" somehow "knew" that there had to be reproduction, why in the world would it have done it in a way that required two organisms coming together? It is spectacularly illogical to base the future of a species on the cooperation of two parties. It is much more practical and efficient to have an organism reproduce on its own. Preservation of the species would rule out the need for two partners.

One last question: Why would a species have a need to reproduce in the first place? It is against its innate sense of self-preservation and there is no gain for the parent. The period of gestation puts the mother at risk since it makes her less agile; the actual birthing process is inherently dangerous to the point of being life threatening; and the need to share food with offspring means less for the parent. Also, why would nature give mothers the fanatical instinct to protect their eggs or offspring even at the risk of their own lives? Doesn't that sense of altruism run counter to their instinct for survival?

The basis of any theory of evolution is the emergence of life through random, chance occurrences. But how do random, chance occurrences create harmony, balance and interdependency? If something was created by chance would it work in perfect unison or would it have severe faults and imperfections?

Do we really believe that randomly tossing paint onto a canvas will produce a work of genius on par with a Dutch master? Is it reasonable to believe that Mount Rushmore, through a process of natural erosion, came to resemble four presidents of the United States and not just four random faces? And in the very country where they held office?

We all know intuitively that random, chaotic occurrences do not produce refined, beautiful or harmonious results. Randomness is generally a destructive force that produces accidents or damage. And yet, we are instructed to believe that everything about our world—the food chain, the cycles of nature, the oceans, delicious food, luscious aromas, beauty, color, music, kindness, generosity and love—all just happened by accident.

Are we really to believe that DNA, with its intricacy and sophistication—one microscopic drop holds the entire genetic code to build a human being, and the genetic information of every creature on Earth could fit in a teaspoon with room to spare—came about by random occurrence? Or that even the smallest elements, like proteins, genes or single-celled organisms that are light years beyond man's creative and scientific capabilities, came about by accident?

If we weren't programmed by society to see the theory of evolution as scientific and intellectual and the theory of creation as ignorant and reactionary, we would have the same reaction to evolution as our European tourist had to the comments he heard regarding the works of Michelangelo, Beethoven and da Vinci. I would show you a human being with myriad systems operating independently within his body, all performing needed functions and each indispensable, each having within it numerous parts and functions all operating in unison and harmony, and then I would tell you, "It all just happened. No one planned it and no one made it."

The evidence that the universe, and specifically our planet, was designed is abundantly visible. Trees shed their leaves in the winter when we need the sun and grow their leaves in the summer when we need shade; fruit does not attain its full color or fall from the tree until it is ripe and ready for us to eat, and before then it is green and hard to dislodge; dead organic matter breaks down in a way that is beneficial to the soil and fertilizes living foliage. There is clearly some design to our world. Everything fits together and works in harmony.

Conscience

There is another human element for which evolution cannot account: Every human being possesses what is called a "moral imperative." We want to do the right thing, and we want to be considered good.

Where does this need come from? Why do people need to justify or explain away their incorrect actions? So, you did the wrong thing. So what?

How do we explain the fact that we all have limits to what we will do to save our own lives? Or that we will risk or forfeit our lives in given situations? It doesn't have to be the usual example of killing someone to save your own life. How about the numerous cases of people running into burning buildings to save people or diving into icy rivers to pull people out, *people that they might not know,* fully aware that they might not survive?

How do we explain the sense of moral outrage that every human shares? Why does it bother us when atrocities occur half a world away? Why should it bother us if it doesn't affect us in the least? Why do people rush to help or send contributions to survivors of natural disasters?

How do we explain why every Jew, to the last man and woman, when asked to hypothetically choose whether they would have preferred to be a Nazi guard in a concentration camp or an inmate who would eventually have been killed in a gas chamber, chooses the latter?

Further, why are people haunted by a sense of guilt for actions long past? Do we believe, as Darwin finally proposed and as many atheistic philosophers and scientists claim, that our sense of morality is just a sensation produced by chemical reactions in the brain? If so, we could just alter our chemicals and have no qualms about, regrets over or reluctance to do anything. If we knew how to control our chemicals, we could leave the scene of a hit and run accident without the slightest guilt because we would know that whatever we might feel is only a sort of mental indigestion.

Those who postulate a godless theory of creation have no explanation for our moral sense and our conscience. How does one explain the desperate need that human beings have to be good if the world is only material and the existence of life only a chemical mishap? Why don't plants, fish or animals—our supposed ancestors and present day cousins—share this need? A dog doesn't need to be good. It needs to eat. It behaves well to avoid getting hit with the newspaper. Is it logical to assume that of all the millions of species that "evolved", only human beings have this trait? And, according to the theory of evolution, what benefit would a moral sense provide to humans? It only interferes with survival by making us less selfish and introducing unworldly factors into decisions. According to evolution, human being should operate according to the rules of the animal kingdom.

But we do not. We humans base our actions on what we perceive to be right. We would be embarrassed to go through life explaining that our actions are the result of what we *felt like* doing. And when we say that we are trying to do what is right, aren't we saying that we are trying to live according to a system that transcends existence and our desires? We are not embarrassed to claim that we chose a certain CD because we like the musician but we would be embarrassed to say we stole it from the store because we felt like it. The choice between stealing and not stealing is an altogether different question than the choice between jazz and bluegrass.

Evolution also lacks any explanation for why only humans, amongst the millions of species that inhabit this planet, pursue and need spirituality. Art, music, literature and philosophy are utterly absent from the animal kingdom. Groundhogs don't plant flowers around their dens to pretty them up. Mom and dad hippopotamus don't hire a babysitter so they can spend some quality time alone. Whales might "sing," but it is a form of communication and all their songs sound the same. Human beings can communicate without song, which represents something altogether different for us. When we do use songs, ours sound unbelievably diverse.

The reason for modern day science's lack of explanation is because morality exists only in the spiritual realm, not the physical one. This is why we will sacrifice physical comfort, security and even our lives to do the right thing. The spiritual pleasure far outweighs any physical gain we might receive from acting immorally. There is an entire state of existence—a spiritual one—that is unique to human being and is beyond the abilities of the physical sciences to understand.

For 200 years the Western world has built its definition of knowledge on a scientific base. To be accepted as fact, something must be proven or verified using physical means and yardsticks. But science cannot measure the human spirit, emotions or soul and therefore is limited in what it can offer. By defining knowledge in a physical way, the Western world has consciously chosen to ignore the other more important and more powerful component of life: Spirituality.

The New Religion

When the freethinkers of the scientific world were waging their just war against an obscurant Catholic Church, they had no way of knowing that science would become the new religion.

Over the last 200 years science has come to replace religion as the object of man's faith. We have been programmed, sometimes overtly but most times subtly, to see scientists as men and women of valor who only seek the truth, who approach their work with remote objectivity and dispassionately accept the results of their findings. This, of course, is nonsense. Scientists are people like the rest of us. They have weaknesses, egos, biases and sensitivities. How often have we read about scientists falsifying data or plagiarizing in order to gain glory? They can also suffer from cognitive dissonance and downright stubbornness, and a scientist's marriage and home life have the same issues and challenges as anyone else's.

But to be fair to scientists, why should we expect anything else? They are not computers. They will not be any more impartial, when threatened, than a non-scientist.

Conversely, religion has been portrayed, especially in the last century, as the last holdout of the simple minded, the superstitious, the backward and the ignorant. For a modern Jew, the issue has been framed as one against the other, with the Jew having to choose a side with which he or she will identify. It's no wonder that most Jews see evolution as truth and everything else as fairy tale. And it's no surprise which side the modern Jew sees as normal and which seems weird.

But these issues have been falsely framed. Judaism does not have a religion-versus-science mindset, nor do we see a conflict. Our conflict is with ideology, not science. And the subject of evolution is loaded with ideology.

How so?

There are really only two positions. One is that life began abruptly in many different forms all with their own distinct features—fish with fins and scales, birds with feathers and wings, egg-laying amphibians with skin and mammals with hair and mammary glands. The other is that inanimate chemicals somehow came to life and slowly (or abruptly, depending on which theory you subscribe to) became more and more developed and sophisticated, culminating with the thinking human being.

So far, science has only proven the first.

Evolutionists have no explanation for what is referred to as the Cambrian explosion, which was the sudden appearance, approximately 530 million years ago, of all the major groups of life—insect, arthropod, fish, bird and mammal—all with their organs, internal systems and body parts intact and functional. Paleontological records show that life suddenly burst upon the scene at a unique point in history without any evidence of having existed previously. This has led to many extreme, desperate ideas. For example, Francis Crick, who won a Nobel Prize for discovering the double-helix structure of DNA, commented on this fact by speculating that life on earth was "seeded" by intelligent alien life.

What science has proven is what is called microevolution or changes within a species. Fossils show that horses have changed over the years, dogs, cats and rodents, too. They have adapted to changes in climate and habitat. The marked differences between an African elephant, rhinoceros and lion and their Asian counterparts are living examples. No matter how far back we go there is still no evidence of one species evolving into another species. Woolly mammoths are just a different type of elephant, saber-toothed tigers another type of cat. Even going back to dinosaurs—these are just different types of lizards, birds and fish.

Therefore, belief in any theory of an evolution of the species, despite its mathematical impossibility and the absolute lack of any fossil evidence, is the definition of a false religion since it requires leaps of faith in devotion to a false idea.

This is why people say that they "believe" in evolution. That is a funny term to use in science. Since when does someone "believe" in a scientific fact? Does a person "believe" in gravity? Like a blindfolded man who follows the person ahead of him by placing his hand on his shoulder, today's garden-variety believer in evolution depends on the "scientists" who have "proven" evolution. He cannot intelligently articulate or discuss the subject. He knows nothing about the leaps of faith built into the evolutionary model. He does not know the debates and disagreements within the scientific community—that there is nothing even approaching unanimity in the scientific world regarding the possibility that evolution ever occurred and that there are thousands of brilliant scientists throughout the world who think the whole idea is bunk.

Non-Orthodox Jews today believe in evolution the way the non-Jewish world believes in their religions: blindly. The completely speculative nature of Darwin's original theory and all the subsequent revisions is ignored. The utter lack of even an iota of evidence is ignored. The mathematical proofs that make fantastic the idea of even one small mutation are ignored. Darwin's own doubts and the problems he wrestled with are swept under the rug and the illusion is fostered that the theory of evolution was proven over 100 years ago, and that all subsequent discoveries continue to prove it and that there is no debate within the scientific community.

The masses have accepted the theory as fact even though there is no evidence to support it and all evidence in fact, disproves it. It is hard to find a greater example of brainwashing in today's world.

So, are we to believe that only one side of the debate is motivated by ideology while the other is simply pursuing the scientific truth? Science has developed its own belief system with its own "holy" doctrine and it will fight any questioning of its tenets. The scientific establishment's shrill opposition to the teaching of any other possibility of the origin of life is no different than the Church's prosecution of Galileo and Kepler. When something cannot be reasonably and rationally discussed or defended, the only other option is to stigmatize the other opinions or physically silence the opposition (like denying tenure).

Science should be a no-holds-barred quest for the truth without any sacred cows or preconceived notions. It should not be a search for explanations that are consistent with predetermined philosophy.

Evolution will eventually run its course, but it will take time. Like all false ideas it will collapse under its own weight. But what gives it such power of survival in the meantime? Why do we accept a random, accidental explanation for the existence of all of life but laugh at the person who would suggest the same for the origin of Mount Rushmore?

The answer is that we don't have an emotional need to believe anything about Mount Rushmore and therefore can view it objectively. But regarding our very existence we have a strong need to believe in evolution and therefore will leap to the conclusion and latch on to it even though it is preposterous.

Throughout history, any rejection of G-d always ran into the same difficulty—how to explain the existence of life on this planet. This posed the greatest refutation to all heretics. As long as the only explanation for life was that it was created by a higher being, humanity was bound by the laws of that higher being. This doesn't mean that the higher being could not be redefined to suit man's purposes, he certainly was, but the existence of a creator always implied meaning and purpose.

The theory of evolution finally provided the intellectual opening for those who wanted to be liberated from G-d and His morality. With evolution man could be redefined not as a unique creation of G-d, but simply as a highly developed primate, a link in an ongoing chain stretching back millennia and forth into eternity.

There are no morals in the physical world. Animals are not "bad" because they kill or eat other animals and the whole notion of morality cannot be applied to chemical reactions or natural phenomena. Lightning is not "bad" or "good." If human beings are just extensions of this system, then it follows logically that we also cannot be judged morally, and the whole concept of right and wrong loses its meaning.

The idea that man evolved from ape, and therefore, is not any more special or obligated in his behavior than an ape frees human beings from any transcendental morality. Once our origins are rewritten, we are then free to rewrite the moral rules by which we live. The theory of evolution successfully kicks G-d out of the picture. It is ideology, not science, that was behind the acceptance and promulgation of this idea and it is ideology that still drives the issue today. Belief in evolution is essential to those who want flexible morals.

This is why people react so viscerally when evolution is challenged—it is a very real and direct threat to both the way they view themselves and their way of life. Their reactions have nothing to do with the science *per se*. Subconsciously, they understand that a rejection of evolution and everything it has come to mean would have profound moral implications on a personal level. This is where the threat lies and this is why society must embrace evolution so loudly and so vigorously.

Aldous Huxley, author of *Brave New World*, wrote an article entitled "Confession of a Professed Atheist" in Report Magazine in June, 1966, in which he made a startling and incredibly honest admission:

> I took it for granted that there was no meaning. This was partly due to the fact that I shared the common belief that the scientific picture of an abstraction from reality was a true picture of reality as a whole; partly also to other non-intellectual reasons. I had motives for not wanting the world to have meaning; consequently assumed that it had none, and was able without any difficulty to find satisfying reasons for this assumption…
>
> For myself as, no doubt, for most of my contemporaries, the philosophy of meaninglessness was essentially an instrument of liberation. The liberation we desired was simultaneously liberation from a certain political and economic system and liberation from a certain system of morality. We objected to the morality because it interfered with our sexual freedom; we objected to the political and economic system because it was unjust. The supporters of these systems claimed that in some way they embodied the meaning (a Christian meaning, they insisted) of the world. There was one admirably simple method of confuting these people and at the same time justifying ourselves in our political and erotic revolt: we could deny that the world had any meaning whatsoever.

Scientific discoveries and advances somehow became reasons not to believe in G-d—as if antibiotics, ultrasounds and electron microscopes somehow refute His existence. One camp begins with the premise that religion is the result of fear and ignorance and once mankind gains knowledge and understanding there is no longer any purpose to religion. In fact, at that point, it is at best a crutch and at worst an impediment to further understanding.

Orthodox Jews, on the other hand, do not begin with that premise and therefore increased knowledge and understanding do not have a negative bearing on our relationship with G-d and His Torah. If anything, it deepens our appreciation of the genius of creation. Discoveries make our lives easier, healthier and more comfortable but in no way refute the existence of G-d or alter the meaning of life.

Social Darwinism

Ironically, because of Darwin's fame his name has been associated with ideas that have nothing to do with his research or his opinions. The term "social Darwinism" was not used until after he died. The term "survival of the fittest" was also not coined by him but by a fellow Englishman named Herbert Spencer, who argued that government charity would only artificially and unnaturally perpetuate inferior people and prevent the natural ordering of society. This was a popular idea in England in the mid to late 1800s.

Darwin himself did not approve of the idea of natural selection being applied to social policy, although he did point out that society, through inoculations and medical advances, was allowing those with "weak constitutions"—those who, years earlier, would have died from natural causes—to survive and reproduce. Nevertheless, he did feel that the more-advanced races and cultures would eventually subsume their inferior counterparts as part of the natural selection process.

Regardless of whether Darwin agreed with what came to be known as social Darwinism, his theory and the way in which it was subsequently embraced by those who wanted to strip society of all moral restraints, quickly and directly led to a despotic barbarism that had not been seen in civilized society for over 2,000 years.

The demise of religious belief led directly to the rise of the various "isms" of the nineteenth and twentieth centuries for, without a transcendental meaning, man had to create one. All the "isms" were firmly secular and so reflected the lowest impulses in humankind. In fact, official atheism inevitably leads to barbarism because it denies a human being's intrinsic value and subsequently devalues human life.

An atheist recognizes no higher authority and is not able to or does not see the need to practice restraint in his application of power. This is the reason why the atheistic philosophies of the twentieth century—namely, Communism and Nazism—killed vastly greater numbers of people than any religious regime ever could. There were no boundaries. The ideologies of Marxism, which was based on economic theory, and Nazism, which was based on genetic and racial theory, were quickly soaked in the blood of millions of innocents.

The irony is that secular people like to bemoan the millions killed in the name of religion, but it is just the opposite that is true. Secularism is the most destructive philosophy on Earth. No religion ever killed the numbers that the atheistic philosophies killed.

There are two reasons why totalitarian regimes must be atheistic. First, so much suffering in the name of economics or nationalism could not condoned by a society based on a belief in G-d. The people wouldn't see it as necessary and would probably believe it to be against G-d's wishes. Second, religion is an obstacle to the complete subjugation of the population. It is a competing philosophy. To a totalitarian regime, there can be no higher authority than the rulers. Therefore, war must be waged against religion.

The danger of atheism can be demonstrated by contrasting the American and French revolutions. The American Revolution was carried out by believers. The Declaration of Independence begins by declaring that all men "are endowed by their Creator with certain inalienable rights." The French Revolution, on the other hand, was violently anti-clerical and its Declaration of Human Rights has no reference to G-d whatsoever.

Consequently, the results were quite different. The United States evolved into a tolerant, just society that respected religion and its practice and encouraged tolerance amongst its citizens. France quickly descended into a bloody madness that saw its leading citizens beheaded, its institutions ravaged and its society shattered. Its civil upheaval continued on for 151 years through four different constitutions, three dynasties, two republics, three revolutions, one coup, one attempted coup, two civil wars and various financial and judicial scandals until it finally collapsed after only in six weeks of war in 1940.

I have described the history of the idea of evolution and how it came to be accepted as unassailable fact in order to introduce the issues that are discussed in the next chapter.

The redefining of human as ape, as just the most advanced animal on an ongoing evolutionary scale, an idea that Orthodox Jews viscerally reject, destroyed any idea of a G-d-ordained specialness to our lives and laid the groundwork for a moral upheaval and societal transformation that was faster and more abrupt than any seen before in human history.

Chapter Nine
Marriage and Intimacy

Marriage

As we saw in chapter seven, G-d created men and women with different strengths and weaknesses, interests, motivations, needs and desires.

To fully develop as spiritually well-rounded people, men and women need each other. The environment in which a man and a woman come together, grow together and function as a unit for their mutual betterment is marriage. Since a marriage is so essential to our spiritual development, the Torah places great emphasis on the need for what is called "*shalom bayit*"—literally, "peace of the home." But this idea of peace is more than just getting along and not fighting. "We get along, we don't fight" is a description of a roommate relationship, not a marriage.

The Hebrew word "*shalom*" has the same etymological root as "*shalem*," which means complete. True peace means the harmonious functioning of all diverse elements. This is true whether one is applying the term to international relations, the internal situation of a single country, the functioning of a household or even of the mind of a single individual. It means more than a lack of conflict; it means everything acting in unison towards a goal. Obviously, this includes not fighting, but that is only the first step.

The only way to attain true unity in a marriage is to clearly understand and appreciate the other party. Without an understanding of the true natures of men and women, a marriage will be rocky and hard to maintain. And since the natures of men and women have been redefined falsely over the last forty years, it is no wonder that marriage is in so much trouble.

The most crucial element in a successful marriage is the most basic: People have to know why they get married in the first place. When asked why they marry, people will usually answer, "For love," "For companionship," or "To have a family." But these do not really answer the question since one can find love and companionship and have a family without getting married. And, if men and women are committed to each other only to raise children, what happens when they are finished with that task?

So, the question remains: Why get married?

The answer is that we get married in order to give—selflessly and altruistically. If people have any other intentions when they marry, they will inevitably be disappointed. The extent to which they are misguided when they marry is the extent to which they will be disappointed. Some people are mildly disappointed, some people much more so.

If a person goes into a relationship looking for someone who will make him feel a certain way, he is looking to receive. And that is the absolutely wrong way to go into a marriage. If you are looking to receive, disappointment and bitterness will be your lot in life. A person who makes his or her spouse feel special, appreciated, understood, physically loved, accepted, desired, respected and protected will have a very happy life. And he or she will receive the same and more in return.

This is why living together is just a cheap imitation of marriage. Deep down it is a self-centered act; because there is no real commitment, either side can just walk away. When we marry, we make a real commitment. Without a real commitment we cannot give in the manner that develops and matures us in the way that we need and the way G-d intended. Marriage is a lifetime commitment and it must be approached that way. Otherwise, there is no incentive to work at it.

This explains one of the reasons why divorce is so prevalent in Western society today. Since society is focused on fun and good times, much of dating is a process of finding someone who is fun and enjoyable to be with. However that does not prepare people for the real world of marriage. Marriage is not a "fun" thing; it is a relationship that requires effort. Contrary to the fairy tales we were raised on and the message in all romantic books, movies and television shows, there is no such thing as a "happily ever after." No one lives happily ever after unless they work at it *ever after*. Every marriage has issues and requires adjustments and compromises, and G-d intended it to be that way. Marriage is the integration of two different human beings and almost two different species, and so it will inevitably have bumps, some of which will get smoothed out and some of which never will. The growth comes in the ways in which we smooth out the former and the ways we live with the latter.

Another reason for the high divorce rate is that we aren't looking for our mates correctly. We desire soul mates, not body mates and certainly not roommates. The more we are in touch with our souls and act like souls, the easier it is to find our soul mates. When people say that they want to be loved for who they are, this is what they mean. They want to be loved for what they truly are beneath the pose, the clothing, the car, the money, the job, the reputation and so on. This is why people who focus on looks often have strings of broken relationships. Beneath it all, they don't know who they are and neither do their partners. So, they never really connect.

Love

So, where does love come in? As we saw earlier, love is the emotion we feel when we identify someone by his or her virtues. It can be felt at different strengths. You might love a friend, but not as much as you would your child. Love actually is a result of commitment and giving; the more you give to a person, the more you will love that person. Two people who like each other and come together to raise a family with sincerity will develop a deep and abiding love for each other through giving to each other and through focusing on each other's virtues. The more they put their spouses before themselves, the greater the love they will create.

Another key element in marriage and an engine for growth is emotional intimacy. Though marriage requires it, it can be quite painful because it strips away the facades that we create for the rest of the world to see. They say love is blind but I think that the person who coined that phrase lived in a cave by himself. He certainly had no real-world experience with love. In reality, love has X-ray vision and the magnification power of an electron microscope.

Think of the people who love you the most. I am certain that they can itemize every one of your faults and shortcomings. Certainly any married person reading this could fill a book with stories and examples of their spouse's faults. But it doesn't matter because we identify those we love with their virtues, which is why we love them and vice versa.

This is much different than infatuation, which is an emotional tidal wave that doesn't allow a person to think clearly. One who is infatuated cannot come up with any faults in the object of his or her desire; this is why infatuation is dangerous in a relationship and always leads to disappointment when the faults, eventually and inevitably, come into focus. We do not fall in and out of love because love is based on knowledge. But we do fall in and out of infatuation because it is based on emotion.

Emotional intimacy, if healthy and nurtured properly, sets off a chain reaction that changes the way a person views and interacts with the rest of the world. A person in a healthy, loving relationship is vastly different from someone who is not in a relationship. And a person in a bad relationship is even worse off because his or her sense of intimacy has been damaged.

For a man, emotional intimacy is the hardest part of a relationship because it so very internal and a man's nature is not to go in that direction. But a man has to understand that he is reintegrating a part of himself that was cut away. It is not another being that he is coexisting with; it is another side of himself, and he needs that other part. He is a cripple without it.

The Talmud describes a man without a wife with the following statement: "Any man who lives without a wife lives without joy, without blessing and without goodness." It then quotes another opinion, which adds the words "without Torah and without a wall" (i.e., protection against the craziness of the world). Finally a third opinion adds "without peace."

It doesn't sound like this guy is missing a cleaning lady, cook or concubine. Such women might provide certain benefits, but they don't bring joy, blessing, goodness, peace or protection. Without a wife to love and care for, a man has no song; there is nothing uplifting or beautiful about his life. And, interestingly, he also has no Torah, even if he has spent his whole life studying it. To become great in Torah, one needs joy, and the single man doesn't have any.

A successful marriage also requires a woman to be aware of a man's emotional needs, and ironically this is frequently overlooked. A man, by virtue of his nature and characteristics, is usually the leader in the relationship. But this role is in no way one of domination or repression because as we have seen, it is not a real relationship if one party is completely subordinated. (An unspoken truth is that women *want* their husbands to lead.) He must also feel valuable and appreciated. He has taken on a great deal of responsibility not just financially but psychologically and emotionally, and eventually, everything that happens in the family falls into his lap. He must always be there for each individual member of his family, including, and especially, his wife. If he is not sincerely appreciated he will withdraw and stop fulfilling his needed role.

I once heard a rabbi speaking under the *chuppah* (wedding canopy) at a wedding. He was advising the newly married couple on how to compromise. This was his example: "Let's say the wife likes to vacation at the beach but the husband likes to vacation in the mountains. So, you compromise—you go to the beach."

Naturally, he got a good laugh. But this man was a weakling and a fool. Besides the fact that he was pandering to the women in the audience (who I am sure were the only ones laughing), he just set up this couple to fight and resent each other. Why should the husband's needs and desires have no weight? Doesn't this man who works hard and carries his family financially and emotionally have a right to enjoy his vacation?

Here's what my advice would have been: "So, you compromise—one year you go to the beach and one year you go to the mountains. And when you go to beach, you (looking at the husband) should say to yourself, 'I prefer the mountains but my wife loves the beach, and so it is my pleasure to give this to her because I appreciate everything she does. It is my pleasure to see her enjoy herself.' And when you go to the mountains, you (looking at the wife) should say to yourself, 'I prefer the beach but my husband loves the mountains and so it is my pleasure to give this to him because I appreciate everything he does. It is my pleasure to see him enjoy himself.' That is how two people love each other."

And on the other hand, while a woman must heed her husband's emotional needs, so must the man sincerely appreciate his wife's extraordinary efforts. We don't subscribe to the demeaning definition of the perfect woman as one who waxes her legs and waxes her floors—i.e., she keeps a great house and looks terrific while doing it. The woman of the house works incredibly hard. Not only would a man need to hire three or four people to do what she does but even with them, he would not be able to replace her. Only a wife can create a nurturing home environment and give her children the love and attention that is so crucial to their mental health. She literally creates people.

It is under a woman's warm guidance and watchful eye that her family grows and flourishes. The home she creates is a protective sanctuary where her children enter as day-old infants and leave as young adults; where she molds their morals and ethics and shapes their personalities and characters. And it is under her loving care that these children learn who they are and how to interact with other human beings. A person's entire life is shaped by his or her experiences in childhood and this task rests almost exclusively with the woman of the house. A man cannot do what she does. To most of humanity, their home is the source of their greatest happiness and their warmest memories.

And, incredibly, the benefits of a woman's efforts in maintaining her family extend far beyond her husband and children. She is, in fact, the foundation on which all of civilization is built because, just as a building is built brick by brick, civilizations are built on the family structure. Destroy the family unit and society will crumble into a mound of sand and rubble. Within the family one receives his moral training; he learns to give, to consider the needs of other people and to compromise. These traits are the basis of a healthy society and without the family environment, civilization begins to acquire a jungle-like atmosphere inhabited by packs of animals, interested only in their own needs and desires.

Physical Relations

Sex is one topic that needs no introduction. But it does need a lot of explanation, especially regarding how it fits into a life of Torah and *mitzvot*.

The sex drive is one of a human being's most powerful drives. After air, water and food (in that order), a person's most pressing physical urge is for sex—which seems odd. It is understandable that the body would crave air, water and food because they're essential for survival. But why would it crave sex? There are no direct benefits from it. People can live without it without any adverse physical effects. They don't die or even become less healthy due to a lack of it.

And there are other weird aspects to sex. For instance, the drive seems insatiable. There is a limit to how much air a person can breathe and how much water and food a person can consume. But sex seems to have no limit. It is a physical drive without the usual boundaries that accompany physical drives, which indicates that there might be something more to it than mere physical gratification.

In addition, sex is inextricably tied to our emotions. Our normal breathing has no emotional effect on us. A good meal can be uplifting, especially if it is followed by a good cigar, but a bad meal will not leave us with emotional problems. Sex, on the other hand, goes very deep and when not used in the proper manner can cause profound scars and emotional trauma. Misused sex, whether within a relationship or outside of one, can be life altering.

So, what exactly is sex?

The Torah views sex as the ultimate and deepest connection with another human being. It is the closest thing to completion, to a physical union that was the original state of a human being before he was split into male and female versions.

It also is the act that produces life, which is the most godlike thing we can do.

This is why it is so powerful: because it is so profound and so sublime. This is also why its misuse is so damaging. Anything that can take us high can also bring us low. The higher the potential, the lower the potential.

The power of sex can be compared to electricity, which, when generated and conducted properly, is a wonderful thing that brings light, warmth and thousands of other benefits to people. But when electricity is not generated and conducted properly, it is a highly destructive force capable of inflicting great pain and even death.

Similarly, when sex is channeled through a marriage it nurtures, builds and warms. But when sex exists outside a marriage, it is like a downed power line—wild, destructive and, in the end, uncontrollable. (This is why, historically, societies continue to grow more and more decadent before collapsing. There is no turning back.)

And, just like electricity, sex is either doing good or doing harm. It has a wonderful and indispensable role to play but only within certain parameters. The Torah posits that sex is either good for us or bad for us as individuals and as a society. There is no such thing as neutral sex.

The actual damage that misused sex does differs between men and women. For a man, sex is an external experience; the act occurs entirely outside of his body. When he misuses sex, it affects the way he relates to and interacts with other people. Because this misuse involves manipulation and using another person for his own gratification, he will become arrogant and self-centered and will increasingly see people as objects to satisfy his needs.

For a woman, however, sex is an internal experience and so when she misuses it, it affects the way she feels about herself and how open she will be with others. Such a woman will feel negatively about herself; she will become calloused and more hesitant or unwilling to open herself up to men. She will also tend towards depression, knowing deep down that she has been used.

A man who regrets past sexual behavior will not want to discuss it and will refrain from doing it again. But a woman has a much deeper and internalized residue. She will see her past actions as reflections of herself. There is a lingering aftertaste that she must contend with. A man's guilt will never focus on how he might have hurt himself.

The Torah's Unique Approach

The first point that must be emphasized, reemphasized and then reemphasized again is that nowhere in the Torah's philosophies of life is sex considered bad or dirty or a sin or anything else that any other religion labels it. We consider it a wonderful and beautiful activity that, in the right context, we are meant to enjoy and freely partake in without guilt, tension or reluctance.

There is no asceticism in Judaism. There are no monasteries; there is no celibacy. We are not commanded to withdraw from normal, physical life. In fact, we are forbidden to withdraw to the mountaintop. To live a full Jewish life we are required to live in communities with other people and to marry and produce children. Celibacy is forbidden in Judaism; it is not a higher way of life.

In fact, the *mitzvot* of the Torah elevate and ennoble the physical life. The way we deal with our physical needs and possessions such as food, clothing and money is what lifts us out of an animal-like existence. Unlike other "religions," Judaism is not built around temples, churches and priests. It is built around a nation going about its daily business in the home, the market, the school and the workplace. The way we deal with everyday life and its moral challenges and struggles is what makes us a holy people. This is true, and even more so, when it comes to sex.

The question commonly asked is why should G-d care what you do in the privacy of your own bedroom? The answer is obvious: He is a loving G-d who cares about his children, and he only wants us involved in positive, beneficial actions. G-d cares about what you do in your bedroom just as He cares what you do anywhere else. In this way He is no different from any human parent who loves his or her child. Nothing a child does is beyond the interests of a parent, especially what the child does behind locked doors. This is because what a person does in the privacy of his own bedroom can affect him significantly. It can alter his personality and change his character. And this is why G-d is concerned with our sex lives.

Good sex is positive and reinforcing; bad sex is negative and destructive. On this point everyone agrees. The divisions are on where the definitions apply. The proponents of the sexual revolution will tell you that sex between consenting adults can never be bad for them. The Torah says it certainly can be. In fact, the Torah clearly states that only sex between a man and a woman within the bonds of marriage is beneficial because only through the relationship of husband and wife can sex serve its intended purpose—the bonding of a man and a woman. Outside of this relationship it will only cause harm regardless of how much physical enjoyment the participants might experience —even if the harm is not immediately noticeable. Just because it feels good doesn't mean it is good for us. The Torah rejects hedonism because hedonistic acts only serve to reinforce the untruth that we are essentially animals. The Torah's restrictions on sexual license are for our own good. They channel our sexual passions in a productive and fulfilling direction rather than having us spend our lives flailing around like a dog in heat.

Refraining from premarital sex also ensures that lust does not play a role in determining a marriage partner—i.e., that a man is not marrying a woman for the wrong reason. This protects the woman. It is absolutely essential that a man be attracted to the woman he marries but any consummation of that attraction takes place after they are married. When sex is introduced into the relationship before marriage, the essential element of the relationship, the aspect that bonds the two together, is introduced too early, when there is no commitment. In such a case it does not perform its purpose; rather, its presence interferes with the proper development of the relationship. The cart has gone before the horse.

The prohibition of premarital sex also sends strong messages to young Orthodox men and women. For the latter it reassures her that her body is not public property and does not exist for the pleasure of others. Because of this she will not be pressured to do things too soon; she will not engage in any type of sexual activity before marriage because she will understand that "good times," "fun" or even "love" are meaningless translations of hormonal impulses that nine times out of ten will only leave her feeling used. An Orthodox woman understands that a wedding band on her finger is the minimum sign of commitment. She understands that even though a man can pledge his eternal love, his definition of "eternity" might be until he gets bored or finds someone better looking or more interesting.

To the young Orthodox man, the prohibition conveys the message that people are not there merely to satisfy his desires. And he is taught the self-control that is vital to a moral life. He comes to understand that only through the ruling of his passions and the mastery of his desires will he be able to channel his drives and achieve greatness.

By nature, men are seekers, conquerors and explorers and these traits also apply to the way they view women. Why did Oriental potentates have harems? The answer is simply because they could (although in Europe, the Catholic Church would not tolerate such open decadence). This urge to have it all does not only stem from base physical desires; it also comes from a man's basic nature. He needs to explore the world.

To again use the example of the television remote, a woman searches for a man the same way she searches for a TV show. Once she finds one with whom she is comfortable and who provides for her emotional needs she is content and not interested in any other man. Men, on the other hand, do not suddenly become disinterested in other women once they find mates. The unbridled male regards women the same way he views the many channels he can watch: He wants to check out and sample them all.

You will often hear women complain that "men just don't get it," but this is not true. Men get it and they get it loud and clear. By getting physical outside the structure of marriage, women have taken away all incentive for a man to make a commitment. They have given him the leeway to procrastinate or avoid responsibility without suffering any consequences.

So how does the average male evolve from an ill-mannered boor into a refined gentleman? First, I'll tell you how he does not, and that is through adopting a façade. All too often we see how civilization can easily break down under pressure. The veneer cracks and submerged passions erupt.

Another way that a man does not become refined is through guilt, harassment or a domineering wife. A man can only refine himself and his refinement is a product of the hard work of subjugating his physical drives and desires to his spiritual will. When he becomes his own master he can then direct his life's efforts onto what he *wants* to do rather than what he *feels like* doing. It is a lifelong process without a finish line since there are always greater heights to attain. It's a process of steady, gradual growth.

That being said, there is certainly a minimum required level of refinement for a Jewish life. You will not find Orthodox men or boys standing around, leering at women or girls passing by. You will not find them with their tongues hanging out like dogs in the midday sun. You will not see Orthodox men or boys suddenly stopping their conversations in mid-sentence to ogle a woman walking by, eyeing her up and down like they were checking out a new car. Our heads won't snap around, we won't whistle, our necks won't strain to follow anyone down the street. We don't buy pornography.

Will individual Orthodox men or boys slip up once in a while? Absolutely. But these occurrences are just that—slipups, not a "boys will be boys," wink-wink, acceptable form of behavior. We are not prudes, nor do we think that sex is dirty or evil. We just don't engage in this type of behavior because it is below someone who was created in G-d's image, and we understand how self-destructive it is. And by the way, slipping up does not make one a hypocrite. Hypocrisy means being dishonest; slipping up is just being weak at that moment.

Even within a marriage there are times when sex is proscribed. For example, a husband and wife do not have physical contact during menstruation, which forces the husband to relate to his wife and love her as a person. Sex can easily become confused with love even though one does not necessarily require the other. There are many people we love, such as parents, siblings and children, without involving sex. And a sexual relationship can exist where there is an absence of affection.

The Torah insists that a man love his wife outside the parameters of physical contact because it helps him see her for the person she truly is and not just as a physical partner. Each month, every Orthodox man rediscovers his wife.

The Western View

The Jewish philosophy of sex directly clashes with the modern, Western view of sex, which considers it a matter of personal choice and no one else's business. What we need to understand is how sex came to be viewed as having nothing to do with morality—and how that affects us.

Firstly, it is, of course, true that sex is a personal choice. But society does not define this as a choice between right and wrong; instead it equates the choice to opting for either plain or peanut M&Ms—either way is fine, it's just a personal preference. The Torah, however, views it as a moral choice between right and wrong, that requires the use of freewill.

Secondly, as we have seen, sex has very real and very serious emotional consequences and what happens in the bedroom has a deep impact on everything else in society. Basically, if one lives in a sewer he will inevitably get dirty. Because of this, not one of us would want to live in a society where brothers marry sisters, nor would we want to live in a society where all marriages are "open"—i.e., where adultery is accepted as completely legitimate and openly discussed.

Since the 1960s the prevailing view of sex in Western society has undergone a radical revision. For nearly 1,500 years, sexual morality was firmly planted as a cornerstone of Western society. Then, suddenly, in the 1960s, there was an upheaval of huge proportions. Sex was redefined as a personal lifestyle choice and not an issue of morality. No longer was it understood to be a profound act laden with meaning and consequences; rather it was redefined as a casual act that was assumed to be part of any dating relationship or worse, a natural, physical act of passion devoid of any real emotional or spiritual consequence.

What force on Earth was able to overturn 1,500 years of moral instruction? Unbelievably, it wasn't a cataclysmic event like a famine or a plague. Nor was it an occupation by a foreign empire with radically different ideas. It was just a simple little pill. And this little pill set off a chain reaction that has not yet subsided.

It also caused unexpected moral clashes over two other issues that came to the surface almost unexpectedly: abortion and homosexuality. It is no coincidence that these two issues, which are at the heart of the cultural battles in the United States today, are both sex related. In fact these two issues boil down to the same one issue that the invention of the birth-control pill provoked—the license to practice unrestricted sex whether it be premarital, extramarital or anything else that a person chooses.

In the following few pages I will attempt to briefly show how society has changed over the past forty years. This is very important to know since what happened to society's sense of morality affects us on a personal level in both thought and deed. Needless to say, there are many ideas that people accept as "normal" or "understood" that are really very recent changes in society.

It is also important to understand that since Orthodox Jews do not follow conventional wisdom but instead maintain the high levels of holiness and spirituality as defined by the Torah, they did not change their morals, opinions or behavior when the rest of Western civilization went through its convulsions.

And, as all of this becomes clear, the reader will understand why Orthodox Jews are consistently represented on the other side of the moral debate from almost all non-Orthodox and secular Jewish organizations.

The Pill and the Sexual Revolution

In 1960, one year after Gregory Pincus discovered that the hormone progesterone prevented conception and formulated it into a pill, the FDA approved a drug called Enovid as the first oral contraceptive. Until that point progesterone had only been used for menstrual disorders.

In 1961, the drug company Searle, which owned the patent, began promoting Enovid to doctors as a contraceptive. For the first time in human history, a woman could take a little pill once a day and never get pregnant regardless of where, when or how much sex she engaged in. There were no longer any consequences. It shouldn't take a great deal of imagination to visualize the effect such a pill could have on a society.

Since our beginning, human beings have had to deal with the obvious consequence of extramarital sex—pregnancy. This has been especially problematic for unwed women. Throughout history, all types of birth control methods were concocted and many of them worked some of the time. But there were still very real risks to promiscuous behavior. What would happen if suddenly there would be no consequences to indulging in our strongest, most-relentless, most-pleasurable and most-addicting physical desire? What could keep everything from bursting open?

In a secular society, nothing. This is because sex is a physical drive and the only way to control our physical drives is to make them subservient to our spiritual drives. That takes belief in a higher power and in reward and punishment. Without this, there is no force on Earth that can stop the dam from bursting. A human-created "morality" will never work since it will, in the end, always bend to accommodate and justify people's wishes and desires. Without a G-d-given morality there is no way for a man to overcome the constant hunger for more and more sex.

This is why the existence of the pill has not affected moral behavior in Orthodox Jewish society. The fact that it exists has no bearing on how we should behave. But to a society that had become more and more secular to the point of even viewing itself as a group of evolved apes, there was no reason not to take advantage of it.

Many embraced the opportunities the pill provided and rallied for "progress," "change" and "liberation." Others saw an explosion of immorality that was debasing society and stripping humanity of its higher meaning. The resultant clash was the head-on collision we call the '60s. This clash of values is the reason for the ongoing culture war in the United States.

Among the most vocal and passionate promoters of the idea of freedom from morality have been Hollywood and the entertainment media; they canonized the '60s as a time of innocence and self-discovery, beginning with the "summer of love" in 1967, when the youth were encouraged to "turn on, tune in and drop out." If you watch any documentary on that era, you would think that every teenager and young adult was participating and that they were doing so out of a sense of higher purpose; that they were finding their true selves through "liberation." But this is a false picture. The '60s (which sort of began in 1966 and sort of ended in 1975) were, in truth, a time of great tension and anxiety. Drugs took an unbelievable toll on people. The most active drug-wise are now either brain dead or have died from overdoses or by choking on their own vomit. Violence was widespread; cities were engulfed in riots and national figures were gunned down in numbers never seen before or since. It seemed to many people at the time that society was literally coming apart.

The baby-boomer generation that supposedly only wanted to love everyone, give peace a chance and change the world did, in fact, do so but it wasn't for the better. The consequences of the turbulence are still being felt today. Soon after "make love not war" became the mantra, the rates of divorce, high-school dropouts, drug use, abortion, sexual diseases and crime shot up.

Why did this happen? Because the true legacy of the '60s is self-indulgence and that only leads to selfishness. The point of the upheaval was to destroy the old order—i.e., right and wrong—to allow for sexual license. When one's philosophy is merely to satisfy his animal lusts, his world revolves around himself. All he knows or cares about is himself and his needs. The values of previous generations, such as loyalty, patriotism, integrity, self-negation and sacrificing for the common good, all went out the window.

And the entertainment industry, by tantalizing and manipulating teen-age hormones, succeeded in changing society's view of right and wrong *vis a vis* sex. By the time I graduated high school in 1979 no one was serious about virginity. It wasn't a question of *if* a person would have sex before marriage; it was a question of *when*.

Abortion and the Right to Privacy

The ability to practice unbridled sex that the pill provided came with an ironic side effect: unwanted pregnancy. It turned out that not everyone who was participating in the sexual revolution was using the pill. Either they were using something that was not as effective or they were using nothing at all. And the greater the number of sexuality active people, the greater the number of unwanted pregnancies there were.

This was not a small problem for two reasons. First of all, getting pregnant completely undid the idea of unfettered freedom to do what you wanted. This was a very real and inconvenient consequence, and the one that supposedly had been eliminated. Secondly, unwed motherhood was still very much a stigma in proper society and that was not going to change overnight.

There are only two solutions to an unwanted pregnancy: Complete it or end (abort) it. But at the time of the sexual revolution, notwithstanding the legal prohibitions, abortion was still considered murder by many and certainly beneath the dignity of a medical practitioner and those who performed abortions practiced in secret. It was unthinkable to an ethical doctor to use his medical knowledge to kill an unborn baby. The reason abortion was relegated to back alleys was because it was so morally abhorrent to upstanding citizens.

Since the best way of avoiding unwanted pregnancies—abstinence— was no longer a serious option, it was inevitable that a legitimate way would have to be created to allow women to get out of pregnancies. Society's view of abortion would have to change.

This happened in three ways. First was the assault on the language used. We can't go around killing babies, so we redefined the idea. It was no longer a *baby*; it was simply a *fetus*. Though, of course, it is only a fetus when we want to abort it. Try going up to a pregnant woman and asking her, "How is the fetus doing?" and you'll see what kind of look you get. Or try consoling a woman who just miscarried by saying, "Sorry you lost the fetus." When it's wanted, it's a baby. When it isn't wanted, it's a fetus.

Second, abortion was redefined as a medical procedure. According to this new doublespeak, aborting a fetus is no different from having one's tonsils removed. Of course, there are obvious dissimilarities. First, this "tonsil" is sucking its thumb. Second, this redefinition ignores the psychological trauma of the abortion. Psychologists deal on a daily basis with women consumed by guilt over their decisions to have abortions; I've never heard of anyone seeing a psychologist because they had their tonsils removed. And this definition also ignores the high turnover rate among workers at abortion clinics as opposed to other types of clinics and medical facilities. It seems that it is psychologically very trying to watch fetus after fetus be thrown into a garbage bag.

Lastly, abortion was reframed as a rights issue, just as there were human rights and civil rights there were now reproductive rights. It was a woman's body and she had a right to decide what to do with the fetus. It was her body and it was unfair and unjust to burden her with an unwanted pregnancy or for society to tell her what to do or what not to do.

(This insistence, by the way, that a woman has the right to make any decision regarding her body is contrary to Jewish belief: She does not, nor does a man. Our bodies do not belong to us. They are on loan, and so we must take care of them and treat them with respect even after our souls have left. This is why Judaism insists on treating the deceased with great respect and why both Jewish men and women are prohibited from mutilating themselves, marring their bodies or even getting tattoos. And we must guard our health as we would a precious gift.)

Redefining a baby and an abortion as a fetus and a procedure paved the way to having abortion legally protected. This happened in 1973, when the United States Supreme Court ruled, in Roe v. Wade, that a woman's right to have an abortion was protected under the constitutional right to privacy as interpreted in the Fourteenth Amendment. But this "legal right" only makes any sense if it is not a baby and it is not being killed. No one has a right under the Fourteenth Amendment to kill a baby in the privacy of their own home. Since the ruling is based on these definitions, it is clear why the issue is still so contentious. Many people do not accept these new definitions.

It should not come as any surprise that Jewish law does not permit abortion on demand. It does, however, permit it at times and even requires in certain situations (such as when the mother will die unless the baby is aborted). This topic is complicated and nuanced but for our purposes we must understand that the idea of aborting a baby because a woman became pregnant as a result of her own freewill decisions contradicts almost everything the Torah stands for. To literally destroy human life because it will inconvenience us is barbaric.

The usual retort to this statement is to bring up the cases of rape and incest. These are very real and painful situations and cannot be dismissed. But—and please read this sentence over and over until it sinks in—no Orthodox Jew ever supported outlawing abortion. It is a necessary medical procedure at times. What reason would there be to outlaw it? The Torah only speaks of the morality of the act. In some cases it is the right thing to do and in some cases it is the wrong thing to do.

In the tragic cases of incest or rape, it might very well be necessary sometimes to abort the child to save the mother's mental health, which is equally as important as her life. But sometimes, it might not be so necessary. Each situation must be evaluated individually. I began the last chapter by stating that the Popes and the preachers do not speak for us. Here I add that the politicians also do not speak for us. The Torah is neither Republican nor Democrat and neither party's platform represents the Torah viewpoint.

Homosexuality

The second issue to inadvertently morph out of the sexual revolution was homosexuality. This is a subject that causes great discomfort. Many people, out of good-heartedness, will defend the rights of homosexuals to live their lives according to their own decisions—but will need to hold their nose while doing so. This is because the vast, overwhelming percentage of people not living in New York, Los Angeles or San Francisco finds homosexuality a deeply nauseating idea. And despite what the media tries to portray, the vast, overwhelming percentage of parents do not want their children to be homosexual and would give all their money and both of their arms if that would prevent it from happening. (Have you ever met anyone who *wants* his or her child to be homosexual?)

Of course, until the sexual revolution, this was not an issue. Homosexuality was relegated to the fringes of society and conducted underground. Even the most progressive-thinking people did not defend homosexuality openly and publicly. Why, then, the sudden need to rehabilitate the concept of homosexuality?

The answer has nothing to do with homosexuality *per se*. Just like abortion, it has everything to do with the overall issue of sexual freedom.

The sexual revolution led directly to the forced acceptance of homosexuality because people painted themselves into a corner. After extramarital sex became accepted, the need to view and defend all sex as a right became inevitable. If the concepts of right and wrong were removed from the discussion of sex (which allowed for extramarital sex), how, on principle, could homosexuality be considered wrong? And inversely, if society would consider homosexuality wrong, what would prevent society from expanding its moral judgment to other sexual issues?

This subconscious logic drove the issue and homosexuality, slowly and again through the political left and entertainment industry, became more visual and more promoted. What is remarkable is that even after a concerted effort by these elements there is still a strong resistance to mainstreaming homosexuality. This is not reflected in polls on the issue itself because people have already been brainwashed to think that if they are against homosexuality then they are "bad" people. It is reflected in the polls on the issue of legalizing homosexual marriages, the opposition to which is overwhelming.

Acceptance of homosexuality opens up a serious can of worms. If it is legitimate and must be accepted by society, it must follow that there is really no sex between consenting adults that is wrong. If that is the case, what is wrong with incest between consenting adults? Or wife swapping between consenting couples? Or polygamy? Once anything goes, there is no end to what has to be accepted in defense of sexual "freedom."

Imagine for a moment that the house next door to you is sold to a new buyer. He is a single man in his thirties, good looking and with a high-paying job in a respected profession. He is very friendly and loves to throw around a ball with the neighborhood children. He also loves dogs and has a number of them living in the house.

But you start to notice that there is a conspicuous lack of women in his life. He has male friends who drop by from time to time but no female friends. So you come to the conclusion that he is gay. *All right,* you say to yourself, *who am I to judge? I am an enlightened, modern person and I should accept people for what they are.* But, almost reflexively, you start to hesitate when you see him talking to your boys. How close is his relationship with them? What kind of influence will he have?

Then, one fall day, while taking a break from raking leaves, you have a friendly chat with him over the fence dividing your yards. It turns out that your suspicions were unfounded. He is not a homosexual after all. In fact, he tells you, he has never been physically attracted to men, nor to women for that matter. He is only attracted to animals—canines in particular. Oh, and when he said he loved dogs, he meant that literally. And all those dogs in his house? Well, he refers to them jokingly as his "harem."

At what point during his monologue do you begin to throw up? And how many minutes will pass before a "for sale" sign goes up on your front lawn? Will you ever let your children play with him again? Or even talk to him?

Now I ask you, what bothers you about this man's lifestyle? Maybe he's happy. Who are you to tell him that he cannot find true love and happiness with a member of another species? Are you a specist? (Yes, that is a real word.)

In the beginning of the effort to force an acceptance of homosexuality, it was billed as another type of "right." Just as society had embraced civil rights and women's rights, the proponents of homosexuality assumed that by painting the issue in familiar colors, society would embrace it as well. But its advocates underestimated the Western revulsion to homosexuality.

So, they changed tactics. Instead of a personal lifestyle choice, homosexuality was transmuted into a biological disposition. Through this tactic, they attempted to manipulate public opinion in two ways. The first was to transform sympathy into legitimacy. In other words, a homosexual had no more choice about his orientation than he did about his height or eye color. He was merely a victim of circumstances. The second was to create a false dichotomy: either you are with them or against them; there is no middle ground. Therefore, to oppose his lifestyle and right to live as he chooses is to be mean spirited, hateful and downright bigoted. How can you be against innocent people for being born a certain way? They are not doing anything wrong; they simply have no choice. It's genetics.

(But it is unnatural. The anus is clearly not designed to be penetrated—it has no natural lubrication and repeated entry causes pain and injury. This makes the act a more animalistic type of behavior which is why the movement, despite what the media tries to portray, is represented by extreme debauchery and perversion.)

It truth, there is really no evidence of a biologically based homosexuality. If anything, it is psychologically coerced through environmental factors, sometimes at a very early age. More often than not, homosexuality is a result of a terrible relationship between a man and his father. In fact, this common denominator is so widespread among male homosexuals that psychologists have coined a new phrase, "triadic families," to describe a family wherein the father is absent, distant or emotionally abusive and the mother is emotionally needy (therefore smothering her son to gain the affection she doesn't get from her husband). This sick environment does not allow a boy to develop normally and instead imbues him with feelings of weakness and a sense of inadequacy with the opposite sex. He craves his father's love, as any boy does, but never receives it. And he can never fulfill his mother's needs because only a husband, not a son, can do that.

In a society that legitimizes homosexuality, emotional problems that would materialize in other ways find an outlet there. This is why the number of homosexuals greatly differs from one society to the next. Wherever and whenever homosexuality is legitimized more and more people engage in it. The genetic argument also ignores the body of psychiatry that cures homosexuals. And for every study showing the innateness of homosexuality, there is another showing that sexuality can change according to circumstances, such as isolation (prisons, monasteries or ships), titillation (too much heterosexual sex) or social strictures (Arab societies). And it seems that not only homosexuals engage in homosexual sex; the epidemic of AIDS among heterosexuals in Africa and South America—both areas of the world where male virility is a virtue—demonstrates the existence of homosexual activity amongst otherwise heterosexual men. (Studies also show that most homosexuals in the United States and Europe have also had heterosexual relationships.)

We all know people who were once straight and now are not. They will tell you that they were always felt different. That might be true but "different" and "homosexual" are not necessarily the same thing. First of all, every teenager feels *different* at some point in his adolescence. And secondly, we all know homosexuals who would have turned out a lot different if their circumstances had been different. The ability to declare themselves to be something altogether different from heterosexuals allows them to turn their problems into virtues and feel better about themselves.

I stress all this because of the suffocating insistence by "enlightened" society that homosexuality is inborn and the implication, and even at times the open accusation, that those who do not fully accept this theory are hate-filled bigots. The Torah, by commanding us to refrain from such behavior—it is explicitly prohibited and one of the 613 *mitzvot* is to refrain from it—clearly states that it is a moral choice.

This view of homosexuality as a moral choice and not a biological *fait accompli* is borne out by looking at its history. The ancient world was immersed in homosexuality, in both the East and the West. The Egyptians,

Carthaginians, Phoenicians and Persians were known for it. Homosexuality was a fundamental part of life in Greece and Rome and was even considered a higher form of love in those societies than that between a man and a woman. The Jews, alone amongst all the peoples of the ancient world, continuously stood in opposition to this practice. And later it was Christianity, using the Torah as a template for morality, that continued the opposition and spread it throughout the globe.

The advent of Christianity ended the acceptance of the practice amongst the Europeans including the Greeks, Romans, Gauls, Celts, Britons and Scandinavians, to name a few. In the Americas, until the arrival of Christianity, it was practiced by many native Indian tribes including the Aztecs, Mayans and Incas. Until a few hundred years ago, also coinciding with the arrival of the Christian Europeans, it was commonly accepted in many parts of Asia including China, Japan, Thailand, Vietnam, Laos and Cambodia. The epidemic of AIDS in Africa, which remains to this day mostly tribal and animist, shows the extent of the practice there.

What is very telling is that today, as the Western world becomes more and more secular, homosexuality is back and gaining increased acceptance. This shows, once again, that only a G-d-given moral system can restrain human passions and desires. There is no logical, rational or intellectual way to do so. As G-d is removed farther and farther from the functioning of society, there will inevitably arise all types of behavior once considered vile.

I mentioned earlier that what happens in the bedroom affects all of society.

But how does the acceptance of homosexuality affect people who aren't homosexual?

The answer is deeply and this is because heterosexuality and homosexuality are diametric opposites. One is about life, the other death. Heterosexuality states that life has inherent meaning beyond our own selves. Homosexuality states that life has no meaning besides the satisfaction of our desires.

I'll explain.

First, let's look at it from a strictly physiological approach. Through heterosexual intercourse, the man's seed travels to the woman's womb, a place of nurturing and growth. In this womb a woman's eggs can be fertilized, triggering a miraculous transformation from zygote to human being. The man's seed is destined for a place from where life emerges. It is an act that, if unhindered, has the potential to create life.

During homosexual sex, the man's seed is deposited in the colon, a place designed for the collection of waste. There, in this place of death and decay, the seed arrives only to be mixed with the feces and byproducts of yesterday's meals before being excreted along with it. It is an act that, by its nature, sends the seed, the life-giving force, literally to the dung heap to die. One act sends the seed to create life; the other sends the seed to the toilet.

Let's look at it another way by comparing two scenarios. In the first, twenty people, ten men and ten women in their twenties, are left on an uninhabited island with the assignment to build a permanent life there. They have all the tools and expertise needed to survive and there is plenty of food and water.

In the second scenario, twenty homosexuals of one gender, also in their twenties, are left on an uninhabited island with the same assignment. They have the same tools and expertise and their island also has plenty of food and water. We return to both islands 100 years later. What do we find?

On the first island, we find hundreds of inhabitants. We find schools, clinics, shops, playgrounds, art, music and literature. We find a functioning society with a system of government and an economy that provides for the common good. The sounds of the hustle and bustle of life fill the air, mixed with sounds of children at play.

On the second island, we find only an eerie silence broken occasionally by the sounds of birds or the wind rustling the leaves on the trees. There are no sounds of human life, no hustle, no bustle and no children. We cannot locate anyone. Not a single person. We find a few old huts, long abandoned and partially reclaimed by the jungle. Up on a hillside, we find a small, overgrown cemetery with not twenty graves but nineteen, since the last person to die had no one to bury him and his body was left to the insects and the wild beasts of the island to finish off. The original twenty are long dead and there is no meaningful testimony to their ever having walked the Earth.

On one island a vibrant, living society; on the other a graveyard. This is the difference between heterosexuality and homosexuality. One represents life, the other death. One is fruitful and creates life; one is sterile and does not.

There is another very pernicious message that flows from the legitimization of abortion and homosexuality: the devaluation of children.

Abortion rights activists promote their agenda as pro-child but this is an Orwellian distortion similar to the people's republics of the Communist world. Abortion, by definition, accords children only a relative value; i.e., if I want one, good, but if I don't want one, bad. Once that type of decision is accepted as valid and the killing of unborn children as legitimate, then children in general are in big trouble. They have lost their inherent value.

The acceptance of homosexuality further reduces the value of children to zero because a society that equates a sterile lifestyle with a fruitful lifestyle is making a statement. **It is stating loudly and clearly that the fruit have no value**.

On the issues of abortion and homosexuality, the same lines are drawn between those who believe in G-d-given morality and those who do not. In fact, the belief in a G-d-given morality has become the Mason-Dixon Line of social issues and will always be the determiner of one's moral positions. Both of these issues necessitate the need to accept and define the concept of right and wrong. And as we have seen, everyone wants to do the right thing and will justify his or her actions or twist the definitions and the viewpoints until he or she is redefined as doing good. The result of the sexual revolution was that these two subjects, previously considered odious and revolting, had to be redefined and accepted in order to allow people to enjoy the fruits of sexual liberation.

There is an interesting point that correlates to this discussion of morality. In the United States another divisive social issue is capital punishment. The views of the opposing sides are revealing and seem to be mismatched. Why is it that the same people who are against abortion are in favor of the death penalty and those who are for abortion are against the death penalty? Wouldn't it make more sense for the people who are against abortion also to be against the death penalty because they don't believe in killing, while those in favor of abortion are also in favor of the death penalty because they don't object to killing? Why the switch?

Where is the logic in being for the killing of unborn children but against the killing of murderers? And is it logical that the vast majority (according to polls) of those who consider themselves religious are in favor of the death penalty while those who consider themselves atheist or agnostic are against it? Shouldn't it be the other way around? Shouldn't it be that those who believe in G-d also believe in the sanctity of life and oppose the death penalty, while those who believe our existence is the result of evolutionary mutations, and therefore without sanctity, have no objection?

All these questions can be answered with one explanation. The real issue at hand is whether there is an absolute right and wrong. Opponents of the death penalty are stating that there is no transcendental morality and that right and wrong are only subjective rules that society creates to maintain a sense of order. Therefore, transgressions must be punished. Dangerous people should be locked away because otherwise society cannot function, but putting someone to death is way too harsh because that is an absolute statement of right and wrong.

Those who identify themselves as religious understand that there is a transcendental right and wrong and that some actions, like murdering someone in cold blood, are absolutely wrong. They do not share the discomfort of the nonbeliever in meting out strong punishment as a deterrent or as a statement because they understand the need for civilization to operate within certain boundaries, and they have no qualms about passing judgment on the actions of its citizens.

So one side—the side with relative morals and without a belief in absolute truth—will not tolerate the death penalty but will find a way to permit abortion due to other emotional and practical needs. The other side—the side that believes in absolute truth and has a set of absolute, G-d-given morals—will use the death penalty for the benefit of society but will not be able to tolerate the killing of fetuses due to the very same moral code.

The Separation of Church and State

If society could get away with drunken orgies as a way of worshiping a god, they would embrace it and most people, especially the men, would be very religious. This was the situation in much of the world until our influence began to be felt. But the Jewish people have been far too successful in their historic mission for anyone to seriously advance such an idea. So, for the allowance of free sex, all moral judgment must be eliminated. And to do this a solidly secular society must be created—one that has G-d removed from all aspects of public life.

In the United States, this has been done by manipulating the idea of a separation of church and state.

Is it a coincidence that the side of the church-state argument that agitates for a strict separation—i.e., the side that wants the country solidly secular—is also pro-abortion and pro-homosexuality? And that the side that does not—i.e., the side that does not want the country solidly secular—is anti-abortion and anti-homosexual?

A short history is in order because the idea of the separation of church and state has meant no less than three radically different things in the last

200 years. And one needs to know that this concept is only being used as a tool to secularize society.

The popular mantra, which is repeated *ad nauseum,* is that the First Amendment to the Constitution requires the separation of church and state. This is 100-percent untrue. The Constitution requires no such separation.

Here is the First Amendment:

> Congress shall make no law respecting an establishment of religion, or prohibiting the free exercise thereof; or abridging the freedom of speech, or of the press; or the right of the people peaceably to assemble, and to petition the Government for a redress of grievances.

The First Amendment is clearly a list of restrictions on the national government. It cannot infringe on a citizen's personal religious observance. It cannot abridge a citizen's rights to free speech, to assembly or to petition the government. It cannot censor the press. And it cannot establish a state religion. And that is all. The founding fathers wanted to ensure that religion would not be used by political leaders as a tool for tyranny, as it had been in Europe.

So, where did the idea of a separation between church and state originate? On January 1, 1802, Thomas Jefferson wrote a letter to the Baptist Association of Danbury, Connecticut, in reply to a letter they had sent to congratulate him on his election to the presidency. The Baptists at that time were a religious minority in a state dominated by what were then called Congregationalists. The Congregationalists were part of the Protestant elite that became the WASPy elite known as Mainline Protestantism. These elites also counted among themselves Episcopalians and Presbyterians but not Baptists or any type of fundamentalist or evangelical.

The Danbury Baptists felt discriminated against and supported Jefferson because of his well-known advocacy of religious liberty. In a sentence that clearly was intended as a show support for their struggle against the religious/political establishment, he wrote:

> Believing with you that religion is a matter which lies solely between Man & his God, that he owes account to none other for his faith or his worship, that the legitimate powers of government reach actions only, & not opinions, I contemplate with sovereign reverence that act of the

> whole American people which declared that their legis-
> lature should "make no law respecting an establishment
> of religion, or prohibiting the free exercise thereof," thus
> building a wall of separation between Church & State.

This is the first time the phrase was ever used; it is not found in the Constitution. The wall that Jefferson was referring to was intended to protect
religion from the government, not eliminate it from society ("...that the
legitimate powers of government reach actions only, & not opinions"). Religion was not to be walled *in*; the government was to be walled *out*. Religion
was the society and government was the intruder. Today the meaning has
been inverted—religion has to be walled out.

As extraordinary as the Constitution is, it contains a fatal flaw: It was
written by human beings and therefore open to all kinds of twisting and
manipulations. Judges can suddenly decide that it says something it doesn't
or mean something that was never intended. G-d can come to be outlawed
by the First Amendment and abortion can become a right in the Fourteenth Amendment.

Yet anyone with even a superficial understanding of the philosophical
beliefs of the founding fathers would immediately recognize that today's
interpretation is bogus. The Declaration of Independence begins by stating, "...all men are created equal, that they are endowed by their Creator
with certain unalienable rights..." (Today, such a document would probably be declared unconstitutional). The military hires and trains chaplains
and Christmas Day is a national holiday; Congress begins each session
with an invocation. The founding fathers would have viewed a secular,
godless society as barbaric and so sought to protect religion, knowing it
was essential for an enlightened society.

The first mention of the "wall" in a Supreme Court ruling was in the
1947 case *Everson v. Board of Education*. In it, the Supreme Court "agreed
that the First Amendment, *properly interpreted,* had erected a wall of separation between Church and State" (italics mine). But what was meant by "a
wall of separation" in 1947 and what it is commonly understood to mean
today are worlds apart.

What is surprising and not widely known is that the original push for
the separation of church and state was in reaction to Catholic immigration. It's hard to imagine today but the blue-blooded mainline Protestant
elite abhorred Catholicism and saw its growth in the United States as a
real threat to the country and their way of life. They particularly feared

the Catholic Church, which was seen as immensely rich and immensely powerful.

In their minds, if the Catholic Church was successfully excluded, America as a free, independent nation would be preserved. These beliefs, by the way were not totally unfounded. The Catholic Church had been the major force of repression in Europe for centuries. Most of the advanced nations were Protestant (England, Scotland, Holland, Scandinavia and Germany) and most of the backward nations (Spain, Portugal, Italy, Ireland and Poland) were Catholic. Ecclesiastical authority was seen as a threat to democracy and prosperity.

The movement to protect the United States from the Catholic Church, packaged as a movement to separate church and state, actually started in the 1830s when the first wave of Catholic Irish and mostly Catholic German immigrants began to arrive. After the great influx of 1880 to 1927, when millions of Catholics (particularly Italians) entered the country, the issue reemerged with renewed vigor. There was actually a group called "Protestants and Other Americans United for the Separation of Church and State." As late as 1960, John Kennedy's Catholicism was a major campaign issue. Would he obey the Constitution or the Pope?

The Ku Klux Klan, mostly known for hating blacks and Jews, was also extremely anti-Catholic. In fact, one of the Klan's tenets was the separation of church and state and it was so basic a part of their beliefs that it was even included in its membership oaths. Obviously, to a group known for burning crosses, this had a different meaning than what it does today.

The Klan reached the height of its membership in the 1920s, just as the immigration issue was at its hottest. Its members also included future Justice Hugo Black, a member of an Alabama chapter and the author of the Supreme Court's 1947 ruling. Black and his anti-Catholic allies would be shocked to see what their favorite term—the separation of church and state—has come to mean.

Until the 1960s, religion was considered a pillar of the American way of life. Because of its official atheistic stance, Communism was often referred to as "godless Communism," as if to say that such a philosophy was abhorrent to a civilized person. In fact, as a reaction to Communism, the words "under G-d" were added to the Pledge of Allegiance and the words "In G-d We Trust" were added to our paper money (they had been on our coins since 1865). Throughout American history, leaders from all walks of life openly spoke of G-d, and prayers were said in public schools, at graduation ceremonies and even at high school football games. Then, suddenly, all this was wrong and even against the Constitution.

And so a term that originally meant a protection of religion from government intrusion morphed first into an anti-Catholic cause and finally into an anti-religious one that has come to mean that public affirmation of G-d is prohibited by the Constitution.

The underlying intent of all of this activism is made clear in the virulent opposition to the teaching of intelligent design in public schools. Intelligent design posits that the world is too complex to have evolved and that the scientific evidence does not support any theory of evolution. Since mentioning G-d in public schools is against the law, they suffice by using the term "higher intelligence." But this is rejected by the secular, liberal courts because they recognize that the intelligence behind intelligent design can only be G-d. And according to their interpretation of the Constitution, that is illegal. Which means that if you want to teach that life was seeded by aliens, it is perfectly okay but if you want to say that G-d was involved, it is against the law.

Political Correctness

The last fifteen or so pages have been a bit critical of morality in the Western world. But the purpose of this book is not to critique any society; it is to unwrap the world of Torah thought and practice to non-Orthodox Jews. I felt that to fully do so I needed to address, along with the major philosophies and widely held opinions prevalent among non-Orthodox Jews, the issues that fall under the heading of "morality".

I have endeavored to show how the invention of the birth control pill led to three things. It increased pre-marital sex which led to unwanted pregnancies which led to abortion as a right. It created an environment that required a neutering of society's moral code which was accomplished through manipulating the concept of a separation of church and state and which succeeded in the delegitimizing and outlawing of G-d. And lastly, the idea of sex being beyond the scope of right and wrong led to the introduction and grudging acceptance of homosexuality into mainstream society.

There is one last topic that must be addressed in this chapter because it has been running in the background the entire time: political correctness.

The reason I feel compelled to discuss it is because of the damage that it is doing to the Jewish people. Over the last few decades Western society has, ironically, become increasingly rigid. Topics that were once freely discussed are now verboten and the very mention of something, even if it's true, can destroy a person's career and reputation. This type of thought control, which is enforced through personal intimidation and character assassination, prevents a healthy exchange of valid opinions and analysis of grand ideas. People will censor themselves and force themselves into positions to avoid being called, or even suspected of being, a racist or a sexist or a homophobe or a religious fanatic or the worst possible label of all—intolerant. People don't allow themselves their own opinions because disagreement becomes classified as "hate".

This is never a positive environment for Jews because rarely do the opinions and mores of society correspond to the Torah. Nevertheless, throughout history Jews always proclaimed the truth. This is because the Jewish people have never been interested in being politically correct. We are only interested in being morally correct. You can never be a light unto the nations by being politically correct because by definition that means flying with the prevailing winds. It means following, not leading. It means conforming, and leaders don't conform—they lead.

Political correctness is, in fact, the diametric opposite of the moral charge of the Jewish people. A Jewish people that is politically correct has abandoned its purpose in the world.

The fact that so many people act or think a certain way means nothing to the Jews. We just don't care if "everybody's doing it." That is not a factor. In fact our entire history is built on the foundation of one man—Avraham—who defied the entire world.

What people do does not determine what is right and what is wrong, and truth is never determined by numbers. People once sacrificed their children to appease their gods. If we Jews went by the numbers, we would have joined the Christians or the Moslems long ago. If we had been politically correct in Greece we would have had no trouble with boys wrestling naked or with inferior infants being put out to die. If we had been politically correct in Rome we would have had no problem with religious orgies or gladiators.

But in fact it was the Jews, alone amongst all the nations, who opposed these immoral practices and resisted them, even taking up arms to fight at times when they were forced on us. While all the conquered nations joined in the so-called fun, we stood aloof. And it is precisely because of this that the world came to realize that these actions and many others were wrong. Because we did not partake in these practices, they are today considered barbaric.

The world understands that the Jewish nation, the nation in possession of G-d's instructions, is the world's moral gyroscope. Had the Jews been politically correct about idol worship and said things like, "Who are we to judge?" or, "One man's idol worshipper is another man's believer," or "Everyone has a right to their opinion even if I don't agree," the world today would still be filled with idol worship and its attendant abominations, such as human sacrifice. The words "human" and "rights" would not be used in the same sentence.

Today's various immoralities are touted by secular Jewish organizations as Jewish values but they are not. In fact, they are contrary to everything the Torah and the Jewish people have stood for over the last 3,800 years since Abraham.

The decline of a civilization follows a pattern. It begins with accumulation of wealth, which leads to a focus on and making a value of material goods and comforts—i.e., decadence. This, in turn, leads to arrogance, self-aggrandizement and the illusion of self-sufficiency which inevitably leads to a rejection of any G-d-given morality.

When a man's spiritual nature is suppressed or denied, he only has his animal nature left. This side of him will convince him that gratifying his sensuous and lustful urges are legitimate goals and he becomes self-centered, manipulative and even dangerous. And society becomes increasingly coarser, meaner and more biting. Our minds, instead of being our masters, become slaves to our lusts. And there is no end to lust; it feeds on itself.

In such an environment, sex becomes the dominant, driving force and everything in society becomes sexualized. In the ancient world the gods themselves were portrayed as lustful beings that engaged in sex with other gods and with mortals. (Today, we see how sex has come to permeate every type of entertainment as well as advertising, fashion and even public discourse.)

When society elevates physical pleasure to a value and it becomes a person's highest aspiration, both marriage and children come to be seen as unnecessary and even as burdens. Marriage, as we have seen, by definition requires work and very often will be uncomfortable. So, if the benefits are available elsewhere, why bother with the pain? A man can hire a cleaning service and eat out. He can be single but never sleep alone. He might eventually get married but when it gets uncomfortable, he has no reason to stick around.

Raising children requires time and effort and it is not always easy or comfortable. It also requires a great deal of money. If physical pleasure is the name of the game, children will definitely get in the way. And so birthrates begin to decline. In fact, historically, as soon as a society acquires wealth, the birthrate drops. The Roman Empire, at its height, was so decadent and homosexuality so widespread that the Emperor, Augustus, actually had to enact a law requiring men to take wives because the birth rate had dropped to levels that would prevent Rome from fielding an army. But it didn't work. By the last years of the empire, a great percentage of the Roman legions were not Roman or even from the Italian peninsula but made up of Germans and other conquered peoples.

Loosening the bonds of morality might seem like progress but it does not elevate or improve society. It doesn't increase freedom or make people happier. It is only through an acknowledgement of G-d that man progresses. *Tikkun Olam*—the perfecting of the world—will only be achieved through a commitment to G-d and His Torah.

Promiscuity destroys the family, destroys the sanctity of marriage and destroys the value of children. Why are secular Jews at the forefront of movements that produce such horrible results? Why do Jewish organizations jump to the front of the crowd and loudly proclaim their devotion to such destructive ideas? Why do secular Jewish organizations promote the stigmatization of religious groups as fanatics?

(The term "fanatic" is quite revealing. What exactly is a fanatic? And why are there are no such things are secular fanatics? I have never seen that term used. According to today's media and entertainment industry, a fanatic is anyone who takes religion seriously and thinks it should play a major role in life. A religious person who opposes abortion but would never vote to restrict it is OK because he is "tolerant," but a religious person who opposes abortion and would vote to restrict it is a fanatic.)

Today, the Orthodox continue to do what generations of Jews did before them, they stand apart and say "no." This refusal to follow the gentiles infuriates secular Jews because, by not joining in, the Orthodox are implying that those Jews who mimic the values and behavior of the gentile society are also doing wrong. But so be it; there is no other way for a people charged with the moral wellbeing of mankind to act.

Where should the Jewish people stand in such an environment of moral decay? What should our position be? What message should we proclaim? Should we justify every step down into the dark abyss or protest such behavior and, by word and deed, lead humanity away from its own destruction?

What is the role of the Jewish People in this situation?

The same it has always been and must be: a voice of moral truth.

If we abandon our role as the beacon of mankind, we are condemning the world to a permanent Dark Age.

PART THREE

The Jews and the World

Chapter Ten
The Jews and the Nations

Introduction

The chapters that comprise the rest of this book need a short introduction. Until this point we have been discussing topics of belief and practice—what we could refer to as "internal issues" that concern only the Jewish people, what we believe and how we manifest those beliefs. But as we have seen, our entire national existence is, in fact, a mission to return the world to an acknowledgement, an acceptance and a love of our Creator, who loves us.

To date we have been only partially successful although we will, in the end, be completely successful. What we have accomplished so far has been a result of a circuitous route that we have taken through history and which has brought us into contact with all the movers and shakers of human history. The following chapters explain why we took that route, how we took that route and where it will end.

Covenant

It is possible to describe the entire population of the world—over six billion people—with two words: Jew and gentile. Now, is it reasonable to be able to use one word to describe 99.7 percent of the world and another for the remaining 0.3 percent? It would seem that even the non-Jewish nations see us as something more than just unique. It seems more accurate to say that the non-Jewish nations understand that there is something existentially different about the Jewish nation, so much so that they describe our statistically negligible, almost nonexistent nation with its own word and lump the rest of humanity together with another word.

Why is this so? What is so fundamentally different about the Jewish people? The answer is one word: covenant.

We saw in chapter four how humanity, beginning in the third generation, allowed itself to be seduced and pulled from the proper path. Within ten generations mankind was past the point of return and G-d started over by saving one family—Noach, his wife, sons and daughters-in-law—and wiping out the rest of mankind in the flood. But the story repeated itself and within another ten generations mankind was back to where it had been prior to the flood.

The only difference this time was the existence of one man, Avraham, who understood the truth. He rejected the various forms of idol worship practiced in his hometown of Ur and his homeland of Babylonia (the ruins of the Ziggurats from his time are still standing in the deserts of Iraq). Instead he sought out the true G-d and once he came to understand the truth, he dedicated his life to bringing it to the rest of the world.

This changed the course of history because, as a result, Avraham and his descendents, whom he would instruct in the truth, would from then on be "G-d's people," responsible for the dissemination of the truth and ultimately the fate of mankind. The purpose of creation would be fulfilled through the actions of these people.

When Avraham was ninety-nine years old, G-d came to him and commanded him to circumcise himself. This is the sign of the covenant, in Hebrew a *brit* or *bris*, depending on the pronunciation, and it represents the dampening of the physical drive and the strengthening of the spiritual drive. It was an acknowledgement of Avraham's level of spiritual perfection, now his body would now also be "perfect".

What is a covenant? The Torah defines it as a solemn, binding agreement between two parties with each party having obligations to fulfill. Our obligation would be to keep the flame of truth burning in this world by living according to G-d's commandments. By doing so, we would become G-d's people and merit an abundance of special blessings and benefits.

There are two aspects that differentiate our covenant with G-d from a simple agreement or contract. First, unlike a contract it cannot be nullified. In a contract, if one side does not fulfill its obligations, the contract is voided and the relationship is over. Not this covenant—it is forever. There are penalties for non-performance but the relationship remains unchanged. And second, since G-d is eternal and this covenant is eternal, the Jewish people became eternal. No matter what we do or is done to us, we will always survive.

Avraham knew very well what the result of this covenant would be—his descendents would be singled out from the rest of mankind. They would have a different and special relationship with G-d that would be marked on the bodies of the male members of the nation. And as G-d's representatives, we would bear the brunt of the world's resentment both of G-d's moral imperative and of our special position.

If we kept our end of the covenant, we would have no trouble. But if we did not, if we forsook His Torah and His commandments and tried to live our lives like all the other nations, then we would be exposed to the anger of the nations.

From the moment Avraham circumcised himself, his family was bound to a sacred agreement with G-d that could never be changed or nullified. History was set on a course that is still unfolding. But to understand what is happening one must be familiar with the first book of the Torah, Bereshit (Genesis). In fact not only does the Torah provide the means to make sense of the world but it is absolutely impossible to understand any geopolitical developments, especially anti-Semitism, unless one has learned Bereshit. In it, all the nations of the world come into being and all the main players are introduced. It is the format for human history.

Avraham's offspring, both the line that would become the Jewish people and the two lines that would become our enemies, are the ultimate determiners of world history.

How did these differing family lines come into being? Avraham spent his life in his hometown of Ur (modern-day Iraq), in Charan (modern-day Syria) and in Canaan (modern-day Israel), trying to create a movement to bring the world back, after generations of idol worship, to a recognition of the one true G-d. He and his wife, Sarah, succeeded in attracting throngs of followers who had come to see the insanity of polytheism and accepted the truth but who, over the years, had gone off on their separate ways. Perhaps the social pressure had been too strong.

Later, in his old age, Avraham still had one loyal follower, a man named Eliezer of Damascus, but Avraham did not see in him the ability to carry the torch after he was gone. What he needed was offspring.

Sarah had not borne him children and at her suggestion, he had taken another wife, named Hagar. She was the daughter of Pharaoh and had followed Avraham and Sarah out of Egypt after they briefly had gone there for food during a famine in Canaan. Hagar bore Avraham a son named Yishmael (Ishmael in English). Despite Avraham's love and guidance, Yishmael did not follow in his father's footsteps. Instead he chose to conduct himself in line with the beliefs and actions of the Canaanite society, which was deeply corrupt.

Immediately after Avraham circumcised himself, G-d informed him that Yishmael would not be the torchbearer that Avraham had hoped for. Instead, Sarah would bear a son, Yitzchak (Isaac), who would carry on his work. Yishmael, however, did not just fade away. According to the Torah he was the father of the Arab nation and amazingly, since the fact stretches back close to 4,000 years, the Arabs are in agreement. However, they change the story slightly: According to the Koran, Avraham rejected Yitzchak and chose Yishmael, and from him the Arabs descended. In their version, they are the chosen people, not the Jews. The descendents of Yishmael will forever hate the descendents of Yitzchak, but they will not be the most serious enemy.

The Torah continues. Yitzchak grew up under his father's wing and emulated him. Avraham's dream of returning mankind to the relationship it originally had with G-d would live on in his son. Yitzchak took a wife, Rivkah (Rebecca), who, after twenty years of marriage finally conceived—but the pregnancy was troubled. There seemed to be a battle being waged in her womb and she sensed that something unusual was happening. She went to a prophet to inquire why she was suffering and was told that she was carrying twins—and not just ordinary twins. She was told, "Two nations are in your womb, and two ideologies will separate themselves from within you, and one ideology will (always) be mightier than the other, and the older will serve the younger."

Yitzchak's twin sons, Yaakov (Jacob) and Eisav (Esau), took radically different paths, both of which are still followed today by their respective descendants.

The Torah teaches us that the descendents of Yaakov and Eisav will wage an ideological battle for the hearts and souls of mankind. The two brothers are diametrically opposed in their approaches to the meaning of life and they will be locked in an ongoing ideological battle that will run throughout history until the coming of the Messiah, when the descendents of Yaakov will ultimately triumph.

Yaakov, the younger twin, proposes that life is eternal and meaningful and essentially spiritual; that all important things in life—love, happiness, self-respect, integrity, friendship—are spiritual; that mankind is one big family in which each person has basic and inalienable rights. Yaakov undertakes to make the world a place wherein we love our neighbors, care for the weak and the sick, and provide for the widow and the orphan. Yaakov proposes beating swords into plowshares and proclaims to the world that we are all children of a loving G-d who created the world for our pleasure and who only wants our good.

Eisav, the older twin, proposes that life is fleeting and meaningless. The Torah recounts how he sold the right of the firstborn (the right to serve as the cohen or priest in the temple) for a meal (actually, a bowl of beans) because, as he said, "I am going to die, why do I need it?" Strength, power and wealth are important to Eisav. He is completely physical. Spiritual values are meaningless, unproductive and a waste of time to him; leadership is determined not by character but by might. To Eisav, mankind is not a family but a hierarchic herd, the strong on the top, the weaker on the bottom.

In Eisav's realm all of life is a struggle, a competition with winners and losers, and that is the only true way to determine one's worth. To Eisav war is glorious; his heroes are the blood shedders. While Yaakov created a way of life that would allow everyone to grow and develop, Eisav and his descendants have created systems and philosophies that crush people beneath the iron fist of authoritarian rule, a bleak world of haves and have-nots devoid of any concept of G-d-given rights.

By the age of fifteen, Eisav had completely absorbed the decadent and cruel ways of the Canaanites. He had already committed theft, rape and murder. Conversely, Yaakov was completely dedicated to the ways of Avraham and Yitzchak. G-d again made a choice and told Yitzchak that Yaakov would continue the mission; Eisav would have no part in it.

When Yitzchak, blind and fearing he was near death, called in Eisav to bless him with physical sustenance, Rivkah overheard it and, much more aware than Yitzchak of the debased character of her son, stepped in to prevent it. She sent in Yaakov to receive the blessing in Eisav's stead. When the deception was revealed, Yitzchak, seeing the hand of G-d in what had occurred, acquiesced to Yaakov's being the recipient. He subsequently gave Eisav a lesser blessing, but Eisav's hatred for Yaakov was forever cast. He swore to kill Yaakov as soon as Yitzchak was dead.

G-d later changed Yaakov's name to Yisrael (Israel) after he had sired twelve sons, the progenitors of the twelve tribes of the Jewish nation. This is why the Jewish people are called the Children of Israel or the Nation of Israel.

But who are the descendants of Eisav? Originally Eisav lived in the Land of Seir, which lies south of Israel. Eventually his people migrated to Europe and settled on a peninsula that jutted out into the Mediterranean. On this fertile land grew a city called Rome and, from this city, the descendents of Eisav conquered an immense empire that dominated Europe and most of the known world. The Europeans of today are dominated by descendents of Eisav. They carry on his philosophies and beliefs and, as history has amply proven, his intense hatred of the descendants of Yaakov.

Amongst the family of nations, as amongst individuals, there are leaders and there are followers. As part of G-d's master plan the greatest leaders amongst the nations grew from the same roots as the Jews, and they are the ones with the most hatred for us. The Europeans and Arabs have shaped the course of history and will determine its future. The other nations in Asia, Africa and the Americas will be involved but only in supporting roles, not as the main antagonists. The Jews do not need to be concerned about the Chinese or the Africans, for example. We only need to be concerned how they act in concert with the Europeans or Arabs.

The Nation of Israel

The twelve tribes proliferated but the Jewish people were still not a *people*—just a large, extended family. We did not become a nation until we were forged into one during the servitude of Egypt. This, in and of itself, is remarkable. We were born as a nation not like other nations that emerged as their stars were rising but while we were in slavery—the nadir of a nation's existence and one that usually spells its doom. The birth of the Jewish people was in itself a supernatural event.

We entered Egypt as tribes and left as a nation and the Torah was given to us as a "nation," not as a family or a federation of tribes. The Jewish nation was to have the impact on the other nations through its ideas and actions.

But what makes us a nation? We don't fit the standard definition. We are comprised of different colors, languages, cultures, philosophies and backgrounds. So, what makes us a people? Historians define a nation as a group that shares four things:

1. A common land
2. A common language
3. A common culture
4. A common history

For 2,500 years the Jewish nation has lacked all four. We have been scattered to the corners of the world. We speak different languages and in fact, most Jews in the world cannot even speak to another Jew unless they use English. What binds a French Jew to a Brazilian Jew to an Iranian Jew? How is it that Jews who identify as Jews feel connected to each other and to a greater Jewish people? What do they have in common? Except for the moniker "Jew," they share little else.

The answer is simple: We are a people only because of our covenant with G-d and the fact that we possess His Torah. Nothing else matters. Not the fact that we speak over 100 languages, are members of tens of different cultures and have experienced different histories depending on where we've lived.

Amazingly, it is the Torah that provides all four of the prerequisites of nationhood.

Our common land is the Land of Israel. Three times a day we pray to G-d to gather in the exiles and return us to our land. We are constantly learning about the Land of Israel and its special place in Jewish law and Jewish life. We are all tied to it because we so fervently want to return to it. It is as if we never left, we are still there because our hearts are still there.

Our common language is Hebrew. It is the language of the Torah. We learn in it and pray in it regardless of the languages of our host cultures. Our books are written in it and our children are fluent in it.

Our common culture is the one created by *Halacha* or Jewish law. Every Jew, regardless of his location, eats only kosher food, prays the same prayers, has the same *tefillin* and Shabbat and festivals and believes in the same G-d. In many ways we have more in common with each other, even though we may be separated by thousands of miles, than we do with our gentile neighbors.

And our common history begins with Avraham, Yitzchak and Yaakov, proceeds through the Egyptian bondage and exodus, through the years recorded in the Bible (First Temple Period and a little beyond). Our formative years were spent together and we all share the same foundations.

This is why the Jewish people were able to endure thousands of years of dispersion and still maintain a strong national identity. Wherever we carried the Torah, we transplanted our land, language, culture and history.

Exile

Because the two branches that descended from Avraham—Yishmael and Eisav—are the final determiners of history, when Israel was punished with its final and most serious exile (with the destruction of the Second Temple by the Romans in 67 AD) it was into these nations that we were sent. (As a result, we have developed into two general branches —Ashkenazi or European and Sephardi or Middle Eastern.)

Our exile is not a capricious act of punishment. It works towards the same purpose as everything else about Jewish existence: perfecting the world. We did not fulfill our mission while living in the Land of Israel and therefore, to have the required effect on mankind, we had to be scattered around the world. By sending us into the midst of the pagan Europeans and later, the pagan Arabs, G-d was ensuring that these nations, which would have the most impact on world history, would come to recognize the one G-d and see to it that the entire world came to understand the truth as well.

Do you think it is a coincidence that besides Judaism, Christianity and Islam are the only religions in the world that speak of one G-d and a revelation? Isn't it a bit strange that out of the thousands of known religions, there are only three that do this? For the other fifty percent of mankind, comprised of Hindus, Buddhists, animists, tribalists, Sikhs, Jains, Shintoists, Zoroastrians, shamans and so on, there is no such thing as a revelation from G-d. He did not speak to anyone, did not express His will, did not reveal a set of laws and does not require daily adherence to any type of code.

And isn't it ironic that the two other religions that speak of one G-d and a revelation both began and developed in regions of the world where the Jews lived in great numbers—Europe and the Middle East? And that there are no such concepts in the regions where Jews did not live in great numbers?

This is because the idea of a G-d who revealed His will to His creations became a tenet of Christianity and Islam only as a result of their exposure to the Jews. Obviously, both of these religions are loaded with falsehoods but their faults do not diminish the tremendous improvements they have brought to the gentile world. Christianity was a trade up for the pagan Europeans and Islam was a trade up for the pagan Arabs. And both were trade ups for the animists of the Third World.

And as part of G-d's plan, these two religions have spread with missionary zeal well beyond their original borders to bring the world under the cloak of their teachings. They have successfully anchored the world into a belief in one G-d. And it is no coincidence that both of their lineages trace back to Avraham.

You might ask if it was preordained that we would wander the world in a state of exile in order to bring about this recognition of G-d. The answer is absolutely not. Everything that happens to the Jewish people, just like everything that happens to individuals, is the results of our freewill choices. Our job is to be a light to the nations. If we do not accomplish that by living a certain type of life in the Land of Israel, we will be spit out into the nations and forced to live in their lands to bring about this recognition. And if we do not bring about this recognition by the way we live, we will bring it about by the way we die, whether it's being burnt at the stake for not accepting Christianity or being beheaded for not accepting Islam or being gassed for just being Jews.

Still, it is clearly better to avoid exile. It is also advisable to get out of exile as quickly as possible but again, that is all dependent on our freewill decisions. Life is real and our decisions affect history. G-d will return us to the Land of Israel just as He pushed us out of it. He exiled us because we were not living the type of life we needed to in order to stay in the Holy Land. If we change ourselves for the better we will find ourselves back in Israel, living in peace and prosperity, in short order.

Needless to say, being forced to live amongst people who violently hate you can be a dangerous and unpleasant experience. And we endured this not once but twice. The first exile sent us to the east and the second to the west. But the first of these exiles only came after nearly 1,000 years of living in the Land of Israel. Here's the timeline in a nutshell:

After Yehoshua (Joshua), who succeed Moshe, conquered the Land of Israel forty years after leaving Egypt, the Nation of Israel lived solely in the Land of Israel. For close to 1,000 years there was no significant settlement beyond its borders. Individuals might have come and gone, trading posts might have been established, but there was no such thing as a Jewish community outside of Israel.

This changed as result of a series of invasions and forced exiles. The first expulsions were perpetrated by the Assyrian Empire (located in today's Syria and northern Iraq) over a period of eighteen years, from 3187 to 3205 on the Jewish calendar, corresponding to the years 574 BC to 556 BC. In total, ten out of the twelve tribes were forcibly relocated to the eastern regions of the Assyrian empire, never to return.

Over the next 400 years one empire was swallowed by another and each conquest had a direct effect on the Jews. Assyria was the first to go, swallowed by the Babylonian Empire on its eastern border. A hundred and fifty years after the ten tribes were banished, the Babylonian emperor Nebuchadnezzar conquered the remaining two tribes—Yehuda (Judah) and Binyamin (Benjamin)—and put an end to Jewish political independence. In the Jewish year 3338, corresponding to 422 BC, the First Temple was destroyed and the bulk of Jewish society was driven in chains to Babylon (the leaders of society had already been taken fifteen years earlier). Eventually most of the land's inhabitants were taken. Jews were now living throughout what is today Syria and Iraq.

The Babylonian Empire was soon swallowed by its eastern neighbor—the Persian Empire, located in what is today Iran. Cyrus (or Koresh in Hebrew) allowed the Jews to return to Israel and rebuild the Temple, though it was a shadow of its former self, as was the Jewish Commonwealth. Most of the Jews remained in their exiled lands or continued to migrate eastward into today's Iran.

Until 1948, there were significant and honored communities in Iraq and Iran that could trace their histories back 2,500 years. But it was here that our eastward migration basically ended. Because the next empire, Greece, was situated to the west of Israel, we stopped moving eastward. There were never great numbers of Jews in Afghanistan, Pakistan and India.

In Greece, or more accurately in Macedonia, a young prince named Alexander came to power upon his father's death and set out to literally conquer the world. He destroyed the Persian Empire and inherited all its possessions, including Israel. The Jews then came under the rule of Greece. Since the Jews did not physically oppose Alexander when he marched into Israel, he allowed them to remain unmolested. We then started a westward trek into the Greek Islands and mainland, what is today western Turkey, the Balkans, southern Italy and North Africa.

After Alexander's death, the Greek Empire was divided amongst his generals into four autonomous fiefdoms and all of them were eventually conquered, over a span of a few hundred years, by Rome. In the year 3700 (61 BC), the Romans marched into Israel. For the Jews, Rome represented and still represents the greatest threat to our existence; under their rule, which continues to this day, we have suffered the most.

The Romans were not benign rulers. They did not allow us to live our lives according to our ways, and their restrictions on practicing Judaism eventually caused the Jews to take up arms in the year 3826 (66 AD). The revolt was fierce and bloody; it took twelve Roman divisions to finally subdue the small Jewish population though it had only taken ten to subdue all of Gaul (today's France). Retribution was swift and intense.

In the year 3828 on the Jewish calendar, corresponding to the year 68 AD, the Romans destroyed the Second Temple and much of the Jewish life in Israel. In the battles and ensuing massacres of civilians, the Romans annihilated approximately one-third of world Jewry—percentage-wise, more than were killed during the Holocaust. Much of the surviving population was forcibly exiled, sold into slavery or left by choice due to the widespread destruction.

Approximately seventy years later, in the year 3892 (132 AD), in reaction to continued persecution, the remaining Jews again rose up against their Roman oppressors but were again crushed. This time the Romans set about ensuring that the Jews would never trouble them again. Jerusalem was destroyed altogether and a Roman city named Aelia Capitolina was built on the site. The earth was salted to prevent re-habitation and, in an attempt to sever the Jews permanently from their land, the name of the country was officially changed on all Roman maps. Instead of Judea, as it had been known for centuries, the territory was henceforth called Palestina, using the name of the ancient and long-gone Philistines and disregarding the fact that it had been the land of the Jews for the previous 1,340 years.

Although some remnant would always remain in the Land of Israel, the Jews began a wide-ranging migration that would take us to the four corners of the Earth.

With the expansion of the Roman Empire, Jews settled throughout the Italian peninsula, Hungary and the Balkans, the Black Sea area (today's Romania and Bulgaria) and up into southern Central Europe—particularly what is today Austria, and Bohemia and Moravia, today known as the Czech Republic and Slovakia. Jewish settlement also expanded into Spain and France and, by the time the Roman Empire collapsed in 476 AD, stretched from Spain to Iran and from Northern Europe to North Africa. We were living in every part of the known world.

You might think that after centuries of living together with the gentile nations we would have eventually been accepted. But that was not the case. In fact, the longer we stayed, the more intense the hostility became. When the Germans set out in 1939 to kill every Jew in Europe, we had been living amongst them on and off for over 1,500 years.

Life was so unbearable in Europe that it is actually possible to track Jewish migration on the continent. Over the course of a thousand years we continuously traveled eastward to seek sanctuary. This is the reason why, when Jewish life in Europe effectively came to an end during the Holocaust, we were disproportionately concentrated in Eastern Europe. Before the war there weren't large Jewish populations in Germany, Austria, France and the Low Countries and there were no Jews at all in Spain and Portugal, but there were millions in Poland, Hungary, Byelorussia, the Baltic States and the Ukraine. Our populations had built up in these lands in our eastward search for safe haven during the Middle Ages and, eventually, there simply was no place to go farther east.

Assimilation and Intermarriage

As was noted, living amongst people who have a violent hatred for you can be a dangerous and unpleasant experience. In such a scenario, there are two general ways to deal with the situation. One is to stand your ground.

This would be based on a clear understanding that you have done nothing wrong to these people and a deeper understanding of why you are enduring such an ordeal. Another way is to try to appease the haters and deny or diminish one's distinction in order not to stand out.

Throughout our history, the vast majority of Jews have taken the first approach. Some exceptions have converted to Christianity or Islam, either under duress or simply to gain some type of advantage. But as we will see in the next chapter, when Europe went through tectonic changes and suddenly seemed more or less open to the Jews, many Jews, out of confusion or a desire for a better financial life, took the bait.

Assimilation is a fatal disease for a people that is supposed to stand apart and live a higher, more-moral and more-spiritual life as an example for the rest of the world. Being like everyone else obviously does not fulfill that role and the effects of trying to do so are two-fold. The first is the rapid loss of our brothers and sisters from the fold. The second, ironically, is anti-Semitism.

Millions of Jews have disappeared in this century besides those who have been killed. According to the American Jewish Historical Society, in 1940, the Jewish population of the United States was 4.8 million. Today it is estimated to be between only 5.2 million and 6 million and that low figure is despite the influx of nearly 500,000 Jewish immigrants from the former Soviet Union and Israel.

So, where did everyone go? By a normal rate of increase, there should be between twenty and twenty five million Jews in the United States today. It hurts to say but these millions of descendents either aren't Jewish or don't know that they are Jewish.

The absorption of non-Jewish values also distorts our thinking. For example, the shifting of values from family first to career first has sent the Jewish birthrate spiraling down into the negative numbers. More Jews die each year in the United States than are born. Jewish women get married later than their non-Jewish contemporaries and have fewer children. The fixations on education and career are pursued at the cost of other Jewish values like having a family or even being happy.

Assimilation was also rampant in prewar Europe, before Hitler put an end to it. By the time he came to power, over fifty percent of German Jews were intermarried and most of those who were not practiced little Jewish observance. This situation was mirrored throughout Europe, where tens of once-great communities had shrunk to piddling remnants of their former selves.

Statistically speaking, if Hitler had never come to power and the situation had been allowed to continue, there would have been almost no demographic difference between the Europe of today and the Europe that would have been. Assimilation would have wiped out as many Jews as did the Holocaust.

It doesn't require a calculator to see the future. With the present inter-marriage rate of close to seventy percent among non-Orthodox Jews, there will be very few descendants in one or two generations. The Orthodox, on the other hand, with a negligible rate of intermarriage and an average of six children per family, will produce the Jewish future. The descendants of those who assimilate will be swept downstream into the vast ocean of humanity, where they will disappear. Unless rescued, they will be lost forever.

One of the common accusations against the Torah is that it isolates the Jews from their host society. This is true to an extent because, since we are so small in number, a certain amount of separateness is essential for both our survival and our effectiveness. Separation prevents us from being swallowed up and it also prevents us from being misled by being immersed among vastly greater numbers of people acting differently.

Acting and dressing like everyone else in a non-Jewish host country and living its people's lifestyle without a solid knowledge of the Torah, its values and its morals leads to absorption of non-Jewish values, which inevitably leads to assimilation. When Jews begin to identify with non-Jews, being Jewish loses value. A person with this outlook will, very justifiably, ask himself: *Why bother being Jewish at all? Where are the benefits? Why should I have to feel different?* Being Jewish comes to be seen as a detriment and a hindrance; it only brings ostracization, hatred and ridicule, and sometimes even violence. Other nations seem to be living normally but the Jews are always looking over their shoulders.

Jews without a strong understanding of Jewish values will come to identify with the purveyors of other values and internalize them. They simply will stop identifying as Jews and start identifying as whatever else—Americans, rights activists, Democrats, attorneys, sports fans and even Israelis. Without the Torah, Jews become confused. And if they live in an anti-Jewish or anti-Israeli environment, it is only a matter of time until they absorb and accept the anti-Semitism.

There is no clearer example of this than the erosion of support for Israel amongst Western Jews. Like arsenic that accumulates over time in the body until it becomes a lethal dose, the news media poisons the minds of American Jews towards the state of Israel. Most American Jews cannot pinpoint exactly what it was or even when it happened but suddenly they no longer viewed Israel as the underdog even though it is vastly outnumbered in terms of men and arms and certainly cannot compete with the Arabs financially or for world opinion. Yet, Israel is labeled the aggressor, the occupier and the oppressor. There is no sympathy for Israel when it suffers because it is "not pursuing peace"—which, according to this view, the poor Arabs have been longing for since 1948.

During the period of time from 2000 to 2003, when over 1,000 Israelis died as a result of sometimes-daily suicide bombings, I often heard Jews defending Israel with the words, "I don't agree with everything Israel does, but…" This disclaimer speaks volumes. Why begin with such a statement? If another country were suffering a similar onslaught and was trying to defend itself would a person begin with such a disclaimer? Or would he simply state that that country should take matters into its own hands because no civilized country can live under such circumstance, nor should it have to?

Why have Jews become defensive about defending Israel? Is it perhaps due to the fact that they are defending a country that has been demonized, and whose every move is criticized?

The younger Jews are even more susceptible. The average college student walks onto campus for his freshman year and steps into a radicalized environment. Depending on which university he attends he is either faced with open hostility or just a cold welcome. Universities are now breeding grounds for anti-Israel and anti-Semitic political positions; there is strong support for the Palestinian cause among the faculty members and among the vocal, left-leaning student organizations (especially the foreign students).

Most of these professors came into adulthood in the 1960s and 1970s and are overwhelmingly tilted to the left. Where Israel was once viewed as the little underdog that took in its refugees and made the desert bloom, to these professors it is an imperialist nation that is oppressing and subjugating the poor Palestinian people. In the mixed-up world of left-wing thought, the Palestinians are the new Jews—i.e., the suffering underdog that any person with a conscience must defend.

Add to this Arab money, which pours into Middle Eastern studies departments throughout the country, and the always-present undercurrent of anti-Semitism and you have a psychologically unsafe environment for a Jewish student already confused about his identity.

And since he is soft-hearted and soft-headed (ignorant of the facts of recent Middle Eastern history) he is a sitting duck for propagandists and activists who will appeal to his sense of justice and pull on his heart strings. He will have no answers and he will bend to social pressure. And besides, it's become chic to be anti-Zionist.

How pathetic and sad it is to see Jews marching in opposition to Israel. Imagine seeing Italians marching against Italy and siding with those murdering innocent Italians. Or Mexicans marching against Mexico in favor of its enemy. Such people have been broken.

The combination of a confused identity and a glaring lack of knowledge about what the Jewish people are, what we stand for and what we possess leads to intermarriage. If a person does not think that there is anything special about being Jewish, he or she will not value marrying a Jew. And since we make up three percent of the population of the United States, chances are we will come into contact with quite a few non-Jews, many of whom are intelligent, witty, charming, pleasant, kind and good-looking. It is quite understandable that Jews would like them.

People might feel a certain pride in being Jewish but without the ability to translate that feeling into concrete thoughts and ideas, it will not have a lasting effect. What every Jew needs to understand is that being Jewish is not an ethnicity. We don't encourage Jews to marry Jews because we are arrogantly chauvinist and view others as below us. Jews need to marry Jews because we have unique spiritual characteristics and only two Jews can build a home based on our values that will be an incubator for creating other people with these values. There is nothing wrong with non-Jews but they cannot serve the same role as a spouse or parent in a Jewish home.

This is why the Orthodox, who understand our role, do not intermarry, but the non-Orthodox do.

Anti-Semitism

The second aspect of assimilation is anti-Semitism, even though it is somewhat counterintuitive because it is common for people to hate the "other" and like the "like." Outsiders are resented and different people are scorned, but someone who looks, talks and behaves like everyone else and has the same interests as everyone else blends in and is eventually accepted...unless that person is a Jew.

The Roman Emperor Hadrian once mockingly asked one of our sages, "Is one sheep greater than seventy wolves?" referring to the Jews position among the nations of the world. A flock of seventy sheep is in danger if there is even one wolf about, so how could one sheep survive if surrounded by so many wolves? It would only be a matter of seconds before the sheep met its end.

For a sheep to survive 2,000 years while surrounded by seventy wolves takes more than just brains and tenacity. It takes ongoing, open miracles.

An understanding of the inherent spiritual difference between Jews and non-Jews provides the true and complete answer—and the only answer—to the question of anti-Semitism. Anti-Semitism is baffling to non-Orthodox Jews because it is so virulent, so universal and so enduring, and because it is so irrational. Orthodox Jews, however, understand the issue much differently and respond to it much differently. These differences reflect contrasting views of the Jewish people and their place among the family of nations. Hopefully this will be clear by the end of this chapter.

Anti-Semitism is an entirely illogical and inexplicable phenomenon unless one is willing to include a spiritual element in the search for an answer. This is why there is no question for the Orthodox and no answer for the non-Orthodox. Secular attempts to rationally understand anti-Semitism will always produce incomplete and unsatisfying answers and attempts to counter it will only produce short-term stopgap measures. To admit that anti-Semitism is unique is to admit that the Jews are unique. For a secular Jew that is an uncomfortable and even an unacceptable position. For an Orthodox Jew it is as basic and as understood as the *Aleph Beit*.

Without understanding the spiritual realities of the world, anti-Semitism will inevitably remain an enigma. How is it that the Jews are the object of persecution regardless of our geographic location, economic situation or political persuasion? Wherever we live, whatever we do or whatever we believe, we invariably become resented in every society. If we compiled a list of anti-Semitic accusations two things would be quickly noted. Firstly, the list would contain many contradictions, and secondly, none of the charges would fully explain why we are universally hated and persecuted.

We are hated because we are Communists and because we are capitalists. We are hated because we are poor parasites and because we control all the money. We are hated because we don't contribute to society and for controlling the government and the press. We are hated because we are pushy and arrogant and because we are weak and passive.

Such irrationality indicates that there is something deeper driving this emotion.

Imagine that you are applying for a job. At your interview they tell you flat out that without computer skills they won't even consider your resume. So, you go right out and enroll in computer courses and in a month you have the necessary skills. You go back and they are pleased to see that you now have the computer skills they had required. However, they can't hire you because you do not dress appropriately for the job and your wardrobe is not up to par. You go out and buy a whole new wardrobe and they are pleased, but now they tell you that the real reason they cannot hire you is because of the way you wear your hair. It just isn't the image that the company is trying to foster and they are terribly sorry.

So you go and get your hair cut and styled to fit their fashion. In fact you style your hair exactly the way the president of the company wears his. You go back once again, expecting the job, however, now they inform you that the real reason why they cannot hire you is that your previous work experience was in sales and they were really looking for someone with an accounting background all along. But thank you for your interest.

Isn't it obvious that the reasons given were not really reasons at all but excuses to mask an underlying reason? Anti-Semitism is no different. Throughout history the "reasons" for anti-Semitism have changed but the underlying hatred has not.

Historically, European anti-Semitism began long before Christianity and it's a mistake to attribute it to religious indoctrination. The pagan Greeks held Judaism in special contempt because it, alone among ancient religions, posed a threat to their man-centered and man-controlled world-view. A religion possessing G-d's revealed will cannot co-exist with a system that only values ideas that originate in the mind of man. Also, the Jews, again alone amongst the conquered nations of their empire, did not kneel before the altar of Hellenism and did not accept Greek culture and philosophy as superior to a life of Torah and *mitzvot*. Alexandria in Egypt, the leading fount of Hellenistic chauvinism outside of Athens, became a hotbed of anti-Jewish feelings and its leading writers attacked the Jews with defamations that lived on in Greek and later Roman writings—accusations that the Jews were misanthropes or a band of Egyptian lepers who escaped and that they worshiped the golden head of an ass.

Pagan Rome surpassed the Greeks in its revulsion of the Jewish people. Famous Roman authors and orators contributed to the annals of anti-Semitic screeds: Apollonius Molon, teacher of Cicero and Julius Caesar; Democritus, who introduced the smear of ritual murder and Apion, Cicero and Seneca, all of whom had only derogatory things to say about us. Tacitus, the famous historian, wrote that Jewish institutions were "sinister, shameful, and have survived only because of their perversity. Of all enslaved peoples the Jews are the most contemptible, loathsome. All that we hold sacred is profane to them; all that is licit to them is impure to us."

We often suffered at the hands of Roman emperors and their legions before they eventually destroyed the Second Temple and tried to blot out our connection to the Land of Israel.

For most of European history since the adoption of Christianity, the main anti-Semitic accusation leveled against the Jews in Europe was that we killed Jesus. But according to the Christians' own source, the New Testament, it was the Romans who killed him; the Jews are only recorded as instigating and encouraging it. So wouldn't it be logical to expect to find both the Romans and the Jews vilified in Church writings? Wouldn't you expect the Romans to be considered cursed for killing G-d? Why are the instigators (according to their version) worse than the perpetrators? Why aren't the Romans regarded as the children of Satan and perhaps the Italians as their hated descendants? Since there is not an iota of any resentment against the Romans it seems reasonable to doubt whether the killing of Jesus is the real issue. (This, of course, assumes that the New Testament is verifiable, which it isn't. Since the whole account was written 300 years after the purported events, it has the same historicity as the tale of George Washington chopping down a cherry tree.)

Furthermore, if the killing of Jesus were the issue, it would be reasonable to expect that once Europe became less religious, its anti-Semitism would also wane. But this did not happen. Not only did it not lessen; it became more virulent and more deadly.

The killing-of-Jesus theory also would not fully explain Arab and Moslem anti-Semitism. Although they regard Jesus as a prophet, they don't mention his death when they rant about killing the Jews. In fact we see historically that once Christianity lost its central role in much of Western European society, Jew hatred did not wane at all but simply mutated from a religious issue into two new forms of anti-Semitism—the first based on nationalism and the second on genetics.

National anti-Semitism was a reaction to the rights and freedoms the Jews began to enjoy in the Napoleonic era. Although on the surface the Jews started to seem like everyone else they were still different in their language, religion and, in the eyes of the gentiles, loyalties. In other words they were not really German, French, Austrian and so on but rather a separate and unique people who could not be fully trusted.

Interestingly, this accusation was not new at all. It had been leveled against the Jews by Pharaoh when he proposed enslaving the Jews because "…the Jewish nation is numerous and stronger than us. Let us be wise with it lest it increase and, when war will approach, join our enemies and fight against us…" (Exodus 1:9-10). It was used again about 800 years later by

Haman in Persia, when he convinced Achashverosh to let him exterminate the Jews (Purim): "There is one nation scattered and (yet) separate among the nations in all the lands of your kingdom, their laws are different from every other nation and the laws of the king they do not fulfill..." (Esther 3:8).

However after the rise of Christianity and the Catholic Church, the killing-of-Jesus issue was more potent and more effective and was therefore used almost exclusively. It was only when religion started to wane that the national issue became the weapon of choice once again.

This "reason" is, of course, just as kooky as the others. If one would take just a cursory look at modern history, say over the last 225 years, how many examples could you find of disloyalty on the part of the Jews to their host countries? You actually would find just the opposite. You would instead find the Jews to be an overtly loyal and patriotic segment of the population. There is not one case in history wherein the Jews acted as a fifth column.

Furthermore, it is one thing to suspect a foreign group in your midst that looks and dresses differently and even speaks a different language (which Jews did in Eastern Europe). But why would anyone suspect an assimilated Jew in Western Europe who wants nothing more than to live amongst his or her gentile neighbors in peace? What would be the basis of accusing such a person of being disloyal or of not being "one of us"?

Ironically, it would have been hard to find Jews more patriotic to their fatherland than the German Jews. During the First World War, they volunteered for the army and for civil causes in disproportionately large numbers. Their Reform rabbis and leadership encouraged them to fight for the fatherland and even went so far as to tell young Jewish men going off to war not to have qualms about killing French Jews because they were the enemy of the fatherland. In fact, historians have pointed out that without three Jewish individuals, Germany would not have been able to fight the war at all:

- Albert Ballin, who prior to the war had developed the Hamburg-Amerika Line into one the world's great shipping fleets. His ships gave the Germans the ability to run the Allied blockade.
- Fritz Haber, who discovered the process for producing nitric acid and synthetic ammonia. This provided Germany the ability to produce munitions after the British blockade successfully cut off Germany's seaborne trade.

- Walter Rathenau, who organized the entire German economy on a war footing and miraculously kept it supplied with raw materials up until the final days of the war. (Rathenau was despised by the Nazis and later was assassinated by them in 1922, but this did not stop Walter Speer, the Nazi minister of armaments, from openly admitting that he used Rathenau's model as the blueprint for Nazi Germany's war economy.)

Imagine how confusing this must have been at the time. For 1,500 years the "reason" we were hated was because we had "killed Jesus." Then, the Enlightenment blossomed and the Church's influence on life in Western Europe declined. The walls of the ghettos were torn down and the Jews were given equal rights. And what resulted? Anti-Semitism in a whole new form.

And then, ironically, as Jews became more assimilated even to the point of converting, anti-Semitism morphed again. Throughout Europe, in the nineteenth and early twentieth centuries, there was actually a great deal of conversion to Christianity among the Jews, especially the wealthy Jews. From France to Russia, Jews who had already jettisoned their Jewish baggage saw no reason to continue to be labeled as Jews and be barred from reaching the highest levels of society. Baptism was the golden ticket and thousands of Jews used it.

To a Jew trying to escape anti-Semitism, this should have been the ultimate cure. He was no longer a member of the Jewish community nor spoke a Jewish language. He did not identify as a Jew and, in fact, sat with his fellow Germans or Poles in the church pews. He had completely melted in to the point where he was almost indistinguishable from the gentiles in his country—he had the same attitudes, customs and identification. It was foolproof...except for one thing: a Jew is a Jew is a Jew.

The gentile reaction to this eager attempt at assimilation was racial Anti-Semitism. It posited that, although the Jew looked, dressed, acted and even prayed like a gentile, he was still and always would be a member of a different race.

So it was that in the late 1800s and early 1900s, at precisely the same time that many Jews were doing everything they could to be less and less Jewish and in precisely the country—Germany—where the Jews were trying the hardest to assimilate, the theory that the Jews are genetically different took hold and grew. Can this irony be explained away as mere coincidence, or is a pattern emerging?

The question of race mixing became a subject of polite conversation: *Do we really want "them," with their different blood and inferior physical characteristics, mixing with our race and diluting its purity?* Unfortunately for the Jew trying to escape his Jewishness, there was no escape from this theory despite its scientific speciousness. The Jews aren't a race any more than the Canadians are. And in fact there is probably not a more heterogeneous people in the world. There are Jews of every different shape, size and color.

Put to scrutiny, the "reasons" for anti-Semitism fall apart. In the end, we are not hated because we are pushy or materialistic or because we are financially successful or because we killed Jesus or because we are a different nationality or race. After hearing about all these "reasons" for thousands of years, we see nothing that approaches a rational explanation or even a common thread. Rather, anti-Semitism is revealed for what it is: a spiritual virus that constantly mutates to fit the circumstances of its environment.

The sages of the Talmud teach that the word "Sinai," as in Mount Sinai, is derived from the Hebrew word "*seenah,*" which means hatred. Once we received the Torah, the die was cast. Our message and even our presence produce a great deal of resentment.

To non-Orthodox Jews this is all incomprehensible; yet Orthodox Jews have always known that the rationales and reasons given for anti-Semitism were never based in reality. We know deep down that no matter what we do the world will always come up with a new reason for its hostility. It will manifest itself differently in different cultures, but it will be there nonetheless until the Messianic era.

And this affliction, like everything else G-d does, is for our ultimate benefit. Because the Jewish people have a mission and a purpose, our existence is intrinsically linked to the continued existence of creation. If there were not a Jewish people, there would be no point to all of it and creation would cease to exist. This is because, without the Jews, G-d's intention for mankind could never be fulfilled. Therefore G-d has built in, so to speak, a failsafe system that gets triggered when we feel so comfortable in our surroundings that we start emulating our non-Jewish hosts and begin to slough off our greater purpose. That is why there are so many instances in our history where our situation suddenly changed from one of repose and acceptance to one of murderous hostility. Without the enmity of our neighbors, we would have disappeared long ago.

In other words, our exile did not take us to ends of the earth so that we should become part of all the other nations. It took us to the ends of the Earth so we should be Jews amongst the nations. Similarly, our exile did not take us to the United States so that we should become Americans. It took us to United States so that we should be Jews amongst Americans. When we start to see ourselves as "American," watch out, trouble is not too far behind.

Amalek and the Germans

There is another person who needs to be mentioned in order to understand the course of history. Eisav had a grandson named Amalek who inherited all the traits and philosophies of Eisav but in a concentrated and more potent form. The Nation of Amalek doesn't just hate the Jews; they want to kill every last man, woman and child.

Within a month of the Jews' departure from Egypt, the Amaleki people attacked them. Distinguished by their cruelty and savagery, Amalek's people attacked the Jews from the rear, preying on the slower, weaker elements. After killing a Jewish man they would cut off his *brit milah,* and throw it skyward shouting mockingly, "Here is your covenant, take it back."

Under the military leadership of Yehoshua (Joshua), Amalek was severely beaten back, losing the cream of its nation and its leadership. Nevertheless, forty years later, as the nation of Israel was about to enter the Land of Israel, the Nation of Amalek attacked again in a last-ditch attempt to prevent Israel from settling on their land. Again they were defeated.

Amalek is the anti-Jew. Actually, he is anti-G-d but since he can't physically fight G-d he fights the Jews. If you really hate G-d and His desire for an enlightened mankind, and you want to make sure it never happens, there is only one way to stop it: Kill all the Jews. All of them, not even one can survive. Why? Because if any survive, they will recover and start spreading their message all over again.

The battle with Amalek is not over. His philosophies are the most diametrically opposed to ours; he is deeply cynical and has no use for the truth. Conversely, we are deeply sincere and are passionate about the truth.

And like matter and anti-matter cannot coexist, neither can Israel and Amalek. The final struggle for the hearts, souls and minds of mankind will be between the Jews and Amalek. Which will triumph, the light or the darkness? Truth or power? Will humanity see itself as a soul or as a body, a spiritual being or just a different kind of animal? What is man and his purpose? Does life have an ultimate purpose or is our existence short, nasty, brutish and meaningless?

The Nation of Amalek attacked us as we headed from Egypt to Israel because they understand that the Jewish people in the Land of Israel would be too potent a force to defeat. Therefore, they endeavored to prevent us from entering the land.

The second time that Amalek tried to eliminate the Jewish people was when an Amalekite was prime minister of the Persian Empire. His name was Haman, and this is the story of Purim.

At that time in history, the Jewish people were at the end of their first exile and the reconstruction of the Second Temple in Jerusalem had already begun under the permission of the previous Persian emperor, Koresh (Cyrus). Haman, through the manipulation of Emperor Achashverosh, tried and failed to have the Jews exterminated.

Can you think of another time in history when the Jewish people were beginning to return to their land and someone arose with a plan to exterminate us?

Fifteen hundred years ago, the sages of the Talmud identified the Germanic tribes as being the descendents of Amalek. If you want to understand the true nature of anti-Semitism, the anti-G-d philosophy, listen to the author of *Mein Kampf.* He understood the threat that the Jewish Nation posed to people like him:

- "The struggle for world domination will be fought entirely between us, between Germans and Jews. All else is facade and illusion. Behind England stands Israel, and behind France, and behind the United States. Even when we have driven the Jew out of Germany, he remains our world enemy…" [1]
- "The internal expurgation of the Jewish spirit is not possible in any platonic way. For the Jewish spirit is the product of the Jewish person… Unless we expel the Jewish people soon, they will have judaized our people within a very short time…" [2]
- "If only one country, for whatever reason, tolerates a Jewish family in it, that family will become the germ center for fresh sedition. If one little Jewish boy survives without any Jewish education, with no synagogue and no Hebrew school, it [Judaism] is in his soul. Even if there had never been a synagogue or a Jewish school or an Old Testament, the Jewish spirit would still exist and

exert its influence. It has been there from the beginning and there is no Jew, not a single one, who does not personify it..." [3]

- "...there can be no compromise—there are only two possibilities: either victory of the Aryan or annihilation of the Aryan and victory of the Jew..." [4]
- "And assuredly this world is moving toward a great revolution. The question can only be whether it will redound to the benefit of Aryan humanity or to the profit of the eternal Jew." [5]
- "Either Germany sinks and we, through our despicable cowardice, sink with it or else we dare to enter on the fight against death and devil and rise up against the fate that has been planned for us. Then we shall see which is the stronger: The spirit of international Jewry or the will of Germany." [6]

Adolf Hitler had a deep and uncanny understanding of the essence of the Jew and his role in the spiritual and moral development of mankind. His main arguments for the elimination of the Jews were entirely accurate and therefore purely evil. Hitler looked at the world and saw what the Jew had done. In his sick mind, Jewish ideas had completely poisoned mankind and distorted its thinking. The diseased ideas of kindness and compassion had perpetuated the weak at the expense of the strong. And who had introduced all this into the world? The Jew.

- "Conscience is a Jewish invention; it is a blemish like circumcision..." [7]
- "Providence has ordained that I should be the greatest liberator of humanity. I am freeing man from the restraints of an intelligence that has taken charge, from the dirty and degrading self-mortification of a false vision called conscience and morality, and from the demands of a freedom and independence which only a very few can bear..." [8]
- "And the Right has further completely forgotten that democracy is fundamentally not German, it is Jewish. It has completely forgotten that this Jewish democracy with its majority decisions has always been, without

exception, only a means towards the destruction of any existing Aryan leadership..." [9]

- "Only a knowledge of the Jews provides the key with which to comprehend the inner, and consequently real, aims of Social Democracy." [10]

- "In a natural order, the classes are peoples superimposed on one another in strata, instead of living as neighbors. To this order we shall return as soon as the after effects of liberalism have been removed..." [11]

- "After all these centuries of whining about protection of the poor and lowly, it is about time we decided to protect the strong against the inferior..." [12]

- "...preservation is bound up with the rigid law of necessity and the right of victory of the best and stronger in this world. Those who want to live, let them fight, and those who do not want to fight in this world of eternal struggle do not deserve to live. Even if this were hard —that it is how it is." [13]

- "...a man must never fall into the lunacy of believing that he has really risen to be lord and master of Nature...he must understand the fundamental necessity of Nature's rule and realize how much his existence is subjected to these laws of eternal fight and upward struggle. Then he will feel that in a universe where planets revolve around suns and moons turn about planets, where force alone forever masters weakness, compelling it to be an obedient slave or else crushing it, there can be no special laws for man. For him, too, the eternal principles of this ultimate wisdom hold sway. He can try to comprehend them; but escape them, never." [14]

- "Mankind has grown great in eternal struggle, and only in eternal peace does it perish." [15]

To change this he had to eliminate the source. Barring that, he would never liberate humanity. As long as the Jews survived, he couldn't triumph. We were an impassable obstacle. The whole concept of morality and conscience had to be destroyed. The struggle had nothing to do with religious belief. Even if a Jew has nothing to do with Judaism, as was the case with most

German Jews, there is something in his soul that will affect his surroundings and those who come into contact with him.

The anti-Semitism of the Germans during the Holocaust is often explained away as a tool used by the Nazis to unite and uplift a broken and dispirited people. This scapegoat theory is used because a secular Jew cannot find an explanation for such unprovoked and premeditated evil. But such an explanation doesn't really hold water.

We are asked to believe that the once-proud and mighty German nation suffered a humiliating defeat at the end of the First World War. The sudden collapse of the German war machine combined with the punitive reparations imposed by the victors crushed German morale. Germany was forced to pay huge monetary reparations to the winning countries; it was disarmed, and chunks of its territory were occupied by the Allies. Other areas were permanently annexed by surrounding countries such as the newly emergent Poland.

After the worldwide economic collapse of 1929 that devastated their economy, the German people could bear it no longer. From this morass of bitterness, pain and anger rose a demagogue who vilified the Jews as the cause of all of Germany's misfortunes. This scapegoat allowed the people to regain their sense of pride and dignity. How could the master race have been brought so low, they reasoned? Only by the machinations of the Jew, who wouldn't allow Germany to rise and challenge their world domination!

The first problem with this explanation is that Germany was not alone on the losing side of World War One. The Austro-Hungarian and Ottoman Empires also lost and in fact were dismantled. Somehow they were able to adjust without resorting to atrocities.

Also, the entire world was suffering from the Depression. In the United States, twenty-five percent of the workforce was unemployed in 1933. Yet Americans did not feel the need to invade Mexico and slaughter entire villages in order to feel better about themselves.

If the maligning of the Jews was only a means, one might expect it to have tapered off once the Nazis had obtained their objectives. Or perhaps it would have been maintained as a unifying measure. But what is very revealing is that what we refer to as "the Holocaust" took place entirely *after* the Jews had been effectively eliminated from German life.

From 1933 to 1939, the Third Reich had enacted various laws and regulations, many of them referred to as the "Nuremberg Laws," that completely eliminated Jews from every aspect of life in Germany and thereby stripped them of all their power and influence. Jews had been removed from civil service. They could not practice law or medicine. Synagogues had been closed and eventually destroyed. Jews were barred from public transportation, beaches, even parks and expelled from all public schools and universities. The racial laws forbade marriage or any physical relations between Jews and Aryans. A Jew could not own a business, employ an Aryan or file insurance claims.

If the purpose of the Germans' anti-Semitism was just to weed the Jews out of German society and encourage emigration, by 1939 it had been wildly successful. During those six years fifty percent of German Jews had left the country and those that remained were no longer racially mixing and no longer had any economic, cultural or political power whatsoever. If these were truly the Germans' issues, they had been solved.

It was only after the Germans had achieved their goal of "saving" Germany from the Jews that they began moving beyond their borders by annexing Austria and swallowing Czechoslovakia. Once they had isolated the Jews in Germany, they then undertook to physically annihilate them in Germany and the rest of Europe.

Hitler's actions prove that he saw all Jews as a threat to Germany. In his mind, Jews in Poland, France, Greece, the United States and Great Britain were a mortal threat to the existence of the German (read "Amalek") nation.

When choices of triage had to be made during the final years of the war when Germany was fighting for its life, Hitler consistently chose to kill Jews rather than protect Germany militarily. Badly needed military supplies were consistently diverted to the extermination efforts. The starkest example of this policy occurred in 1944 when troops, trains and supplies that were desperately needed on the collapsing eastern front against Russia were instead sent to Hungary to kill Jews.

Hitler did this knowing full well that the Russians were marching on Germany and the end was perilously near. The Jews couldn't just have been a scapegoat; nobody risks military defeat to kill a scapegoat. Ultimately, Hitler was fighting a battle against the idea of a G-d who imposes an absolute system of morality and demands free-will choices and responsibility from each and every human being. Until his dying breath, he didn't waver. The last line of his last will and testament reads, "Above all I charge the leaders of the nation and those under them to scrupulous observance of the laws of race and to merciless opposition to the universal poisoner of all peoples, international Jewry." A few minutes later he shot himself.

This hatred of a moral G-d is not only the root of Hitler's and the German's anti-Semitism but of all anti-Semitism throughout the history.

Anti-Semites can't stand what we stand for, and a Jew who doesn't know this will never have peace.

All the so-called reasons for anti-Semitism—we killed G-d, we control the world and so on—are just window dressing. Anti-Semitism is a spiritual sickness; it's a disease of the soul. That is why, most of the time, non-Jews don't have clear understandings of what's bothering them about us. And that is why the so-called "reasons" wildly vary.

Anti-Semitism is not a function of what we say or do or how we vote. It is a function of our existence. Without understanding this we find ourselves constantly answering the anti-Semites' ridiculous charges and accusations which only justifies their insanity and gives it credence. We pin our hopes on dialogue—understanding their positions and trying to make them see ours—but it's as winnable as arguing with a madman.

And because anti-Semitism is a spiritual disease it is an instant indicator of something wrong in a society: It's a warning that you are in the presence of evil. The Jews are the canary in the coalmine: When society starts to turn on us you know something bad is about to happen.

This understanding also explains why no one else over the past 2,000 years has been able to express himself as honestly as Hitler did. To be honest about why you hate the Jews you'd have to be able to admit that you hate G-d and His laws, and neither a religion nor religious people can officially say that.

But Hitler could, and did so openly: "They refer to me as an uneducated barbarian. Yes, we are barbarians. We want to be barbarians; it is an honored title to us. We shall rejuvenate the world. This world is near its end." [16] Most people, especially royalty, clergy and anyone who sees himself as enlightened, would not find the label flattering. Hitler had no such qualms and therefore could be brutally honest.

Understanding the root causes of anti-Semitism also sheds a light on Jewish anti-Semitism. Yes, there definitely is such a thing. It manifests itself as self-hate and a dislike of Orthodox Jews. Why do so many non-Orthodox Jews, many of whom have almost nothing to do with Orthodox Jews, feel an irritation towards Orthodox Jews? Are the Orthodox, by their way of life and their values, perhaps reminding them of something they do not want to hear? Can it be that Jews become annoyed when they are reminded of the higher purpose of the Jewish people or irritated when reminded that there are Jews who do not aspire to be accepted by their gentile neighbors, preferring instead to cling to the greatness inherent in a truly Jewish life?

It's something to think about, and I'll tell you something else: Even in the Orthodox world, which spans a wide range of religious degrees, the more "Orthodox" the group, i.e., the more it rejects Western culture, the more it is resented by other groups to its left on the spectrum. It seems that the more one is viewed as promoting the message, the more he is disliked.

All of this leads to a very fundamental question: Why would a person resist the instructions of a loving G-d who only wants our good? Why wouldn't we want a message that civilizes and elevates us? The answer has to do with perception. Part of us—the body—sees G-d's instructions as repressing and restricting. The soul sees them for what they are: true liberation from the slavery of the body and its meaningless desires. The soul actually desires to listen to G-d but is not free to do so unless the body cooperates. So, the more one identifies with the body, the more he or she will resist and resent any representation of G-d's plan for mankind.

Without a Torah, man is the highest authority and the final arbiter of right and wrong, good and evil. With a Torah, he's not. Without a Torah, he can conjure up any kind of religion or belief system and justify it. With a Torah, he can't. Without a Torah, he can act anyway he wants. With a Torah, he can't; he first must make sure he's doing the right thing. This is why every great empire has seen the tiny Jewish nation as a threat or an enemy.

Some wonder how it is possible that a people that has contributed so much to mankind has suffered so much persecution in return. The answer is in the question.

Our greatest contributions are not contradictions to anti-Semitism; they are the cause of it. The civilizing of mankind is only appreciated by those who want to be civilized. Adolf Hitler looked at the twentieth century and saw a world in which the message of the Jews was on the rise. The ideas of humanitarianism, equality before the law, the inalienable rights of each individual, democracy, the brotherhood of man and world peace were taking hold. These ideas were becoming part of the fabric of mankind. Hitler, who viewed himself as a barbarian, correctly identified his enemies.

The Jewish people are and have always been a light unto the nations. That is very threatening to someone who wants the world to be a dark place.

Chapter Eleven
The Modern Age

The Really Big Picture

Now that we have discussed assimilation, intermarriage and anti-Semitism, it seems the proper time to address the divide that exists today within the Jewish people and see how we came to be divided.

What exactly is an Orthodox Jew? Or a Reform Jew? Or a Conservative Jew? What do these terms mean and how did they come into being in the first place?

Depending on when you want to begin counting, the Jewish People are at least 3,322 years old. That is because 3,322 years ago, in the Jewish year 2448, corresponding to 1312 BC, we left Egypt and headed into the Sinai desert. If you prefer to consider the start of our history with the birth of Avraham, add on another 500 years.

It might be surprising to learn that for nearly 3,100 of our over 3,300 years there was no such thing as a "branch" of Judaism. Some breakaway movements, beginning in the Greek and Roman eras and continuing until around the year 1,000 AD, attempted to redefine Judaism to make it fit the times, and sometimes these movements had large followings, but they only succeeded in ruining themselves. They all disappeared many centuries ago; none of us are descended from them.

The present-day notion of "branches" of Judaism only began in the early 1800s when the Reform movement established itself. Until then the definition of a Jew was universal. No matter where a Jew lived, he lived according to the commandments in the Torah. A Jew ate only kosher food, kept the Shabbat, learned Torah and maintained all the laws and customs that had been passed down from the time of Moshe (Moses). Every Jewish man covered his head, prayed three times a day and owned *tefillin*. Every Jewish wife lit Shabbat candles. A Jew could walk into any synagogue in the world and know what was going on.

Then, something happened that eventually caused the Jewish people to split into different divisions with very different approaches to G-d and religion. And those events of 200 years ago continue to affect us today on a daily basis.

Life in Exile

By the late 1700s Jews were living everywhere from England to Iran and from Denmark to Egypt. Some Jews had even come to the New World with the Dutch and the English. No matter where we lived, though, our situation was never easy.

In the Arab and Moslem lands, after the rise of Islam in the 600s, the Jews were delegated to the status of *dhimmi*—a second class of inferior rights assigned to non-Moslems. We were taxed oppressively and our behavior and practices were restricted. For instance, a Jew walking in the street could not pass on the right side of a Moslem and no synagogue could be built higher than a mosque. And, periodically, we had to deal with violent mobs and fanatic rulers. It was no picnic, but it was nothing compared to life in Europe.

Life for the Jews in Europe can be accurately described as 2,000 years of attacks, restrictions, extortions, humiliations, massacres and expulsions with periodic intervals of calm. At any given time, somewhere in Europe, we were suffering.

When times were good, Jews throughout Europe were subjected to harsh decrees and oppressive taxes. Restrictions were placed on what professions we were allowed to practice, whether we could own land, what clothing we had to wear or could not wear, where we were allowed to live within cities (if at all) and, at times, even how many marriages and births were allowed per family. For example, in 1750 Frederick II of Prussia limited the Jews of Frankfurt to twelve weddings a year and only if both of the couple had reached the age of twenty-five, a marital age that had been decreed specifically for Jews.

During the intervals of calm, Jews were grateful for their good fortune. When times were bad, whole communities were pillaged and/or massacred. During the Crusades entire communities were burnt alive at the stake. Jews were commonly expelled with only what they could carry on their backs. Children were often stolen to be baptized. *Pogroms,* for any reason or pretext, were not unusual. A Jew could be arrested and tortured on the flimsiest of charges. Life and death very often depended on the mood and disposition of the local prince or bishop.

The ghettos in which Jews were forced to live did not grow along with the population. In Frankfurt, Germany, for example, the Jewish Quarter was established in 1462. More accurately it was a single street called "Judengasse," or "Jew's Alley." This street would remain the Jewish neighborhood for the next 350 years. As the population grew, the houses were either subdivided or enlarged by adding story upon story and digging basement under basement.

Whereas the Judengasse housed 150 people when it was established, by the 1600s it housed over 3,000. Jews had to be within the walls of the ghetto by sundown, when the authorities locked its gates, or they would be arrested. Jews were not allowed to live anywhere else in the city until the ghetto was finally abolished in 1811.

None of these persecutions happened without the collusion of the Christian authorities. Mostly, it was the Popes and the Catholic hierarchy that pounded the drum. But even after the Reformation in the 1500s, the Protestant leaders acted in the same fashion. Martin Luther openly called for our persecution when we didn't follow him.

It is important to know what life was like for us in Europe so we can understand how we reacted when things changed so radically.

Radical Changes in Europe and the Rise of Secularism

What happened to change the status of the Jew from hated strangers locked behind ghetto walls to equals citizen in free societies? The before and after pictures are radically different.

This topic could fill many books but for the purposes of this chapter we need to know only two things: First, it was not an overnight change but a gradual one that occurred over a span of over 300 years and only broke through the surface in the late 1700s. And second, and more important, it wasn't a change *vis à vis* the Jews *per se*; anti-Semitism was still very strong but there was a change in the way European society viewed religion and specifically Christianity. The strong Christian element in our persecutions meant that when Europe's relationship with Christianity changed, so would the situation of the Jews.

Ever since the Roman Emperor Constantine declared Christianity to be the state religion of the Empire in 312 AD, the Roman Catholic Church was always a partner in ruling Europe. Sometimes it was in league with the temporal rulers; sometimes it struggled with the rulers; but either way it was immensely powerful and immensely wealthy. It openly sided with the monarchs and the nobility that lorded over the peasantry and in turn was allowed to collect huge sums in taxes, tithes and payoffs. The Church grew more and more wealthy and more and more corrupt while the average peasant could look forward to spending his forty-year life span in hunger, sickness and abject poverty.

For a number of reasons, including the Black Plague which caused a crisis of faith and the Avignon Papacy which disillusioned the faithful, Europe began to stir in the late 1300s and early 1400s in a period we call "the Renaissance," which is French for rebirth. The world then was nothing like it is today and ideas took centuries, not hours, to take hold and affect change.

In Italy, the humanists looked to ancient Rome instead of the Church for ideas and enlightenment, and art began to seem more human and more humane. (They coined the term "Middle Ages" to denote the years between the end of the Roman Empire and the beginning of the Renaissance.) But in Italy, the loosening did not spark the violence and rebellion that would soon explode on its northern border.

The first real, open challenge to the reign of the Church occurred in 1517 when Martin Luther nailed his *Ninety-Five Theses* onto a church door in Wittenberg, Germany. This would prove to be the first crack in the dike. Disgusted by the corrupt practices of the Catholic Church, Luther set out to create a purer Christianity that would not have any of what he considered phony additions to the religion that had only been added to empower the Church and enslave the people. One of his major objections was to the practice of "indulgences" where, for a set price, a Christian could buy himself and his relatives out of hell. Pope Leo X was so in need of money to build today's Vatican in the early 1500s that he actively promoted these "indulgences" and directly contributed to the rise of Protestantism.

Luther's Protestantism would have no saints, no confession to priests and no Latin in the service. Luther translated the Bible into German in defiance of the Church, which mandated that it only be written and read in Latin so the common folk could not understand it. In fact it was a capital offense to translate the Bible from Latin into any other language. (Gutenberg's Bible was printed in Latin.)

This direct challenge to the Pope's authority set off a wave of wars on the continent, which culminated in the Thirty Years' War of 1618 to 1648, a bloodbath that eventually involved every major power in continental Europe. When the war ended in 1648 with the Treaty of Westphalia,

Protestantism was established as a legitimate form of Christianity. For the papacy, it was a tremendous setback.

Almost concurrently, another major challenge faced the Church. In 1534, Henry VIII of England broke with the Church due to its refusal to grant him a divorce from Catherine of Aragon so he could marry Anne Boleyn. Henry VIII's action led to an on-again, off-again religious civil war that only ended in 1689 with the establishment of the House of Orange and an act of Parliament that required the king and queen of England to be members of the Church of England.

The Pope lost both the battle for Germany and the battle for England and from then on, the Church would see a gradual but steady rolling back of its power and authority both temporally and morally.

The Protestant Reformation and the establishment of the Church of England set off a chain reaction against the stifling, oppressive and corrupt Catholic Church. The cynicism, hypocrisy and cruelty with which the Church had conducted itself during its reign of power had created a deep-seated animosity.

Since the Church had long opposed free inquiry, it had created an environment wherein religion and intellectual pursuits could not coexist. Due to its understandable insecurity and the very real threats to its authority from investigation, the Church endeavored to keep people ignorant. It was Church versus science, Church versus literature and Church versus political reform. The Church became the enemy of progress and this anti-intellectual environment led to strong anticlerical feelings among those who aspired to be intellectually free.

Martin Luther might have denounced the Church, broken away and created an alternative form of Christianity but others were content to simply break away. Europe began to emerge from the intellectual coma imposed on it by the Church and this era, which has been dubbed "the Age of Reason," contained a strong element of revolt against the Church, its teachings and its principles and European society slowly became more and more secularized during the 1600s and the 1700s. (Judaism would later be thrown in with "religion" and "organized religion" but in truth Judaism never had any of the insecurities or paranoia that the Church did. Nor was it in agreement with any of the Church's philosophical or intellectual principles.)

In philosophy, thought shifted away from the supernatural to the natural. Reason, deduction and even mathematics became the intellectual foundations of the day. G-d was no longer the center of philosophical discussions and in science, the empirical approach became the standard, inherently dismissing any acknowledgment of a spiritual component in life. Economics was born as a branch of science.

Christianity had brought G-d to a pagan Europe and now the drift away from the Church would lead not only to a rejection of Christianity but also to a rejection of G-d Himself. Intellectual society circled back to the Greek world of thought, where it had been prior to the formation of Christianity. Man again became the center of the universe and the final arbiter of truth.

Mankind, it was proposed, could attain an enlightened society through the use of reason and a modern, rational man had no need for old superstitions. These fires were stoked further during the years leading up to the French Revolution when writers like Voltaire openly mocked Christianity and the Church. These ideas gained much prominence and validity due to the French Revolution and were later embraced by Napoleon, who spread them throughout Europe on his march to Moscow.

Europe, in the nineteenth century, was very fertile ground for new ideas. The old Russian and Austro-Hungarian empires were tottering as many small nations that had been long dominated by them were beginning to get restless. The German and Italian states were beginning their national stirrings and would eventually unify and create new national identities. And the Industrial Revolution and the subsequent growth of cities were tearing up much of the fabric of the old order.

In short, the world was changing at an incredible speed.

The Siren's Call

All of this affected the Jews living in Western and Central Europe very significantly.

Although the Jews had gradually gained better treatment starting in the middle of the century in places like France and some of the German kingdoms where the Church had been weakened, the pace now quickened considerably. The throwing off of the old order inevitably included discarding the Church's doctrines, which included its attitude towards the Jews. France, after the revolution, was the first to grant its Jews citizenship and equal rights and was soon copied by other countries. Societies that saw themselves as modern and enlightened did not want to be identified with the "dark" practices of the Church.

Throughout Europe, ghetto walls were razed and social and economic restrictions on the Jews were slowly abolished. The secularization of Europe changed the Jewish world in ways that are hard to exaggerate. After close to 1,500 years of brutality at the hands of the gentiles, the Jews were suddenly offered freedom and equality.

The Jews had always been the other, the scapegoats for kings, bishops and debtors. They had suffered beatings, oppressive taxes, expulsions and humiliating restrictions. Then, suddenly, they went from being pariahs to being fellow citizens.

Many European Jews thought they could finally escape the endless persecutions and violence that had plagued them for centuries. Instead of oppression there would be acceptance; instead of hatred, fraternity. They could coexist as equals in a free and open society. It was a whole new world.

For many the sudden change was disorienting. For a Jew who felt true spiritual happiness, despite the living conditions of the ghetto, and who had a real relationship with G-d, Torah learning and *mitzvah* observance, the newfound freedom was appreciated, but was not seen as anything other than a welcome end to discrimination and persecution. However, if they did not have these spiritual benefits then the door being held open by non-Jewish society was far too seductive. No one could have imagined the size of the crowd that would surge through it.

The Beginning of Assimilation

In 1783 a man named Moses Mendelssohn published a translation of the Torah into the German language. It is now seen, in hindsight, as *the* watershed moment in modern Jewish history.

Mendelssohn was an Orthodox Jew born in Dessau, Germany, in 1729, but he had moved to Berlin at the age of fourteen when his rabbi and teacher took a position there. He was very soon drawn into the intellectual ferment of the salon scene that was buzzing in the Prussian capital. He learned mathematics, Latin and German and befriended many of the leading German intellectuals of the time including Gotthold Lessing and Immanuel Kant. He fell in love with German culture.

Today the idea of translating the Torah might seem like a non-issue but at the time it was an extremely radical and controversial step for a very simple reason: There was absolutely no reason to translate the Torah into German. Jews studied it and understood it in the original Hebrew as they had for thousands of years. Mendelssohn's intention in translating the Torah into German was not to assist Jewish scholarship because if that had been his goal, he would have written his commentary in Hebrew as had always been the practice of the Jewish people. The few exceptions in our history where a book or commentary was written in Aramaic or Arabic or Yiddish or German were because those were the commonly spoken languages at the time and the author wanted to reach the unlearned. Today, many books and commentaries are published in English for that same reason.

However, in 1783, no Jew in Europe used German as his spoken language, he used Yiddish. It is clear from this and from Mendelssohn's later comments and writings that his intention was to introduce the German language to the Jewish people so that they, as he'd done after he'd learned German, could have access to his beloved European culture. This would allow the Jews to integrate into German society.

It represented, for the first time in close to 2,000 years of Jewish exile, a proactive and purposeful attempt to assimilate into the society and culture of the gentile host country. There had been times in Jewish history when Jews in a specific place had assimilated into the host country, the most famous being the years in Spain and Portugal in the fourteenth and fifteenth centuries, before the expulsions. However, this had taken place gradually and almost by accident, never with intention. Not since the time of the Greeks had there been such an overt and willful attempt to mimic the host gentile society and meld into it.

Although at the time it would have required an almost prophetic insight to see where Mendelssohn's translation would lead, many of the leading rabbis in Europe did see and, in an attempt to prevent further damage, energetically did everything they could to oppose him. But they were unable to stop what had already started and was quickly gaining momentum.

The immediate result of Mendelssohn's actions and of the school of thought that developed around him—called the Haskalah in Hebrew, the Enlightenment in English—was a hemorrhaging of Jews into gentile society.

Why did this happen? Three reasons.

Firstly, Mendelsohn and his disciples were very vocal about their rejection of rabbinical authority. In a letter to a Protestant deacon he wrote:

> I will not deny that I have perceived in my religion human additions and abuses which, unfortunately, do too much to dim its luster. What friend of truth can boast that his religion is free from all damaging human embellishments? All of us who seek Truth recognize the lethal breath of

> hypocrisy and superstition and wish we could expunge it
> without doing harm to the true and the good.

By proclaiming that Judaism needed to be developed and improved, Mendelssohn was, in no uncertain terms, saying that many of the beliefs and traditions of the previous generations were flawed or worse.

Secondly, Mendelssohn and his followers were enamored of European culture, putting it on a par with Judaism. This confused those with fragile connections and further weakened their Jewish identities. If religion and culture were of equal value, why bother with religion?

And thirdly, despite the political freedoms, the Germans were still anti-Semitic and Jews found that their Jewishness was still a liability. The Germans were, however, willing to accept Jews who converted to Christianity. This caused enormous stress on the followers of Mendelssohn who so loved the arts and sciences. They were enticed by the sweet gentile fruit and eager to be fully accepted by their non-Jewish countrymen, yet they were still Jews and therefore social outsiders.

Almost immediately there was a stampede to the baptismal font, where thousands eagerly converted. These Jews quickly dropped all connections to the Jewish community, married out and disappeared. Four of Mendelssohn's six children converted, and all of his grandchildren, save one, were practicing Christians (composer Felix Mendelssohn was a grandson). Many of the leading figures in Germany in the 1800s were baptized Jews or descendents of baptized Jews—Karl Marx probably being the most famous.

The number of converts was more numerous than we would like to admit. It is estimated that between 1819 and 1823 alone over one-third of the Jews living in Berlin converted. This group has no bearing on modern Jewish existence except as a source of sadness and shame. They are gone forever. Descendents of martyrs who suffered and died to be Jewish, proclaiming G-d's existence with their dying breaths, and of generations of heroes who absorbed torments and tortures in order to perpetuate their holy way of life, they simply walked away when given the opportunity.

Others were eager to assimilate but not anxious to convert, considering it a humiliation. They wanted to keep some semblance of Jewishness but they very quickly ran into some inherent problems. A Jew who kept the Shabbat could not mix into a society that worked six days and rested on Sunday. A Jew who kept kosher could not eat in the homes and restaurants of gentiles. A Jew who kept his Hebrew or Yiddish name and unique manner of dress stood out. Jews had their own holidays and did not partake in the gentile ones. Certainly the prohibition against intermarrying made it hard to see yourself like "everybody else"; it's hard to claim that you are just like everybody else when you're not allowed to marry them.

These rules had always made the Jews a distinct element within any society but in Germany in the early 1800s, they presented a big problem to a large segment of the Jewish population. They did not want to give up their Jewish identities, yet they wanted to live like non-Jews. There was a just one huge obstacle standing in the way of their desires: Judaism itself. So, they came up with a solution. Judaism would have to change.

The result would come to be known as Reform Judaism.

The Rise of Reform

In order to be able to create a malleable Judaism the leaders of the nascent Reform movement knew one thing very clearly: The *mitzvot* (commandments) of the Torah had to be discredited. If Jews saw them as G-d given and obligatory, there was no way to change them. However, if they were redefined as manmade and part of antiquity, they could easily be changed or even eliminated as the situation needed. Therefore, they set out to do what had never been done before in history of the world.

After 3,100 years of being a light unto the nations and the conscience of the world, a group of Jews stood up and loudly proclaimed something that had never been said before, not by Jew or non-Jew. The Torah, they asserted, was written by men, not G-d. As we saw earlier, even Christianity and Islam believed that the Jews received the Torah on Mount Sinai and still maintain that to this day.

Obviously this leads to some questions. We know why this was done but how did they get away with it? And why was such a claim never attempted before in history?

Let's look at the circumstances. Is it a coincidence that Reform Judaism began precisely where and when Jews were being offered previously unimagined liberties and where Jewish observance would be an impediment to these liberties? Does one have to do with the other or is it a mere coincidence?

Why did this philosophy not emerge in any of the centuries before? Why didn't we "realize" that the Torah was just a bunch of ancient laws that had no bearing on life when we were being slaughtered by the hundreds of thousands in Christian and Arab lands precisely because we would not abandon the Torah? It seems to me that that would have been an opportune time to figure it out.

Or, perhaps, did the attitudes and opinions of the non-Jews in Europe at that time directly affect our attitudes and opinions?

I think the answer is obvious. The reason why this type of philosophy never arose in another time or place is twofold. First, there was no need for it—a secular gentile society that was willing to accept Jews as equals had never existed before. But once there was such a society it necessitated the need for such a movement. After the emotional need arose, the intellectual justifications were found.

And the second reason why they were able to get away with claiming that 3,000 years of Jewish tradition was mere fiction is that enlightened European society had already taken that position with regard to Christianity. The modern era had already seen the rejection of the idea of a divinely ordained religion and of G-d Himself. Once the gentiles did it, Jews could now be so bold as to do the same and feel enlightened at the same time. The non-Jews had delegitimized the Bible therefore the Jews could also get away with it. Such a philosophy would have been highly offensive in past centuries.

The founders of Reform Judaism set out to redesign Judaism into something that would fit comfortably in a Christian society and as a result, early Reform Judaism became no more than a cheap copy of Protestantism. And that is no accident. Reform Judaism began in Germany, the same country where the Reformation began (same word—Reform, Reformation). Both were revolts against the established religion and, interestingly, both involved translating the Bible into German.

Shabbat services were moved from Saturday to Sunday; organs, choirs and stained glass were installed in the synagogues and the *yarmulke* and the *tallit* were not only discarded but actually forbidden. The bareheaded rabbis wore vestments modeled on Christian priestly garb. Hymns were sung. Confirmation, a Christian rite, was introduced. The prayer book was rewritten to delete all references to Jerusalem and a return to Zion and was published in only the German language, without any Hebrew (because a good German prays in German). The synagogues where all this occurred were renamed "temples." In hindsight, it is clear that the rule guiding these changes was that any aspect of Jewish observance that had a Christian counterpart was retained and anything that did not was discarded.

On a personal level, Shabbat observance and daily prayer were eliminated. There was no further requirement to fast on Yom Kippur, or to wear *tzitzit* or *tefillin*. Women were told that they should not bother with Shabbat candles or kosher homes. Circumcision was officially discouraged, at times even denounced as barbaric, and abandoned in droves.

Modern styles of dress were adopted in order to make Jews look more like non-Jews. All outward trappings of being a Jew were gone. Jews were literally told to be "a Jew at home and a man on the street." Many Reform Jews preferred to be called "Germans of Mosaic (as in Moses) background." Later, Jews in other communities also adopted this stance. Incredibly there were even Jews in Poland before the Holocaust who referred to themselves as "Poles of Mosaic background."

On a philosophical level, the concepts of a G-d-given Torah, a chosen people and a belief in an eventual messianic redemption from exile were disavowed. Jews were no longer a people but simply a religion. Germany was the fatherland, not Zion. Nothing at all had occurred on Mount Sinai and all of Judaism was a human creation based on some sort of ongoing quasi-divine revelation.

There then emerged two kinds of Jews: the Reform Jews and the ones labeled pejoratively by the Reform as "Orthodox" Jews.

Throughout Germany, community after community dropped thousands of years of Jewish tradition as the Reform movement created a new religion and a new Jewish identity. Now, a Jew could be a Jew without having anything to do with the *mitzvot*—a very destructive idea because a serious alternative definition of a Jew was never proposed. (This is because, by definition, another one cannot exist.)

The secularization of Jewish communities was not limited to Germany. It spread to France, Holland, Belgium, the Austro-Hungarian Empire (Austrian, Czech, Polish, Slovak, Hungarian and Balkan communities), the Russian Empire (Russian, Polish, Byelorussian, Lithuanian and Baltic communities) and England. Soon Jews were assimilating and disappearing in all these communities.

Emigrants brought this secular philosophy to the New World; the British and French empires brought it to the great Sephardic communities in Morocco, Egypt, Syria, Iraq and Iran; and the early Zionists settlers transplanted it to Israel. (Although in a slightly different form—the early Zionists had no need for the façade of Reform Judaism. They simply threw off all Judaism and religious belief and attempted to create a new Jewish identity based on nationalism and a connection to the land. This is explained in the next chapter.)

It should come as no surprise that after a few years of actively mimicking the gentiles, the Reform Jews also began dropping all pretenses to being Jewish and began intermarrying with the local gentile population. One of the first leaders of Reform Judaism in Germany, a man named Israel Jacobson, had ten children, most of whom converted. His son, Dr. Hermann

Jacobson, the first boy confirmed in the Berlin Temple, became one of the leaders of Berlin's Catholic community.

The Jews of Europe quickly became very secular and within a century, for the first time in our history, most Jews were not observant of the *mitzvot* of the Torah. The effects were very wide and very deep. Family photographs from Europe in the years up until World War II often show religious parents and secular children.

The modern Jewish era continued to evolve. The minds of Jews cut from the moorings of the Torah were fertile ground for all kinds of new philosophies brewing in Europe such as the socialist, communist and various nationalist movements in which Jews quickly rose to positions of leadership. Zionism sprang up as a Jewish counterpart to the nationalistic movements in Europe and Reform Judaism splintered and gave birth to Conservative Judaism. To say there was no unity would be an understatement.

Chasidim and Their Style of Dress

During this period, the Chasidim (the Hebrew plural of the singular, Chasid) adopted their code of dress. (In English, the word is sometimes spelled Hasid just as Chanukah is spelled Hanukah. But it is pronounced with the guttural "ch" that sounds like someone clearing his throat.)

During our years of slavery in Egypt—the very first experience the Jewish people had of living among non-Jews—we avoided assimilation by standing fast on three issues: our names, our language and our clothes. The Talmud describes how these three points maintained our sense of identity. When we looked into the mirror, we saw a Jew. When someone called our name, we heard that we were a Jew. And when we spoke or thought in Hebrew, we existed as a Jew. Our identity was constantly reinforced.

On the other hand, if we dress like non-Jews, speak the same language as non-Jews and share the same names as non-Jews, the opposite message is reinforced. We are constantly reminded that we are no different from them.

Until the modern era, all Jews throughout the world differentiated themselves in these three ways. And today, the Orthodox continue to do so. We are identifiable by our clothing, most of all our *yarmulkes* and the modest way women dress. We have Hebrew or Yiddish names, and Yiddish, a combination of Hebrew and German with a sprinkling of Slavic words, is still spoken in many Orthodox homes, although the numbers are dropping. Until most Sephardic Jews moved to Israel after 1948, Ladino, a combination of Hebrew and Spanish, was their spoken language.

In fact, throughout history, Jews have often spoken a distinct language or dialect that was a combination of Hebrew and the host language. Yiddish and Ladino were the most universal but Jews living in Provence, Piedmont, Catalan, Aragon, Greece, Crimea, Georgia and Persia all once had their own languages or dialects that were half Hebrew; these languages were unique to them and were not shared by the non-Jews amongst whom they lived. There was also a Judeo-Arabic language that varied by region.

When the modern era burst open, there were groups of Jews in Eastern Europe who felt that the danger of assimilation was so dire, they undertook added stringencies to isolate themselves.

The roots of Chasidism are based in the Ukraine and the movement began in the late 1600s. Eventually it spread to the rest of Russia, Poland, Byelorussia, Hungary and Romania. At the beginning they dressed no differently than any other Jew in the area. But when they saw the dangers of getting swept up in the illusion of "equality," they decided to do the opposite. They were not going to budge. This is why they still dress in the style of eighteenth-century Polish nobility.

Historically, Jews have never had a specific unchanging style of dress that they wore regardless of where and when they lived. We are not walking around in robes as we did in antiquity. We also are not dressing in Roman togas or the styles of medieval Spain. Why did some Jews suddenly decide "no further?" They did this to protect themselves from being part of any new movement or "ism" and from becoming identified with the modern, secular world.

But it is only the Chasidim's manner of dress that hasn't changed. Every other aspect of their lives is modern. They are not riding around on horses and buggies. Their homes are up to date; they drive cars, operate businesses, use computers and utilize every modern convenience. But they did not want to be part of a general, integrated society. So when the ghetto walls came down they took measures to make it impossible to integrate. And they have succeeded. You can spot them a mile away.

Even among many Orthodox Jews who are not Chasidim, there is still a custom to wear hats, nowadays almost always black. This is because until the 1960s, all men and even boys wore some type of hat or head covering in public. It was only when John Kennedy refused to wear one that this manner of dress came to an end. Wearing a hat is a more formal way of dressing, and the casual style of dress that became the norm during the years of the sexual revolution was not adopted by many Orthodox Jews.

Conservative Judaism

Years of pulling in one direction by the Reform movement were bound to cause some fracturing. The first crack appeared in 1846, when a school opened in Breslau, Germany (today Wroclaw, Poland) called the Jewish Theological Seminary. It is considered the beginning of Conservative movement and it began as a reaction to the excesses of the Reform movement.

There were Jews who were not comfortable intermarrying or frying up bacon for breakfast. Nor did they view circumcision as a barbaric rite. The seminary taught what was then called "Positive-Historical Judaism." It was an attempt to straddle a middle ground but it never gained a significant following in Germany and eventually closed.

However, the pressures were still there and the rupture finally occurred in the United States, where Reform Judaism had grown with the huge German-Jewish immigration in the 1840s and 1850s. There were two events that caused the split.

The first occurred in 1883 and came to be known as the "Treifa (unkosher) Banquet." At the ceremony for the first graduating class of the Hebrew Union College, a seminary founded in Cincinnati to ordain Reform rabbis, the dinner menu included clams, shrimp and frogs' legs. This caused an uproar. Although it seems hard to understand in light of everything that had been developing in Europe, the American Jews were not of the same cloth as their European counterparts. American Jews did not face the same barriers and discrimination as European Jews. While there was certainly anti-Semitism, it was unofficial and not universal. A gentlemen's agreement is a far cry from a walled-in ghetto.

Since American Jews could maintain much of their heritage without it becoming an impediment to advancement, they had no reason or desire to butcher it. Also, America took its religion much more seriously than did Europe and had a warmer regard for it. Religion in America was not identified with repression and exploitation.

The second event was the publication of the Pittsburgh Platform of 1885. This document became the official doctrine of American Reform Judaism. In it, the Bible was described as "reflecting the primitive ideas of its own age." Practices that "are not adapted to the views and habits of modern civilization" such as those that "regulate diet, priestly purity and dress" were rejected because they "originated in ages and under the influence of ideas entirely foreign to our present mental and spiritual state."

Although asserting that the soul is immortal, the platform rejected the concept of heaven and hell—i.e., reward and punishment. It also categorically opposed Zionism and the settlement and building up of Israel. Since the Jews were not a people, it insinuated, why should they have their own country?

All this was way too radical for many American Jews and in 1886, the Jewish Theological Seminary (named for its predecessor in Breslau) opened in New York City. Popular opinion, due to the growing settlement in Israel and the rise of Hitler, eventually forced the Reform leadership to reverse their position and embrace Zionism when it published the Columbus (Ohio) Platform in 1937.

The stated goal of the Conservative Movement—so named because it aimed to conserve the traditions instead of reforming them—was to draw a middle ground based on *Halacha* or Jewish law. As a result of its public embrace of Jewish law and tradition, Conservative Judaism was the most popular branch in the United States from its inception until very recently, when it slipped behind Reform. This recent decline makes sense since Conservatives try to straddle a divide that continues to shift. It has itself split twice in recent years. In 1968, there was a break-off to the left (Reconstructionist) and in 1985, to the right (the Union for Traditional Judaism).

An Honest Assessment

Now that we have surveyed the last two hundred years, it is worthwhile stepping back and, for the sake of truth, evaluating the results. Where have the events of the last two and a half centuries left us?

Besides the splintering of the Jewish people into various groups, polls show that nearly forty percent of Jews have no affiliation at all. And of the remaining percentages that do belong to some type of non-Orthodox synagogue, how many can really claim to know the tenets of their movements? Or, to be more honest, how many really care at all?

Personally, I grew up in a home that belonged to a Conservative synagogue because we weren't Orthodox and Reform Judaism was not an option for my traditionally-minded parents. They could not conceive of going to a synagogue that served unkosher food and had a bareheaded rabbi who prayed in English. But we had no idea what Conservative Judaism officially believed, nor did we care. I can probably count on one hand all the Conservative Jews I have met who had any idea what the beliefs of the Conservative movement were or had any interest in living by them.

Today, all non-Orthodox denominations allow their members a wide array of views on the basic tenets of the religion. Officially, Reform Judaism defines revelation as "a continuous process, confined to no one group and to no one age." It long ago disposed of any idea of a personal G-d who requires certain behavior from us. Its 1885 Pittsburgh Platform spoke of a "God Idea."

Since Reform philosophy denies any commandments, there is only emotion to fall back on and the result is that the movement has been hemorrhaging men and has become, in essence, a movement of women. Today, the majority of its rabbinical students and synagogue officers are women and the percentage is increasing. Its sole focus on social issues assures that many will leave the fold. Who needs a religion to be active in social issues?

The Conservative movement officially maintains that the Torah is of divine origin but acknowledges that it has been influenced by other cultures. The Revelation at Mount Sinai was the clearest form of revelation, they say, but other more-subtle ones have occurred and continue to occur today.

What this means is that regardless of what the Reform and Conservative movements claim to be their tenets today, it could all change tomorrow. And whatever they do happen to believe today is not even binding on its followers—not even its rabbis. These movements continue to change according to the fluctuations of the larger gentile society, but this is ultimately suicidal. If, at any time in history, Judaism had ever conformed to the times it would have disappeared long ago. It survived and flourished precisely because it did *not* conform.

Both the Reform movement and the Conservative movement claim to be parts of the *mesorah,* or the transmission of Judaism, but—and I am sorry if this sounds harsh—this is a dishonest claim. Their contribution has been the elimination of the foundations of Judaism, which is the observance of the *mitzvot* and the resulting relationship with G-d, replacing them with words about Israel, social justice and the like.

In fact, a closer look shows that on the contrary, the engine for these movements had always been the social movements taking place in their immediate non-Jewish surroundings. Think about it, the Reform movement started as a way to assimilate and blend in with greater German society and so its leaders fashioned a Judaism that was in many ways indistinguishable from Protestantism. The Conservative Movement tried to make a landing midway between Orthodox Judaism and the Reformed version. But both movements, at heart, either look to the non-Jews as models or respond to their constituents' wishes that have been formed by assimilation into non-Jewish society.

For example, why did it take so long for the Reform movement to become "enlightened" enough to accept open homosexuality into its ranks and clergy? Why didn't they consider homosexuality and sexual freedom as pillars of their philosophy in 1830 or 1900 or even 1960? Why weren't they promoting abortion as a woman's right for the last 180 years? Why did it take until 1972 to ordain a woman rabbi?

The reason why is simply that such behavior was not accepted by the "enlightened" gentile society in which they lived. But as soon the gentile society did accept such behavior, without missing a beat, the moralists of this movement jumped in to declare these actions as rights. The Reform leadership won't dare introduce any changes in practice or philosophy until the gentiles around them are doing it, and then they enshrine them as Jewish values and rights.

The Conservative movement's espousal of "continuing revelation," means that the movement will land far from the goal that it originally set for itself—a middle ground. In the 1950s, as its constituency began moving to the suburbs, where the synagogues were no longer within walking distance, the rabbis of the Conservative movement responded by permitting driving on Shabbat—but *only* to the *nearest* synagogue and *only* if the person would otherwise not be able to attend services. (I have never met a Conservative Jew who abides by that rule.) Once the Reform movement ordained women, the Conservatives had no choice and began doing so in 1986.

Once a movement has to scamper to legitimize the behavior of its members, it has lost any position of moral leadership. You can no longer look to it for definitions of right and wrong because it is only defining right and wrong around what people are doing.

In fact, any morals or ethics, when removed from a Torah context, will not last. It is analogous to a cut flower that looks great but since it has been removed from its source of nutrients, its death is inevitable. Yes, it's beautiful and it smells wonderful but it is also on borrowed time. It is only a matter of time until it will die. It is not a question of *if*; it is a question of *when*.

Today there is great pressure from the Conservative membership to mimic Reform in issues like patrilineal descent and the acceptance of homosexuality and, frankly, it is only a matter of time. If they don't change with the times they will be considered less progressive and lose membership. In the end, like the Reform movement, they will always come around to justify what their adherents are already doing.

But in reality, whether they do or do not mimic the Reform movement is entirely academic. The vast majority of Conservative Jews have no interest in the debate. An enormous chasm has opened between the official positions of the leadership and the everyday practice of its laypeople. Many leaders of the movement have already admitted that almost all Jews who call themselves Conservative do not feel bound by *Halacha* or tradition. And, in fact, the Conservative movement has officially stated that just because one belongs to a Conservative synagogue doesn't necessarily make him a Conservative Jew. Their members may possess warmer feelings to things Jewish and therefore have greater awareness and a bit more observance of some laws, traditions or rituals in their lives, but in no way is there an ironclad obligation to observe.

And even though it took some years, the lines between all these non-Orthodox movements are getting very blurry. In fact, there are almost no differences between the daily lives of Reform Jews, Conservative Jew and unaffiliated Jews. Their synagogues function differently, but that has very little relevance for the majority of their members, who show up three times a year. Have you ever heard of a Conservative parent objecting to his or her child marrying a Reform Jew or vice versa? Can you imagine a mother saying that she didn't like her daughter's boyfriend because he never went to Hebrew School?

Today's Reform and Conservative movements and for that matter, secular Jewish organizations have, despite their lip service, abandoned any claim to moral leadership. In a sense, they are the ultimate followers. Instead of acting as moral leaders, they walk lockstep with the rest of "enlightened" non-Jewish society. A movement that copies the nations cannot lead the nations. They provide no true moral and spiritual guidance. They are not lights to the nations; they are merely the taillights on the caboose.

Anything can be said to be in the name of Judaism, Jewish values or Jewish ethics. What are the criteria for stating that something is a Jewish value? Does it have anything to do with the Torah, or is it determined by a vote of a committee comprised of social workers and psychologists? Leadership that looks to the editorial pages of *The New York Times* for instruction before pronouncing the latest morality is not leadership. Their "*mitzvot*" keep changing with the times. It was once workers' rights, then civil rights; now it is a mix of environmentalism and multiculturalism. I guarantee it will be something different in a few years.

Today's Reform movement states that it is at the forefront of the "ongoing defense of the wall of separation of church and state." But since when is the elimination of G-d from life a Jewish value or ethic? We are the children of Avraham, who became the great forefather of the Jewish nation precisely because he spent his life devoted to teaching the world about G-d and bringing Him back, so to speak, into the world after generations of idol worship had all but eliminated the knowledge of Him. What does it say about the rabbis and leaders of the Reform and Conservative movements who are so vocal and seem to be at the forefront of such opinion making?

When firing a rifle at a target in the distance, a tilt of even one degree on the part of the shooter can mean a miss of inches or even feet, depending on the distance to the target. If one is firing an artillery shell, one degree can mean miles. Setting a space probe one degree off path can eventually mean an error of millions of miles. The greater the distance, the greater the miss. The orientation of history follows the same physical law.

In Jewish history it is clear that even a slight deviation from the Torah will not be so apparent when close to the event but will become very obvious over a period of time, and always lead to the disappearance of those following that trajectory. Once the Torah was redefined as a manmade document, every Jew was free to take it or leave it, in whole or in part.

Today the vast majority of Reform and Conservative Jews do not feel a religious obligation to fulfill any of the *mitzvot*. These are not considered the requirements to be a good Jew. The result is that the spirituality and the meaning have been gutted from their Judaism leaving only a thin shell that offers no real satisfaction. This is apparent in the vastly disproportionate number of Jews in other religions, movements and cults. In fact, there are so many Jews practicing Buddhism today that a new term has been coined: Bujews.

Jews who eat bacon for breakfast, cheeseburgers for lunch and lobster for dinner will not be able to inspire or lead the Jewish people. They might wield power for a period of time but soon the masses will start listening with only one ear and eventually will wander off, attracted by someone or something more interesting. This is exactly what is occurring today. Empty words have only produced a mass exodus of the younger generations. People have voted with their feet.

Facing their abject failure to inspire their youth to, at the very least, marry Jews, the Reform and Conservative movements have embarked on what they call outreach—i.e., reaching out to non-Jewish spouses to attract and involve them in an attempt to hold on to the next generation. They mask their decay by couching their efforts in an Orwellian glossary of terms such as "inclusive," "welcoming" and "pluralistic." What I don't understand is, if they couldn't inspire the parents, why do they think they will be able to inspire the children. What are they attracting them to? They state (rather pompously, in my opinion) that "a Judaism frozen in time is an heirloom, not a living fountain." These efforts, they claim, will make the Jewish people stronger and more vital. I wonder if anyone even believes what they are saying.

If you are confused by all of this, don't worry—so am I. And, I venture to say, so are most Jews.

So, today we have a divide. One side believes the Torah is from G-d and that the purpose of our lives is to develop a relationship with him and fulfill his commandments. The other side believes the Torah is an outdated, manmade document that has no bearing on modern life and that everyone is free to pick and choose what they want to do or not do, as if the Torah were a menu in a Chinese restaurant. One group eats in non-kosher restaurants while the other only eats according to the laws of *Kashrut*. One group is shopping and going to the beach on Saturday while the other keeps the Shabbat. One group openly embraces intermarriage while the other sees it as unmitigated disaster.

This schizophrenic existence has caused an enormous rift that has led to significant misunderstandings and a good deal of negativity towards Orthodox Jews and often towards Judaism itself on the part of non-Orthodox Jews.

Orthodox Jews are seen as monolithic and centrally controlled but the opposite is true. In fact, there are so many philosophies, movements and gradations of thought in the Orthodox world that it is difficult to keep track of them. This decentralization is evidenced by the process of rabbinical ordination. If one wants to become a Reform rabbi, there is only one way. He must attend the Hebrew Union College. If one wants to be a Conservative rabbi, there is only one way. He must attend the Jewish Theological Seminary. But if one wants to be an Orthodox rabbi, he can attend any one of the hundreds (if not thousands) of *yeshivas* throughout the world and get ordained. Orthodox Judaism is not an institutionalized or top-down philosophy. It reflects the varied assortment of ideas and individuals that comprise the Jewish people.

Another deep-seated misconception is that Orthodox Jews do not consider non-Orthodox Jews to be Jewish. Unfortunately the fires of this nonsense are very often fanned by people with political agendas. But it is not true. (If that were the case, I wouldn't have written this book.) A rejection of non-Orthodox doctrine and practice is not a rejection of non-Orthodox Jews. The Conservative movement does not accept Reform converts. If you convert through a Reform rabbi and want to join a Conservative synagogue, you will need to convert again. Does this mean that the Conservative movement does not consider the Reform Jews to be Jews? Of course not. And if Orthodox Jews didn't consider non-Orthodox Jews to be Jewish, there would be no attempt to reach them and educate them as there is in Israel and throughout the world. Every Jew is a diamond and every *mitzvah* that he does is beloved by G-d.

Observance of the *mitzvot* is not a zero-sum game, nor is it all or nothing. Any *mitzvah* that is done is an eternal merit to that soul. If the only thing a person does is put a *mezuzah* on the front door that is certainly better than having no *mezuzah!* Is there more to do? Of course, but what Jew (especially an Orthodox Jew) who has his head screwed on properly is going to belittle the fulfillment of that *mitzvah?*

This synopsis explains why I have chosen to use the term "non-Orthodox" for this book—because after 250 years of noise and tumult and a lot of rancor and bitterness, it is clear that in reality and in practice, there are only two types of Jew in the world: those who accept the Torah as G-d given and feel personally obligated to fulfill all the *mitzvot* in the Torah and those who do not. This explains why Orthodox Jews never speak of branches of Judaism. Rather, they speak of the "observant" (of the *mitzvot*) and the "nonobservant." Instead of branches, there is, in actuality, a divide in which each side holds opposing views of the most fundamental aspects of Jewish identity.

This is all a result of the European emancipation and the stresses it created.

And it is an awful tragedy.

Chapter Twelve
The Land of Israel and the State of Israel

Love of the Land

In planning this book I chose to discuss those issues and ideas that I felt were the most puzzling to non-Orthodox Jews and the issues that were the most divisive (and therefore most in need of explanation). I tried to put myself in my old shoes. What did I once find incomprehensible about Orthodox Jews and what bothered me? How did I feel when I read about Orthodox Jews in the newspaper (especially while I was in Israel) or when I met a few of them? I remember having many questions about their clothing, what I interpreted to be their aloofness and clannishness and their opposition to many things that I thought any "normal" person would agree with. Two issues that I became acquainted with while living in Israel and that I just could not understand were their supposed opposition to the State of Israel and their supposed non-participation in the army. I say supposed to both of these because they both turn out to be very untrue.

Of course, I had little familiarity with the history of the Jewish people or any idea what the Torah was. I could not have told you who came first, Noach or Abraham or Moshe. I could not understand Hebrew (I had learned to read and write it in Hebrew school but that was all), nor could I articulate what Jews believed or why.

My six months on a secular *kibbutz* in 1981 and my subsequent months of backpacking around the country actually led me to Aish HaTorah. This was because I came to believe that there was something deeper and more meaningful to being Jewish than what I was seeing or what I knew. I had always had a fascination with the Holocaust and was a little familiar with historical anti-Semitism and I suppose the irrationality of it all drove my inquisitiveness.

I had also been very disappointed when I lived on the *kibbutz*. I had gone to Israel with stars in my eyes and thought I would be living among people who were idealistic and content. What I found was, for the most part, the opposite. The young people I met on the *kibbutz* were in love with Western music and Western culture. Being Jewish was not their main identity and when it was, it felt like it had been forced upon them and they were trapped in it. It did not seem like something they embraced with pride. They knew less about Jewish history and the Jewish religion than I did.

However, I was very proud of being Jewish and fell deeply in love with Israel. And for me, one of the hardest issues that I had to wrestle with after I began learning in a *yeshiva* was some Orthodox Jews' opposition to Zionism. To me, it was a no-brainer. Who wasn't a Zionist? Arabs weren't and anti-Semites weren't, and that just proved the point.

In the United States, I'd had very little exposure to Orthodox Jews and those I had known, including some second cousins, were what are termed "modern Orthodox." A love of Israel was a pillar of their faith. It wasn't until I went to Israel that I discovered an entire segment of Orthodox society that was not made up of flag wavers and did not go into the army. I am grateful that I did not develop a hatred for them despite the virulent feelings against them on the *kibbutz* and in the Israeli media. I just didn't understand what they were thinking. Or, to be more accurate, I couldn't understand how seemingly intelligent people (after all they *were* Jews) could be so wrong.

But as I matured in years, temperament and intellect, I soon realized that the history and existence of the State of Israel was not as black and white as it was presented, that the Orthodox were branded as things they weren't and that opinions were ascribed to them that they did not espouse. I also learned that in regard to Israel, there are so many shadings, gradations and nuances to the "Orthodox view" that the term has no real meaning.

There is one point that needs to be made at the outset and that is that amongst all Orthodox Jews, regardless of political leanings, from the most left wing to the most right wing, there is an unbelievably deep and passionate love of the Land of Israel. In fact, I do not know any adult Orthodox Jew who has not been to Israel at least once. And I know many who go as often as they can. I also know many who have moved there with their families. Israel is a part of an Orthodox Jew's life and has been throughout history. However, when it comes to political Zionism, that is where the road forks.

Hopefully, by the end of this chapter I will have made the issues and disagreements clear and understandable. To do this, though, we need to clearly understand the meaning of the land, the history of the land and the history of the modern Zionist movement.

The Meaning of the Land

The idea that a nation should have a homeland seems quite natural. A homeland is indispensable to a nation's self-image and identity. In fact, it is hard to imagine how a nation could function as a nation without a homeland.

However, like everything else in this world, the rules that apply to the Jewish nation are different than those that apply to all the other nations. The concept and purpose of a homeland for the Jewish nation is radically different than those of a homeland for the rest of the world's nations.

G-d did not promise the Land of Israel to Avraham and his descendants so that we could have our own cities, merchant fleet, highways, radio stations and national airline. And He certainly did not promise Avraham the Land of Israel so we could conduct ourselves like all the other nations, with their violence, immorality and meaningless distractions. We might have all the accoutrements of nationhood like cities, merchant fleet, highways, radio stations and a national airline, but only as a means of fulfilling our mission, not as means in and of themselves.

G-d promised the Land of Israel to Avraham and his descendants so we could create a unique and exceptional society on Earth and live a life of closeness to Him. By creating a holy society we would provide an example for the rest of humanity. The nations would learn how to conduct their affairs—legal, financial, social, cultural and so on—by modeling themselves on the morality of the Jewish nation. The purpose of creation would thereby be fulfilled.

We are told repeatedly throughout the Torah that if we keep the *mitzvot* we will enjoy prosperity and longevity in the land. The fertility of the land does not depend on our agricultural expertise or cycles of nature, nor does our safety in the land depend on our military prowess or secure borders. It depends solely on our keeping our end of the bargain that we made at Mount Sinai.

The Land of Israel is, therefore, given to us on condition. As we saw earlier, Moshe had predicted that the Jewish people would prosper, grow fat and rebel against G-d's direction. G-d's response would be a series of troubles and crises designed to snap the Jewish people out of their illusions and bring about a national reordering of priorities. If they did not wake up they would eventually be exiled.

This is the formula. If we use the land properly we will prosper, but if decide to use the Holy Land for a life that is not in consonance with G-d's expressed purpose, we will be ejected (Deut. 11:13-21).

Throughout the Torah, the holiness of the land is continuously emphasized, as if to say that an unholy life cannot be tolerated by the land itself. In one place in the Torah, where the laws of proscribed sexual and marital relationships are listed, G-d says that if we conduct ourselves immorally the land itself will become defiled and it will literally "vomit" us out (Lev. 18:28), just as a human being will throw up rotten food.

A clear indication of this conditional relationship is the very profound fact that Mount Sinai is not located in the Land of Israel. The Jewish people received the Torah *outside* the Land of Israel, and only when we had the Torah were we brought into the land—i.e., we entered the land already in possession of the Torah and leading a life of *mitzvot*. Possession of the land is predicated upon the fulfillment of the Torah. The purpose of the land is the ultimate fulfillment of the Torah.

Another important point is that getting expelled does not mean that we relinquish ownership. The Land of Israel belongs to the Children of Israel regardless of whether or not we are present. We own the deed, and squatters do not acquire any rights to it. This is evidenced by Moshe's prophecies promising that we will eventually be returned to the land.

In fact, as we saw earlier, once the Jewish people are evicted, the land will dry up and die and not allow another nation to settle it. It will be put on the shelf, so to speak, to await the return of its rightful owner.

But on a deeper level, the Land of Israel is essential to our lives for another reason. It is in this land that G-d's presence is felt more keenly. It is only in this land that a person's spirituality can reach its full flower. This is why G-d commanded Avraham to go there, and this is why prophecy is only attainable in Israel. It is the natural environment for a life of righteousness, piety and love for one's fellow Jew.

Just as certain regions of the world are renowned for producing the highest-quality or most-delicious produce while others places cannot, Israel's national product is spiritual, not physical. The Talmud states that the air alone makes a person wise. For this reason, the Talmud also teaches us that it is preferable to live in Israel among non-Jews than to live outside of Israel among Jews. In addition, many of the 613 *mitzvot* can only be performed and fulfilled in Israel.

But just like the vines in Italy and France, the olives in Greece and the tea in India must be cultivated and cared for, so must our product be properly grown and maintained. Without a life of Torah and *mitzvot*, the natural "fruit" of Israel will not grow to its full potential and might actually be ruined.

The History of the Land

The truth of Moshe's prophecies that the Land of Israel would go into a state of suspended animation after the Jews were exiled has been amply testified to by visitors to the land throughout history. The fact that no nation ever developed there is proof enough. Never in history has a fertile, conquered land ever been abandoned. The Romans settled throughout Europe. The Arabs (from Arabia) settled throughout their conquered territories—Spain, North Africa, Syria and Iraq—and lived alongside the Greeks, Romans, Babylonians and other native peoples who were remnants of previous empires. They established or built up grand cities like Granada in Spain and Baghdad. But Israel was left in ruins.

As late as the 1800s, visitors still found only a desolate wilderness. The British Consul General, James Finn, wrote in 1857 that "the country is in a considerable degree empty of inhabitants." He added that the land's "greatest need is that of a body of population."

In 1867, Mark Twain visited Israel as part of a tour of Europe and the Middle East. He traveled through the land and later wrote about it in his travelogue, *The Innocents Abroad*. Listen to his description:

Regarding the Dan region in the northern Galil:

> Here were evidences of cultivation-a rare sight in this country-an acre or two of rich soil studded with last season's dead cornstalks of the thickness of your thumb and very wide apart... Close to it was a stream, and on its banks a great herd of curious-looking Syrian goats and sheep were gratefully eating gravel... I only suppose they were eating gravel, because there did not appear to be anything else for them to eat... We saw water then, but nowhere in all the waste around us was a foot of shade and we were scorched to death...this blistering, naked, treeless land... There is not a solitary village throughout its whole extant-not for thirty miles in either direction...One may ride ten miles hereabouts and not see ten human beings.[17]

As he traveled through the lower Galilee:

> We traversed some miles of desolate country whose soil is rich enough, but given over wholly to weeds; a silent,

mournful expanse, wherein we saw only three person-Arabs with nothing on but a long, coarse shirt...It's hard to realize that this silent plain had once resounded with martial music and trembled to the tramp of armed men... A desolation is here that not even imagination can grace with the pomp of life and action. We reached Tabor safely...we never saw a human on the whole route, much less lawless hordes of Bedouins.[18]

This is how he concluded his account of his visit:

Of all the lands there are for dismal scenery, I think Palestine must be the prince. The hills are barren, they are dull of color, they are unpicturesque in shape. The valleys are unsightly deserts fringed with a feeble vegetation that has an expression about it of being sorrowful and despondent... It is a hopeless, dreary, heart-broken land...

Palestine sits in sackcloth and ashes. Over it broods the spell of a curse that has withered its fields and fettered its energies... Nazareth is forlorn; about that ford of Jordan where the hosts of Israel entered the Promised Land with songs of rejoicing, one finds only a squalid camp of fantastic Bedouins of the desert; Jericho, the accursed, lies a moldering ruin, to-day, even as Joshua's miracle left it more than three thousand years ago...Renowned Jerusalem itself, the stateliest name in history, has lost all its ancient grandeur, and is become a pauper village...The noted Sea of Galilee...was long ago deserted by the devotees of war and commerce, and its borders are a silent wilderness...

Palestine is desolate and unlovely. And why should it be otherwise? Can the curse of the Deity beautify a land?

Palestine is no more of this work-day world. It is sacred to poetry and tradition—it is dream-land.[19]

Arthur Stanley, a British cartographer, wrote in 1881 after his visit: "In Judea it is hardly an exaggeration to say that for miles and miles there was no appearance of life or habitation."

This might sound odd considering how violently the Arabs fulminate about how holy Jerusalem is to them and how Palestine has always hosted an Arab civilization that was displaced by the Zionists. But, as is usually the case today, what the Arabs claim does not agree with the facts.

How holy is Jerusalem to Moslems? To begin with, the Koran never mentions Jerusalem by name.

At the time of the writing of the Koran, the city of Jerusalem had been called by that name—Jerusalem—for at least 1,000 years, going back to the time of King David. It was a fairly well-known city with a lot of history and there is no reason why the Koran wouldn't call it by name. There are many other cities mentioned in the Koran and they are all mentioned by name.

Our Bible, on the other hand, refers to Jerusalem by name 667 times.

The Moslems claim that when the Koran spoke of "Al Aksa" it was referring to Jerusalem. The term "Al Aksa" literally means "the farthest" or "the most remote" and it is mentioned in the Koran only once and in a vague way. The verse states, "Blessed be He who brought His servant at night from the holy sanctuary to the outermost sanctuary (Al-Masjid al-Aksa)." That's it. That's the sum total of the Koran's love of Jerusalem. Then it goes on to another topic altogether.

Moslems claim that this refers to when Mohammed supposedly ascended to heaven alive on his white steed. What is not known, even to many Moslems, is that this supposed event is not mentioned at all in the Koran. Based on this verse, it became part of Arab folklore long after his death. It has as much basis in fact as Remus and Romulus being weaned by a wolf or the Egyptian pharaohs' claim to be descendents of gods.

When he supposedly did this, in 632 AD, he had already conquered all of Arabia and had established Islam as the state religion.

The religion revolved, then as now, around the holy sites in Mecca and Medina, both in Arabia. Jerusalem and the rest of Palestine were far away. In fact, the Arabs did not conquer Palestine until 638 AD, six years after Mohammed's death, when they took it from the (Christian) Byzantine Empire and made it part of an Arab-Moslem empire.The Arabs had no name of their own for this region and simply adopted the Roman name Palastina, which they pronounced as "Falastin" since there is no "p" sound in the Arabic language. After that, much of the mixed population of Falastin converted to Islam and adopted the Arabic language—or were killed.

Doesn't it seem a little strange that Mohammed would suddenly fly from Arabia, the heartland of Islam, to Jerusalem, a Byzantine city that was not part of his empire and where there was not one Moslem or mosque, and depart this Earth from the Temple Mount where a church stood at the time? He might as well have departed from Athens, Rome or any other Christian city.

So, how did "the farthest mosque" and Jerusalem become synonymous?

In 638 AD, when Jerusalem was conquered by the Arabs, the caliph, Omar Ibn al-Khattab, asked Sophronius, the Greek patriarch who ruled the city, to show him the Masjid Dawud or Mosque of David. He was taken to a building on the southern end of the Temple Mount, which historians speculate was a Jewish building that dated back to the Second Temple period. He entered and, according to Arab tradition, cleared away some of the rubbish that had accumulated inside over hundreds of years of neglect and prayed there.

However, construction of an actual mosque did not begin until at least fifty years later under the caliph of Damascus, Abd al-Malik, and was only finished later by his son, al-Walid, who also ruled from Damascus, in the year 705 AD. This is the site that is now claimed as the third-holiest site in Islam. It is **NOT** the gold-domed mosque in the middle of the Temple Mount but the dark-domed mosque at its southern end.

Al-Malik named it the Al-Aksa Mosque for political reasons. He was in a power struggle with his counterparts in Arabia and was attempting to wrest control of the Moslem world away from them. Until that time, there was no tradition in Islam that the term "Al-Aksa" referred to Jerusalem. Al Aksa was simply an unknown, mystical place.

In 691 AD, al-Malik completed the gold-domed mosque that now adorns all the travel posters. He built this mosque on the exact site where the two Jewish temples had stood. Why did he do this? For the same reason the Christians had also built a church there: to demonstrate that they represented the true religion. A church on the site of the Jewish temple proved that Christianity had supplanted Judaism and a mosque on that site proved that Islam had supplanted both of them. Both understood that Jerusalem represents the truth.

To this day, Moslems face Mecca when they pray, not Jerusalem as Jews throughout the world do. One cannot help but find it ironic that when the time comes to pray, those Arabs on the Temple Mount will turn their backs to the mosque, kneel down and pray toward Mecca.

For the next 1,200 years or so, the land lay in waste. Arab rulers made no attempt to build up or beautify the city, nor did the Moslem Ottoman Turks, who ruled the land for 400 years (1517 to 1917).

In 1099, Christian crusaders from Europe conquered Palestine in the First Crusade. Over the next two centuries, Christians and Moslems battled for control of the land, which seesawed back and forth between them. Even at their height, the crusader kingdoms never developed national identities. They remained military outposts of Christian Europe—no settlers arrived or were even considered—and lasted less than 200 years before finally collapsing under Arab assault.

The Arabs, even after they re-conquered Palestine, gave it in no special religious or national significance. It was merely a part of the contiguous Moslem land mass. When Salah-A-Din (Saladin in English) captured Jerusalem from the crusaders in 1187 he did not bestow on it any type of importance; in fact he did not even allow its destroyed walls to be rebuilt. Instead he chose Ramla as his regional capital. (The crusaders had designated Akko (Acre) as theirs. Earlier in history, the Romans had used Caesaria. Only the Jews have ever established Jerusalem as their capital.)

In 1249 the Egyptian sultan al Kamil, ruler of Palestine, ceded Jerusalem, along with Nazareth and Bethlehem, to Emperor Frederick II of the Holy Roman Empire as part of a peace treaty ending the sixth Crusade. This alone was an incredible admission that Jerusalem had no true significance to Moslems. But the Sultan's words are even more demonstrative. At the time, he stated, "I have ceded nothing but ruined churches and wrecked buildings." So, not only was the city of no religious importance to Moslems, it was also a ruin. If Jerusalem was truly a great Arab city or one of religious significance to Moslems, it would have resembled Cairo, Damascus or Baghdad, which all have long and rich histories.

The people who lived there were always subjects of a distant caliph who ruled them from his capital, which was originally Damascus. Later it was Cairo, then Baghdad and eventually Istanbul. If Jerusalem was of any importance, religious or political, wouldn't there have been a caliphate of Jerusalem?

As late as 1900 Jerusalem was still a small, backwater town seemingly abandoned by history. It was never a destination of religious pilgrimage for Moslems. Even during the period between 1948 and 1967, when the Temple Mount was in Jordanian hands, very few Islamic religious leaders of any status visited, and certainly no one from the Saudi royal family. A Moslem who makes the *Haj* or pilgrimage to Mecca can add the honorary title of Al-Haj to his name for the rest of his life. A similar trip to Jerusalem is of absolutely no religious significance.

What is abundantly clear from all historical records is that from the time the Jews were exiled by the Romans, the area known as Palestine was never the homeland of another nation. Palestine never existed as a country. There has never been a land known as "Palestine" that has been governed by Palestinians. It never had defined borders or a native culture. You can search the libraries of the world and you will not find one volume on the history of the Palestinian people. They never existed.

Look at maps of the Middle East from the 1800s and no two show the same boundaries. Some include Lebanon as part of Palestine and some even include Syria. Palestine had the same loose meaning as "the Maghreb" or "the Midwest." It was a geographical term, used to designate the region during those times in history when there was no nation or state there. Every book published before the 1950s describes Palestine as a region.

Political Zionism

The last time that the entire Jewish people lived together in the Land of Israel was in the year 3408 or 423 BC, the year of the destruction of the First Temple by the Babylonians. Since that time, the Jews have longed for an ingathering of the exiles and a return to our homeland, so we can fulfill the Torah in its entirety and with complete love and dedication. Three times a day, every day for the last 2,500 years, Jews have petitioned G-d for this—it is included in our daily prayers. We end our Yom Kippur prayers and our Passover Seders with the prayer, "Next year in Jerusalem."

Although most Jews live in exile, there was never a time when the Land of Israel was completely empty of Jews. Immediately after the Roman destruction, some stubbornly stayed and were willing to live in deprivation in Israel rather than more comfortably outside of it. This tenacity and gumption, always present in the Jewish character, led many pious Jews throughout the centuries, including some of our greatest scholars, to take the arduous journey to settle in Israel. Many Jews expelled from Spain in 1492 also made their way to Israel and settled in Jerusalem and Tzfat (Safed in English).

A real and organized movement to begin resettling the land did not begin with modern political Zionism in the mid 1800s. It began long before the term was even coined. The period of modern settlement actually began in 1700 when one of the leading European rabbis, Rabbi Yehuda HaChassid, settled in Jerusalem and built the Churva synagogue in what became the Jewish Quarter. It stood until the Jordanians destroyed it in 1948 and has since been rebuilt.

In the late 1700s groups organized by the leading rabbis of Europe began to settle in Israel. Originally they settled in Jerusalem, which, at the time, was only what is now referred to as the "Old City"—the area bounded by the walls built between 1538 and 1540 by the Ottoman ruler Suleiman. In 1860, due to overcrowding, Jews began founding settlements outside the walls such as Meah Shearim and Yemin Moshe, both of which eventually became part of greater Jerusalem. Some were even founded in other parts of the country—most famously Petach Tikvah.

As hard as it is to imagine, the founding of these settlements was life threatening. It meant leaving the safety of the city and moving out into the hardscrabble dirt wasteland where dangers like scorpions, disease and marauders lurked. Some people were so afraid that they returned to the city at night. Many died of disease as they literally built a settlement out of nothing in a wilderness.

As we have seen, the nineteenth century was a time of great turmoil in the Jewish world. Unheard of opportunities were suddenly available to Jews and many leapt into the gentile world headfirst and disappeared. But many did not and although they had been "liberated" from religious "superstitions" and "ignorance", they still strongly identified as and actually took pride in being Jews. Some became Reform Jews; others began to dream of a Jewish homeland.

This dream was the product of three factors. The first, simply, was that their ancestors and probably even their parents were still praying three times a day for the restoration of the Jewish people to the Land of Israel. The idea was not new. Second, Jews were still persecuted unfairly despite the so-called equality they received. What is official state policy and what is actually practiced can sometimes be quite different; also, the levels of emancipation varied by country or principality.

The third factor was that in the 1800s many peoples in Europe began to agitate for national independence, some successfully. This was still the time of empires, and Central and Eastern Europe were dominated by three of them: the Austro-Hungarian, the Russian and the Ottoman Turkish. Many of the nation states that we take for granted today, such as Greece, Poland, Hungary, Finland, Romania, Bulgaria and the Czech Republic, did not exist. They were provinces of these empires.

During this time, the various Italian states merged to become a united Italy and the idea of a united Germany, instead of 300 different kingdoms and principalities, began to gain hold in the minds of many Germans. The idea of the restoration of homelands was one of the major political views of the day. So, why not also the Jews?

Even in the United States, the idea of restoring the Jews to Palestine was a widely held belief among many prominent citizens. The idea of the Jews returning to their homeland actually had been developing in England and the United States for some time. In fact, some Protestant theologians in England had propounded the idea as far back as the early years after the Reformation. Protestants rejected the idea that a man—the Pope—was the ultimate spiritual authority and final arbiter of all things religious. Instead they turned to the Bible itself—"scriptures," as they called it—where line after line and book after book was filled with prophecies of the Jews' return to Zion. And, since the Protestants insisted on printing the Bible in the language of the people, not Latin, people began to understand what they read.

Many Puritans leaders held the same view and brought it to the United States, where they imagined themselves as the new Jews coming to the Promised Land. They gave their children biblical names and called their settlements after places in the Bible such as Bethlehem, New Canaan and Bethel. Increase Mather, a president of Harvard, wrote over 100 books in his lifetime. His first, and one that went through many revisions in his lifetime, was titled *The Mystery of Israel's Salvation*; in it he spoke of the idea of the Jews returning to their homeland. The Jews, he wrote, "...who have been trampled upon by all nations, shall shortly become the most glorious nation in the whole world and all other nations shall have them in great esteem and honour." This idea became known as "restorationism"; "restorationists" believed in and promoted the idea of restoring Palestine to the Jews. It was strongest in New England.

In 1818, John Adams wrote in a letter to Mordechai Noah, a playwright, a former consul to the Kingdom of Tunis and the most-prominent American Jew of his time, "I really wish the Jews in Judea an independent nation." Abraham Lincoln said in 1863, during a meeting with Henry Wentworth Monk, the most influential Canadian restorationist of his time, "Restoring the Jews to their homeland is a noble dream shared by many Americans."

In 1891, a Christian Restorationist, William Blackstone, organized a petition, now known as the Blackstone Memorial, asking President Benjamin Harrison and Secretary of State James Blaine to:

> ...use their good offices and influence with the Governments of
> their Imperial Majesties—
> Alexander III, Czar of Russia
> Victoria, Queen of Great Britain and Empress of India
> William II, Emperor of Germany
> Francis Joseph, Emperor of Austro-Hungary
> Abdul Hamid II, Sultan of Turkey
> His Royal Majesty, Humbert, King of Italy
> Her Royal Majesty Marie Christiana, Queen Regent of Spain
>
> and the Government of the Republic of France and with the
> Governments of Belgium, Holland, Denmark, Sweden, Portugal,
> Roumainia, Servia, Bulgaria and Greece.

> To secure the holding at an early date, of an international conference to consider the condition of the Israelites and their claims to Palestine as their ancient home, and to promote, in all other just and proper ways, the alleviation of their suffering condition.

It was signed by approximately 400 prominent Americans from Chicago, Boston, New York, Philadelphia, Baltimore and Washington, DC—mayors, newspaper editors, clergyman (mostly non-Jewish), leading businessmen and bankers. It also included members of Congress from Texas, Indiana, Ohio, Missouri, California, New York and Pennsylvania. The signers included the chief justice of the Supreme Court and the speaker of the House of Representatives as well such names as William McKinley, John D. Rockefeller, J. P. Morgan and Charles Scribner.

Their logic was simple:

> Why shall not the powers which under the treaty of Berlin, in 1878, gave Bulgaria to the Bulgarians and Servia to the Servians now give Palestine back to the Jews? These provinces, as well as Roumania, Montenegro and Greece, were wrested from the Turks and given to their natural owners. Does not Palestine as rightfully belong to the Jews?

While it had little effect politically, it received widespread coverage in the newspapers. In response, President Harrison stated, "It is impossible for one who has studied all the services of the Hebrew people to avoid the faith that they will one day be restored to their historic national home." Blackstone made a similar appeal to Woodrow Wilson during World War One. Wilson, a Presbyterian minister's son, was in agreement and later supported the Balfour Declaration.

In England in the 1800s, the restorationist belief was not as widespread but among believers it was fervent. The most-influential person in the British movement was a man named Anthony Cooper, later named Lord Shaftsbury. He literally spent his life writing, speaking and lobbying his friends in the government for the fulfillment of the idea. The Church of Scotland came onboard and in 1839 actually sent a delegation to Palestine to report on the condition of the Jews living there. One man who was born in Scotland and was a member of the Church of Scotland was Arthur Balfour. According to his sister who wrote his biography, he was a lifelong admirer of the Jewish people and often spoke sympathetically of the problems the Jews faced in this world.

Lord Balfour became famous among the Jewish people when, as foreign minister, he issued the Balfour Declaration on November 2, 1917. It stated, "His Majesty's Government view with favor the establishment in Palestine of a national home for the Jewish People, and will use their best endeavors to facilitate the achievement of this object..."

It had not been easy and had required a great deal of political maneuvering and persuasion to convince the war cabinet to issue the declaration. Balfour's lifelong friend, Prime Minister David Lloyd George, was no less enthusiastic about the idea and later remarked, "I was taught in school far more about the history of the Jews than about the history of my own land. I could tell you all the kings of Israel. But I doubt whether I could have named half a dozen of the kings of England and no more of the kings of Wales."

In the mid-to-late 1800s many Jews in Eastern Europe and even in England and the United States organized circles and cooperatives under the auspices of groups like Chibat Tzion (which later became Chovevei Tzion) and BILU (a Hebrew acronym) and founded the towns of Rishon LeTzion, Chadera and Rechovot. The Russian *pogroms* of 1881 to 1884 intensified their efforts and led to what is called the First Aliyah, which began in 1882.

Just so the chronology is crystal clear, all of this occurred long before Theodore Herzl arrived on the scene. The idea and the practice of Jews resettling the Land of Israel did not originate with Herzl or his creation, the World Zionist Congress. In fact, the new word "Zionism"—using one of the Bible's names for Israel (*Tziyon*, or Zion in English) to describe the Jewish nationalist movement—wasn't introduced until 1893.

Theodore Herzl, a Hungarian Jew who was raised in Vienna, had his brainstorm about a Jewish state when he covered the Dreyfus trial in Paris in 1894 as a reporter for an Austrian newspaper. In that case Alfred Dreyfus, a Jewish French military officer, was falsely convicted of treason on trumped-up charges. It was clearly a case of anti-Semitism and the unfairness of the trial and the anti-Semitic mobs roaming Paris shouting "kill the Jews" shocked the thoroughly assimilated Herzl. He concluded that only with a homeland and a "normal" national life would the Jews ever be considered equal amongst the nations. In 1896, he published a book entitled *The Jewish State*, which encapsulated the idea of a modern Jewish political state along the lines of other countries.

His idea of a Jewish homeland in Palestine was not novel or unique—by that time Jews had been settling in Israel for close to 200 years—but his book focused on the idea of statehood in a simple and convincing manner. People read the book and began to think that a resurgent Israel was not such a pipe dream after all. The fact that Herzl was an assimilated Western Jew, as opposed to a Russian or Polish Jew, helped his lobbying efforts in Western capitals. Using his organizational skills he founded the World Zionist Congress, which had its first meeting in Basel, Switzerland, in August 1897.

Herzl was completely unfamiliar with basic Judaism and even felt no connection to the Land of Israel. His goal was not to return the Jewish people to their land for the purpose of serving G-d, and Judaism played no part in his thinking. In fact his first suggestion to solve the Jewish question had actually been a mass conversion to Christianity. (Some of his children did, in fact, convert to Christianity and all of them intermarried.) He only wanted a separate Jewish country and was even willing to accept the Uganda Plan, in which the British government was willing to set aside 5,000 square miles in what is today Kenya for the purpose of Jewish settlement. (This was called the Uganda Plan because in 1903, Kenya was part of Britain's greater Uganda Territory.)

In the beginning the Zionists were a mixed bag. When the first Zionist Congress convened, it was fairly inclusive and had some Orthodox representation. But most Orthodox Jews opposed participating in a secular-run movement and absented themselves. They understood that the problems faced by the Jews in their exile were not a function of being stateless and weak. Therefore, the idea of a state formulated along the lines of other nations would solve nothing and, in fact, could create monumental problems.

Many German and Reform groups also boycotted the Congress out of philosophical opposition to the very idea—Jews were co-religionists but not a separate people. In fact the meeting was originally planned for Munich but intense pressure from German Jews had the meeting moved over the Swiss border.

Herzl died six years later, in 1904, at the age of forty-four and the movement was taken over by a socialist element with a specific agenda. Very soon the tenor changed and it became a kind of secular, anti-religious movement similar to the many socialist and Marxist movements that were spreading in the main cities of Europe. Many of the early leaders came from Russia and Poland (which was then part of the Russian Empire) and shared many of the anti-religious opinions that later became policy in the Soviet Union.

At that point the Orthodox response splintered into many different viewpoints ranging from accommodation to outright opposition to the secular Zionist movement. The range of opinion continues to this day with a wide spectrum of thought and many divergent opinions on how to view and interact with the modern State of Israel. Some lean towards accommodation; some are strongly opposed to any dealing whatsoever. The majority fall somewhere in between. But one thing that all parties agree on is that having secular leadership of the Jewish State is not optimum to say the least. Every Orthodox Jew believes that the State of Israel should run according to the laws of the Torah and all firmly believe that this will eventually happen.

The Zionist movement of David Ben-Gurion and Chaim Weizman, although professing to represent the age-old longing of the Jewish people for their homeland, actually had a specific agenda that can be summed up in three points. The first was to guarantee the security of the Jews worldwide. The Jews would have a protector, through strength of arms, in the form of the State of Israel. Second, the Jews would become "normalized." They would take their rightful place amongst the family of man, no longer outcasts or pariahs. And, lastly, they would create a new Jew—strong, proud, self-confident and self-sufficient—who wouldn't cower and grovel before the non-Jews.

G-d, the Torah and the *mitzvot* had no place in this agenda. In fact, religious Jews became the characterization of all that the Zionists wanted to purge in their efforts to create the "new Jew." "*Shtetl*" Jews were openly mocked and held up to derision. Young Israelis were taught to despise their own forefathers, who had endured trials and suffering that they could not imagine. Caricatures of bent-over old men, afraid of their own shadows, were used to drive this point home.

Non-Jews had never singled out the "ghetto Jew" or the "*shtetl* Jew"; it was the secular socialist Zionist movement that introduced this image. If you have ever heard any negative remarks or opinions about the old European Jews or the Jews of the old *shtetl*, you should know that you have been propagandized. All of this mockery is a creation of Jewish self-hate.

Had it not been for the uncompromising hostility of the Arabs, which forced the secular Zionists to tone down their rhetoric, temper their behavior and appeal to world Jewry for help and support, world Jewry would have soon come to see the virulent hatred that the early Zionists had for

Judaism and Jewish tradition. Unbelievably, G-d is not even mentioned in the Israeli Declaration of Independence; as a compromise the term "Rock of Israel" was used.

When I lived on the *kibbutz* (the *kibbutzim* were the ideological centers of secular Zionism) I was told straight out that all the customs and traditions that were practiced in the exile were now null and void. Their purpose had only been to maintain the Jews as a unique people and now that we were back in our land we could just drop it all. Even though at the time I was not religiously observant, the ludicrousness of the statement was very clear.

I also happened to be living on the *kibbutz* when Yom HaAtzmaut (Independence Day) fell out. The *kibbutz* celebrated with a barbeque where the only food offered was pork. It didn't take a genius to look around at the Jewish men, women and children sitting around on the grass, eating their pork chops, to know that something was very wrong with the picture. (I refused to eat the pork—I did not eat it at home and did not come to Israel to start eating it—and asked for something else, but, unfortunately, there was only one item on the menu.)

The core belief of political Zionism was that, if the Jewish people had their own homeland with their own government, army, police force, cities, financial markets, agriculture and so on, anti-Semitism would disappear. They truly believed this. But this was obviously not based on anything in the Torah, and Orthodox Jews scoffed at such an idea, knowing, as we saw in chapter ten, that anti-Semitism has nothing to do with that. Many leading Rabbis even considered the secular Zionists' forceful establishment of an independent political entity in the midst of millions of hostile Arabs a mortal threat to the Jewish people, correctly fearing that it would lead to great bloodshed.

Those Orthodox Jews who have chosen not to wave the flag have done so because they will not substitute a foreign, anti-religious philosophy for the *mitzvot* of the Torah. They know that Zionism, like every other "ism," will come and go but the Torah is eternal.

They also see secular Zionism as a historical hijacking. Think about it: If the Jews had prayed three times a day for 2,500 years for an ingathering of the exiles and a rebuilding of Jerusalem, what idea did Zionism offer that was new? If the Jews had been settling the Land of Israel since the late 1700s, what did Zionism contribute?

Those opposed to secular Zionism understand that the mission and destiny of the Jewish people is radically different from those of all other nations. Creating a gentile-style nation with all its attendant social problems will accomplish nothing beneficial in the long run and is bound to fail. The Jews are not meant to be "normalized"; they are meant to be a light unto the other nations.

We are familiar with the term "let my people go" but that is only half the sentence. When Moshe stood before Pharaoh, he told him in, G-d's name, to "let my people go so they should serve Me." That is the only reason we are to be free; that is the purpose of our existence. We were not freed from Egypt in order to conduct ourselves just like the Egyptians except in another country. And we were not brought into Canaan in order to act like the Canaanites. And we will not be gathered in from the four corners of the world in the future in order to act like the rest of the world.

Those who are uninformed have been led to believe that if a person is not a Zionist then he is against the Jewish people having a country of their own. But this is not the case at all. Orthodox Jews fervently believe that we should have political independence and hope and wait for the day when truly we will have it. However, they just don't believe it should be constituted along non-Jewish lines, governed by non-Jewish laws and led by non-believers who subscribe to non-Jewish ideas.

They also know that without leadership that is firmly anchored in a loyalty to the Torah and the Jews' special mission, bad things are eventually going to happen.

Meltdown

On one hand, Zionism is probably the most successful political movement of the last 100 years. Where there was once a dusty, disease-ridden, sparsely populated wasteland, there is now a modern, prosperous nation teeming with millions of people. And this was done despite the almost-total lack of natural resources (certainly no oil), the absorption of millions of refugees, four wars and a constant state of hostility with its neighbors.

However, in my opinion, this has nothing to do with Zionism or any other political philosophy. It has to do with the nature of the Jewish people. It is the same drive and tenacity that the Jews have had to employ throughout their thousands of years of exile.

In the years of European exile, say from 500 AD until the Second World War, there were over 100 recorded expulsions of Jews—an average of one every 14.4 years. Sometimes they were only expelled from cities or provinces but very often they were sent away from entire kingdoms, such as the expulsions from England in 1290, France in 1306, Hungary in 1349, Austria in 1421, Lithuania in 1445, Spain in 1492, Portugal in 1497, Prussia in 1510 and the Papal States in 1569, to name just a few.

Starting over has become an almost constant state of being for us. The same drive that Holocaust survivors used when they arrived in their new homes—whether in the United States, Canada, Argentina, Australia or wherever—and rebuilt their lives, provided for their families and, in more than a few cases, became very wealthy is the same drive that the Jews in Israel put to use to build their country. Jews can do this with or without Zionism.

On the other hand, Zionism has been an unbelievable failure.

Not only has the Zionist promise of the end to anti-Semitism not happened but the opposite has occurred: Anti-Semitism has evolved from a local issue to an international issue. Israel is constantly on the front page of every newspaper in the world and is the focus of most of the United Nations' proceedings and resolutions. Israel is (and therefore Jews are) portrayed negatively throughout the world press. Countries such as Botswana, Vietnam and Iceland, countries where nary a Jew ever walked, have opinions and votes on Israeli/Jewish issues.

In a cruel twist on the secular dream, it is becoming apparent that the very existence of the State of Israel is generating anti-Semitism. The fear of most Orthodox leaders—that secular Zionism would eventually backfire—has come to fruition. In fact, it could be argued that Israel is one of the most dangerous places in the world for a Jew to live.

And, in what must be a bitter irony to the older generations of Zionists, Israel has come to occupy the same position among the nations that Jews as individuals occupied in Europe before the State was established: it is an outcast.

Israel proclaims, "Look at us! We are just like any other nation." To which the nations of the world respond, "No, you're not." These other nations understand what most secular Zionists have always refused to acknowledge: that we are unique and unlike the other nations. This is why we are not accepted into the family of nations but are set apart.

In fact, Israel is such an outcast among the nations that it is the only country in the world that does not have internationally recognized borders and whose own declared capital is not recognized as such by the rest of the world. Imagine, Israel claims its borders and the world says "no." Israel designates its capital and the world says "no."

The early Zionists sincerely believed that the health of the Jewish people depended on the health of their state but history is proving the opposite—that the health of the state is dependent on the health of the Jewish people.

The very uncomfortable, boiled-down fact is that Zionism has failed to inspire the Jewish people. It has failed to do so because it is an inherently false philosophy, and false philosophies never succeed and never last. The evidence of Zionism's failure is readily apparent. Its creed was that worldwide Jewry should return to Zion—the Land of Israel—and build a national life there. The Zionist leaders thought that Jews worldwide would come streaming into their new workers' paradise but nothing of the sort happened. Over sixty years have passed since the founding of the State of Israel and not only do the overwhelming majority of Jews in the world not even consider the possibility of moving there, but most have never even visited the country and never will.

Today the Jews who move to Israel are either Orthodox and therefore inspired by the Torah and not a political philosophy or are the victims of oppression in their host countries. What these two groups have in common is the knowledge that they are strangers in the exile. Secular Jews who are not oppressed live under the illusion that they are "at home" wherever they happen to be living at this juncture on the timeline. However, this is an illusion that will eventually and inevitably be shattered, especially for the Jews in the Western democracies and the United States.

Even in Israel, most Israelis have given up. The old days of Zionist idealism are gone, replaced with a postmodern cynicism and self-indulgence that is more similar to Western European counties like Sweden or the Netherlands than the Israel of the previous generation. Classical Zionism is viewed as a tired, spent and discredited idea. The term used today is "post-Zionism," whatever that means. This is the bitter fruit of a sick tree.

The Israeli school system provides little or no Jewish education and as a result the average Israeli knows less about Judaism than many educated non-Jews. For years it taught that Jewish history basically ended with the destruction of the Second Temple by the Romans in 67 B.C. and only picked up again in the 1800s with the Zionist movement. Today it is run by the guilt-ridden liberal elite, which has changed the school curricula to include a great deal of Arab propaganda and historical revision.

The media run by the same liberal elite constantly mocks religious Jews and their customs. A militantly secular Supreme Court is intent on divorcing Israeli life from Judaism and Jewish practices by allowing civil marriages, malls to be open on Shabbat and the importation of pig products and other unkosher food. Since the Law of Return, which allows any Jew to become a citizen of Israel immediately, defines a Jew as anyone with even one Jewish grandparent (a violation of Torah Law, which defines a Jew as someone with a Jewish mother), Israel is now home to over 500,000 non-Jewish Russians, many of whom openly wear crosses around their necks. Swastikas are frequently seen on the walls of absorption centers and recently a violent neo-Nazi group was discovered operating in Israel.

The State of Israel has bequeathed to its Sabra generations a rootless secularism that has no ties to the past and is therefore full of lingering doubts as to the morality of a claim to what they have come to see as Arab land. The secular Zionists, in their quest to create the new Jew, tried to cut the Jews off from their own history, heritage and destiny. Any society without idealism will inevitably decline despite its wealth or power. But such a society surrounded by hostile, bloodthirsty enemies certainly does not have long to live. Israel is a country that is basically running on fumes.

And how could it be otherwise? Only the Jewish people can have a claim to the Land of Israel. There can be no such thing as an Israeli claim to the land. Only a people that traces itself uninterrupted back through 2,000 years of exile, through the Second Temple Period, through the Babylonian exile, through the First Temple Period and back to Mount Sinai, back through the Egyptian bondage, all the way back to our forefathers Avraham, Yitzchak and Yaakov, to whom the land was promised, can make a claim to the Land of Israel. A group that sought to remake the Jews in a gentile image has no legitimate claim.

This experiment has turned into a disaster that is very rapidly imploding before our very eyes. Since Israel's secular leadership does not possess any moral claim to the land they are in a process of meltdown. As we watch, the secular political establishment in Israel continues to back pedal over previously held principles in response to Arab, European and American pressure (no negotiating with terrorists, no Palestinian state, no negotiating while under fire, no negotiations on Jerusalem, no unilateral withdrawals). They fall over themselves to "restart" "peace negotiations" that never started and never provided peace, offering concession after concession and one "confidence-building measure" after another to the Palestinians, who have not once reciprocated. It is an expanding catastrophe that has not yet reached its climax. All of this is viewed by Orthodox Jews with the deepest anger at the perpetrators and the deepest pain for those who have suffered.

Contrast today's situation to the raid on Entebbe. In three decades Israel has gone from freeing hostages to freeing terrorists. Those who murder and maim Jewish children are no longer hunted down; instead they are called "negotiating partners" and "peace partners," offered parts of the Land of Israel and given money and arms. In fact had any terrorist been captured at Entebbe instead of killed, surely he would have been released by now.

A big part of this meltdown has been the overwrought, almost pathetic longing for peace. While this idea is a quite normal desire in life, it does not apply to the Jewish nation in exile. Until the Messianic era (see next chapter), we are still considered to be in exile despite the existence of the State of Israel. This is because the existence of the State of Israel does not really have political independence. Despite the bravado, an Israeli prime minister is not free to act, even in the defense of the country, without considering the effects on Israel's international standing and the response of the world and getting permission from the United States, upon which it is dependent for its very existence.

There will be no peace for Israel, just as there hasn't been peace for the Jews for the last 2,000 years, until our final chapter—even if we live in the Land of Israel. The nonstop pining for and singing about this elusive and impossible peace has created a no-win situation for the Israeli public who grow increasingly desperate. Picture a forlorn and dejected man yearning for an unrequited love while the object of his desire laughs at his weakness and you have a picture of the Middle East situation.

Again, this illusion only afflicts the secular population. The Orthodox population understands the deeper currents running through our history, and their heads aren't full of fantasies. That is why the secular population is emotionally deflated and continues to leave the country while the Orthodox continue to move to Israel.

In conclusion, the present State of Israel does not embody the Torah's ideals for a national Jewish existence, nor does it represent the redemption that has been the yearning of every Jewish heart for the last 2,500 years. Nevertheless, it exists, and G-d forbid that it should fall. We must do everything possible to strengthen and protect it and work to alleviate the suffering of our brothers and sisters who live there. Eventually, as the hearts and minds of the Jews of Israel and throughout the world return to the Torah, we will one day have a different sort of state—one that embodies our deepest hopes and dreams; a strong, prosperous and secure independence that will be, finally and forever, truly free.

The Five Rules of the Middle East "Conflict"

Because Orthodox Jews understand what is really going on, they react to the situation in the Middle East differently from non-Orthodox Jews. For example, the Orthodox provided the most vociferous opposition to the Oslo Accords and even when they blew up, literally, in the faces of the Israelis, the Orthodox never stopped visiting Israel, moving there or sending their children to study there. (Ironically, the Reform movement, which supported Oslo most loudly, was the first to announce the cessation of its visiting teen programs in Israel because of the violence.)

When one views the world through the lenses of the Torah many things become crystal clear that would otherwise be confounding. This includes what the world likes to call the "Middle East conflict".

I have distilled the underlying elements of the "conflict" into what I term the "The Five Rules of the Middle East Conflict." These points represent the fulcrum on which the Middle East turns. Without understanding them, nothing that happens over there will ever make sense. The Orthodox operate with these rules as assumptions. The secular Israeli leadership does not, and that is why they are losing. They are not even fighting the real battle because they are constantly being duped by the feints, diversions and prevarications of the Arabs and their allies.

The Five Rules of the Middle East Conflict are:

1. The conflict in the Middle East has nothing to do with the Palestinians and everything to do with the existence of Israel.
2. The Arabs do not want peace—they want victory.
3. Europe is anti-Semitic.
4. The media is not interested in the truth.
5. There is no secular solution to the Middle East "conflict."

1. The conflict in the Middle East has nothing to do with the Palestinians and everything to do with the existence of Israel.

The Arab propagandists have done a brilliant job of reframing the issue of the Arab-Israeli conflict. It is now known as the "Israeli-Palestinian conflict." Palestinian terrorism, we are told, stems from the "occupation," and peace will only come to the Middle East when Israel withdraws from the lands seized in 1967. At that point, Israel and the new state of Palestine will be able to live side by side in peace and mutual understanding.

This line of reasoning works wonders with people who are ignorant of history, want the problem to go away because it is uncomfortable and want to see things work out fairly (no one likes to see someone's homeland stolen). This description covers most non-Jewish Americans and, unfortunately, many younger American Jews. This is why the Palestinian "cause" is gaining legitimacy. If it is accepted that the Israelis are occupying someone else's land, they will never win an argument. That is why the Israelis are losing the PR war.

This reframing contains many sleights of hand. Many people now believe that Israel is the aggressor nation in the conflict, as if the one democracy in the Middle East has been guilty of harassing the twenty-two Arab dictatorships. The Arabs commonly use words like "stolen" and "returned," which alter the color of the issue. "Liberation" of an "occupied" homeland sounds so much more valiant and moral than declaring your intention to destroy a country and slaughter its inhabitants.

In 1947, the United Nations, in what could be argued has been the only real political accomplishment in its history, voted to divide what remained of the British Mandate of Palestine into two states—one Jewish and one Arab. I use the term "what remained" because originally the British Mandate included what is today the Kingdom of Jordan. This kingdom was created by the British in 1922, when Abdullah from the Hashemite clan of Arabia, an ally of Great Britain, lost the struggle to rule Arabia to Ibn Saud's clan (hence the name Saudi Arabia) and was forced to flee his ancestral domain. The British simply created a kingdom for him that was comprised of all of Mandatory Palestine east of the Jordan River.

There was no historic Arabic name for this land, so it was simply named after the river, which delineated its western border. If you look at the shape of the country you will notice that its borders are all straight lines except for the border formed by the river. That's because they were drawn on a map in London. It juts out to the east to protect the oil pipeline that ran from British Iraq to British Palestine.

The Jews immediately accepted the UN vote even though the borders of the proposed state were untenable. They were willing to make a go of it, but not the Arabs. On May 15, 1948, when the last Union Jack was lowered in the territory, five Arab armies—Egypt, Iraq, Jordan, Lebanon and Syria, with added manpower from Saudi Arabian and Yemeni contingents—invaded to destroy the Jewish state. Notice that there was no Palestinian army.

They did not succeed in destroying the infant state but did manage to seize some territory for themselves—Egypt took the Gaza and Jordan took what became known as the West Bank (so named by the Jordanians, since their country now straddled the Jordan River and had an east bank and a west bank). Notice that these areas were not incorporated as a country named Palestine for the supposed Palestinians.

These Arab conquests were not recognized diplomatically by any nation in the world except two: Great Britain and Pakistan. Even the other Arab counties didn't offer recognition. Jordan expelled all the Jewish residents of the seized territories including the half of Jerusalem it controlled and destroyed every synagogue and Jewish holy site in the city.

When the Arabs again instigated a war to destroy Israel in 1967, Egypt and Jordan lost these territories. In other words, the "occupied territories" were not "taken" from the Palestinians, they were taken from Egypt and Jordan, who had only controlled them for all of nineteen years.

At no time during the 1948-49 conflict did any of the governments of any of the Arab countries waging war against the small group of pitifully armed Jewish fighters ever declare their intentions to rid the land of the Jewish usurpers and restore the land to its rightful owners, the Palestinian people. In fact, from the years 1948 to 1967, when the lands that Israel seized in 1967 were still in Arab hands, the Arabs never spoke of it, nor did they offer the land to the Palestinians. The Palestinians never suggested it either. There is an obvious question here: If these lands are the key to peace, why wasn't a Palestinian state established by the Arabs when they had the land?

The answer is crystal clear. The issue is not the land "taken" in 1967. The issue is the land "taken" in 1948. Israel's existence is the issue. Or, more precisely, the issue is the return of the Jews to their homeland. That is why Jews were killed in pogroms in 1920, 1921, 1929 and 1936, in cities like Jerusalem, Chevron (Hebron), Yafo (Jaffa) and Tzfat (Safed). (Were the Arabs angry because they knew that in forty or fifty years Jews would settle the West Bank?) That is why Israel was attacked in 1948 and 1973 and forced into life-or-death situations in 1956 and 1967. That is why Arab terrorism has been a fact of life for Israelis since its inception—not since 1967. And that is why the Palestine Liberation Organization wasn't even founded until 1964, when it was created by the KGB as just another means to harass Israel. What was it founded to liberate anyway? Not the West Bank and Gaza, which at the time was in Arab hands.

This is also the reason why the Palestinians have rejected outright any type of state in the West Bank and Gaza whenever it has been offered.

There are other very pertinent facts that somehow no longer get mentioned. The Six Day war ended on June 10, 1967. On June 19, the Israeli cabinet met and decided to offer the Sinai back to Egypt and the Golan Heights back to Syria in exchange for peace accords. The Arab response came in September of that year, when the Arab League met in Khartoum, Sudan, and declared the "Three Nos": no peace with Israel, no negotiations with Israel and no recognition of Israel.

At that time there were almost no settlers in the West Bank and Gaza to act as "obstacles" to peace. In fact as late as 1972 there were only approximately 800 settlers in the territories and most of them were secular and living in *kibbutzim* that were established in the Jordan River Valley. Only after Israel was attacked in 1973 did the settler movement begin in earnest. It seems that the Israelis were willing to give up some of their homeland for peace but once they saw that peace was not going to be had, they figured they might as well settle the newly acquired parts of the Land of Israel. This inconvenient fact belies the oft-repeated assertion that the settlers are the obstacle to peace. There was no peace long before there were settlers and there would be no peace even if there were no settlers.

And despite the affectations of solidarity and brotherly love, there is, on the contrary, an enormous body of evidence to show that not only are the Arabs truly not interested in establishing a country called "Palestine" but they really don't give a flying falafel about their Palestinian brothers at all. Since 1948, the Arabs who left Israel at the behest of the Arab leaders or of their own volition have been classified as refugees. What do nations do when their "brothers" become refugees? They take them in, don't they?

Germany took in millions of German refugees after World War Two. In the years following World War One, Greece took in nearly three million Greek refugees who were expelled from the Ionian coast—the western coast of what is today Turkey. These Ionian Greeks had lived there for over 3,000 years. Tens of millions of refugees were created when the nations of India and Pakistan were carved out of the British Raj. Most of the Hindus headed to India and most of the Moslems to Pakistan.

But what did the Arabs do? They forced the refugees into camps and kept them there. The Palestinians are barred by law from ever becoming citizens in any Arab country with the exception of Jordan. When the Gaza Strip was under Egyptian administration, the Palestinians living there were denied Egyptian citizenship and remained stateless. Palestinians live and work throughout the Arab world yet neither they nor their children can acquire citizenship.

In the years immediately following World War Two, there were approximately 100 million refugees worldwide. The Palestinian Arab group is the only one in the world that has not been absorbed or integrated. During that same time, millions of Jewish refugees from around the world have been absorbed into the tiny nation of Israel. Most of these Jews left their homes with only what they could carry. There isn't one Jewish refugee in the world today even though the Jew is the definitive refugee.

Obviously, the Arabs do this for a reason: It keeps the wound open and the issue alive. If the Palestinian Arabs simply melted into their adopted countries, the Arab governments would lose the ability to maintain pressure on Israel. But what does it say about their brotherly love? The camps are filthy, disease ridden and run with open sewage. How can it be that today there are still millions of destitute "refugees" living in squalor in these camps?

In 1950, the United Nations Relief and Work Agency (UNRWA) defined a Palestinian Arab as one who had lived in Palestine a minimum of two years before 1948. That's it. This means that if you moved to Palestine in 1945 from, say, Morocco, and left in 1948, you were now a Palestinian refugee who had been deprived of his ancestral homeland. In addition, not only were the actual refugees defined as refugees but their children, their grandchildren and all their descendents forever more were also classified as refugees—the only group in the world with such an arrangement. The number of people UNRWA defines as refugees has gone from 600,000 in 1948 to nearly four million today. It is the only class of refugees in the world that has grown, not shrunk.

One and a half million of these so-called refugees still live in fifty-eight different camps in the Middle East—Lebanon (twelve), Syria, (nine), Jordan (ten), the West Bank (nineteen) and Gaza (eight). In Syria and Lebanon they cannot move out of the camps or leave to attain employment or education. The UNRWA budget is $340 million annually, of which Arab states contribute less than two percent. (The United States supplies one-third and the rest is funded by the EU and Canada.)

In fact, now that the Palestinians have autonomy over the vast majority of the territories, why haven't the Gulf states, with their billions of petrodollars, come in and built towns and cities for these people? Just imagine what their wealth could achieve.

Of course this all begs a much more significant question: How is it that there are refugee camps in the West Bank and Gaza? Isn't that part of "Palestine"? How can one be a refugee in his own country? Aren't they already living in their homeland?

2. The Arabs do not want peace—they want victory.

When the Arabs insist that they want peace, I always wonder when that became their desire. It certainly wasn't in 1948, 1956, 1967 or 1973. And if they want peace, why would they still maintain the Arab boycott of Israel? Why not just sit down and negotiate? Israel has already proven that it will do so and will cede territory as part of a peace deal.

I also don't recall seeing one peace rally or peace march in any Arab country. Not one in the last sixty years in not one of the twenty-two Arab countries. In fact, there is no Arab peace movement at all, nor is there even one organization dedicated to peace or mutual understanding with Israel.

If there were such a desire for peace, wouldn't the withdrawal of Israel from territories bring a reduction in hostilities, not an increase? As of this writing, Israel is under constant rocket attack or threat of attack from Gaza and Lebanon—the two places from which it recently withdrew its troops. And if the Palestinians wanted peace, why do their textbooks show maps without a state of Israel and with a state of Palestine in its place?

The call for peace began when the Arabs realized that they could not conquer Israel on the battlefield. An alternative method would have to be devised. Only after the Six Day War did the Arab countries start referring to the pre-1967 borders. They saw a rollback as the first step in weakening an Israel they could not defeat outright. In this way they based themselves on an episode in the Koran.

Mohammed, in his quest to conquer all of Arabia, ran into a tribe called the Koraish, which ruled Mecca and which he could not defeat. So, he sued for peace. The resultant agreement, the Treaty of Hudaibiyah, signed in 628 AD, allowed Moslems to pray in Mecca. It was supposed to be a ten-year treaty but Mohammed's intentions were never to respect his word. He bided his time until he sensed that the Moslems were strong enough to overpower the Koraish. After two years, he attacked them, overpowered them and slaughtered them to the last man.

While in the West this would seem sneaky and dishonorable, to the Arabs it is an example of cunning and smarts. Arafat himself would often speak of the Oslo Accords as modern-day examples of the Koraish treaty. The actions of the Palestinians since the signing in 1993 leave no doubt that they are following in Mohammed's footsteps.

There is another aspect to their behavior that demonstrates that what drives the Arabs is the sole desire to destroy Israel and nothing else. Since the implementation of the Oslo Accords, the Palestinian Authority has had autonomy over ninety-nine percent of the landmass of the West Bank and ninety-eight percent of the Palestinian population. What an opportunity! With the billions of dollars contributed by the world, primarily the Europeans, they could have built housing, founded technological colleges, established manufacturing centers, resettled the refugees living in Lebanon, Syria and Jordan, taken down the fetid camps and basically created a *fait accompli* for an eventual state.

(Look at what the refugees from Mao Tse-tung were able to accomplish in Hong Kong—a barren rock with no natural resources. Starting in the 1950's, the Chinese transformed a small British colony into a glittering, modern city and international financial center with a higher standard of living than Britain itself.)

But the Arabs did none of these because those are not their goals. Why did terrorism surge *after* Oslo? Why did the suicide bombings begin *after* Oslo? Simple; because they could. Once Israel withdrew they had the ability to carry out their true goals. They had the autonomy and the funding—a free hand and official sanction. (Similarly, Al-Qaeda was founded *after* the Soviet withdrawal from Afghanistan. The Arabs were convinced that they had defeated one superpower and now they would defeat the other.)

The underlying reason for these phenomena is that world conquest is a fundamental tenet of Islam. In its worldview, the world is divided into believers and nonbelievers and the believers are commanded to conquer the nonbelievers and Islamicize them. It is hard to imagine how this belief can coexist with any other. This is why any gain or concession only fuels the flames, not dampens them.

And, regardless of your political views, the following two sentences are not debatable: If the Arabs were to put down their weapons today, there would be no more violence. If Israel were to put down its weapons today, there would no more Israel.

Because of Islam's mandate for world conquest, in the eyes of believers any place that was ever conquered by Moslems is forever considered Moslem land. So, that means that the Middle East is a Moslem region. At the time of the first Crusade, the Land of Israel had only been under Moslem rule for a little over 400 years. Nevertheless, the infidels were coming to steal holy Moslem land. The Arabs see everything in this context. They still view Spain as a lost province that will one day be reclaimed.

Today Islam stretches across two-thirds of the planet, from Morocco to Indonesia. The Moslems almost conquered Europe but were twice turned back, once by the Franks in southern France in 732 and later by the Austrians and Poles at the Battle of Vienna in 1683. They conquered the

Byzantine Empire and the Persians. Cities such as Constantinople (Istanbul) in Turkey and Alexandria in Egypt, which were entirely Greek and Western in nature, were swallowed up and are now Moslem.

Since 1948, the Arabs have been comparing the state of Israel to the crusader kingdoms. To the Arabs, the Jews coming from Poland, Russia and the rest of Europe were foreign interlopers who had no roots and no place in the Middle East. (Think about it: Didn't ships arrive full of Europeans?) In their minds, it was just a matter of time until they were defeated outright or weakened and overrun.

Ironically, they are correct to a point. The secular state of Israel will not last in its present form. However, the Jewish people aren't going anywhere. They will stay and flourish and what emerges from the seedpod that is the present secular state will be a lot worse for the Arabs than anything they have experienced to date.

3. Europe is anti-Semitic.

I focus specifically on Europe because the Europeans are the enablers of all that goes on in the UN and in world diplomacy. They play the spoiler role in world affairs in order to assert themselves and much of the Third World, especially former European colonies, looks to them for leadership in world affairs. They are the role models for the leftists in the United States and on campuses throughout the world and they fund, to the tune of hundreds of millions of dollars, both the leftist NGOs (non-governmental organizations) in Israel that agitate on behalf of the Palestinians and the Palestinian Authority itself. All of the Palestinian media that poison young minds and the school textbooks with their distorted history and hate speech—ignoring the existence of the state of Israel and exhorting children to become martyrs—are paid for with euros. The checks to cover the costs of constant lawsuits, brought by Israeli NGOs trying to use legal means to hamstring Israel's ability to defend itself, are sent from London, Stockholm, Oslo, Copenhagen, Dublin, Amsterdam and Brussels, to name just a few.

The United States does not share the European love of the Arabs and is much less willing to threaten Israel. It must be remembered that every European country—with the ironic exception of Germany—maintains some type of arms embargo of Israel, which can only buy the arms to defend itself from the United States.

Of course a student of Jewish history knows how Yaakov is viewed by his twin brother, Eisav. The history of the 2,000 years of Jewish settlement in Europe reads like an account of a race of serial killers. As recently as sixty years ago, Europeans—not just Germans but also eager collaborators in every German-occupied country—actively hunted down and murdered every Jew they could find.

The bestiality of the Holocaust years caused the Europeans a considerable amount of shame and in the early years of the State of Israel they tried to buy back their souls. But it didn't last more than twenty years. After the Six Day War most of Western Europe tilted towards the Arabs.

Great Britain, which could claim it had nothing to do with the Holocaust, had been pro-Arab since the end of World War One, when T. E. Lawrence (Lawrence of Arabia) secured the Arabs as allies against the Ottoman Turkish Empire; an enemy of Great Britain which, at the time, ruled over Arabia and most of the Arab lands. The British had been overtly pro-Arab in their administration of Palestine under the League of Nations mandate. In fact, during that period the British referred to the Jewish population of Palestine as "Palestinians" including even those who served in the British Army in World War Two. To call them Jews would have implied too much. The Arabs, on the other hand, were called...Arabs. (Meaning that under the British, they were two types of inhabitants of Mandatory Palestine: Palestinians and Arabs.)

In 1939, in an attempt to appease the Arabs and forestall an Arab-German alliance, the British government issued the infamous White Paper, which prohibited all Jewish immigration into Palestine. At the same time, they permitted or ignored massive illegal immigration into Palestine from Jordan, Syria, Egypt and North Africa. On May 23, 1939, in a speech against the White Paper in the House of Commons, Winston Churchill noted that "so far from being persecuted, the Arabs have crowded into the country and multiplied..."

Why had there been such a massive influx of Arabs? Economic opportunity. The labors of the Jewish pioneers created better conditions and new economic opportunities, which in turn attracted poor Arab migrants from many parts of the Middle East.

This latent European anti-Semitism explains why, in their peace rallies, there are vastly more anti-Semitic statements than there are pro-Palestinian statements. (And Arab anti-Semitism would explain why, in official Arab media, there are vastly more anti-Semitic statements and caricatures than there are pro-Palestinian statements.)

This latent anti-Semitism also explains why, of all the nations on Earth, Israel is the only one that is routinely compared to the Nazis.

It also explains why, according to polls, Europeans view Israel as the greatest threat to world peace. Forget for a moment the insanity of such an opinion and let's say that they viewed Israel as the problem in the just the Middle East. Is it reasonable to think that all the problems in the Middle East are caused by a tiny country of five million people in a sea of 800 million? The margin of error in the Arab world's census is actually greater than Israel's population figure.

This latent anti-Semitism also creates a biased environment wherein Israel can do no right and the sins of the Arabs are overlooked or explained away. So, Palestinians are allowed to purposely target civilians in schools, in restaurants and on buses but if civilians are accidentally killed during Israeli retaliation it is a "crime against humanity." Or, it is "disproportional" or a "lack of restraint." The message that this sends is that if Israel fights back it risks condemnation and even sanctions. Calls by European trade unions for boycotts of Israeli products are commonly heard. They seem to be unaware of the massive human rights violation in most of the Arab world. Ever hear one of them call for a boycott of Russian goods because reporters there are constantly being murdered in broad daylight by shadowy figures who never seem to get caught? Or of Chinese goods in protest of the jailing of dissidents?

This message also tells the Arabs that there is no need for moderation. Meaning that despite Israeli concession after Israeli concession, the Europeans, instead of cutting Israel some slack and demanding that the Arabs reciprocate, only increase their demands and threats against Israel. According to the UN, when it comes to the State of Israel, no matter the circumstances, it is still at fault. How many nations are condemned by the United Nations for defending itself or for repelling an outside invasion force? Only the Jewish nation in 1973. What did we do wrong? We survived. All of this allows the Arabs to bide their time and run out the clock.

And even though there are numerous occupied peoples around the world seeking statehood or some sort of national autonomy, including the Tibetans, Kurds and Chechens, there seem to be no expressions of solidarity with Chechen separatists, calls for divestiture from China or rallies in European cities on behalf of the Moslems killed in Bosnia.

4. The media is not interested in the truth.

The worldwide media, by its very makeup, is not a truth-seeking device. It is a business and therefore a ratings-craved, sensationalist device. Breathless reporting of injustice accompanied by staged photos and sound bites trans-lates into excitement, which translates into viewership, which translates into ad sales, which translates into profits. So, they will report on the Israeli "occupation" of the territories as if it were the greatest crime in world history and ignore the simple and logical fact that land is seized when aggressive states attack their neighbors and lose.

This disingenuous quest for ratings (and reporters' quests for fame, glory and Pulitzer Prizes) is the reason why the media routinely prints mis-leading definitions and terminology, unbalanced or fabricated reporting and outright distortions. It will omit facts to make a story slant a certain way or sound more convincing, draw false conclusions and print specula-tive and unsubstantiated stories as fact. Israel's position and responses are given a lukewarm hearing at best.

Since there is no accountability for what the media writes or broadcasts, it will act with impunity and with no regard for personal reputations. This is because most reporters are out to "save the world" and are so convinced of their own moral rectitude that they feel justified in everything they say and do. Truth is not as important as its own agenda. And the left's agenda is not pro-Israel.

In fact, this slant is really the most sinister element in the media coverage of Israel: Most reporters identify with the left. I once saw a poll of American reporters that had ninety percent voting Democrat and ten percent voting Republican. (European reporters don't need to be polled; all you have to do is read their reporting.) And the left has abandoned its support of Israel and wholeheartedly embraced the cause of the oppressed, downtrodden Palestinians and, by extension, the anti-American, Arab view of the world.

This, in and of itself, is counterintuitive since, no matter what type of "rights" the left claims to support, the only place in the Middle East where they will find those rights is in Israel. But the type of person with sympa-thetic views of radicals, revolutionaries and Che Guevara-type martyrs will not be able to see both sides of the conflict.

Those who are anti-Israel and/or pro-Palestinian fall into one of three categories: weak of mind—they don't know the facts; weak of charac-ter—they don't have the fortitude to stand up for truth; or anti-Semitic. I suspect modern journalists of being all three. Then, there is the fear factor. Reporters who do their jobs—*really* do their jobs—in Arab countries and especially in the Palestinian territories get themselves killed. Therefore they will never pose the hard questions. Here are some that *should* be asked:

Why do Arabs spend such an inordinate amount of their daily lives hating a nation that takes up one percent of the Middle East?

Why is it that to date not a single suicide bomber has been an *imam* or a member of his family, or a family member of any Palestinian leader?

Why should we believe that an independent state of Palestine would be a secular, democratic state when there is not one secular, democratic state in the Arab world? How do you explain that Arabs have more rights, privileges and opportunities as Israeli citizens than as citizens of any Arab state in the Middle East? Or that Israeli Arabs enjoy the highest standard of living of any Arab in the Middle East? Or that the only free Arabic press is in Israel?

Are we really to believe that every society in the Arab world, a vast, oil-rich region stretching thousands of miles, is stunted and miserable because of how the Jews are "mistreating" the Palestinians? Is it reasonable to believe that the hostilities between Iraq and Iran, Iraq and Kuwait, Iraq and Syria, Turkey and Syria, Syria and Lebanon, Syria and Jordan, Egypt and Yemen and Egypt and Libya, just to name a few, are the result of Israel's "oppression" of the Palestinians?

If the Israelis treat the Arabs like Nazis, why is Arabic an official language of the State of Israel? How do you explain how, without oil, a large population, friendly relations with its neighbors or vast real estate, the Jews have built the most powerful economy, the mightiest military and the only industrial and democratic nation in the entire Middle East—and on a tiny piece of land that was an arid wilderness just sixty years ago?

Such questions usually earn the questioner a bullet to the head.

5. There is no secular solution to the Middle East "conflict."

Forgetting for a moment G-d's role in all of this and looking at the situation on a purely natural level, Israel is certainly doomed. Today in Israel there are close to five and a half million Jews—less than the number killed in the Holocaust. The Arabs total over 100 million. And roughly sixty percent of that population is under the age of twenty-five.

There is an information explosion in the Arab world consisting of satellite TV and the Internet. These sixty million Arabs are being brought up watching events unfold and vicariously experiencing the "humiliation" of the Palestinians and, by extension, the entire Arab nation at the hands of the Israelis. How will Israel survive this generation and all the coming generations who will grow up similarly?

Al-Jazeera openly distorts the news and, on days when there are no new Arab casualties, they rerun old footage. An entire generation is being raised in outrage and fury and is becoming radicalized. What will happen when the tottering old regimes in Egypt, Jordan and Syria are washed away by a rising tide of radicalism? Imagine the scenario of Israel bordered by these Islamic states, governed by people who embrace martyrdom.

Israel's very existence as an open, technologically advanced, growing, prosperous, participatory democracy smack dab in the middle of the most backward region on the planet is an unending source of humiliation to the much-wealthier Arabs—and that is not going to go away. Blessed with billions of dollars in annual revenue, Arab countries still rank at the bottom of the United Nations' surveys of literacy, health, life expectancy and economic and political freedom. Faced with these facts, the easiest position to assume is one of righteous rage focused against those who have succeeded. Hence the storyline that once Israel is gone, the rage will settle down and the Arab world will revert back to its natural state as a humane and enlightened civilization.

The truth is that if, G-d forbid, Israel were to fall, the Arabs would immediately revert back to what they have always been doing—warring amongst themselves.

Historically, wars are won when one side feels compelled to give up on its goals. If neither side gives up, the fighting either continues or temporarily dies down and can potentially resume at any time. Since 1948, both sides have retained their goals: The Arabs fight to eliminate Israel, and Israel fights to win the acceptance of its neighbors. But how long can a country fight for acceptance? And with the Arabs it is clearly not going to happen, even with all the peace treaties in the world, because they take the long view of history. They see it as a continuum, not as distinct periods of peace and war. And they don't honor treaties.

To the Arabs, the present conflict is just a continuation of what began in the seventh century, when Islam exploded out of the Arabian Peninsula and began its quest for world domination. In their minds, the present conflict has only one inevitable end—the destruction of Israel—even if it takes a few hundred years.

The Arabs are fighting an offensive battle, the Israelis a defensive one. Offensive battles, even if not successful, are purposeful and can be inspiring. But how long can people fight defensively before wearing out? The Arabs are patient, intense and determined and they use any means at their disposal—propaganda, economic warfare, open warfare, terrorism—to push forward. They have nothing to lose. They can be violent and barbaric because their society accepts such behavior and the Western world excuses it. It's almost like they can't fail. They just haven't succeeded yet.

The Israelis, on the other hand, withstand the blows in the hope that the Arabs will tire and come to accept their existence. There is no way they can win; they can only survive. And this desire is really so silly. What is so sacred about peace treaties and diplomatic recognition? Treaties can always be abrogated and recognition rescinded. Israel has had a treaty with Egypt since 1979, and what has it brought in the way of economic or cultural relations? Egypt leads the campaign to expose Israel's nuclear capabilities and has publicly announced that if other Arab countries were at war with Israel it could not be expected to refrain from aiding its Arab brothers. Its government-run press is the most vocal in the Arab world in anti-Jewish and anti-Israel propaganda.

So, how should Israel promote its agenda (i.e., acceptance)? It desires to do so through negotiations. But negotiations, by their very nature, imply compromise. And Israel will never be saved through compromise. Why? Because the enemies of Israel aim to completely obliterate it. Therefore, compromising only weakens our position but does not soften their position. There is no compromise between existing and not existing. And besides, how many countries would consider recognition of its right to exist as a concession or diplomatic victory? Shouldn't a nation's right to exist be axiomatic?

To our enemies, compromising is just the first step in the process. Every compromise we make brings their goals closer.

So, the Israelis try to manage the situation since they cannot resolve it. This lack of control of the situation has lead, after decades, to delusional behavior on the part of its leadership. Desperate for an end to the siege they were living under, the Israeli government literally created an illusory peace partner where none existed—the PLO. And they stuck to this illusion despite everything the Palestinians did, said, taught their children or broadcasted in Arabic. Instead, they clung to anything that the Palestinians said in English as "proof" of their true intentions while trying not to notice that the Palestinian Authority routinely named and continues to name schools, summer camps, sporting events, streets and public squares after blood-shedding terrorists. The whole process is pathetic and humiliating.

But what can be expected from a secular leadership that has no idea why there should even be a Jewish State in the first place? The most common refrain is that Israel serves as a sanctuary for Jews throughout the world. But for the most part, Jews live free, secure and comfortable lives around the Western world. Today a Jew might even feel safer in Toronto than in Tel Aviv. So, who needs Israel? What if all the Jews in Israel could be safely resettled in the West? What would be the rationale for enduring the extreme pain of the present situation? The Holocaust? An event that happened two generations ago?

Israel has become a middle-class, advanced society and, lacking an inspired belief in the purpose of its existence, will not be able to bear the psychological strain of a war of attrition. What can Israel hope for in the future? What are its goals in negotiations? Not to get blown up?

In the meantime, dedicated terrorists with a single, clear goal will continue to wear away at Israeli resolve. They have the benefit of ruthlessness, something almost impossible to sustain in a democracy. They will not debate the morality of using a certain type of weapon or how to treat prisoners. They will simply continue to draw blood until Israel is dead.

And as the pain becomes greater, the delusional qualities will increase. More and more Israelis will come to accept the Arabs' arguments and will begin to identify with them. (In psychology this is termed the "Stockholm Syndrome," although I think regarding Israel it should be called the "Oslo Syndrome.") Since Israel is an open society where all opinions can be heard, the Arabs will continue to take advantage of the secular Israelis' moral confusion to make their case loudly and more assertively at Israeli resolve.

And, outside of Israel, the situation is more dangerous than ever. Fanatical religious groups who are not afraid to die are now encamped on all of Israel's de facto borders—Gaza, the West Bank and Southern Lebanon. These are people who believe that they will be rewarded in the afterlife for killing Jews. How do you fight such people?

The north of Israel lives under a constant missile threat from Lebanon and the south of Israel lives under missile threats from the Gaza. Iran is developing long-range missiles capable of striking Israel while at the same time pursuing nuclear capability. Pakistan, a very unstable country, possesses nuclear technology and has already shown that it will share the technology with other Moslem nations.

Time is not on our side. Nor are the numbers. Nor are the odds.

Nothing any Israeli leader will do will change any of the facts. And so any Israeli leader will have to squarely face the fact that the Arabs want complete and total victory, that their grievance and resentments have nothing to do with 1967 and that the Europeans and the world media will not be fair or supportive of the truth. Israel will slowly sink into paralysis.

This is why there cannot be a secular solution. The type of strength needed to face the truth of this situation only comes from a rock-solid belief in the G-d of Israel, His Torah and His covenant with the Jewish people. A leader who believes in anything else will eventually break.

Israel's long-term existence is a certainty but its future will unfold in ways unfathomable to secular Zionists. The mission of the Jewish people going back to Avraham will be fulfilled and the world will change and Israel will be the place from where it all happens. Our entire past has been one long, miraculous process that has defied every known natural law.

Our future will be no different.

Chapter Thirteen
The Messiah and the End of History

Step One: The State of Israel

If the previous chapter left you a little depressed about the future—and I don't know how it couldn't—I hope that this chapter will lift your spirits.

Now that the Jewish nation is back in its land, we will not be leaving again. The story of its resettlement beginning in the 1700s and continuing through the original Orthodox settlers, the Zionist movement, the refugees from the Holocaust, the Russian immigration of the 1990s and the continuing Orthodox influx and population growth is paving the way for Israel's ultimate redemption.

And so, ironically, the irreligious and the anti-religious settlers who drained the swamps, plowed new farmland and built cities were really working on G-d's behest without ever knowing it. They laid the foundation for the return of the entire Jewish people to the Land of Israel. Now, when the Messiah finally does come, the Jews from around the world will have an airport to land in, cars and highways to use and homes and buildings in which to live. The Land of Israel has been transformed from a scrubby wasteland into a fertile homeland from where the Jews will ultimately fulfill their mission.

A question that has been asked since 1948 is: Why did G-d have it transpire that the State of Israel would be founded by irreligious Jews? Since the Torah should play the central role in the Jewish society that will be created in Israel, and since fulfilling the Torah is the point of our living in Israel at all, it doesn't make sense that the state would be founded by people who would work against that direction.

There is no clear answer to this question. But perhaps we could answer it this way:

The destruction of European Jewry had been foreseen by more than a few rabbis and thinkers in the years leading up to the Holocaust. During that time assimilation was epidemic and as a result many Jews developed a different image of themselves. Perhaps, after the Holocaust, a state comprised of Orthodox Jews would have been a foreign and unappealing idea to the secular survivors. They would not have been able to relate to it.

But by having Israel operate as a secular entity, G-d arranged the remedy before the illness. Israel provided these broken-hearted Jews both an option for settlement as well as an idea from which they could find inspiration for the future. The secular Holocaust survivors (the Orthodox would come anyway) could look at the Israeli Jews, looking and acting like their secular European counterparts, and feel there was hope for the future, that not everything had been lost. The sense of devastation in the Jewish world after the Holocaust and the depth of despondence on the part of the survivors were immense and it is certain that the establishment of the state prevented another million Jews from assimilating out of deep despair.

The Jewish Concept of History

Let's first begin with the Jewish idea of history and then we'll discuss specifically the Jewish idea of the redeemer of mankind, which will only make sense in that context.

The purpose of all of human history since the fateful decision of Adam and Chava has been to rectify their mistake and create a G-d-oriented, spiritually-run world. Mankind consistently shirked its mission and purpose, preferring to busy itself with G-d proxies, G-d imitations and make-believe gods until Avraham took responsibility. From that moment it was the role of his descendents—the Jewish people—to get humanity back to the Garden. And though it seems that the rest of the world wants to get back to the Garden just so they could take their clothes off, we want to get back to be able to live real lives.

All of history is merely the development of mankind towards this goal.

Atheists love to point out the moral advances of society as proof of the obsolescence of religion without understanding that it is religion, and specifically the Torah, that has driven mankind's progress away from pagan savagery.

Change does not occur without a catalyst, and the Jews have been the force behind mankind's progress. What the world calls "modern enlightenment" is only the process of Jewish ideals and values filtering into the greater non-Jewish society. As Jewish values penetrate society and seep into the recesses of people's consciousnesses, humanity progresses towards its ultimate goal.

Historians have often asked why, in the course of history, some cultures have advanced while others have remained primitive. Why is European culture, in Europe and the New World, performing *in utero* heart surgery on fetuses, coding data onto silicon chips, launching satellites into orbit and sending space probes beyond our solar system while, in much of the Third World, men in loin clothes and painted faces crouch around open fires and hunt with spears? While Africa might seem the poster child for this type of life, it is not limited to one race. This same description can be applied to Aborigines in Australia, Polynesian Islanders in the Pacific and most Indian tribes in Central and South America. Much of Central Asia is similarly primitive although dressed a bit differently due to the climate. Take European influence, know-how and technology out of the Third World and what will you have? Subsistence living. Interestingly, this same description could be applied to a great deal of Europe during the time of the Romans. What change occurred in Europe but not elsewhere?

Historians have given many reasons usually based on access to natural resources, physical conditions and climate. But I believe the answer lies in two words: the Bible. An overview of world civilizations shows specifically that the people who became Christian advanced and those who were ignorant of the Bible did not. In our day and age these Bible-ignorant societies are still living more or less the way their ancestors did millennia ago.

Today, if a nation wants to be considered advanced, it must become what is referred to as "Westernized." This means more than wearing Western-style clothes, using electrical appliances and going to nightclubs. To be "Western", a society must introduce a legal system and a political system that reflects the basic belief that human beings have inherent, G-d-given rights and wherein all are equal before the law. In such a society, human rights such as free speech and the right to assembly are respected, leaders rule only with the consent of the people and private property is protected.

These ideas did not materialize out of thin air, nor did either the Greeks or the Romans formulate them. Neither of these societies believed human beings had inherent, G-d-given rights. These ideas come from the Bible.

Greece was intellectually advanced and Rome a marvel of engineering but both had barbaric and cruel elements that modern man would find repulsive. The Greeks waxed philosophical about the search for truth and yet had no qualms about killing children who were less than perfect. The Romans invented indoor plumbing and laid thousands of miles of roads and aqueducts but saw nothing objectionable about enslaving captives and working them to death. The Greeks and the Romans might have been the progenitors of Western architecture, engineering, science and entertainment but they were not the progenitors of Western values.

Western values came from the Torah through a proxy—Christianity—that spread basic Jewish philosophies, using the Bible, throughout Europe. It is deficient and full of distortions, but it nevertheless had a profound effect.

With the exception of Christian Europe, none of the areas of the world conquered by either the Greek or Roman Empire developed into the leading civilizations of the world. Nor did either empire bequeath to the world a galaxy of enlightened societies. Both empires were brutal and greedy and when they collapsed they left nothing but ruins. But this shouldn't be surprising. A pagan society that is ruled by gods who murder, steal and rape other men's wives cannot leave anything but murder, theft and rape as their legacies.

It was only once Christianity, possessing Jewish ideas, spread throughout the Roman Empire that enlightened ideas began to germinate. The results were not immediate but within a few hundred years, Europe was so far ahead of any other society that it was able to control and colonize most of the world. Today a non-Christian country like Japan, China or India can become a world leader but only as a result of mimicking Christian Europe.

The Third World is a violent and cruel place to live because, until recently, there has been no Jewish influence, directly or indirectly. It does not possess the sense of individual self-restraint that is necessary for the functioning of a civilized society. Without a concept of deferred gratification, which is inherent in a law-based religion that believes in ultimate reward and punishment, members of a society cannot cooperate for the common good. Rather, they must fend for themselves and compete with one another.

Looking from the end of history backward, it is clear that the Jewish people have not been influenced by history but rather that history has been influenced by the Jewish people. Holding firm to our immutable Torah we have travelled through the world and through the ages, seeding mankind with the necessary ideas and ideals that will eventually lead to its ultimate purpose. The practical applications of the Torah laws will vary depending on time, place and situation (new technologies, for example) but the underlying principles never change. The thinking of a Torah Jew today is no different from that of a Torah Jew from 1,000, 2,000 or 3,000 years ago. Only the circumstances and challenges are different.

Because we are bound to such a crucial mission, our national existence will not operate under the natural laws that affect other nations. Unlike the histories of other nations, which wax and wane and eventually disappear or become reduced to footnotes, the journey of the Jewish people is directed always upward towards an ultimate goal. Whether our fortunes are up or down, we are still progressing towards a brilliant summit.

This idea is illustrated in a comparison between the Jewish and Western calendars. The Jewish calendar year begins in the fall, at the turning of the seasons. The summer is over and winter is ahead. The year begins at a downturn of sorts and progresses through the cold, dark winter until it emerges in the spring, a symbolic rebirth, and finishes in the summer when the world is most alive and fruitful. The Jewish day mirrors this path: It begins at sundown and immediately goes into the dark night until it emerges in the newborn day and finishes in the afternoon. Both the day and the year symbolize a journey that begins in one place but ends in an entirely different one. There is meaning to the journey.

The Western calendar year begins on January 1, in the middle of the cold, dark winter. It travels the cycle through the newborn spring and into the lively summer but then dies again in the fall and finishes exactly where it began—in the cold, dead winter. Similarly, the calendar day begins at 12:00 a.m., in the middle of the dark night. It proceeds through the morning and has a wonderful, bright afternoon but soon enough the sun sets and the day ends exactly where it began—in the deep, dark night. In both of these cases, the journey had no meaning, it was just an exciting ride.

The nations of the world similarly conclude where they began. They start simply, rise up, take center stage and enjoy a period of grandeur but inevitably wane and soon fade away. They have had their proverbial moment in the sun.

The Jewish nation, on the other hand, will end its history on its highest note. Our journey through history is identical to our marking of time. We started in daylight only to be plunged into a long, cold, dark exile but as sure as day follows night, we will arrive at our destination and end our journey in the bright sunlight that will bring real joy and real peace to a tired and spent world.

And because the Jews are eternal, we understand that we are always living in a fleeting moment. We understand that the here and now will very quickly become the then and there. So, while the nations of the world revel in their glory and their power, the Jews watch and know that it's only a matter of time until these nations join the ash heap of history along with every other power that once strut, chest out, across the stage.

Putting aside the ancient and obvious examples of Babylon, Greece and Rome, how many other modern nations were once great powers? The Serbs in the 1300s were the masters of the Balkans; Poland once ruled over Lithuania and the Ukraine. Sweden in the 1600s was so mighty that Russia greatly feared it and parts of England and France were controlled by the Danes. The mere mention of the Mongols in the Middle Ages gave men the shakes—they swept eastward out of Mongolia, swallowing all of Russia, the Ukraine and Hungary and conquering as far as Poland before unilaterally halting their advance and turning back due to internal issues. A few hundred years ago, Spain was a superpower and Portugal was one of the world's mightiest maritime and commercial powers. Until 1948, the sun never set on the British Empire.

The Turks, at their height, ruled an empire of over thirty million people. The modern nations of Romania, Albania, Serbia, Croatia, Slovenia, Bosnia, Hungary, Bulgaria, Greece, Cyprus, Syria, Iraq, Lebanon, Israel, Jordan, Saudi Arabia, Egypt, Sudan, Libya, Tunisia and Algeria are all successor states to the Ottoman Empire.

And these are the nations that are still around. What about great nations like the Parthians, the Chaldeans, the Bactrians and the Scythians? The list of once-powerful nations that no longer exist at all is also quite long.

Many non-Jews have noted the Jews' unique journey. King Louis XIV of France once asked the French philosopher Blaise Pascal to give him proof of the supernatural, to which Pascal is reputed to have answered, "The Jews, your Majesty, the Jews."

Leo Tolstoy considered this question in a book entitled *The Final Resolution*, published in 1908. In it he said this of the Jews:

> What is the Jew?... What kind of unique creature is this whom all the rulers of all the nations of the world have disgraced and crushed and expelled and destroyed; persecuted, burned and drowned, and who, despite their anger and their fury, continues to live and to flourish. What is this Jew whom they have never succeeded in enticing with all the enticements in the world, whose oppressors and persecutors only suggested that he deny (and disown) his religion and cast aside the faithfulness of his ancestors?!

The Jew—is the symbol of eternity... He is the one who for so long had guarded the prophetic message and transmitted it to all mankind. A people such as this can never disappear. The Jew is eternal. He is the embodiment of eternity.

A few years earlier, in March of 1898, Mark Twain published a long article, entitled *"Concerning the Jews,"* in *Harper's Magazine*. His concluding quote has become famous:

To conclude—if the statistics are right, the Jews constitute but one per cent of the human race. It suggests a nebulous dim puff of stardust lost in the blaze of the Milky Way. Properly the Jew ought hardly to be heard of; but he is heard of, has always been heard of. He is as prominent on the planet as any other people, and his commercial importance is extravagantly out of proportion to the smallness of his bulk. His contributions to the world's list of great names in literature, science, art, music, finance, medicine, and abstruse learning are also away out of proportion to the weakness of his numbers.

He has made a marvelous fight in this world, in all the ages; and has done it with his hands tied behind him. He could be vain of himself, and be excused for it. The Egyptian, the Babylonian, and the Persian rose, filled the planet with sound and splendor, then faded to dream-stuff and passed away; the Greek and the Roman followed, and made a vast noise, and they are gone; other peoples have sprung up and held their torch high for a time, but it burned out, and they sit in twilight now, or have vanished.

The Jew saw them all, beat them all, and is now what he always was, exhibiting no decadence, no infirmities of age, no weakening of his parts, no slowing of his energies, no dulling of his alert and aggressive mind. All things are mortal but the Jew; all other forces pass, but he remains. What is the secret of his immortality?

The answer to Mr. Twain's question is that we are immortal because we have a covenant with G-d; everyone and everything else will go the way of the world. Power based on the accumulation of wealth and the indulgence of sensual pleasures cannot endure. Only that which is built on truth, justice and righteousness is eternal.

Mashiach

The word "Messiah" comes from the Hebrew word *Mashiach,* which means anointed—as in oil poured on one's head. The reason why this future ruler of the Jewish people is called the *Mashiach* is because Jewish kings are coronated with the anointment of oil, hence he will be anointed. The English word "Messiah" has no meaning; it is just an anglicized version of the Hebrew word.

For our purposes we need to use the Hebrew word because the English word has been so tainted to the Jewish ear that it is hard to discuss the topic without seeing a bleeding man nailed to crossed beams. It also summons to mind very un-Jewish concepts of the Messiah that will only distort our understanding of the truth.

How does Judaism understand the *Mashiach?* First of all, and maybe most importantly, he will be a normal human being, born of a human mother *and human father* and he will eventually die. He will grow up like all other boys, play in the playground and scrape his knees when he falls. But as he matures into adulthood, he will direct himself, using his free will, to great spiritual heights. Just as all great Jews in our history, such as Avraham, Moshe and King David, he will be self-made in the sense that his decisions and his conduct will create his greatness.

The *Mashiach* will also be a direct descendent of King David and will re-establish the House of David. He will inspire the Jews to return to Israel—the ingathering of the exile—and there will no longer be any Jews living beyond the borders of Israel. He will lead the Jewish people with kindness, strength, humility and great wisdom and understanding. He will teach us and the world, through word and deed, the real truths of life, peeling away layer upon layer of the rancid scar tissue that has accumulated on mankind's collective mind over nearly 6,000 years of falsehoods and distortions. There will be no more wars. He will eventually attain prophecy when prophecy returns to the Jewish people during his rule. The Jewish people will return from the four corners of the world and establish a nation based on the Torah. The Temple will be rebuilt on the Temple Mount. (All those travel posters will have to be reprinted.)

We await his "coming" eagerly but for no other reason than so we can learn Torah unimpeded and live the full Jewish lives for which we were intended. Yes, there will be physical benefits, such as honor and wealth, that the Jewish nation will inevitably receive as a result of the changes in the world, but they will pale in comparison to the sheer joy of living that will define life at that time.

The two main differences between now and then will be:

    a. The world will know and accept the truth.
    b. The Jews will no longer be persecuted.

Otherwise, everything in the physical world will be the same. You will need to go to work to earn a living; if you get sick you will need a doctor. If you bang your head on a kitchen cabinet that someone left open, you will get a bump.

In the Jewish system of belief, the *Mashiach* and the Messianic Era are not concepts of physical improvement; they are concepts of spiritual improvement and perfection. All the resources of society will be directed towards that goal. Culture—art, poetry, music, literature, even movies and television—will no longer glorify nihilism and perversion. It will ennoble society and reinforce the positive instead of being a means to denigrate and debauch it. Nor will culture dwell on the modern concept of existential loneliness which, since it is caused by distance from G-d and a lack of meaning in life, will no longer be a concern. Modern art, which is anxious and restless, and represents the world and especially human beings in disjointed and distorted images, will instead express man's inner joy and his inherent goodness.

In the Modern Era, with its focus on the physical world and neglect of the spiritual world, messianic movements have always been manifested in physical ways or built around "saviors". Science became the vehicle for the modern false messianic movements that went out to "Save the World!"

In the 1960s bestsellers were proclaiming that the "population bomb" (that was the title of the leading book on the subject and it became a popular term) would destroy life on this planet. We would run out of food, water, forests and energy; even the soil would be drained of its minerals by the overpopulation of the world. This was serious science and it became a *cause celebre*. Of course it wasn't even close to being true. Today's population is a billion people larger, and life has actually improved. Free markets and human ingenuity will always produce solutions.

The latest Chicken Little fad of predicting the end of civilization unless we do something about global warming is no different. All the hysteria ensures is that laws will be enacted that will damage people economically, actions will be taken that are counterproductive and even harmful and a great deal of money will be wasted. But once people have invested themselves into an idea and it becomes a messianic, save-the-world crusade, it is very hard for them to let go. Even another ice age wouldn't convince them.

Today, computer technology assumes that role of messiah; technology (and the Internet), we are told, will change everything for the better and presage a new era for humanity. We are always looking for the Messiah, but in all the wrong places.

Christianity and Islam absorbed the concepts of a messiah and of the ultimate redemption of mankind and have spread them literally to half of the world. The Christians await the second coming (an idea that was needed due to the obvious lack of success during the first coming) and the Moslems, although the Sunnis and the Shiites disagree on the details, await the *mahdi* or twelfth *imam,* who they believe will conquer the world and convert it to Islam. So, half of the world is now waiting for someone.

The Messianic Era will begin a while before the *Mashiach* is actually known; it will not begin with him. It is generally accepted among Orthodox Jews that we are living in that period right now. But how it will progress or when or how it will end, we do not know—nor are we supposed to.

For centuries a series of milestone events have been leading up to the point where the world will live as one under one G-d:

- The Age of Exploration, which brought all of the world's peoples into contact with each other.
- The acceleration of technological know-how over the last two centuries which exploded after World War Two, especially in communication and travel.
- The huge disruptions, movement and suffering of the Jewish people in the twentieth century.
- The beginning of the ingathering of the worldwide dispersion of the Jewish people.

In the Talmud, the final years are referred to as "the birth pangs of the *Mashiach*." Just as a woman's discomfort becomes greater and greater as the actual birth nears, so does the discomfort of the Jewish people and the world at large. The closer we come to the end, the more our "contractions" will increase in number and intensity until the future is finally born.

The End of the Exile

Our long exile is nearly at an end, and the long, convoluted journey has contained lessons both for us and for the rest of the world.

The lessons for the rest of world have been spelled out in some detail in the preceding chapters. But what are the lessons for the Jewish people?

We were sent into the exile to learn with crystal clarity that there is nothing for us outside of G-d and His Torah. Everything else is fleeting, meaningless and illusory.

We have seen the great and mighty wither and collapse before our eyes. The most powerful nations with all their financial, military and technological might have been, in the end, either destroyed or reduced to mediocrity and indigence.

We have been exposed to every conceivable idea and philosophy and despite their popularity or assertions of truth, we have seen them all totter and fall leaving nothing but emptiness in their wake.

We have learned that unless we are unified with love and respect for one another, the outside world will take actions that will generate unity or demonstrate our oneness. The Nazis stuffed religious and nonreligious Jews into the same gas chambers. They saw us as all the same. Do we?

We have seen that unless we cling to the Torah and its G-dly way of life, we will not survive for long as Jews. We have also learned that we do not become more popular or more respected by the non-Jewish world when we abandon our mission.

We have seen that every time we embrace a false ideology (read "idol"), it turns on us and persecutes us. When some Jews converted to Christianity in Spain to avoid persecution, the Spanish instituted the Inquisition to persecute converts. In modern times, we embraced nationalism and the nationalists came after us. We embraced socialism and the socialists came after us.

When we embraced atheism and secularism the Soviet Union, the paragon of godlessness, became our greatest tormentor. Domestically it outlawed Judaism and sent any loyal adherents to suffer in the *gulag*. In foreign affairs, it supported the Arab war machine and funded and trained terrorists. In the United States, we became enamored of secular higher education and elevated it to the loftiest of human endeavors; today, the academics and professors lead the fight against Israel, and college campuses have become some of the most philosophically and even physically dangerous places for Jews.

Since Franklin Roosevelt, the Jews have lined up obediently behind any candidate with a "D" after his name but those with their eyes open are starting to see that the Democratic Party has become the think tank for anti-Israel policies and the home of most of the anti-Israel politicians in Congress. A student of Jewish history knows that it will be the Democratic Party that will eventually turn the United States against Israel.

We marched for civil rights only to find that the black leaders and their rank and file were deeply and openly anti-Semitic, and they have not shown an ounce of gratitude by offering support for any Jewish causes or Israel. Ditto the Women's Rights Movement and all the other liberal causes that have embraced a soft (so far) anti-Semitism as part of leftist ideology. Every time we pin our hopes on something other than G-d, we suffer bitter disappointment.

We have seen that, as long as man considers himself the final arbiter of right and wrong, there is no limit to the depth of his dark side, and that it will always come to rule him.

And, although on the surface this might sound inverted, we have seen the extent to which G-d loves the Jewish people. He simply will not let us go. We are special to Him and He loves us more than the other nations.

Imagine this scene: As you watch, a ball flies out into the street and right behind it runs a child who, without looking, runs into the street after it. A car is driving down the street and must screech to a halt to avoid running over the child. Enraged, the driver bolts from the car and chases the child across a few lawns until he finally grabs the kid by the arm. You see him shaking the boy while yelling angrily.

Who is that man?

It is his father.

A stranger or even an acquaintance would have just given the boy a mean look and driven off muttering to himself. A friend might have sternly rebuked the boy through the open car window. But only the father would care enough to get that upset and actually do something.

Similarly, our national existence is so vital to the world's destiny and G-d's love for us so deep, that He will go to extreme measures to ensure that we continue to exist as a people. The farther we diverge from where we are supposed to be, the more extreme the measures that will be needed in order to bring us back.

These are lessons that we have come to understand through experience as opposed to an intellectual understanding. In a sense, we have learned the hard way. Our exile is painful. We have not been able to live normal lives and have spent 2,000 years waiting for the next shoe to drop. In a sense, we are better for our experiences even though it would have been better to avoid them in the first place. But we have been able to endure the vicissitudes of the last 2,000 years because we know that G-d loves us and there is meaning and an ultimate purpose to everything we have gone through.

The nations have also contributed a great deal to human development but only in a physical sense. Their building, discovering, creating, inventing, conquering and settling would have been utterly meaningless without our contribution. The difference is not one of degree but of essence; our teachings gave their activities meaning. Without the Jewish ideal for humanity, all of their activities and accomplishments would have been no different from digging holes and filling them in and then digging them again to fill them in again, over and over.

Pagan or Not, Here We Come

What will the world be thinking during the time of the *Mashiach?*

Firstly, they will not be Jewish. We do not believe that non-Jews must convert to Judaism, nor have we ever promoted Judaism to non-Jews. There is absolutely no concept that a person must be Jewish to do G-d's will or to go to heaven. We have never had missionaries. This is obviously a dramatic difference from Christian or Moslem doctrine. To a Christian or a Moslem, a non-believer cannot enter heaven and is, in fact, damned to hell for eternity. According to the Torah, a non-Jew's only obligation is to recognize the true G-d and live a moral life.

Our universalism is evidenced, again, by our calendar. Throughout history, nations and religions have marked the years in an ethnocentric manner. Romans dated their years from *"ab urbe condita,"* the founding of the city. Christians count the years from the supposed birth of Jesus, and the Moslems count the years from Mohammed's journey from Mecca to Medina. But the Jewish people do not count the years using anything that is specific to our religion.

If we were like everyone else, you would expect us to count the years from the exodus from Egypt or the day we stood at Mount Sinai or the original conquest of the land under Yehoshua (Joshua). But we don't; we count the years in a more humble and truthful way. We simply count time from when humanity began. This book is being published in what the Jews refer to as the year 5770 from the creation of Adam.

Since Avraham stepped into the breach, we have been waging a battle for the hearts and minds of mankind - to change people's thinking from a pagan philosophy to one of a recognition of the existence of the true G-d and His role as creator, sustainer and supervisor of the world.

There are, after all is said and done, only two schools of thought. One is that G-d is all-powerful, all-knowing, and beneficent. The other is that He is not. (It doesn't matter whether G-d is defined as limited and flawed or if His existence is denied entirely; the resulting philosophies will be, for all intents and purposes, the same. He cannot be looked to for help and man must fight and struggle to survive.)

These two philosophies are diametrically opposed. The first imbues our lives with joy and purpose; the second robs it of all meaning. The first is warm, loving and reassuring; the second, dark and menacing.

Modern secularism is paganism in a different package. It shares the same underlying philosophy because a nonexistent god is the same as a limited one. Both leave mankind at the mercy of the forces of nature and bound by its limitations; and both leave man as the arbiter of right and wrong and the final word on all matters moral.

The Torah, and only the Torah, offers the alternative to the pagan view of life. The world has been pagan since almost the beginning. When history concludes, none of it will be. The world will have the same understanding of G-d that the Jewish people have had for the last 3,800 years, since the time of Avraham.

The Seven Noahide Laws

If a non-Jew's only obligation is to recognize the true G-d and live a moral life, what are the practical rules for doing this? In other words, how will the world operate during the time of the *Mashiach?*

The requirements for non-Jews are referred to as the "Seven Noahide Laws" because they were given to Noach (Noah) when he and his family, from whom all human beings are descended, emerged from the ark after the flood. They are:

1. Do not blaspheme
2. Do not engage in idol worship
3. Do not engage in sexual immorality

4. Do not murder
5. Do not steal
6. Do not eat the limb or flesh taken from an animal before it died
7. Establish courts of law to enforce these prohibitions

This is the template for universal morality and any person from any nation in the world who lives according to the Seven Laws of Noah is fulfilling G-d's requirements of him. Through these seven laws non-Jews create themselves and develop their relationship with the true G-d.

(Actually, six of these *mitzvot* were originally given to Adam. Because mankind was not permitted to eat meat before the flood, the prohibition regarding animal flesh was unnecessary. After the flood, once it was permitted, the prohibition was added.)

These are not just nice sayings, axioms or pithy words of wisdom. Each one is actually more of a category heading containing many detailed regulations. For example, the prohibition of stealing includes many of the same rules that Jews must live by, such as the requirement to have accurate weights and measures and the prohibitions of price gouging and moving boundary markers in order to steal property.

When the *Mashiach* finally comes, the non-Jews will view G-d's commandments the same way the Jews always have—as opportunities to come close to G-d and perfect themselves. They will no longer view them as unfair restrictions that are just impediments to having a good time.

When the *Mashiach* reigns in Jerusalem, the world governments will send delegations to Israel to learn the intricacies of the laws and the philosophies and lessons behind G-d's requirements. The United Nations, no longer spending its time and resources to condemn Israel and aid it enemies, will instead act as a world body pursuing truth and justice at the highest level. The world will look to Jerusalem for truth and inspiration and for lessons in goodness and righteousness.

A Light Unto the Nations

I want to finish this book on an audacious note. It is, no doubt, stirring to look to this vision of the future when the Jewish people will be on the top rather than the bottom, and will openly play the central, vital role in the elevation and perfection of mankind. But simply to say that we will be great people only in the future is untrue. We have always been a great people—despite our human shortcomings - and this is still true today. My last words here will be to drive that home.

We have been maligned and slandered for thousands of years and many of us have come to believe it on some level. But there is no reason to swallow this bitter pill. Spit it out.

I am sure you have heard the question asked: Are Jews morally superior to other nations? The answer is yes, absolutely.

In our post-1960s, everyone-is-beautiful, politically correct world, that kind of statement is strictly forbidden. Well, it might upset some people, not least of all some Jews, but it is irrefutable.

When you think of all that we have given to mankind for its spiritual and even physical benefit and how molested we have been in return, wouldn't you expect the Jewish people to be a bitter, resentful, vengeful people? Why are we not full of hatred?

Yet here we are, 2,000 years after being expelled from our homeland and forced to live among people who don't like us and have mistreated us, and yet we only want the best for them. Do we not sincerely want the world to live in peace and brotherhood? Do we not want to eradicate illness, poverty and oppression? Do we not feel for the suffering of even our enemies?

Where are the Jewish assassins and suicide bombers, wreaking havoc in German pizza parlors, malls, night clubs and restaurants, or in Arab ones? Or on their buses and public transportation? Do any of our enemies live in fear that a Jewish person standing next to them might pull out a knife and attack? Did we target Russians with car bombs and kidnappings when they held three million Jews prisoner in the Soviet Union? Did the Russians even consider these as possibilities?

Has there ever been a period in our history in which we have been the marauders or oppressors? Even the Arabs in Israel walk the streets in safety. Do we vandalize the cemeteries of those who have tortured us? Do we concoct stories to discredit them? Do we attack their churches or mosques? Where is the anger, the resentment, the rage?

If you are reading this and saying to yourself, "Of course not, don't be ridiculous," it is because our moral stature is so apparent and so taken for granted that the very ideas are ludicrous. All of these scenarios can apply to any other nation at any time in history, but not to us.

Is there another people like this today in all the world?

No.

Has there ever been a people like this in all of history?

No.

We are existentially different and, because of that, we function as a guide to the rest of the world.

For hundreds of years, the Jews were effectively kept out of society. The guilds that controlled the industries excluded us. We could not attend universities. In many countries, we could not even own land. We lived without any rights and at the whim of the ruler. And yet, within two generations of emancipation, the Jews were leaders in every single field they entered whether it was business, medicine, the arts, science, law or politics.

As early as 1905, two years after the establishment of the Nobel Prize, two Jews were recipients. In fact, as of this writing, Jews, who comprise 0.3% of the world's population, have won 21% of the Nobel Prizes that have awarded (164 of 779). Broken down, we have won 13% of the literature prizes, 19% of the chemistry prizes, 26% of the physics prizes, 41% of the economics prizes, 28% of the medicine prizes and even 9% of the peace prizes (which is surprising considering we are blamed for all of the world's problems.)

Is it any wonder that a non-Jew would look at all of this and conclude that something is amiss? How is this possible? How can one explain the unnatural success of the Jews? How can it be explained that we are always disproportionably on top and in the forefront?

Many great thinkers have pondered the question and concluded that it is simply G-d's blessings at work. But others, almost understandably, look at all of this objectively and see a worldwide Jewish conspiracy.

The state of Israel has been in existence for sixty years, which means that for sixty years Jews in Israel could live their lives without needing to be concerned with non-Jewish overlords. It is the one-hundredth-smallest country in the world and has one-one-thousandth of the world's population. Yet in a little over half a century it has blown past most of the world in many crucial areas.

On a *per capita* basis Israel has the highest amount of university degrees, the most published scientific papers, the most medical device patents, the most museums, the most personal computers and the most startup companies in the world. *Per capita* it has the second-highest number of books (though I think that might be on the low side; I doubt that this figure includes the volumes of Torah scholarship that line the walls of the homes of nearly twenty percent of Israel's population).

On an absolute basis, Israel has the largest concentration of high-tech companies outside of Silicon Valley. Its military is world renowned and it has the highest standard of living in the Middle East. Almost monthly, new medical discoveries and breakthroughs are announced. It is considered a developed country, *not* a developing country. You do not need to be vaccinated to visit (as you do to visit every single one of the surrounding countries).

This was all accomplished within two generations in a land without natural resources, while in a perpetual state of war, while absorbing, percentage-wise, the largest amount of immigrants in the world, and in spite of a corrupt, socialist government.

In short, we are unstoppable.

And while it is true that the Jewish people have made vast contributions, way out of proportion to our numbers, to the world in the spheres of art, music, literature, finance, medicine and science and have led almost every intellectual, social and political movement of the last two centuries, it is *not* the reason we are a light unto the nations. It's a byproduct of our fundamental mission and drive.

The true accomplishment of the Jewish people has been our moral and intellectual impact. In fact, we have changed the world so significantly and affected the ideas and practices of enlightened civilization so profoundly that we can no longer see it.

Sure, we taught the world that there aren't a slew of gods; nor is G-d the mountain, in the mountain or on the mountain or a piece of carved wood. But our influence has been much more consequential and far-reaching than many realize: human rights, civil rights, universal education, justice and equality before the law (and that all men, even rulers, are subject to the law), world peace, the sanctity of human life, social responsibility, charity, compassion for the less fortunate, the commitment to the continuing development and perfection of society, the concept of a meaning to life and an optimistic hope for the future are all Jewish ideas that were once considered radical and are now taken for granted.

Not one of these ideas existed in any society until the Jewish people received the Torah and began to live a national life based on a radically different set of values than those that were extant in the world at that time.

When we first appeared on the world scene, knowledge of the true G-d had been all but eliminated from the world. Everything was a god—the sun, the moon, stars, animals, even people—and there was a god for everything—love, war, fertility and so on. The world was a place where human beings were bought and sold like chattel, where infants deemed unhealthy or undesirable were killed or left to die, where women were encouraged to become prostitutes for the temples of the gods, where young boys were partnered with older men for sodomistic relationships, where daughters were considered burdens and very often killed, sold or loaned out for their fathers' benefits, where kings had eunuchs to guard their harems, where human beings were sacrificed to deities, where people were killed or made to fight to the death for public spectacle and where the gods were considered to have human weaknesses like lust, anger and pettiness and needed to be patronized or appeased.

These practices were not restricted to certain times or places. They were spread throughout the world and were practiced by both the highest and lowest societies until they came into contact with the Jews or with Jewish ideals. Today the everyday, accepted practices of the ancient world are considered barbaric. It has been a long slog and one that is not yet finished - some of these practices are still found in areas of the world where Jewish influence has, until recently, been negligible.

By reminding the societies in which we lived of the true G-d through living according to His instructions, we were able to eliminate much of the sickness from the human mind. And by surviving against the natural odds and thriving despite everything thrown at us, G-d's existence was revealed to all. Our existence proves that human success and wealth are not dependent on human might and power. Our national existence in the Land of Israel today continues to demonstrate this lesson for even those nations that had never previously heard of a Jew.

Throughout history, the Jewish people have had a transmutative influence on every gentile nation in which we have lived. Our existence challenged their false beliefs and their immoral and brutal societies. Their leaders, both religious and secular, very correctly saw us as a mortal enemy.

In fact, every nation that has ever conquered the Jews or amongst whom the Jews have lived in significant numbers is now monotheistic. Without resorting to missionizing or rhetoric, we have been able to change and improve societies by just living according to the laws of the Torah. Exposure to us inevitably brings about change.

Both European and Arab pagans saw the vast difference between the holy Jewish life and the type of lives they were leading and gradually, they aspired to a higher level. And we have accomplished this while being a statistically negligible presence. (Even in the United States, where we have had enormous influence, we have never comprised more than three percent of the population.)

One of the most transforming ideas that we have introduced into mankind is that of progress. The belief that the future will be better and that mankind is striving towards a higher place is strictly Jewish. Where there is no Jewish influence, there is no concept of progress and people do not look to the future with hope for change and improvement. These societies are not working towards anything but their next meal. Even in much of industrialized Asia, the concept is a recent import. The idea of hope belongs to the Jews.

From the Torah, the world also has learned the concept of good triumphing over evil. Since we know that our message will eventually get through and that humanity will reach its intended goal, we intuitively understand that good will eventually win out over evil. By the way, even secular Jews intuitively know this. The "Golden Age of Hollywood" with its archetypal good triumphing over evil was a Jewish creation. Jews also created the comic book superhero who vanquishes evil. (Superman and Batman were created by Jews and Marvel Comics founded by Jews.)

The Jewish influence has enlightened mankind to the fact that this world will have a happy ending. This philosophy is a far cry from a pagan/ secular view which lacks any concept of good and evil. In the original versions of the old pagan European fairy tales, the outcomes are usually brutal and cruel. For instance, Hansel and Gretel get killed and Little Red Riding Hood gets eaten by the wolf.

For 3,000 years we have lived a different life than the other nations of the world and as a result we have given them a destiny that they could not have otherwise achieved. Their dreams of a better life and a better world are our dreams. We taught them about freedom, progress, justice and hope for the future. We taught them that each individual has inherent rights and dignity. We taught them that life itself has a higher purpose and that we are not mice on a wheel or worker drones toiling through a short, miserable existence. We have taught them social responsibility, the meaning and the necessity of peace and the obligation to love and respect their fellow men.

And, above all else, we taught G-d's children that there is a kind and just Creator who loves us; that He is the creator of all of existence including time and space and that He has created a beautiful world for us.

Amazingly, we taught all of this to the nations of the world while they did everything to shut us up. They penned us in behind walls, tried to forcibly convert us to other religions and stole our children in order to raise them in falsehood. They outlawed the practice of Judaism, expelled us from their lands and massacred us, sometimes burning alive entire Jewish villages—but to no avail. They more they fought, the more they absorbed the truth.

And this process continues today. As recently as 100 years ago, each nation of the world pursued its own interests without regard to any other consideration and often at the expense of its rivals. World unity was not an ideal that a grown-up discussed. However, the Jewish vision of a world at peace and working in harmony is now the template for all international relations. It didn't happen immediately; it took decades and two world wars but like every other enlightened idea that the Jews have consistently and stubbornly proclaimed, it has come to be accepted as an undeniable truth.

The day is coming when the entire world will acknowledge the one true G-d and cast off all the nonsense it has accumulated and clung to over the millennia. All religions—Christianity, Islam, Hinduism, you name it - will cease to exist. There will not be one church in Rome or a single mosque in Mecca. Before you dismiss the idea, reread the above paragraphs.

When this era dawns, the world will begin to see life for what it truly is: a gift and an opportunity. The minds of the world's great thinkers will be directed to understanding truth and not towards self-aggrandizement, the accumulation of wealth or destructive ideas. Children throughout the world will be taught the meaning of life and the true nature of the loving G-d who created them and only wants to do good for them. They will be taught what true freedom is as opposed to license; how to love and be loved; how to care for their fellow man; and the purpose of physical pleasure. They will finally be taught why they were created in the first place. This is how we will conquer the world - we will change their thinking.

When mankind comes to recognize the truth that we are creations of a loving and altruistic Creator on whom we depend for our blessings, our livelihoods and even each breath we take, then and only then will the family of man live happily ever after. *Only* a world based on this knowledge can live in peace and harmony.

But to arrive at our ineluctable destiny in a happy way, the Jewish people must be devoted to G-d and the Torah. If we turn away and instead embrace foreign ideologies and causes, we are criminally negligent and we will suffer needlessly.

Imagine that you knew someone who had the ability to cure a deadly disease from which people were suffering yet did not pursue it because he didn't want to be bothered. Instead, he got a simple nine-to-five job so he could hang out with his buddies down at the sports bar after work. Or, perhaps spend his free time playing golf.

You would be outraged. You would do everything in your power to focus him on the need for a cure. You would flatter him, cajole him, push him, beg him and threaten him—anything to get him to develop that cure. Imagine how much more intense your efforts would be if a loved one were stricken with that disease. Now imagine that your friend didn't budge and instead just went about his mundane life and your loved one died.

What would you think of him? Would you respect him? Would he remain your friend?

This is a description of a person who turned his back on greatness and on a world that desperately needed him and instead callously chose a puny, meaningless life. He opted to be a nothing when he could have been a hero.

How is that different from the Jew who turns his back on his magnificent, historic, ultimately world-saving mission?

The world is counting on us.

Chapter Fourteen
A Few Last Words

I hope that this book has been somewhat enlightening and that it has provided explanations for many of the beliefs and actions of Orthodox Jews.

Hopefully you have learned that Orthodox Jews are not closed-minded, ignorant, hateful or mindlessly dogmatic. Hopefully you have come to understand that the world of the Torah and *mitzvot* is not black and white. It is not all or nothing. Any *mitzvah* a Jew performs is a benefit to him regardless of whether or not he does the other ones. It might be a cliché, but life truly is a journey.

Also, I will also be very gratified if you come away with a clear understanding that Judaism is not just another "religion."

When Karl Marx wrote in 1843 that religion was "the opium (or opiate) of the people" he was looking at Christianity. A religion that asks its followers to take a leap of faith, to believe and obey in spite of obvious questions in exchange for promises of paradise, is a mind-numbing hallucinatory drug. An adherent to such a belief system can be manipulated and exploited while clinging to the illusion that he will be rewarded. It detaches its followers from reality and that is why it is an opiate or, to use a better descriptive, a painkiller.

Judaism, by definition, can never be an opiate. In Judaism, knowing there is a G-d and knowing that He gave the Jewish people a Torah is only the beginning of the journey, not the destination. These beliefs do not guarantee anything. In fact, there are no guarantees at all in Judaism. As we have seen, a Jewish life is one long process of self-creation and self-improvement that begins at birth and does not end until a person's very last breath. It requires constant effort, constant diligence and constant morality. The stakes are high and success is not at all guaranteed. This is no drug.

I also hope that this book has opened up your mind and your heart to your own heritage, which is your birthright, and, perhaps, even spurred you to look into it a bit more. Every single Jew in the world today is part of this unbroken, 3,300-year-old chain. No Jew should be limited with regard to knowledge of his heritage simply because of the circumstances of his birth.

This has not been an easy book to write. On one hand I wanted to hack away at the oxidation that has been imprisoning the minds of modern Jews, keeping them rusted into irrational positions regarding the Torah and *mitzvot*. But, on the other hand, I feared turning off readers by sounding too preachy or doctrinaire which would lead to the accusation that I was acting like a missionary, a common invective directed towards Orthodox Jews involved in Jewish outreach.

There is a bitter irony to being called a missionary by a fellow Jew. Not only is it tantamount to being called a Nazi or a Cossack, because missionaries have always been enemies who stopped at nothing—deviousness, lies and even kidnapping—to "save" Jewish souls, but the term also misstates the whole picture.

The Jewish people were never into saving souls; it is not part of our lexicon. We are not nor have we ever been missionaries. When Orthodox Jews reach out to their secular brothers and sisters, it is purely a heartfelt desire to open their eyes to the wonderful treasure that is their rightful inheritance. The average secular Jew has no inkling of what it means to be a Jew and to the Orthodox that is a catastrophe. Outreach on the part of the Orthodox is an entirely altruistic endeavor. It is based on nothing other than a deep-seated love for Jews and a sense of dismay at a seventy-percent intermarriage rate.

If people can volunteer their time to save dolphins or wetlands or rain forests, why is it so farfetched to think that someone is volunteering to save Jews? I'll tell you why: because we are inundated with Christians who are insincere and Moslems who are violent, and so we assume that all purveyors of religion are cut from the same cloth. Not true. Jews are different. We always have been, we always will be. Hopefully this book has made that clear. So while fundamentalists around the world in every type of belief system—both religious and secular—are quick to spew hatred and intolerance and damn nonbelievers to hell, Orthodox Jews live at peace with the world, believing in the Jews' very unique relationship to G-d. They do so based on very real, very reasonable beliefs that have been handed down, parent to child, for over 3,300 years.

I have always felt a great deal of personal frustration with the way the situation has been framed. Having wandered into a *yeshiva* when I was twenty, and having benefited greatly from my experiences there, I have always wanted to share it with all my friends and my family. I want them to also experience what I experienced when I sat in on classes nearly thirty years ago and watched this unknown world unfold in brilliant color.

But when I open my mouth to say something, I am immediately

branded a missionary! If I meet an old school friend who I haven't seen in fifteen years and I tell him I'm a financial planner and my specialty is using loopholes in the IRS codes to eliminate my clients' taxes, or that I run an investment fund that has generated terrific returns consistently over the last ten years, would he not want to speak with me about the opportunities?

But if I tell him that I can show him how to eliminate the feeling of meaningless that hounds every secular adult, how to have a strong, vibrant marriage, how to teach his children morality and self-esteem, or that he has a soul and it has needs and drives that are unfulfilled and haunting him or that—dare I say it—there is a G-d who created the world solely to give him pleasure, well then I am a missionary. I am quickly labeled and discarded; he can just shut me out.

This is what the Christian missionaries have done to us. Every time I say the word "G-d" I might as well be saying "Jesus." But truth be told, what greater kindness is there than teaching others about truth and reality?

The resentment and, sometimes, outright hostility that Orthodox Jews encounter when trying to introduce their secular brethren to their own heritage is astounding. If I told someone that he dropped his wallet, would he resent me? If I told him that he forgot to pick up two free tickets to the Super Bowl, would he call me names?

Imagine twin brothers separated at birth and adopted by different families. One decides to investigate his roots and discovers that his birth parents left a fortune for him and his brother in their will, should the boys ever turn up. This man claims his stake and goes off looking for his lost brother.

Finally he locates him and travels to meet him, to tell him the good news. The brother is not well off and lives in a rundown neighborhood. The first man is excited to change his brother's life. He arrives in a nice car, wearing nice clothing, because he is now very wealthy. He gets out of his car and as he walks towards his brother, the brother blurts out, "Look at Mr. Fancy Pants, coming here to show us poor slobs how important he is."

The man is stunned but figures his brother will soften up once he hears the news.

"Listen," he says, "I have wonderful news for you. It turns out we are blood brothers and our parents left us an unbelievably valuable inheritance."

But instead of coming around, the brother becomes more irate. "Listen to Mr. High and Mighty, coming to save me! Do I look like I need your money? Are you somehow saying that my life is missing something? You rich people are all the same. You think you're better than everyone and you've got it all. How dare you come here and judge me?"

The man is speechless. There he is, offering his long-lost brother a fortune that will give him everything he ever wanted and bring him back into touch with his extended family, who would love to meet him. But the brother won't give him a hearing and instead is full of resentment and anger. The more the man tries to reason with him and explain to him that it is *his* money, the angrier the brother becomes.

To an impartial observer, the brother is obviously reacting with such emotion to something that is going on in his own head and not to what his brother is doing or saying.

The Talmud states a clear truth: that every Jew believes in G-d. We might fight Him, resent Him, rebel against Him, avoid Him, spite Him, ignore Him or be angry with Him, but we believe in Him. And many times just bringing Him up can cause serious reactions—sometimes even eruptions.

This book has hopefully also explained why many Jews who were born into irreligious or nonobservant families have embraced the Torah life. An uninformed person looking in from the outside finds it hard to fathom. It seems that people with everything going for them suddenly take on dreary, rigid lives.

I recall an incident at Aish HaTorah that, years later, I still find dismaying. The Jerusalem campus was hosting a luncheon for a visiting mission from the Jewish Federation of Los Angeles. One of Aish HaTorah's non-Orthodox board members from Los Angeles, who was also a major donor to the Federation, was visiting Jerusalem and got up to address the gathering. He began by talking about assimilation and intermarriage, and the need to educate the next generation and instill in them a pride in being Jewish. Aish HaTorah, he said, was on the forefront of this effort.

Then, suddenly, in what I felt was an attempt to involve the crowd emotionally, he stressed how Aish HaTorah had saved so many from drugs, cults and all kinds of bad things. The students who had been asked to participate nearly fell off their chairs. You could hear their jaws dropping against the lunch tables. Drugs? Cults? The only cult I was saved from was the American Bar Association. And as for drugs, well, I guess it is true—my home does not have a television.

We were all very embarrassed. I wished he hadn't said it because it wasn't true. Hopefully I am the only person who remembers it. But it did reinforce a truism: Unless a person understands the Torah and the beautiful life it creates, he or she is always on the outside looking in and at some point cannot relate to what is happening on the inside. This man liked Aish HaTorah and supported it financially because on an intellectual level he understood the need, but nevertheless, on some level, he couldn't relate to it.

The idea of a well-balanced, successful person becoming religiously observant is incomprehensible to those unfamiliar with the reality of Torah. Family and friends will view the newly observant—a *ba'al tshuva* in Hebrew—as if he or she is joining a monastery or going off to India to join an ashram. They will pepper the newly observant with questions like, "Why would you do such a thing?" or, "What was missing from your life? You had everything going for you!" using the same puzzled intonation that one would use when asking "Are you crazy?"

What these questioners do not see is that this person has recognized and acted upon the fact that man cannot live by bread alone. There is no enduring satisfaction from material benefits. Eventually the thrills are gone and the music fades and we are still left with the same nagging question: "What was it all for?" The *ba'al tshuva* simply has looked ahead and, anticipating the pain, chose to find the answers now.

The world of Torah can be compared to the ocean. When one views the ocean from above its surface, it is impossible to discern what is taking place below. It stretches out to the horizon in a monotonous expanse devoid of landmarks or distinguishing characteristics. The waves all look alike and a description of one part of the ocean could very well describe any other hundreds of miles of it.

But strap on a mask and a snorkel and peer below the surface or, better yet, put on a mask and an air tank and descend twenty or thirty feet and suddenly a magnificent, rich world of previously unimagined beauty and complexity will open up before your eyes. There is nothing monotonous about an ocean below its surface. It is a fantastic world teeming with all sorts of life forms, from mammals to fish to amphibians to invertebrates in all sizes, shapes and colors. This unbelievable world was always there; it was just that you couldn't see it. But once you have seen it, you will never look at the ocean the same way again.

The world of Torah learning and *mitzvah* observance is an intellectually and spiritually diverse world made up of a cornucopia of interests, ideas and pursuits populated by all types of people with all types of opinions and outlooks. But looking at it from above the surface you will never see this. It requires a dip into the vast ocean that is authentic Jewish life. Once in, your eyes will be opened up to a rich, beautiful and radiant world that you never knew existed.

Endnotes

1, 7, 8, 11, 12

The Voice of Destruction by Hermann Rauschning used by permission of the licenser, Pelican Publishing Company, Inc.

2

Speech at Nuremberg, January 13, 1923

3

Robert Wistrich, *Hitler's Apocalypse,* (from a conversation with Croatian Security Minister Kvaternik, July 21, 1941)

4, 6, 9

Hitler's speech in Munich on 12 April 1922

5, 10, 13, 14, 15, 16

Mein Kampf, Elite Minds Inc.; First edition (July 25, 2009)

17, 18, 19

"Innocents Abroad (The Oxford Mark Twain series)" by Twain M, Fishkin S (1996); permission from Oxford University Press, Inc

Index

Y

Z